PRINCIPLES OF FRENCH CONSTITUTIONAL LAW

Principles of French Constitutional Law offers a concise and accessible account of the key principles and rules of constitutional law in the French legal system, presenting a much-needed up-to-date overview of this rapidly changing subject.

The textbook explores the five essential pillars that underpin the teaching of constitutional law, namely the institutions, legal history, case law, comparative law, and current affairs and developments. It is split into two core sections: Part I examines the basis of French constitutional law, the theoretical developments about key notions of constitutional law such as the state and the constitution, as well as the historical background to French constitutional law. Part II provides students with an understanding of the current Fifth Republic and how constitutional rules are adopted and applied, and how they affect other areas of law and politics. It offers a critical account of the 1958 Constitution's past, present, and future by placing it in its political and socio-historical contexts and critically assessing contemporary developments and constitutional reforms.

Given the growing expansion of this branch of law in the French legal system, this book will be essential reading for anyone studying French Law, Law with French, Comparative Constitutional Law, and European Legal Studies.

Marie-Luce Paris is Associate Professor in Law at UCD Sutherland School of Law, Dublin. She is the Academic Co-Director of the UCD Centre for Human Rights. She is the Academic Director of the UCD French Law Programmes. Paris is a French constitutional law expert, having studied constitutional law in France, and published internationally about the subject and taught it to common law and international students.

"Comprehensive, illuminating and crystal clear, Principles of French Constitutional Law opens a window into the doctrine, history and theory of one of the world's most fascinating and influential constitutions."

—Richard Albert,
Professor of World Constitutions and Director of Constitutional Studies, The University of Texas at Austin, US.

"A must-read for anyone interested in French constitutional law and constitutional law in general. This book is an invaluable, pedagogical and up-to-date reference for lawyers and students. An excellent mastery of French constitutional law!"

—Aurélie Duffy-Meunier,
Professor of Public Law, Aix Marseille University, France.

PRINCIPLES OF FRENCH CONSTITUTIONAL LAW

Marie-Luce Paris

Routledge
Taylor & Francis Group
LONDON AND NEW YORK

Designed cover image: daboost / Getty Images ®

First published 2025
by Routledge
4 Park Square, Milton Park, Abingdon, Oxon OX14 4RN

and by Routledge
605 Third Avenue, New York, NY 10158

Routledge is an imprint of the Taylor & Francis Group, an informa business

British Library Cataloguing-in-Publication Data
A catalogue record for this book is available from the British Library

Library of Congress Cataloging-in-Publication Data
Names: Paris, Marie-Luce, author.
Title: Principles of French constitutional law / Marie-Luce Paris.
Description: Abingdon, Oxon [UK]; New York, NY: Routledge, 2024. |
Includes bibliographical references and index.
Identifiers: LCCN 2024034005 | ISBN 9780415841443 (hardback) |
ISBN 9780415841436 (paperback) | ISBN 9781003268871 (ebook)
Subjects: LCSH: Constitutional law--France. |
Constitutional history--France. | France--Politics and government--1958-
Classification: LCC KJV4079 .P39 2024 | DDC 342.44--dc23/eng/20240724
LC record available at https://lccn.loc.gov/2024034005

ISBN: 978-0-415-84144-3 (hbk)
ISBN: 978-0-415-84143-6 (pbk)
ISBN: 978-1-003-26887-1 (ebk)

DOI: 10.4324/9781003268871

Typeset in Times New Roman
by Deanta Global Publishing Services, Chennai, India

CONTENTS

DETAILED CONTENTS

PREFACE

The book is about French constitutional law, that is, the study of the French Constitution and the political institutions of France. The study encompasses the role and powers of the different political branches, the governing system, as well as the protection of the rights of French citizens. I first had the idea for this book in 2011, four years after I took over the teaching of the course on French Public Law from my UCD colleague Professor James Casey. Professor Casey's influential book *Constitutional Law in Ireland* (Round Hall Press, 3rd edn, 2000) inspired me greatly. At the time, I thought: Why not compile my course notes into a comprehensive resource for students in the French Law Programme and beyond? In other words, wouldn't it be relevant to turn my, now long-running, course into a textbook? As such, this book caters primarily to students enrolled in law programmes which include an element of French Law teaching. Additionally, the book will also appeal to individuals studying law or related disciplines (such as political science, history, comparative legal studies, or European studies) seeking a foundational understanding of principles of French constitutional law. Moreover, legal practitioners, lawyers, and judges desiring a clear, accessible, and up-to-date insight into the public law system of France can benefit from this book.

The outline of this book reflects the typical outline found in most French constitutional law textbooks, which usually consist of a theoretical part and an institutional part. I have in consequence devoted Part I to key theoretical notions (Chapter 1) and historical development (Chapter 2) of French constitutional law. In Part II, the focus is on the Fifth Republic, which is the current political regime of France based on the 1958 Constitution. The topics have been selected to provide an exhaustive overview of a discipline which is very rich and multidimensional, particularly when exploring aspects of political science. Following a chapter on the historical and legal foundations of the French constitutional system (Chapter 3), the subsequent chapters cover the Fifth Republic institutions (Chapter 4), political parties, elections, and referendums (Chapter 5), and constitutional justice and rights protection (Chapter 6). Interspersed figures, tables and boxes offer additional insights into specific issues and, where relevant, present a comparative perspective. While I occasionally draw comparisons to Irish law and other legal systems in my teaching, this book is not a work of comparative law. Nonetheless, the book relies, to differing degrees and in various contexts, on the five essential pillars that underpin the teaching of constitutional law, namely the institutions, legal history, case law, comparative law, and current affairs and developments.

However, this might not be the way constitutional law will be taught and learnt in future years. This is for two reasons: the evolving content of the topic and the changing methods of instruction. Historically, constitutional law has not always been taught in French law schools, at least in that format. In fact, from the end of the nineteenth century, it was primarily taught as a *droit politique*, not really hard law, focusing on the description of institutions and the principles underpinning them. The topic of *droit constitutionnel et institutions politiques*, as it was from the 1950s, received its proper label as simply *droit constitutionnel* at the end of the 1990s when the teaching of the course, under the influence of Professor Louis Favoreu, became less political and more legal. Instead of concentrating on the analysis of the ways in which power is acquired and exercised within the state, it became appropriate to give full importance to the study of two other areas, namely the normative system and the protection of fundamental rights and freedoms. Today, constitutional law remains a fundamental discipline but one which has been legalised, "jurisprudentialised," Europeanised, and internationalised. In a post-modern era, traditional concepts and principles, such as the notions of democracy, the state, or the principle of sovereignty, have been challenged from different corners. Additionally, the objectives and methods of constitutional law have diversified, creating a more interdisciplinary approach to the topic. In other words, because constitutional law has been renewed and enriched with new stakes, teaching the topic has become more complex. Besides, the advancement of artificial intelligence poses a new challenge to the field of constitutional law, as to other fields of law, impacting both research methods and educational strategies. As a result, it is conceivable that constitutional law may undergo further transformation in the future, potentially leading to a reimagined approach to its teaching and study.

All translations from French to English in this book are my own.

The law stated is the law as of 31 March 2024.

Use of AI-based tools

I did not rely on AI tools such as chatbots (e.g., ChatGPT) to create content for this book. The ChatGPT tool was used via its rewrite function to refine parts, but not all, of the content as responsible usage for the purpose of fluency of language. Essentially, I first penned the original text, then used the ChatGPT rewrite feature, and lastly reviewed the text by blending suitable idioms from both my own writing and the ChatGPT tool.

Acknowledgments

I am indebted to a variety of individuals and institutions for their assistance in the writing of this book.

My first thanks are for the UCD Sutherland School of Law for the support provided in the form of a generous research leave at the tail end of the writing as well as for funding obtained through the School Research Competition for research assistance. I am also grateful to the successive Law Deans, School Head of Research, and Research Manager for their moral and, at times, very practical support. Law Deans and many colleagues in the School have supported the UCD French Law Programmes over the years, and I am fully appreciative of that.

I thank the research assistants who have worked with me at various stages of the development of the book. I particularly thank UCD French Law graduate Beth Carthy and doctoral student Maxime Millon, member of the *Centre d'Études et de Recherches Comparatives sur les Constitutions, les Libertés et l'État* (*CERCCLE*) of Bordeaux University. During his time as a visiting researcher at the School, Maxime offered invaluable support with the book's figures and uplifting words of encouragement. I would like to express my gratitude to Justice Gerard Hogan, judge of the Supreme Court of Ireland, for reading my manuscript so carefully and for providing such a powerful foreword.

The pressure of academic life has contributed to unduly delaying the submission of the first manuscript of this book. I am therefore appreciative of the support of my publisher, Routledge, and beholden to Chloe Herbert and Emily Kindleysides in particular for their understanding and incredible patience.

I would not have found the motivation to write this book had it not been for the enthusiasm, interest, and hard work of UCD French Law students. To the many cohorts of past, present, and future students, I am immensely grateful. This book is for you.

On a more personal note, my deepest gratitude goes to my family for their constant support and encouragement over the years.

Marie-Luce Paris
Dublin
June 2024

FOREWORD

Comparative constitutional law is an inherently interesting subject, since it provides the key to understanding the contemporary history and evolution of the modern state. Yet the general lack of knowledge and understanding of the constitutional law of even major countries such as France, Germany, and Italy is striking. While one might have thought that some 70 years of ECHR and EU law might have deepened an awareness of the importance of comparative constitutional law, much more remains to be done. Decisions of continental constitutional courts are, for example, almost never cited by Irish courts even though, as this book shows, they often grapple with very similar issues of popular sovereignty, democratic control, and the rule of law.

Professor Marie-Luce Paris's *Principles of French Constitutional Law* provides a fascinating introduction to French constitutional law. She charts the rise and fall of the various French republics from 1789 onwards to the adoption of the present French Constitution by referendum in September 1958. While there is at times a tendency to gloss over the instability of domestic French politics in the period leading up to the Franco-Prussian war of 1870, this work shows that it was the failure to strike the right balance between executive and legislative powers in the Third and Fourth Republics which was a major part of the constitutional instability which produced the Fifth Republic. This was particularly true of the immediate post-war period when French governments lacked strong parliamentary majorities and were hampered by a lack of clarity as to when the Executive could force the dissolution of Parliament. The separation of powers—and, ultimately, democratic control itself—were further undermined by the excessive use of governmental decrees (*décrets-lois*) as a substitute for legislation.

The Constitution of the Fifth Republic was adopted by referendum in September 1958. It sought to address many of these problems by providing for a stronger executive Head of State, although Professor Paris also notes that the full-scale adoption of the US presidential model would have been seen by many as too "Bonapartist" a move. So, the French system is a hybrid-model with features of both the US system and the traditional UK-style parliamentary democratic model. This explains the complex mechanisms surrounding the right of the President of the Republic to force through legislative change by the use of the article 49 paragraph three decree power over the wishes of Parliament, while at the same time giving the Parliament the right to vote no confidence in the government. As was seen last year with the use of article 49 paragraph three in the case of Pensions Law reform, such votes of no confidence rarely succeed because they trigger the automatic dissolution of Parliament and fresh legislative elections.

Perhaps the most interesting development since 1958 has been the consistent evolution of the *Conseil Constitutionnel.* It was originally conceived as a sort of group of political and legal elites (*les sages*) who would act as arbiters of parliamentary and electoral type-disputes: it was, after all, a constitutional *council,* not a constitutional *court.* The Sarkozy reforms of 2008–2009 have in particular transformed the situation by giving the Council an ex-post form of judicial review of legislative measures, so that it is now well on its way to being a fully fledged constitutional court. There is so much in this book which is of great interest. I can only admire the elegant manner in which Professor Paris has succeeded in capturing the essence of French constitutional law and history in a way which is interesting, concise, and authoritative.

Gerard Hogan
Judge of the Supreme Court of Ireland
24 May 2024

ABBREVIATIONS

CJEU	Court of Justice of the European Union
ECHR	European Convention on Human Rights
ECtHR	European Court of Human Rights
EEA	European Economic Area
EEC	European Economic Community
EP	European Parliament
EU	European Union
ICC	International Criminal Court
ICJ	International Court of Justice
IMF	International Monetary Fund
OUP	Oxford University Press
PCIJ	Permanent Court of International Justice (1922–1945)
PUF	*Presses universitaires de France*
UCD Press	University College Dublin Press
UK	United Kingdom
UN	United Nations
USA	United States of America

LIST AND TRANSLATION OF QUOTES

State and Sovereignty

« L'État, divinité abstraite, aussi insaisissable dans son essence qu'insatiable dans ses appétits. »

Translation: The State, abstract divinity, as elusive in its essence as [it is] insatiable in its appetites.

Source: Abbot Antoine Martinet, from *Statolatrie, ou le Communisme légal* (Hachette 2014) reprising texts from Martinet, *Solution des grands problèmes mis à la portée de tous les esprits : Peut-on encore être homme sans être chrétien* (Jacques Lecoffre and Co 1848).

Constitution and Hierarchy of Norms

« Le respect de la Constitution est non un risque mais un devoir. »

Translation: Respect for the Constitution is not a risk but a duty.

Source: Pierre Mazeaud on his reply to the then minister for Justice, in the context of legislation on electronic tagging (Press Release, 27 September 2005).

Democracy and the Rule of Law

« La démocratie, c'est 'le gouvernement du peuple, par le peuple, pour le peuple.' »

Translation: Democracy is "the government of the people, by the people, for the people."

Source: citation attributed to Abraham Lincoln, *Selected Writings and Speeches of Abraham Lincoln* (Packard & Company 1943).

Separation of Powers and Systems of Government

« Pour qu'on ne puisse abuser du pouvoir, il faut que, par la disposition des choses, le pouvoir arrête le pouvoir. »

Translation: So that power cannot be abused, it is necessary that, through the arrangement of things, power stops power.

Source: Montesquieu, *De l'Esprit des Lois* (1748), Book XI, Chapter IV.

Ancien Régime (before 1789)

« [Louis XIV] est Dieu. Il faut attendre sa volonté avec soumission, et tout espérer de sa justice et de sa bonté, sans impatience, afin d'en avoir plus de mérite. »

Translation: [Louis XIV] is God. We must await his will with submission, and hope for everything from his justice and goodness, without impatience, in order to have more merit.

Source: Duchesse de Montpensier, *Mémoires de Mademoiselle de Montpensier*, 6 tomes, 3 volumes (Jean Frédéric Bernard 1730).

Experimentation with regimes of separation of powers (1789–1870)

« Les Français ont fait en 1789 le plus grand effort auquel se soit jamais livré aucun peuple. »

Translation: In 1789 the French made the greatest effort that any people has ever made.

Source: Alexis de Tocqueville, *L'Ancien Régime et la Révolution* (1856).

Establishment of the parliamentary regime under the Republic (1870–1958)

« Je suis en république, et pour roi j'ai moi-même. »

Translation: I am in a republic, and for king I have myself.

Source: Victor Hugo, *L'Année terrible* (Michel Lévy frères 1872).

Origins and Sources of Inspiration

« D'emblée, la Vème République se trouve placée sous le signe de la rupture et de la continuité. »

Translation: From the outset, the Fifth Republic was characterised by both a break from the past and a seamless continuation of certain aspects.

Source: Frédéric Rouvillois, *Droit constitutionnel : La Vème République* (4th edn, Flammarion 2014) 31.

Main Features and Evolution of the Regime

« Un des caractères essentiels de la Constitution de la Vème République, c'est qu'elle donne une tête à l'État. »

Translation: One of the essential characteristics of the Constitution of the Fifth Republic is that it gives a head to the state.

Source: Charles De Gaulle (Press Conference, 20 September 1962).

The President of the Republic

« Il y a deux organes inutiles : la prostate et le Président de la République. »

Translation: There are two useless organs: the prostate and the President of the Republic.

Source: Georges Clémenceau cited in Adrien Dansette, *Histoire des présidents de la République : de Louis-Napoléon Bonaparte à Charles de Gaulle* (Le Livre contemporain 1960).

Government and Parliament

« Nul gouvernement ne peut être longtemps solide sans une redoutable opposition. »

« Le comptoir d'un café est le parlement du peuple. »

Translation: No government can be long secure without a formidable opposition.

The counter of a café is the parliament of the people.

Source: Benjamin Disraeli, *Collected Edition of the Novels and Tales* (1870).

Quote attributed to Honoré de Balzac (unknown source).

Other Institutions

« Quel mal a éprouvé la France à stabiliser ses institutions ! »

Translation: How difficult it was for France to stabilise its institutions!

Source: Édouard Balladur, *Le Figaro*, 9 February 2015.

Political Parties

« Pour ma part, je dirais simplement : oui aux partis politiques, mais non à l'esprit de parti. »

Translation: For my part, I would simply say that I fully support political parties, but I strongly oppose partisanship.

Source: Raymond Barre, *La Vie française*, 15 December 1980.

Elections and Referendums

« C'est une bonne idée d'avoir choisi le référendum, à condition que la réponse soit oui. »

Translation: It is a good idea to have chosen the referendum, provided the answer is yes.

Source: Valéry Giscard d'Estaing on the occasion of the vote on the Treaty establishing a Constitution for Europe, *Le Monde*, 6 May 2005.

The French Court-System

« Le premier caractère de la puissance judiciaire, chez tous les peuples, est de servir d'arbitre. Pour qu'il y ait lieu à action de la part des tribunaux, il faut qu'il y ait contestation. Pour qu'il y ait juge, il faut qu'il y ait procès. »

Translation: The primary feature of judicial power, in all societies, is to act as a mediator. For there to be action by the courts, there must be a dispute. For there to be a judge, there must be a trial.

Source: Tocqueville, *De la démocratie en Amérique* (1848), Chapter VI.

The Constitutional Council

« Le Conseil [constitutionnel] n'est pas là pour rendre des services politiques, mais pour défendre le droit et protéger les libertés qui sont garanties par la Constitution. »

Translation: The primary purpose of the [Constitutional] Council is not to cater to political interests, but to uphold the law and safeguard the freedoms enshrined in the Constitution.

Source: Jean-Louis Debré, *La Lettre du cadre territorial*, 26 February 2016.

Constitutional Review

« À plusieurs reprises, la QPC a été l'occasion pour le Conseil [constitutionnel] de statuer sur des questions de société. »

Translation: On several occasions, the *QPC* was an opportunity for the [Constitutional] Council to rule on social issues.

Source: *Rapport d'activité 2022*, Conseil Constitutionnel, September 2022, 8.

Principles of Constitutional Justice

« *La Constitution est désormais l'affaire des citoyens.* »

Translation: The Constitution is now the business of the citizens.

Source: Jean-Louis Debré, *Le Monde,* 5 March 2011.

LIST OF FIGURES, TABLES, AND BOXES

The numbering of each figure, table and box corresponds to the chapter in which they are inserted. For example, there are three tables (1.1, 1.2., 1.3.) and two boxes (1.1., 1.2) in Chapter 1, but no figure; there are one figure (2.1) and two tables (2.1, 2.2) in Chapter 2, but no box, etc.

Figures

Tables

Boxes

LEGISLATION

Codes

Civil Code
Code of Administrative Justice
Code of Defence
Code of Judicial Organisation
Criminal Code
Electoral Code
Nationality Code

Constitutional Laws

Constitutional Law No 2024-200 of 8 March 2024 on the freedom to resort to voluntary termination of pregnancy

Constitutional Law No 2008-724 of 23 July 2008 on the modernisation of the institutions of the Fifth Republic

Constitutional Law No 2008-103 of 4 February 2008 amending Title XV of the Constitution-Treaty of Lisbon

Constitutional Law No 2007-239 of 23 February 2007 on prohibition of the death penalty

Constitutional Law No 2007-238 of 23 February 2007 amending Title IX of the Constitution

Constitutional Law No 2007-237 of 23 February 2007 on the electoral body of New Caledonia

Constitutional Law No 2005-205 of 1 March 2005 on the Charter for the Environment

Constitutional Law No 2005-204 of 1 March 2005 Treaty establishing a Constitution for Europe

Constitutional Law No 2003-276 of 28 March 2003 relating to the decentralised organisation of the Republic

Constitutional Law No 2003-267 of 25 March 2003 European arrest warrant

Constitutional Law No 2000-964 of 2 October 2000 relating to the duration of the mandate of the President of the Republic

Constitutional Law No 99-569 of 8 July 1999 on equality between women and men

Constitutional Law No 99-568 of 8 July 1999 International Criminal Court

Constitutional Law No 99-49 of 25 January 1999 Treaty of Amsterdam

Constitutional Law No 98-610 of 20 July 1998 relating to New Caledonia

Constitutional Law No 96-138 of 22 February 1996 social security financing law

Constitutional Law No 95-880 of 4 August 1995 single parliamentary session; adjustment of parliamentary immunities; and expansion of the possibilities of recourse to referendum

Constitutional Law No 93-1256 of 25 Novembre 1993 right of asylum

Constitutional Law No 93-952 of 27 July 1993 revising the Constitution of 4 October 1958 and amending its Titles VIII, IX, X and XVIII

Constitutional Law No 92-554 of 25 June 1992 adding to the Constitution a title: "European Communities and the European Union"

Constitutional Law No 76-527 of 18 June 1976 interim presidency of the Republic

Constitutional Law No 74-904 of 29 October 1974 amending article 61 of the Constitution

Constitutional Law No 63-1327 of 30 December 1963 parliamentary session

Constitutional Law No 62-1292 of 6 November 1962 relating to the election of the President of the Republic by universal suffrage

Constitutional Law No 60-525 of 4 June 1960 states of the Community

Constitutional Law of 3 June 1958 providing for a transitional derogation from the provisions of article 90 of the [1946] Constitution and providing for a referendum

Organic Laws

Organic Law No 2021-27 of 15 January 2021 relating to the Economic, Social and Environmental Council

Organic Law No 2018-1201 of 22 December 2018 relating to the fight against the manipulation of information

Organic Law No 2016-506 of 25 April 2016 on the modernisation of the rules applicable to the presidential election

Organic Law No 2014-1392 of 24 November 2014 implementing article 68 of the Constitution

Organic Law No 2014-125 of 14 February 2014 prohibiting the cumulation of local executive functions with the mandate of deputy or senator

Organic Law No 2013-1114 of 6 December 2013 implementing article 11 of the Constitution

Organic Law No 2013-906 of 11 October 2013 relating to transparency in public life

Organic Law No 2012-272 of 28 February 2012 relating to the reimbursement of campaign expenditures for the presidential election

Organic Law No 2011-410 of 14 April 2011 on the election of deputies and senators

Organic Law No 2011-333 of 29 March 2011 relating to the Defender of Rights

Organic Law No 2009-1523 of 10 December 2009 relating to the application of article 61-1 of the Constitution

Organic Law No 2009-403 of 15 April 2009 relating to the application of articles 34-1, 39 and 44 of the Constitution

Organic Law No 2009-38 of 13 January 2009 implementing article 25 of the Constitution535

Organic Law No 2004-192 of 27 February 2004 on the statute of autonomy of French Polynesia

Organic Law No 2001-692 of 1 August 2001 relating to finance laws

Organic Law No 2001-419 of 15 May 2001 modifying the end of the mandate and powers of the National Assembly

Organic Law No 2000-294 of 5 April 2000 on incompatibilities between electoral mandates

Organic Law No 1999-209 of 19 March 1999 on New Caledonia

Organic Law No 98-404 of 25 May 1998 determining the conditions for the application of article 88-3 of the Constitution relating to the exercise by citizens of the European Union residing in France, other than French nationals, of the right to vote and stand as a candidate in municipal elections, and transposing Directive 94/80/EC of 19 December 1994

Organic Law No 88-226 of 11 March 1988 relating to financial transparency in political life

Organic Law No 58-1100 of 17 November 1958 on the functioning of parliamentary assemblies

Ordinary Laws

Law No 2021-1109 of 24 August 2021 confirming respect for the principles of the Republic

Law No 2019-1461 of 27 December 2019 relating to the involvement in local life and the proximity of public action

Law No 2019-828 of 6 August 2019 on the transformation of the public service

Law No 2019-290 of 10 April 2019 aimed at strengthening and guaranteeing the maintenance of public order during demonstrations

Law No 2019-222 of 23 March 2019 on programming 2018–2022 and reform for justice

Law No 2018-1202 of 22 December 2018 relating to the fight against the manipulation of information

Law No 2018-509 of 25 June 2018 relating to the election of representatives to the European Parliament

Law No 2017-1339 of 15 September 2017 relating to confidence in political life

Law No 2017-286 of 6 March 2017 aimed at reinforcing the accounting obligations of the political parties and the candidates

Law No 2017-1510 of 30 October 2017 strengthening domestic security and the fight against terrorism

Law No 2017-55 of 20 January 2017 on the general status of Independent Administrative Authorities and Independent Public Authorities

Law No 2016-1691 of 9 December 2016 relating to transparency, the fight against corruption, and the modernisation of economic life

Law No 2016-1547 of 18 November 2016 on the modernisation of justice in the twenty-first century

Law No 2016-508 of 25 April 2016 on the modernisation of various provisions applicable to elections

Law No 2015-912 of 24 July 2015 relating to intelligence

Law No 2015-366 of 31 March 2015 aimed at facilitating the exercise, by local elected representatives, of their mandate

Law No 2015-177 of 16 February 2015 on the modernisation and simplification of law and procedures in the areas of justice and home affairs

Law No 2014-126 of 14 February 2014 prohibiting the cumulation of local executive functions with the mandate of representative in the European Parliament

Law No 2013-907 of 11 October 2013 relating to transparency in public life

Law No 2013-702 of 2 August 2013 relating to the election of senators

Law No 2013-659 of 22 July 2013 relating to the representation of French people living outside France

Law No 2013-403 of 17 May 2013 relating to the election of departmental councillors, municipal councillors and community councillors, and modifying the electoral calendar

Law No 2011-1977 of 28 December 2011 on finances for 2012

Law No 2011-525 of 17 May 2011 on the simplification and improvement of the quality of law

Law No 2011-392 of 14 April 2011 on police custody

Law No 2011-334 of 29 March 2011 relating to the Defender of Rights

Law No 2011-140 of 3 February 2011 to strengthen the means of Parliament in terms of monitoring government action and evaluating public policies

Law No 2010-1192 of 11 October 2010 prohibiting the concealment of the face in public space

Law No 2010-1 of 4 January 2010 on the protection of journalists' sources

Law No 2009-39 of 13 January 2009 relating to the commission provided for under article 25 of the Constitution and to the election of deputies

Law No 2004-228 of 15 March 2004 governing, in application of the principle of secularism, the wearing of signs or clothing indicating religious affiliation in public schools, colleges and high schools

Law No 2002-276 of 27 February 2002 relating to local democracy

Law No 2002-214 of 19 February 2002 amending Law No 77-808 of 19 July 1977 relating to the publication and dissemination of certain opinion polls

Law No 2001-1275 of 28 December 2001 on finances for 2002

Law No 2001-504 of 12 June 2001 aimed at strengthening the prevention and repression of sectarian movements that undermine human rights and fundamental freedoms

Law No 2000-719 of 1 August 2000 amending Law No 86-1067 of 30 September 1986 on freedom of communication

Law No 2000-493 of 6 June 2000 aimed at promoting equal access of women and men to electoral mandates and elective functions

Law No 2000-295 of 5 April 2000 on the limitation of multiple electoral mandates and functions and their conditions of exercise

Law No 97-1027 of 10 November 1997 relating to the automatic registration of persons aged eighteen on the electoral lists

Law No 97-1019 of 28 October 1997 reforming the national service

Law No 95-65 of 19 January 1995 relating to the financing of political life

Law No 93-933 of 22 July 1993 reforming the law of nationality

Law No 92-108 of 3 February 1992 relating to the conditions for exercising local offices

Law No 90-55 of 15 January 1990 on the limitation of election expenses and the clarification of the financing of political activities

Law No 88-227 of 11 March 1988 relating to financial transparency in political life

Law No 87-1127 of 31 December 1987 on reforming administrative litigation

Law No 86-1067 of 30 September 1986 on freedom of communication

Law No 86-897 of 1 August 1986 on the reform of the legal regime of the press

Law No 86-1197 of 24 November 1986 relating to the delimitation of constituencies for the election of deputies

Law No 86-825 of 11 July 1986 relating to the election of deputies and authorising the government to delimit electoral constituencies by ordinance

Law No 85-890 of 10 July 1985 amending the electoral code and relating to the election of deputies

Law No 82-213 of 2 March 1982 relating to the rights and freedoms of municipalities, departments, and regions

Law No 77-808 of 19 July 1977 relating to the publication and dissemination of certain opinion polls

Law No 77-729 of 7 July 1977 relating to the election of representatives to the European Parliament

Law No 75-1329 of 31 December 1975 amending certain provisions of the Electoral Code

Law No 74-631 of 5 July 1974 setting the age of legal majority at eighteen

Law No 62-1292 of 6 November 1962 relating to the election of the President of the Republic by universal suffrage

Law No 58-520 of 3 June 1958 relating to the full powers [granted to the De Gaulle Government for a duration of six months]

Law No 56-619 of 23 June 1956 on measures to ensure the development of territories under the Ministry for Overseas France

Law No 55-385 of 3 April 1955 relating to the state of emergency

Law No 53-611 of 11 July 1953 relating to economic and financial recovery

Law No 50-728 of 24 June 1950 repealing the Law of 22 June 1886 relating to members of families who reigned in France

Law No 46-940 of 7 May 1946 proclaiming all nationals of overseas territories citizens

Law of 1 June 1924 implementing French civil legislation in the departments of Bas-Rhin, Haut-Rhin, and Moselle

Law of 28 March 1907 relating to public meetings

Law of 2 January 1907 concerning the public exercise of worship

Law of 9 December 1905 concerning the separation of Church and State

Law of 28 March 1882 on the organisation of primary education

Law of 16 June 1881 establishing free primary education in public schools

Law of 3 April 1878 on the state of siege

Law of 24 May 1872 reorganising the Council of State

Law of 9 August 1849 on the state of siege

Law of 28 *Pluviôse* Year VIII (17 February 1800)

Law of 16 and 24 August 1790 on judicial organisation

Ordinances

Ordinance No 58-1270 of 22 December 1958 on the Organic Law relating to the status of the judiciary

Ordinance No 58-1210 of 13 December 1958 on the Organic Law on the allowance of members of Parliament

Ordinance No 58-1067 of 7 November 1958 on the Organic Law on the Constitutional Council

Ordinance No 45-2441 of 19 October 1945 on the French Nationality Code

Ordinance No 45-1839 of 17 August 1945 relating to the electorate and the eligibility of the military, amending article 33 and repealing article 31 last paragraph of the Law of 5 April 1884 relating to municipal organisation

Ordinance of 21 April 1944 on the organisation of public authorities in France after the liberation

Decrees

Decree No 2022-94 of 31 January 2022 issued for the application of (...) Law No 88-227 of 11 March 1988 as amended relating to financial transparency in political life

Decree No 2017-1063 of 18 May 2017 relating to ministerial cabinets

Decree No 2012-875 of 16 July 2012 on the creation of a commission for the renovation and deontology of public life

Decree No 2009-1730 of 30 December 2009 increasing the limit of election expenditures

Decree No 2001-213 of 8 March 2001 implementing Law No 62-1292 of 6 November 1962 relating to the election of the President of the Republic by universal suffrage

Decree No 98-1048 of 18 November 1998 relating to the evaluation of public policies

Decree No 64-46 of 14 January 1964 relating to strategic air forces

Decree No 63-766 of 30 July 1963 on public administration regulation for the application of Ordinance No 45-1708 of 31 July 1945 and relating to the organisation and functioning of the Council of State

Decree No 53-934 of 30 September 1953 on reforming administrative litigation

Decree of 27 April 1848 relating to the abolition of slavery in the French colonies and possessions

Decree of 5 March 1848 convening electoral assemblies and fixing the number of deputies to be elected

Decree of 6 December 1939 relating to the boards of directors of religious missions in the colonies

Decree of 16 January 1939 establishing overseas boards of directors of religious missions

Decree of 16 *Fructidor* Year III (2 September 1795) which prohibits the courts from hearing acts of administration, and cancels all procedures and judgments made in this regard

Others

Arcom Recommendation No 2021-03 of 6 October 2021 in relation to audio-visual communication services with a view to the 2022 election of the President of the Republic

Circular No 2012-056 of 27 March 2012

CSA Deliberation No 2017-62 of 22 November 2017 on the principle of political pluralism in the radio and television media services

CSA Recommendation No 2011-1 of 4 January 2011 on the principle of political pluralism in radio and television services during an election period

CASES

Constitutional Council

Decision No 2023-857 DC of 14 December 2023 *Loi de programmation des finances publiques pour les années 2023 à 2027*

Decision No 2022-843 DC of 12 August 2022 *Loi portant mesures d'urgence pour la protection du pouvoir d'achat*

Decision No 2022-152 ORGA of 11 March 2022 *Décision portant règlement intérieur sur la procédure suivie devant le Conseil constitutionnel pour les déclarations de conformité à la Constitution*

Decision No 2021-940 QPC of 15 October 2021 *Société Air France [Obligation pour les transporteurs aériens de réacheminer les étrangers auxquels l'entrée en France est refusée]*

Decision No 2021-824 QPC of 5 August 2021 *Loi relative à la gestion de la crise sanitaire*

Decision No 2020-801 DC of 18 June 2020 *Loi visant à lutter contre les contenus haineux sur internet* (*Loi Avia on online hate speech*)

Decision No 2020-841 QPC of 20 May 2020 *La Quadrature du Net et autres [Droit de communication à la Hadopi]*

Decision No 2020-800 DC of 11 May 2020 *Loi prorogeant l'état d'urgence sanitaire et complétant ses dispositions*

Decision No 2020-799 DC of 26 March 2020 *Loi organique d'urgence pour faire face à l'épidémie de covid-19*

Decision No 2019-823 QPC of 31 January 2020 *Union des industries de la protection des plantes [Interdiction de la production, du stockage et de la circulation de certains produits phytopharmaceutiques]*

Decision No 2019-28 ELEC of 21 February 2019 *Observations du Conseil constitutionnel relatives aux élections législatives des 11 et 18 juin 2017*

Decision No 2018-717/718 QPC of 6 July 2018 *M. Cédric H. et autre [Délit d'aide à l'entrée, à la circulation ou au séjour irréguliers d'un étranger]* (*Délit de solidarité*)

Decision No 2017-172 PDR of 20 July 2017 *Observations du Conseil constitutionnel sur l'élection présidentielle des 23 avril et 7 mai 2017*

Decision No 2017-632 QPC of 2 June 2017 *Union nationale des associations de familles de traumatisés crâniens et de cérébro-lésés [Procédure collégiale préalable à la décision de limitation ou d'arrêt des traitements d'une personne hors d'état d'exprimer sa volonté]*

Decision No 2015-470 QPC of 29 May 2015 *Société SAUR SAS [Interdiction d'interrompre la distribution d'eau dans les résidences principales]*

Decision No 2014-12 FNR of 1 July 2014 *Présentation du projet de loi relatif à la délimitation des régions, aux élections régionales et départementales et modifiant le calendrier électoral*

Decision No 2013-340 QPC of 20 September 2013 *M. Alain G. [Assujettissement à l'impôt sur le revenu des indemnités de licenciement ou de mise à la retraite]*

Decision No 2013-26 ELEC of 11 July 2013 *Observations du Conseil constitutionnel relatives aux élections législatives des 10 et 17 juin 2012*

Decision No 2013-156 PDR of 4 July 2013 *Décision du Conseil constitutionnel sur un recours de M. Nicolas Sarkozy dirigé contre la décision du 19 décembre 2012 de la Commission nationale des comptes de campagnes et des financements politiques*

Decision No 2013-669 DC of 17 May 2013 *Loi ouvrant le mariage aux couples de personnes de même sexe*

Decision No 2012-297 QPC of 21 February 2013 *Association pour la promotion et l'expansion de la laïcité [Traitement des pasteurs des églises consistoriales dans les départements du Bas-Rhin, du Haut-Rhin et de la Moselle]*

Decision No 2012-653 DC of 9 August 2012 *Traité sur la stabilité, la coordination et la gouvernance au sein de l'Union économique et monétaire*

Decision No 2011-157 QPC of 5 August 2011 *Société SOMODIA [Interdiction du travail le dimanche en Alsace-Moselle]*

Decision No 2011-125 QPC of 6 May 2011 *Mr Abderrahmane L. [Déferement devant le procureur de la République]*

Decision No 2010-79 QPC of 17 December 2010 *M. Kamel D. [Transposition d'une directive]*

Decision No 2010-618 DC of 9 December 2010 *Loi de réforme des collectivités territoriales*

Decision No 2010-52 QPC of 14 October 2010 *Compagnie agricole de la Crau [Imposition due par une société agricole]*

Decision No 2010-20/21 QPC of 6 August 2010, *M. Jean et autres (Loi Université)*

Decision No 2010-14/22 QPC of 30 July 2010 *M. Daniel W. et autres [Garde à vue]*

Decision No 2010-6/7 QPC of 11 June 2010 *M. Stéphane A. et autres [Article L 7 du code électoral]*

Decision No 2010-605 DC of 12 May 2010 *Loi relative à la concurrence et à la régulation du secteur des jeux d'argent et de hasard en ligne*

Decision No 2010-117 ORGA of 4 February 2010 *Décision portant règlement intérieur sur la procédure suivie devant le Conseil constitutionnel pour les questions prioritaires de constitutionnalité*

Decision No 2009-595 DC of 3 December 2009 *Loi organique relative à l'application de l'article 61-1 de la Constitution*

Decision No 2009-581 DC of 25 June 2009 *Résolution tendant à modifier le règlement de l'Assemblée nationale*

Decision No 2008-573 DC of 8 January 2009 *Loi relative à la commission prévue à l'article 25 de la Constitution et à l'élection des députés*

Decision No 2007-557 DC of 15 November 2007 *Loi relative à la maîtrise de l'immigration, à l'intégration et à l'asile*

Decision No 2006-543 DC of 30 November 2006 *Loi relative au secteur de l'énergie*

Decision No 2006-540 DC of 27 July 2006 *Loi relative au droit d'auteur et aux droits voisins dans la société de l'information*

Decision No 2006-535 DC of 30 March 2006 *Loi pour l'égalité des chances*

Decision No 2005-532 DC of 19 January 2006 *Loi relative à la lutte contre le terrorisme et portant dispositions diverses relatives à la sécurité et aux contrôles frontaliers*

Decision No 2005-31 REF of 24 March 2005 *Monsieur Stéphane HAUCHEMAILLE et Monsieur Alain MEYET*

Decision No 2004-509 DC of 13 January 2005 *Loi de programmation pour la cohésion sociale*

Decision No 2004-499 DC of 29 July 2004 *Loi relative à la protection des personnes physiques à l'égard des traitements de données à caractère personnel et modifiant la loi n° 78-17 du 6 janvier 1978 relative à l'informatique, aux fichiers et aux libertés* (*Protection des données personnelles*)

Decision No 2004-494 DC of 29 April 2004 *Loi relative à la formation professionnelle tout au long de la vie et au dialogue social*

Decision No 2003-468 DC of 3 April 2003 *Loi relative à l'élection des conseillers régionaux et des représentants au Parlement européen ainsi qu'à l'aide publique aux partis politiques*

Decision No 2003-469 DC of 26 March 2003 *Révision constitutionnelle relative à l'organisation décentralisée de la République*

Decision No 2002-461 DC of 29 August 2002 *Loi d'orientation et de programmation pour la justice*

Decision No 2021-940 QPC of 15 October 2021 *Société Air France [Obligation pour les transporteurs aériens de réacheminer les étrangers auxquels l'entrée en France est refusée]*

Decision No 2001-448 DC of 25 July 2001 *Loi organique relative aux lois de finances*

Decision No 2000-24 REF of 23 August 2000 *Monsieur Stéphane HAUCHEMAILLE*

Decision No 2000-23 REF of 23 August 2000 *Monsieur Pierre LARROUTUROU*

Decision No 2000-21 REF of 25 July 2000 *Monsieur Stéphane HAUCHEMAILLE*

Decision No 2000-433 DC of 27 July 2000 *Loi modifiant la loi n° 86-1067 du 30 septembre 1986 relative à la liberté de communication*

Decision No 2000-428 DC of 4 May 2000 *Loi organisant une consultation de la population de Mayotte*

Decision No 99-421 DC of 16 December 1999 *Loi portant habilitation du Gouvernement à procéder, par ordonnances, à l'adoption de la partie législative de certains codes*

Decision No 99-412 DC of 15 June 1999 *Charte européenne des langues régionales ou minoritaires*

Decision No 98-408 DC of 22 January 1999 *Traité portant statut de la Cour pénale internationale*

Decision No 98-407 DC of 14 January 1999 *Loi relative au mode d'élection des conseillers régionaux et des conseillers à l'Assemblée de Corse et au fonctionnement des Conseils régionaux*

Decision No 98-400 DC of 20 May 1998 *Loi organique déterminant les conditions d'application de l'article 88-3 de la Constitution relatif à l'exercice par les citoyens de l'Union européenne résidant en France, autres que les ressortissants français, du droit de vote et d'éligibilité aux élections municipales, et portant transposition de la directive 94/80/CE du 19 décembre 1994*

Decision No 94-359 DC of 19 January 1995 *Loi relative à la diversité de l'habitat*

Decision No 93-322 DC of 28 July 1993 *Loi relative aux établissements publics à caractère scientifique, culturel et professionnel* (*Statut des universités*)

Decision No 94-343/344 DC of 27 July 1994 *Loi relative au respect du corps humain et loi relative au don et à l'utilisation des éléments et produits du corps humain, à l'assistance médicale à la procréation et au diagnostic prénatal*

Decision No 93-325 of 13 August 1993 *Loi relative à la maîtrise de l'immigration et aux conditions d'entrée, d'accueil et de séjour des étrangers en France* (*Maîtrise de l'immigration*)

Decision No 92-313 of 23 September 1992 *Loi autorisant la ratification du traité sur l'Union européenne* (*Maastricht III*)

Decision No 92-312 DC of 2 September 1992 *Traité sur l'Union européenne (Maastricht II)*

Decision No 92-308 DC of 9 April 1992 *Traité sur l'Union européenne* (*Maastricht I*)

Decision No 91-290 DC of 9 May 1991 *Loi portant statut de la collectivité territoriale de Corse*

Decision No 89-271 DC of 11 January 1990 *Loi relative à la limitation des dépenses électorales et à la clarification du financement des activités politiques*

Decision No 88-248 DC of 17 January 1989 *Loi modifiant la loi n° 86-1067 du 30 septembre 1986 relative à la liberté de communication*

Decision No 88-244 DC of 20 July 1988 *Loi portant amnistie*

Decision No 88-14 REF of 9 November 1988 *Proclamation des résultats du référendum du 6 novembre 1988*

Decision No 86-224 DC of 23 January 1987 *Loi transférant à la juridiction judiciaire le contentieux des décisions du Conseil de la concurrence*

Decision No 86-218 DC of 18 November 1986 *Loi relative à la délimitation des circonscriptions pour l'élection des députés*

Decision No 86-217 DC of 18 September 1986 *Loi relative à la liberté de communication*

Decision No 86-208 DC of 2 July 1986 *Loi relative à l'élection des députés et autorisant le Gouvernement à délimiter par ordonnance les circonscriptions électorales* (*Découpage électoral*)

Decision No 85-197 DC of 23 August 1985 *Loi sur l'évolution de la Nouvelle-Calédonie*

Decision No 85-187 DC of 25 January 1985 *Loi relative à l'état d'urgence en Nouvelle-Calédonie et dépendances*

Decision No 83-165 DC of 20 January 1984 *Loi relative à l'enseignement supérieur* (*Libertés universitaires*)

Decision No 82-146 DC of 18 November 1982 *Loi modifiant le code électoral et le code des communes et relative à l'élection des conseillers municipaux et aux conditions d'inscription des Français établis hors de France sur les listes électorales* (*quotas de femmes*)

Decision No 82-141 DC of 27 July 1982 *Loi sur la communication audiovisuelle*

Decision No 82-137 DC of 25 February 1982 *Loi relative aux droits et libertés des communes, des départements et des régions*

Decision No 81-132 DC of 16 January 1982 *Loi de nationalisation* (*Nationalisation*)

Decision No 81-1 ELEC of 11 June 1981 *Monsieur François DELMAS*

Decision No 80-127 DC of 20 January 1981 *Loi renforçant la sécurité et protégeant la liberté des personnes*

Decision No 80-119 DC of 22 July 1980 *Loi portant validation d'actes administratifs*

Decision No 80-117 DC of 22 July 1980 *Loi sur la protection et le contrôle des matières nucléaires*

Decision No 79-105 DC of 25 July 1979 *Loi modifiant les dispositions de la loi n° 74-696 du 7 août 1974 relatives à la continuité du service public de la radio et de la télévision en cas de cessation concertée du travail*

Decision No 78-95 DC of 27 July 1978 *Loi complétant les dispositions de l'article 7 de la loi n° 60-791 du 2 août 1960 relative à l'enseignement et à la formation professionnelle agricole*

Decision No 77-87 DC of 23 November 1977 *Loi complémentaire à la loi n° 59-1557 du 31 décembre 1959 modifiée par la loi n° 71-400 du 1er juin 1971 et relative à la liberté de l'enseignement*

Decision No 75-59 DC of 30 December 1975 *Loi relative aux conséquences de l'autodétermination des îles des Comores*

Decision No 74-54 DC of 15 January 1975 *Loi relative à l'interruption volontaire de la grossesse* (*IVG*)

Decision No 73-51 DC of 27 December 1973 *Loi de finances pour 1974* (*Taxation d'office*)

Decision No 71-44 DC of 16 July 1971 *Loi complétant les dispositions des articles 5 et 7 de la loi du 1er juillet 1901 relative au contrat d'association* (*Liberté d'association*)

Decision No 71-42 DC of 18 May 1971 *Résolution tendant à modifier les articles 2, 3, 5, 6, 7, 8, 11, 13, 14, 17, 21, 22, 29, 32, 36, 42, 45, 59, 72 et 108 du règlement du Sénat, à le compléter par un article 29 bis et un article 109 et à abroger l'article 84 dudit règlement*

Decision No 62-20 of 6 November 1962 *Loi relative à l'élection du Président de la République au suffrage universel direct, adoptée par le référendum du 28 octobre 1962* (*Loi référendaire*)

Decision No 59-5 DC of 15 January 1960 *Résolution modifiant les articles 95 et 96 du règlement de l'Assemblée nationale*

Decision No 59-1 FNR of 27 November 1959 *Proposition de loi déposée par MM. Bajeux et Boulanger, sénateurs, tendant à la stabilisation des fermages (et à abroger le décret n° 59-175 du 7 janvier 1959 relatif au prix des baux à ferme)*

Decision No 59-2 DC of 24 June 1959 *Règlement de l'Assemblée nationale*

Council of State

CE, Sect, 9 June 2010, *Association CAP SUR L'AVENIR 13*, No 327423

CE, Ass., 30 October 1998, *Sarran, Levacher et autres*, Rec. Lebon 368

CE, Ass., 10 September 1992, *Meyet*, Rec. Lebon 327

CE, Ass., 8 February 1974, *Commune de Montory*, Rec. Lebon 93

CE, 23 October 1964, *d'Oriano*, Rec. Lebon 486

CE, Ass., 2 March 1962, *Rubin de Servens*, Rec. Lebon 143

CE, 13 December 1889, *Cadot c/ Ville de Marseille*, Rec. Lebon 1148

Court of Cassation

C. cass, Ass. plén., 20 January 2023, No 22-82.535

C. cass., Crim., 15 December 2010, Bull. crim. I, 2010, No 207

C. cass., Ass. plén., 2 June 2000, *Fraisse*, Bull. Ass. plén. 2000, No 4

European Court of Human Rights

Moulin v France, App No 37104/06, 23 February 2011

Bosphorus Hava Yolları Turizm ve Ticaret Anonim Şirketi (Bosphorus Airways) v Ireland [GC], App No 45036/98, 30 June 2005

Court of Justice of the European Union

The Minister for Justice and Equality v OG and PI (Case C-508/18), EU:C:2019:456, 27 May 2019

The Minister for Justice and Equality and Commissioner of the Garda Síochána (Case C-378/17), EU:C:2018:979, 4 December 2018

Stefano Melloni v Ministerio Fiscal (Case C-399/11), EU:C:2013:107, 26 February 2013

Yassin Abdullah Kadi and Al Barakaat International Foundation v Council of the European Union and Commission of the European Communities (Joined Cases C-402/05 P and C-415/05 P), EU:C:2008:461, 3 September 2008

Omega Spielhallen und Automatenaufstellungs-GmbH v Oberbürgermeisterin der Bundesstadt Bonn (Case C-36/02), EU:C:2004:614, 14 October 2004

Internationale Handelsgesellschaft (Solange I) (Case C-11/70), EU:C:1970:114, 17 December 1970

Flaminio Costa v ENEL (Case 6/64), EU:C:1964:66, 15 July 1964

Van Gend en Loos v Nederlandse Tariefcommissie (Case 26/62), EU:C:1963:1, 5 February 1963

Foreign national courts

Germany

Lisbon Case, BVerfG, cases 2 BvE 2/08

Federal Constitutional Court (*Bundesverfassungsgericht*), Decision of 30 June 2009, 2 BvE 2/08 et al., BVerfGE 123, 267–437

India

Supreme Court, *Kesavananda Bharati v State of Kerala*, (1973) 4 SCC 225

Israel

Supreme Court, Movement for Quality Government in Israel v the Knesset, HCJ 5658/23, 1st January 2024

Supreme Court, *United Mizrahi Bank v Migdal Cooperative Village*, 49(4) PD 221 (1995)

Italy

Constitutional Court (*Corte costituzionale*), Decision No 170 of 8 June 1984, *S.p.a. Granital v Amministrazione delle Finanze dello Stato*

Poland

Treatment of Polish Nationals and Other Persons of Polish Origin or Speech in the Danzig Territory (Advisory Opinion including the text of the declaration by Baron Rolin-Jaequemyns) [1932] PCIJ A/B 44

Spain

Constitutional Court (Spain), Decision on the Treaty establishing a Constitution for Europe (13 December 2004), complemented by Constitutional Court Judgment No 26/2014 of 13 February 2014

UK

Supreme Court, *R (Miller) v Secretary of State for Exiting the European Union* [2016] EWHC 2768 (Admin), [18]

House of Lords Select Committee on the Constitution, *Reviewing the Constitution* (First Report of Session 2001–2002), HL 11, July 2001, [20]

USA

Supreme Court, *Marbury v Madison*, 5 U.S. (1 Cranch) 137 (1803)

PART I

Bases of French Constitutional Law

Part I of this book contains the foundational knowledge necessary to comprehend the field of French constitutional law. This is done in two chapters: Chapter 1 delves into the key notions of French constitutional law, while Chapter 2 describes the rich history of French constitutional development.

DOI: 10.4324/9781003268871-1

1

KEY NOTIONS OF FRENCH CONSTITUTIONAL LAW

Chapter Summary

Constitutional law aims to establish a legal framework for the organisation and exercise of political power. This power is typically wielded within the boundaries of a state. In French constitutional law, the state serves as the fundamental paradigm for examining constitutional law along with the cognate notions of constitution, democracy, and separation of powers. This chapter presents a general overview of these concepts, as well as the principles that are closely associated with them. These principles include the idea of sovereignty, which is linked to the state; the hierarchy of norms, which is connected to the concept of the constitution; the rule of law, which is associated with democracy; and the different systems of government that uphold the principle of separation of powers.

State and Sovereignty

> *"L'État, divinité abstraite, aussi insaisissable dans son essence qu'insatiable dans ses appétits."*[1]

For centuries, the state has been the classical framework for the exercise of political power.[2] In contemporary times, the state remains the most prevalent form of societal organisation, with nearly 200 states existing worldwide.[3] The aspiration to establish an independent state is

1 Antoine Martinet (1776–1839), French churchman [The State, abstract divinity, as elusive in its essence as [it is] insatiable in its appetites].

2 The 1648 Treaty of Westphalia laid down the fundamental principles of the modern state, including sovereignty, non-interference in the internal affairs of other sovereign states, and the right to self-determination.

3 As recognised by the UN. In fact, more than 255 countries exist in the world but not all are officially recognised.

DOI: 10.4324/9781003268871-2

considered the foremost objective for a collective group who share a common territory, history, and values, allowing them to shape their own destiny. As of now, South Sudan holds the distinction of being the newest nation in the world, having gained independence from Sudan in 2011.

The state is both a reality and an abstraction. As a reality, the state is an entity that anyone can relate to in their daily activities when dealing with the public administration or using public services, such as, paying taxes, sending their children to public schools, using public roads etc. As an abstraction, the state represents the foundation which legitimises the exercise of political power and allows the separation between those who govern and those who are governed. Any society, even in its most primitive shape, needs some form of organisation to survive, in the first place, and to ensure more efficient operation, in the second place—such is the manifestation of political power. Political power lasts because of the state. As such, the state is indeed the institutionalised form of political power. The state has been, since the fifteenth century, the instrument of affirmation of sovereignty at the domestic level and international levels. At domestic level, the state, as a legal person, has the power to impose its decisions on citizens and is in charge of public order and, more generally, of ensuring the coherence of society. At international level, the state is responsible for international relations and ensures the independence of the country vis-à-vis other states.

Different theories explain the emergence of states. In classical constitutional law, a state is characterised by three main components: territory, population, and public power. Additionally, a state can take different forms, such as unitary or federal. However, the traditional understanding of the state in terms of its historical justification and organisational structure has been challenged by the emergence of new forms of political power, particularly at the international and supranational levels. The process of European integration and globalisation has significantly influenced domestic legal norms, leading to a re-evaluation of the boundaries of constitutional law beyond the state. Nevertheless, the state remains the paradigm for the exercise of political power based on the principles outlined in its constitution. This section delves into these issues.

The origins of the state

The concept of the state is a relatively new idea that emerged during the sixteenth century through the writings of Niccolò Machiavelli and Jean Bodin.[4] Following a discussion on the historical perspective of state development, this subsection presents the theories that elucidate the origins of the state.

The historical approach to the development of the state. The concept of the state builds upon previous forms of political organisations that deal with relations in society such as the Greek city-state and the Republic in the Antiquity. The development of the state includes two dimensions. Firstly, there is the institutional dimension, that is, the idea that the state refers to a temporal (as opposed to a spiritual), permanent (as opposed to the temporary power of the rulers), unified, independent, and institutionalised power. Such features enable a distinction to be made between the state, taken as an abstract legal entity supposed to last over time, and

4 Niccolò Machiavelli (1469–1527), Italian diplomat and philosopher, *The Prince* (circa 1513); Jean Bodin (1530–1596), French jurist and political philosopher, *The Six Books of the Republic* (1576).

the rulers, who are meant to exercise power only as long as their mandate lasts. Such features also provide for a justification of the state being the only entity entrusted to hold the monopoly of public power (*le monopole de la puissance publique*). The state may be thus defined as an abstract and permanent entity embodied by governmental and administrative bodies that exert power over those who are governed, constituting the legal framework of the exercise of political power, and in which relations in society are regulated. Secondly, there is the normative dimension, meaning that the state produces legal norms and is also subject to them. To prevent abuse of power and respect the rights of those who are governed, the state provides for its own limitations. The exercise of such self-restraint means that the state abides by general principles which precede its creation and are of superior force. These self-restraining rules are normally contained in a constitution or in legislation. In modern parlance, it is referred to as being subject to the rule of law (i.e., *État de droit* in French, or *Rechtsstaat* in German).

Theories about the origins of the state. Theories concerning the inception of the state revolve around a fundamental question: Is the state the result of a natural process or a deliberate creation by humans? Proponents of the former idea point to the theory of the state's natural origin, while proponents of the latter idea refer to the theory of the social contract. In the former scenario, the emergence of the state is seen as an inevitable outcome, representing the inherent evolution of societies and the advancement of human interactions. Conversely, in the latter scenario, the state's origins stem from a collective and conscious decision made by society.

The first theory finds its origins in the sociological theories that have analysed the evolution of human societies and the various ways in which these societies were established, whether over a long period of time or, on the contrary, over a shorter period as a result of violent episodes (e.g., wars, conquests) or not (i.e., alliances). In this regard, the Greek city-states of the Antiquity stand as the most relevant examples in the known history of embryonic state organisations. Closer to us, Carré de Malberg was a proponent of the natural origin of the state. He viewed the state as a natural and spontaneous phenomenon stemming from the need for a society to seek to improve its organisation.[5] Another point of reference here is Marx, who regarded the state as the result of a natural evolution but with "an end" (i.e., bound to disappear). Under Marxist theory, the state's disappearance was dictated by the need to replace the dominating class of bourgeois leaders by the proletariat to establish a new basis for ruling social relations.[6]

The second theory grounds the state in a conscientious act. This theory took shape with the social contract theories as developed by major philosophers during the seventeenth and eighteenth centuries (see Table 1.1 Theories of the social contract). Among them are Thomas Hobbes, John Locke, and Jean-Jacques Rousseau,[7] although the idea of a pact between men had already been evoked by Plato and explored by Althusius, Grotius, Spinoza, and Pufendorf. Here is Rousseau's reasoning with regard to the social contract and the formation of the state.

5 Raymond Carré de Malberg (1861–1935), French jurist and constitutional scholar, *Contributions à la théorie générale de l'État* (1920).

6 Karl Marx (1818–1883), German philosopher and political theorist, *Critique of Hegel's Philosophy of Right* (1843).

7 Thomas Hobbes (1588–1679), English philosopher, *Leviathan* (1651); John Locke (1632–1704), English philosopher, *Two Treaties of Government* (1689–1690), Jean-Jacques Rousseau (1712–1778), Genevan philosopher, *Du Contrat Social* (1762).

TABLE 1.1 Theories of the social contract

Thomas Hobbes (Leviathan, 1651)	*John Locke (Two Treaties of Government 1689/1690)*	*Jean-Jacques Rousseau (On the Social Contract, 1762)*
Relevant excerpts		
"Lastly, the agreement of these creatures is natural; that of men is by covenant only, which is artificial: and therefore, it is no wonder if there be somewhat else required, besides covenant [contract or agreement], to make their agreement constant and lasting; which is a common power to keep them in awe and to direct their actions to the common benefit. The only way to erect such a common power, able to defend them from the invasion of foreigners, and the injuries of one another, (...) is to confer all their power and strength upon one man, or upon one assembly of men, that may reduce all their wills, by plurality of voices, unto one will........ This is more than consent, or concord; it is a real unity of them all in one and the same person, made by covenant of every man with every man, in such manner as if every man should say to every man: I authorise and give up my right of governing myself to this man, or to this assembly of men, on this condition; that you give up, your right to him, and authorise all his actions in like manner. The multitude so united in one person is called a COMMONWEALTH; in Latin CIVITAS" [a state, in modern terms]. *Chapter XVII: Causes and Definition of a Commonwealth*	"Whosoever therefore out of a state of Nature unite into a community, must be understood to give up all the power, necessary to the ends for which they unite into Society, to the majority of the Community, unless they expressly agreed in any number greater than the majority. And this is done by barely agreeing to unite into one political society, which is all the compact that is, or needs be, between the individuals, that enter into, or make up a *common-wealth.* And thus that, which begins and actually constitutes any political society, is nothing but the consent of any number of freemen capable of a majority to unite and incorporate into such a society. And this is that, and that only, which did, or could give beginning to any lawful government in the world." *Second Treatise, § 99*	"I suppose men to have reached the point at which the obstacles in the way of their preservation in the state of nature show their power of resistance to be greater than the resources at the disposal of each individual for his maintenance in that state. That primitive condition can then subsist no longer; and the human race would perish unless it changed its manner of existence. But, as men cannot engender new forces, but only unite and direct existing ones, they have no other means of preserving themselves than the formation, by aggregation, of a sum of forces great enough to overcome the resistance. These they have to bring into play by means of a single motive power, and cause to act in concert. This sum of forces can arise only where several persons come together: but, as the force and liberty of each man are the chief instruments of his self-preservation, how can he pledge them without harming his own interests, and neglecting the care he owes to himself? This difficulty, in its bearing on my present subject, may be stated in the following terms—'The problem is to find a form of association which will defend and protect with the whole common force the person and goods of each associate, and in which each, while uniting himself with all, may still obey himself alone, and remain as free as before.' This is the fundamental problem of which the *social contract* provides the solution. (...) If then we discard from the social compact [contract] what is not of its essence, we shall find that it reduces itself to the following terms— *'Each of us puts his person and all his power in common under the supreme direction of the general will, and, in our corporate capacity, we receive each member as an indivisible part of the whole.'"* *Book I, Chapter 6*

(*Continued*)

TABLE 1.1 Continued

Thomas Hobbes (Leviathan, 1651)	*John Locke (Two Treaties of Government 1689/1690)*	*Jean-Jacques Rousseau (On the Social Contract, 1762)*
Characteristics of the state of nature		
The state of nature, is "a war of every man against every man." There is no security for individuals.	The state of nature is a state of perfect freedom and equality. However, it does not allow the protection of the right of property. Property is defined in a broad sense: it covers the protection of life, freedoms, and goods of individuals.	The state of nature is a state of freedom and equality. It is society which subverts men with the idea of property, which causes inequality.
Objectives of the social contract		
Men [*sic*] have an interest in submitting themselves to an absolute sovereign, the State, which assures, by use of force, social peace. Men, by the social pact, renounce their natural freedoms in exchange for safety, guarantee by a State which protects them against others.	In order to respect the rights and property of an individual from encroachments of their neighbours, laws are necessary or, in other words a political power, a state. To enter into political society and to submit themselves to the laws of a State is a way for individuals to improve the protection of their rights.	In an unequal civil society, individuals have an interest in entering into a contract enabling each individual to be a citizen and to participate in the exercise of sovereignty. Political society is then created and is the result of an association agreed between free and equal individuals.

Firstly, the initial state of man [*sic*] is the state of nature in which men are free and equal. However, this situation of happiness is gradually replaced by a perverted situation in which inequality emerges among men because they follow their natural inclination to dominate others (i.e., masters and slaves, rulers and ruled). A truly just society can only therefore arise from the agreement between willing individuals who understand the usefulness of banding together to be stronger. In a final step, these individuals unite their rights and their goods, and the "society" thus created is placed under the authority of the general will as the basis of the social pact and the foundation of the state. Within such an entity, the individual, who has abandoned everything to the community, finds freedom and equality in return.

What the various social contract theories have in common is the idea that the state is the product of a conscious will of men and women who accept to give up their freedom and rights to the authority of the state in order to ensure, in return, the protection of their person and goods. Social contract theories have never received any concrete application. As theories, they are precisely based on the abstract construct of an agreement (i.e., social pact or contract) that men and women need to renew by accepting, regularly and tacitly, to be part of an organised political society and obey its laws and rulers. However, these theories represent an essential building block to understanding how states have been legally formed over the course of history. The other mode of formation of the state, that is violence, excludes such a legal explanation.

The concept of the state

In the view of Carré de Malberg, the state is described as "a community of individuals, established in a particular territory, and equipped with a structure that grants the group a supreme power to act, command, and coerce when interacting with its members."[8] Thus, in its legal meaning, the state is a legal entity formed by three fundamental components: a territory representing its geographic or material aspect, a population embodying its social or personal aspect, and a public power, also known as state authority, representing its political aspect. This subsection explores these components in turn.

The territory. Inland, maritime, and aerial borders delimit the territory over which the state exercises its authority. The territory provides the necessary geographical space for the population to live on over which the state exercises its authority. Moreover, the territory ensures the cohesion and protection of the population that resides on it. While a state can overcome changes that affect its boundaries, whether these changes divide its territory or remove part of it (e.g., the annexation and occupation of Alsace and Lorraine by Germany after 1870; the partition of Ireland after the Anglo-Irish Treaty in 1921; the concession of Hong Kong by China to the UK until 1997), a state cannot survive without a territory. There is no upper or lower limit to the size of a state territory, and some states are extremely large (e.g., Russia, China, and the USA) while others are tiny (e.g., the Vatican, San Marino, Liechtenstein).

The population. This component can be described as the social group or gathering of natural persons that forms a community and that is distinct from other groups of individuals. This social element is linked to the concept of the nation. Historically, two conceptions of the nation were proposed in European thinking. On the one hand, the German conception of the nation was developed during the nineteenth century. Such a conception proposed a relatively objective definition of the nation based on a common language, a common religion, a common culture, and common traditions but also referred to the race of the people living in the same geographical space. On the other hand, the French conception, notably promoted by Renan,[9] suggested that the formation of a nation was a more complex phenomenon. In addition to the objective criteria identified under the German conception, the nation was perceived as being based on the desire of the people to live together because they shared a common history and, as a group, could relate to key events that forged their sense of belonging together (e.g., people from Alsace-Lorraine in France). In other words, a common heritage, and a personal willingness to share that heritage, define the nation under the French conception. In the words of Renan:

> A nation is a soul, a spiritual principle. Two things, which in truth are but one, constitute this soul or spiritual principle. One lies in the past, one in the present. One is the possession in common of a rich legacy of memories; the other is present-day consent, the desire

8 Raymond Carré de Malberg (1861–1935), French jurist and constitutional scholar, *Contributions à la théorie générale de l'État* (1920).

9 Ernest Renan (1823–1892), French scholar in semitic and civilisation studies.

to live together, the will to perpetuate the value of the heritage that one has received in an undivided form.[10]

The modern conception of the nation is a mix of the objective and subjective conceptions of the nation.

The continuity between the people (i.e., a population living on the same territory),[11] the nation (i.e., a population having a sense of belonging together and wishing to live together), and the state (i.e., people agreeing to bind themselves by a social contract to guarantee their freedom and security) is crucial in understanding the concept of the state: people declared themselves as forming a nation in which individuals held a nationality (as consecrated since the 1789 Revolution) from which national sovereignty was derived (i.e., political power belonging to the nation) and the power and legitimacy of any nation to declare itself a state (i.e., concept of the nation-state). In most European countries, where the model of the nation-state is widespread, the creation of a state was the way to recognise, in legal and political terms, the formation of such nations which already had a dense common history (e.g., German unity in 1850; Italian unity in 1871; French unity as realised under the Third Republic in the period 1875–1940). In other parts of Europe and the world, the reality of the creation of the state is as complex but does not always correspond to the model of the establishment of the nation-state. For example, it is often the case that several populations with strong identities (i.e., ethnicities), which therefore do not constitute a homogeneous group of people susceptible to form a nation, share the same territory under the authority of a state. The boundaries of such states were often imposed under colonisation rules (e.g., Cyprus, India, Rwanda, Sri Lanka). In these cases, the state precedes the creation of a nation. In certain cases, the federal form of government has allowed, notably in western nation-states, the de-escalation of tensions and rivalries between different parts of the population (e.g., Canada, Switzerland, and Belgium).

The authority of the state. The political element of the state is more abstract. It has been referred to under different concepts in the literature such as institutionalised power ("*pouvoir institutionnalisé,*" Georges Burdeau), state power or sovereignty ("*puissance d'État*" or "*souveraineté,*" Carré de Malberg), public authority ("*autorité publique*"), or, merely, political power ("*pouvoir politique*"). The state, as a legal entity, exercises political power. This political element has two main implications: firstly, it allows a community, composed of numerous individuals, to be unified and endow the state with the legal capacity, through its government and administration, to rule; secondly, it makes it possible to consecrate the state in the continuity of time while entrusting its rulers to govern for a limited period. It follows that governments

10 Ernest Renan Conference, *Qu'est-ce qu'une nation ?* 11 March 1882, Sorbonne, Paris.

11 The notions of "population" and "people" are intertwined. As soon as individuals residing on the territory (*population*) decide to live together on the territory and pursue common interests and defend common values, they form a people (*peuple*). There is a principle of indivisibility of the French people under French constitutional law which is linked to the principle of indivisibility of sovereignty as expressed in the principle of indivisibility of the Republic (see below).

must accept acts, decisions, and treaties of previous governments. The other key element of the state in this matter is its sovereignty, which is examined under the relevant section below.

The organisational form of the state

There are two primary forms of state organisation: unitary and federal. The unitary form is the most widespread form of organisation, characterised by principles of unity and centralisation. France serves as a prime example of a unitary state. On the other hand, the federal form has become the prevailing choice for larger states due to its effectiveness and flexibility. Countries such as Australia, Brazil, Canada, Germany, India, Mexico, Russia, South Africa, and the USA have adopted the federal system. Additionally, smaller states such as Austria, Belgium, and Switzerland have embraced federalism to accommodate linguistic or other forms of diversity. This subsection examines the concepts and characteristics of both the unitary and federal state models.

The unitary state. The unitary principle implies the centralisation of all public authorities, meaning the existence of a single government, a single Parliament, and a single judicial power. An example of such centralisation in a unitary state is expressed in article 1 of the French Constitution, which proclaims that "France is an indivisible Republic." However, excessive centralisation may lead to different kinds of challenges regarding the exercise of power, possibly to an inefficient public administration and inequalities between territories (e.g., "Paris and the French desert").[12] Mechanisms such as de-concentration and decentralisation have been developed to remediate such defects by bringing the state public administration closer to the citizens. Besides, the unitary form of state has had to accommodate other forms of delegation due to an increasing claim to regionalism by territorial areas to manage their own affairs (e.g., devolution in the UK).

De-concentration consists in the delegation of several competences from the central government to a state authority which exercises it within a clearly defined territorial framework (e.g., the department, the region). Such delegation is administrative rather than political in the sense that it does not modify the nature of the relations between the state and those it governs. For instance, the French prefect exercises the authority of the state in his/her territorial constituency and is responsible for all de-concentrated public services therein such as agriculture, infrastructure, and equipment etc. The underlying concerns justifying de-concentration relate to the difficulty for the state to administer all aspects of public administration on the whole territory, especially when such a territory is relatively vast. Imperatives of efficiency and democracy call for bringing the administrative decision-maker closer to where the decision applies on the territory. Therefore, the state territory is divided into territorial administrative units, or districts, whose administrators exercise delegated powers on behalf of the state and act as its representative.[13]

12 Jean-François Gravier, *Paris et le Désert Français* (Flammarion 1947). The book explores the unequal distribution of resources between the Parisian area (Île-de-France) and the rest of the country after the Second World War.

13 See the famous quote that symbolically epitomises the concept of de-concentration: "It is still the same hammer that hits, but we have shortened the handle." Uttered after the adoption of the decree of 25 March 1852 on

Decentralisation also consists in a delegation of certain powers from central government to local authorities. However, contrary to de-concentrated authorities, decentralised authorities are distinct and independent from the state. Decentralised local authorities have legal personality and are entrusted with an autonomous decision-making power for the management of local affairs. They consist of a deliberating body and an executive body whose members are elected by local citizens. This form of delegation, which brings citizens closer to where decisions affecting them in their daily life are taken, aims at enhancing local democracy. The autonomy of decentralised authorities therefore results from the following traits: besides the fact that they possess legal personality, decentralised authorities self-administer through their own local bodies and have their own budgetary resources. Decentralised local authorities must, however, respect the laws of the state.

Numerous examples of such decentralised forms of government exist in Europe, such as the local government in the UK and, to a more limited extent, in Ireland.[14] Additionally, Italy is known for its regional governance structure, and Spain has autonomous communities, both of which are often recognised as highly decentralised states. In France, the process of decentralisation has been slow and incremental, starting in the early 1980s. Historically, France has always leaned towards an extreme form of centralisation, ever since revolutionary Jacobinism made its own the principle of indivisibility of the Republic inherited from the *Ancien Régime* to eschew any possible federalist turn. Nevertheless, in its contemporary form, the French state features a degree of decentralisation. Decentralisation or local government, in France, has come about in several steps. In the nineteenth century, the laws of 1871 and 1884 created, respectively, the departments (*départements*) and the municipalities (*communes*). Under the current regime, the Law of 2 March 1982 established the regions (*régions*) as other constitutional local authorities as well as provided for an extensive delegation of powers from the state to local authorities.[15] The 2003 constitutional amendment consecrated the decentralised nature of the French Republic by amending article 1 of the Constitution in the following terms: "France is an indivisible, secular, democratic, and social Republic. The Republic shall ensure equality of all citizens under the law without discrimination based on origin, race, or religion. The Republic respects all beliefs. *Its organisation is decentralised* … (emphasis added)."[16]

The aim of decentralisation is to bring the public administration closer to the citizens to take into account the specificities of the various components of the state's territory. These specificities relate, among others, to the economic dynamism of a particular territory, the place of tourism in such an area, its insularity, its energy resources, its demography etc. Decentralisation can, however, produce perverse effects. When the delegation of powers from the state to

administrative decentralisation, these words are ascribed to Odilon Barrot. Barrot served as the President of the Council of Ministers from 1848 to 1849 during the presidency of Louis Napoléon Bonaparte.

14 Ireland is the epitome of a small, centralised, and unitary state. Local governance services are provided by local authorities at county and city level which work within specific geographic areas, called Local Government Areas. Local authorities have competencies related to housing and building, planning permission, and essential services such as roads and bridges. Regions play a limited role in Ireland. There are three Regional Assemblies, which have particular power in relation to spatial planning and economic development (i.e., Eastern and Midland Regional Assembly, Northern and Western Regional Assembly, and Southern Regional Assembly). For more, see Mark Callanan, *Local Government in the Republic of Ireland* (Institute of Public Administration 2018).

15 Law No 82-213 of 2 March 1982 relating to the rights and freedoms of municipalities, departments, and regions, the so-called "loi Defferre" from the name of its instigator, Gaston Defferre, minister for Home Affairs (1981–1984).

16 Constitutional Law No 2003-276 of 28 March 2003 relating to the decentralised organisation of the Republic.

local authorities, hence the actual disengagement of the state towards local authorities, is not matched by a corresponding transfer of budgetary resources, inequalities between territories can develop. In the end, a lot depends on the strengths and weaknesses of local authorities and the way in which local government is managed.

De-concentration and decentralisation are two distinct processes addressing different needs of the unitary state. However, these processes can be combined since a unitary state, particularly a relatively vast one, which is necessarily de-concentrated, can also accommodate a degree of decentralisation to address deeper democratic concerns. France provides a good example in that regard. The administration of state affairs is done by de-concentration and decentralised authorities: at the regional and departmental levels, a departmental *prefect* (and a regional *prefect*), as per de-concentration, and a *president* of the departmental council (and regional council), as per decentralisation, coexist; at the municipality level, the mayor wears "two hats," that of the state representative, as per de-concentration, and that of the elected executive member in the local authority, as per decentralisation.

A unitary state may also feature an ultra-decentralisation process, or regionalism, leaving to the local authorities (called "regions," "provinces," or "communities," depending on the state concerned) a wide autonomy be it administrative, financial, and even legislative, to the point that their form is closer to that of a federal state rather than a unitary state. In that context, regionalism concerns the transfer, or devolution, to the local government of an autonomous legislative power which is endowed with administrative and financial autonomy. What makes such local government distinct from federated states is that local authorities do not have political decision-making power. Such power remains with the central state; local authorities are not represented in Parliament in a federal type of parliamentary house. Regionalism may be interpreted in different ways. For some, regionalism represents the ultimate outgrowth of decentralisation. For others, regionalism may well be a transitional form between an advanced decentralised state and an upcoming federal form. Alternatively, regionalism may be interpreted as its own form of state, distinct from both the unitary and the federal state.

Spain, Italy, and the UK have allowed this advanced form of decentralised state to develop. Spain, for example, is qualified as "the state of autonomous communities" (*comunidades autónomas)*, based on the principle of territorial autonomy embodied in its different municipalities, provinces, and autonomous communities.[17] Italy is qualified as "the state of regions" (*regioni d'Italia*), based on the territorial division between regions, provinces, and municipalities or communes.[18] Still, in a 2006 referendum, the Italian people rejected a more advanced form of federalism. The UK can be described as "a multinational state" which, under the devolu-

17 Article 2 of the Spanish Constitution: "The Constitution is based on the indissoluble unity of the Spanish Nation, the common and indivisible homeland of all Spaniards; it recognises and guarantees the right to self-government of the nationalities and regions of which it is composed and the solidarity among them all." There are currently 17 autonomous communities in Spain with highly variable and unequal competences. For further details, see Agustín Ruiz Robledo, *Constitutional Law in Spain*, *International Encyclopaedia of Laws* (3rd edn, Wolters Kluwer 2023).

18 Article 114 of the Italian Constitution: "The Republic is divided into Regions, Provinces and Municipalities." There are currently 20 regions endowed with autonomous status in Italy, consisting of 15 ordinary regions and five special regions (namely, Friuli-Venezia Giulia, Sardinia, Sicily, Trentino-Alto Adige, and Val d'Aosta) that enjoy special status with enhanced administrative, financial, fiscal, and legislative autonomy. For further details, see Valerio Onida et alii, *Constitutional Law in Spain*, *International Encyclopaedia of Laws* (3rd edn, Wolters Kluwer 2021).

tion legislation, has transferred a number of powers from the central Parliament (Westminster) to the local parliaments of Scotland (Scottish Parliament), Northern Ireland (Northern Ireland Assembly), Wales (National Assembly for Wales), and to their associated executive bodies, namely the Scottish Government, the Northern Ireland Executive, and the Welsh Government.[19] Despite a number of differences in status among these devolved authorities, one common point is that the devolved authorities cannot exercise sovereign powers. These sovereign powers relate, for example, to constitutional issues, international relations and defence, nuclear energy, and nationality, as opposed to devolved powers which concern areas such as education, agriculture, tourism, the environment, or economic development. Again, devolution differs from federalism in that the devolved powers to the sub-national authority ultimately reside in central government because the state remains de jure a unitary state. Legislation creating devolved parliaments, or assemblies, can be repealed or amended by the central government in the same way as any ordinary law.

The federal state. A federal state is an association of states which superimposes, at two levels, the federal level and the (federated) state level. The federal state is founded on a constitution and consists of several distinct states (i.e., federated states). The federated states have transferred part of their powers, and henceforth sovereignty, to the federal entity. A federal state is characterised by two fundamental features: firstly, a federal constitution, which is the foundational act of the union between the federated states and which the federal entity draws power from; secondly, the juxtaposition of the federal level and state level. Federated states receive various appellations in the different federal states of the world such as "*régions*" and "*communautés*" in Belgium, "provinces" in Canada, "*Länders*" in Germany, "субъекты Российской Федерации" or "subjects of the Federation" in Russia, "*cantons*" in Switzerland, or "States" in the USA.

The federal state is distinct from the co-federal state, or confederation. The confederation is a form of association of states which are independent but decide, for various reasons, to cooperate in certain areas. The main distinctive features of the confederation compared with the federation are the following: the confederation does not entail the creation of a new sovereign state and does not entail the superimposition of two state levels; the confederation is based on a treaty and not a constitution; the confederation exercises competences in limited areas only (e.g., industrial, military, or economic areas) which must be to the advantage of the associated states; the confederation is an intergovernmental form of organisation which requires unanimity in its decision-making process. Examples of confederations are limited to historical ones. It is often the case that such a form of state was a transitional form towards fully fledged federalism. For example, several states of the USA formed a confederation in 1776 before forming a federation in 1787. The same is true for Germany in 1871 and Switzerland in 1848, the latter having retained the name of the Swiss Confederation. Russia appears to be a different case as the disaggregation of the federal state (i.e., dissolution of the Soviet Union) in 1991 led to the creation of the Commonwealth of Independent States (CIS) by Russia, Belarus, and Ukraine.[20]

19 Devolution has also concerned London with the London Assembly and its executive body, the Greater London Authority. For further details, see David Wilson & Chris Game, *Local Government in the United Kingdom* (5th edn, Springer 2018).

20 Ukraine left the CIS in 2018.

The CIS is a confederal type of (regional) organisation composed of ten former USSR republics in Eurasia aimed at encouraging cooperation in the economic, political, and military areas and has certain powers to coordinate trade, finance, security, and law-making.

As a form of state organisation, federalism aims to address two distinct motivations, namely a motivation of association or a motivation of dissociation. The federalism by association type results from the union of independent states which decide to associate themselves by adopting a federal constitution in order to share means and powers while preserving part of their sovereignty. American federalism epitomises federalism by association, which was formed when the former British colonies vowed to resist British rulers and fought for their independence.[21] In the federalism by dissociation type, the federal state results from the partition of a unitary state into several autonomous states, which accept to be bound to each other within the federal framework. Such federalism is exemplified by Belgium, which became a federal state in 1993 to allow more autonomy to its decentralised local authorities. Belgium is currently composed of three regions (i.e., Flanders, Wallonia, and Brussels), three communities (German-speaking, French-speaking, and Flemish-speaking), ten provinces, and 589 municipalities. This makes Belgium's political and administrative structure quite complex. However, the Federal State of Belgium is a fragile construct as it is regularly the object of criticism, notably from certain Flemish provinces demanding more independence.[22]

There are several advantages for establishing a federal state stemming from the idea that "together, we are stronger." More specifically, the federal structure allows the creation of a stronger entity (i.e., the federal state) at the diplomatic, military, and economic levels in addition to the optimisation of the management of key policies and public services (i.e., defence, customs, communications, energy, transport, change etc.). The federal structure also brings the administration closer to its citizens since decisions are made at the most appropriate level in terms of efficiency, thus allowing the local (state) level to decide on the matters that are most relevant to the day-to-day lives of citizens. Besides, the type of vertical separation of powers of the federal structure is arguably a factor of stability and moderation in the relationships between powers. Most importantly, because a state that is part of a federal union keeps its autonomy and identity, the federal structure allows for the various identities and communities that are based on the various linguistic, religious, ethnic, and/or cultural differences within the federation to be respected and heard.

Federalism is based on three principles: superposition, autonomy, and participation.[23] The principle of superposition means that there are two levels of political and legal organisation, namely the federal level and the state level. This principle is itself governed by two regulatory principles, namely the principle of primacy, or supremacy, of federal law, and the principle of direct applicability, or direct effect, of federal law. According to the principle of supremacy, federal law is supreme over (inconsistent) state law. According to the principle of direct effect, federal law is, in principle, directly applicable to all citizens without intervention of the federated states.

21 Other examples of federalism by association include Germany and Switzerland.

22 Other examples of federalism by dissociation include Mexico and Brazil.

23 The idea of the principles of autonomy and participation was developed by Georges Scelle in his *Précis de Droit des Gens* (1932).

The idea behind the principle of autonomy is that the federated states determine, within limits, their own institutional organisation. Each state has their own constitution, as well as their own executive, legislative, and judicial powers. This explains why states may have different legislation in certain areas such as, for example in the USA, on abortion, on the death penalty, or on social policy. States retain their sovereignty at the domestic level on the territory that they govern. In principle, federated states do not enjoy external sovereignty since only the federal state is legally recognised on the international scene. An interesting development came about in relation to the USA under the Trump presidency (2016–2020). Given the decision of Trump to renounce the 2016 Paris Agreement on Climate Change in 2017, several states (namely, California, Washington, and New York) sought to enter into alliances and agreements with states and local authorities in other countries to compensate for the absence of commitment at the American federal level. For example, the governor of California took part in international summits and concluded a number of agreements with Canada, Mexico, and Sweden on matters relating to the environment. This arguably questions the exercise of external sovereignty of the American federation.

The principle of participation, or association, means that federated states remain associated with political decisions at the federal level. This has three implications: firstly, the right of the federated states to take part in the adoption and, most frequently, amending process of the federal constitution (i.e., constituent power); secondly, the right of the federated states to take part in the elaboration of federal laws (i.e., legislative power); thirdly, the right of the federated states to take an equal part in the political decision-making process (i.e., political power) whatever their demographic or geographical size, which is a sine qua non condition of the participation of smaller states.[24] The configuration of the federal Parliament, as a bicameral legislature, reflects this: one House represents the population in its entirety (e.g., House of Representatives in the USA, and *Bundestag* in Germany) while the other House represents the states (e.g., Senate in the USA, and *Bundesrat* in Germany). The states can also be represented in the federal executive power as it is the case in Canada or in Switzerland. The states can participate in the election of the federal executive power as is the case, for instance, in the USA with the election of the US President through the process of the Electoral College based on elections at state level.

The allocation of powers between the states and the federal state is laid down in the federal constitution. The principle of such an allocation is the distinction between general powers (*compétences de droit commun*) and conferred powers (*compétences d'exception* or *d'attribution*). Indeed, instead of enumerating the different powers attributed to each level, the federal constitution resorts to the following distribution principle: if the state level is endowed with general powers, then the federal level is attributed certain specific powers—vice versa, if it is the federal level that is endowed with general powers, then the state level takes "what is left." The first type of allocation corresponds to the association-type of federalism as is the case, for example, in the USA by virtue of the Tenth Amendment to the 1787 Constitution: "The powers not delegated to the United States by the Constitution, nor prohibited by it to the States, are reserved to the States respectively, or to the people." The second type of allocation corresponds to the dissociation-type of federalism as is applied, for example, in Canada and South Africa.

24 The principle of equality is not always strictly applied, and certain adjustments may be considered to address significant demographical disparities, as observed in Austria, Canada, and Germany.

However, the situation is often more complex in practice, with a third group of powers emerging in addition to those reserved to the federal state and those reserved to the states—powers that are shared by the two levels. Subsidiarity is the regulatory principle in that regard whereby federal powers are those which are deemed more rationally and effectively exercised at federal level. These powers include, for example, international relations, defence, diplomacy, and, generally, all powers attached to external sovereignty. The federated states keep powers in areas such as education, culture, family matters, and possibly taxation, insurance, and banking matters, while some areas are better exercised if shared, such as powers as regards the economy, transport, energy, and employment. Obviously, such allocation of powers is different in every federal state and may fluctuate in time within a given federal state depending on constitutional interpretation and practice. The regulatory authority of federalism is a court—a supreme court (e.g., Supreme Court in the USA) or a special constitutional court (e.g., Federal Constitutional Court, *Bundesverfassungsgericht*, or *BverfG*, in Germany). The court's role is to adjudicate, by interpreting the constitution, on conflicts of powers between the federal state and the federated state(s) involved, or between federated states. The court also exercises judicial review of state law as regards their compliance with federal law.

Recent developments in a number of federal states have prompted a reflection on what appears to be a crisis of federalism. Several factors explain this state of affairs: firstly, the dilution of responsibilities resulting from an increasingly blurred allocation of powers between the federal and state levels; secondly, the trend towards an aggregation of powers by the federal state to the detriment of federated states, as is the case in Germany and in Russia; thirdly, the questioning of the federal form itself as the cases of Belgium and Canada show; fourthly, the emergence of derivative forms of federalism which challenge the classical form, Belgium and Russia being good examples in that regard. Reflection on the relevance of federalism is also interesting when talking about the EU in the context of more general developments about other forms of political organisation beyond the state.

Beyond the state: The European Union and other forms of political organisations

Beyond the confines of traditional nation-states, there exist alternative political organisations that warrant consideration. The EU, as a remarkable form of legal integration, serves as an exemplary case in point. Broadly speaking, the concepts of Europeanisation, internationalisation, and globalisation offer fertile ground for scholarly exploration into the potential evolution of constitutional law beyond national borders. Within this subsection, we touch upon several of these ideas.

The European Union: Towards a federal state? The current process of European integration began after the Second World War, although there had been earlier proposals for the establishment of a "United States of Europe." As far back as the nineteenth century, influential figures such as Victor Hugo advocated for a European project, expressing it in the following manner:

> The day will come when we see these two immense groups, the United States of America and *the United States of Europe*, placed opposite each other, reaching out to each other across the seas, exchanging their products, their trade, their industry, their arts, their geniuses (...)

> In our old Europe, England took the first step, and by her age-old example, she said to the people: "You are free!" France took the second step and said to the people: "You are sovereign!" Now let us take the third step, and all together, France England, Belgium, Germany, Italy, Europe, America, let us say to the people: "You are brothers!" (Emphasis added)[25]

Right after the war, Winston Churchill actively advocated for the idea of a unified Europe. However, he held the belief that the UK should not be a participant in this endeavour. Churchill was firmly convinced that a united Europe would serve as a definitive solution to the deep-rooted issues of nationalism and the propensity for war within the continent:

> I wish to speak about the tragedy of Europe, this noble continent, the home of all the great parent races of the Western world, the foundation of Christian faith and ethics, the origin of most of the culture, arts, philosophy, and science both of ancient and modern times. If Europe were once united in the sharing of its common inheritance there would be no limit to the happiness, prosperity, and glory which its 300 million or 400 million people would enjoy. Yet it is from Europe that has sprung that series of frightful nationalistic quarrels (…) What is this sovereign remedy? It is to recreate the European fabric, or as much of it as we can, and to provide it with a structure under which it can dwell in peace, safety, and freedom. We must build *a kind of United States of Europe*. (Emphasis added)[26]

Since the very start of the European construction in the 1950s, the "federalists" have been opposed to the "sovereigntists": while the former advocate for a federal Europe which would see the member states become integrated as federated states into a European federation, the latter's stance is to defend the sovereignty and identity of nation-states. Today, the EU has become a supranational organisation sui generis (i.e., of its own kind), epitomising one of the most developed forms of integration in the world. The EU is founded on two main treaties, namely the Treaty on European Union (effective since the 1992 Maastricht Treaty) and the Treaty on the Functioning of the European Union (effective since the 1957 Treaty of Rome). As a Union based on the rule of law, the EU has legal personality and is a source of law. Its decision-making process is based on a majority voting system and deals with areas of sovereign nature that member states have accepted to transfer to the Union. The EU is endowed with its own institutions consisting of the European Council, the Council of Ministers of the EU, the European Parliament, the European Central Bank, the European Court of Auditors, and the Court of Justice of the EU.[27] The EU Treaties, general principles, and Charter of Fundamental Rights are known as primary legislation.[28] Secondary legislation consists of the acts adopted by the EU. In the landmark cases of *Van Gend en Loos* (1963) and *Costa v ENEL* (1964), the CJEU developed the fundamental doctrines of direct effect and primacy of EU law.[29] The doctrine of direct effect is based on the idea that, if a provision of EU law is directly effective, it gives

25 Victor Hugo Opening Speech, 21 August 1849, International Peace Congress, Paris.

26 Winston Churchill Speech, 19 September 1946, University of Zurich.

27 For more details on the EU institutional framework, see, among others, Dermot Hodson et alii (eds), *The Institutions of the European Union* (5th edn, OUP 2021).

28 International agreements concluded by the EU are subordinate to primary legislation.

29 *Van Gend en Loos v Nederlandse Tariefcommissie* (Case 26/62) [1963] ECR 1; *Costa v ENEL* (Case 6/64) [1964] ECR 585.

rise to rights upon which individuals can rely directly in the domestic courts. The doctrine of supremacy dictates that EU law takes precedence over conflicting provisions of domestic law. The EU has also established a complete system of legal remedies and procedures designed to enable the CJEU to review the legality of EU institutions' acts.

Qualifying what is or, rather, what has become the EU after all these changes, whether prompted by treaties, legislation, or case law, is a difficult endeavour. As a "non-identified political object" ("*objet politique non identifié*"),[30] the EU is not a confederation that would have grown out by reason of its extreme degree of integration. Neither has the EU transitioned towards a fully fledged federation, for several reasons. The EU does not have the features of a sovereign state for reasons linked to the absence of a unified European people and lack of demos as the subject of legitimisation, to the lack of a common and independent foreign policy (and European army), and, to an extent, to the lack of governmental authority. Also, the EU does not display the guarantees attached to federalism such as a federal constitution and a federal Parliament with two Houses ensuring the participation of the federated states in one of the Houses. In short, ever since the failure of the Treaty establishing a Constitution for Europe in 2005, the question of the future development of the EU has been posed.

This is without mentioning the difficult political questions that the EU is facing at the moment not only because of the still-unfolding Brexit and the relationships with the UK, but also because of a general defiance towards what the EU represents and ought to represent for Europeans. Several options can be put forward as regards the evolution of the EU as a form of political organisation. A first option is the, surely controversial, development of the EU towards a form of federalism (i.e., from a pre-federal state to a fully fledged federal state superimposed on the 27 member states). A second option, equally controversial, consists in the EU somehow backtracking towards an intergovernmental logic, that is, of an alliance between sovereign nation-states. A third option is the development of the EU into a *new form* of political organisation, if one concedes that the state, in its current form, is not the ultimate and only form of political organisation that can be envisaged. This poses the question of conciliating sovereignty and federalism, perhaps in the framework of a "federation of nation-states" or "multinational federation."[31] Whatever the option, the particularity of the European project as well as its democratic legitimacy ought to be considered.[32] In any case, all this is dependent on politics, which arguably makes the EU more a prototype of a federal polity in action rather than normatively a federal state in the making.[33] However, the current political climate is certainly

30 The expression was used by Jacques Delors, former president of the EU Commission (1985–1995). Other qualifications have been used to describe the legal nature of the EU such as, "federation of nation-states," "intergovernmental federalism," or "pre-federal organisation."

31 See, for example, Olivier Beaud, "Conceptions of the State" in Michel Rosenfeld & András Sajó (eds), *The Oxford Handbook on Comparative Constitutional Law* (OUP 2012) 269.

32 The German Federal Constitutional Court notes the legal nature of the EU, and its conciliation with the democratic principle, in the seminal *Lisbon Case* about the compatibility of the German Act approving the Lisbon Treaty with the 1947 Basic Law. According to the German Federal Constitutional Court, the EU does not constitute a federal state, but a union of rule (*Herrschaftsverband*) founded on international law, and permanently supported by the intention of the sovereign democratic member states. The primary responsibility for integration rests in the hands of the national constitutional bodies which act on behalf of the peoples. Consequently, a better association of national parliaments in the EU decision-making process is required to allow the approval of the Lisbon Treaty. See *Lisbon Case*, BVerfG, cases 2 BvE 2/08 and others from 30 June 2009.

33 Eva G Heidbreder, "Federalism in the European Union" in Soeren Keil & Sabine Kropp (eds), *Emerging Federal Structures in the Post-Cold War Era* (Palgrave Macmillan 2022) 277.

not conducive to serene and judicious thinking about reforming the EU. The Union needs a new impetus to instil a renewed interest for its citizens, especially after the turmoil of the 2008 financial crisis, the puzzling aftermath of the 2016 Brexit vote, and the multifaceted challenges of the 2020–2021 Covid-19 crisis. This is without mentioning greater geopolitical challenges linked to the climate change crisis, the continuing migration crisis since 2015, the ongoing conflict in Ukraine since February 2022, and the repercussions of the war in the Middle East since October 2023.

Europeanisation, internationalisation, and globalisation: Constitutional law beyond the state? The progress made in European integration has had a significant impact on the state and its related concepts, particularly from an academic perspective. The traditional connection between the state and its constitution, and therefore constitutional law, has been challenged. With the EU now subjected to numerous constitution-like rules, does this necessarily imply that the EU is evolving into a state? Is it possible to have a constitution without a state? Can constitutional law be studied and conceptualised without reference to the theory of the state? If so, what rules would govern a new type of political entity that is not a state? These thought-provoking questions urge us to explore political organisations that go beyond the traditional state-model, especially given the increasing influence of internationalisation and globalisation on the state's governance capacity. In essence, these inquiries extend beyond the realm of European integration and give rise to new concerns, thus fostering the revitalisation of constitutional law.[34]

Two series of observations conclude the above developments on the notion of the state. Firstly, it seems that federal states undergo a movement of centralisation while unitary states are subject, on the contrary, to a movement of disaggregation due to the processes of deconcentration and decentralisation. The second observation follows on from the first one and relates to the "existential" crisis faced by the state due, in large part, to the effect of globalisation. The decline of the state, in the context of the so-called "post-nation state era," is a well-known phenomenon.[35] The state still exercises the core of its sovereign powers (i.e., police, justice, diplomacy, international relations, and defence) but seems less able to be a welfare state. The modern state is not the only public actor anymore, either because it does not want to be (because of the imperatives of liberalism and competition) or because it is not able to fulfil such a role (because of the influence of other powers and norms at international and European levels). Other actors, notably from the private sector, including in the charity sector, have somewhat taken over. The upshot is that the role of the state is changing towards that of a regulator of society within the respect of the rule of law.

Sovereignty

Originating from the Latin word *superus*, sovereignty encompasses the notion of a supreme entity possessing ultimate authority that surpasses any other governing body. Consequently,

34 Ran Hirschl, "From Comparative Constitutional Law to Comparative Constitutional Studies" (2013) 11 (1) *International Journal of Constitutional Law* 1.

35 Special issue, *The End of the Nation-State* (2011) 24 (1–2) *International Journal of Politics, Culture, and Society*.

sovereignty is inherently intertwined with the concept of power. This subsection addresses the concept of sovereignty and explores the underlying theories associated with it.

The concept of sovereignty. Since the sixteenth century and the start of the seventeenth century, the works of Jean Bodin (*Les Six Livres de la République*, 1576) and Charles Loyseau (*Les Œuvres de Maistre Charles Loyseau, Traités des Seigneuries, des Offices et des Ordres*, 1600–1610) contributed to the emergence of the concept of sovereignty. Sovereignty is intrinsically linked to that of the state to such an extent that some view sovereignty as the essence of the state. In constitutional law terms, sovereignty refers to an entity endowed with a supreme ruling power featuring a dual dimension: a dimension that is internal to the state, and a dimension that is external to the state.

Internal sovereignty refers to the supreme power enjoyed by the state over its people and its territory. No other power enjoys equivalent supremacy. This makes the state the only legitimate source of power, enabled to make laws and to ensure their implementation by having recourse to the public force, if need be. This last feature, that of commanding the public force (i.e., the police and the armed forces), is indeed distinctive of the sovereign power as the holder of the so-called "monopoly of legitimate physical violence," as coined by Max Veber.[36] Internal sovereignty is indivisible (i.e., it cannot be shared), inalienable, and imprescriptible (i.e., it cannot be renounced or even delegated). The exercise of internal sovereignty entails the exercise of sovereign-related powers (*pouvoirs régaliens*) such as the power to levy taxes, to issue currency, to ensure defence and national security on the territory, to conclude international treaties, and to render justice—in other words, all the competences that the state exercises through its legislative, executive, and judicial powers. As the constituent power (*pouvoir constituant*), the state determines the conditions of its own organisation and the exercise of such powers, meaning that the state has the "competence of competence." In that sense, the state is "the alpha and omega" of the legal order whose primary mission is to ensure the cohesion and proper functioning of the national community.

External sovereignty refers to the supremacy of the state on the international plan. The state is independent politically and geographically vis-à-vis other states and is not subordinated to any of them. External sovereignty is based on the principle that all states enjoy equality of status on the international scene. In other words, the state is subject to no external authority, and its power is supreme (i.e., there is no superior normative authority) and independent (i.e., it cannot proceed from any external authority). However, limits may curtail the external sovereignty of the state. In practice, the state must deal with the supremacy of other states in the conduct of international relations, on the one hand, and to respect rules of international law which it did not (directly) adopt but agreed to adhere to when joining international and European organisations, on the other hand. Examples include participation in the UN (1945 Charter of the United Nations) whereby state parties accepted to be bound by the principles of international law about the maintenance of international peace and security, the promotion of the well-being of the peoples of the world, and international cooperation to these ends; participation in NATO (1949 Treaty of Washington) whereby state parties agreed to pool their competences in the military area; or participation in the World Trade Organisation (1994 Marrakesh Declaration and Final

36 Max Veber (1864–1920), German economist and sociologist. Max Veber, *The Politician and the Scientist* 1919 (*Le savant et le politique*, Julien Freund tr, Plon 1959).

Act) whereby state parties agreed to be subject to common commercial rules. As for the EU, member states have agreed, in an advanced form of integration and supranational organisation, to transfer several sovereign powers to the European institutions in, for example, the area of monetary policy and the area of asylum and immigration policy. In other cases, limits to external sovereignty are not necessarily the state's own *fait* (deed) but when the state becomes governed by other states or international organisations. This is the case, for example, of the economic supervision operated by the IMF. This concerns mainly developing countries but not only those. Ireland, for example, after the 2011 bailout following the 2008 financial crisis, saw its banking system supervised by the so-called "European troika" composed of the IMF, the EU Commission, and the European Central Bank.

In short, the concept of state sovereignty refers to the state's ultimate authority and independence within its own territory, separate from other states. This traditional understanding has faced challenges from two opposing forces. Firstly, the "inward pull" comes from within, exemplified by the decentralisation of state power. Secondly, the "outward pull" arises from external influences such as international organisations, international law, and the effects of globalisation. These factors together have raised questions about the classical notion of state sovereignty.

Theories about sovereignty. The study of sovereignty can be illustrated effectively through French constitutional history. This historical context serves as an excellent platform to examine various theories on the subject.[37] The significant turning point came with the 1789 Revolution, which brought an end to the belief in divine-right kingship, wherein the King held absolute sovereign power. Following the 1789 Revolution, two prominent theories emerged, both offering alternative arrangements for the exercise of sovereignty. The first theory advocated for placing sovereignty in the hands of the people, known as the theory of popular sovereignty. The second theory suggested vesting sovereignty in the nation, known as the theory of national sovereignty (see Table 1.2 Theories of sovereignty).

Challenging the sovereignty of the King. The sovereignty of the King was theorised by Jean Bodin as the absolute and perpetual power endowed on the Prince (King), who was subject to natural and divine laws only.[38] Under the *Ancien Régime*, power came from God. Entrusted with such divine power, the King was identified with political power and regarded as the only legitimate ruler as consecrated in the famous phrase "*l'État, c'est moi*."[39] Such a political regime was called the absolute monarchy of divine right. However, philosophers of the Enlightenment sought to challenge absolutism, notably by proposing to dissociate the person of the King from the entity endowed with the power to govern. According to them, the King's power had to be limited: the King could not be regarded as the permanent embodiment of political power but rather as the temporary holder of such power. If the source of power was no longer divine, the ensuing question was: What was to be the source of power? While, on the theoretical level, the

37 See also Chapter 2 on the history of French constitutional law.

38 Jean Bodin, *The Six Books of the Republic* (*Les Six Livres de la République* 1576).

39 "The state, that is me." This quote is attributed, perhaps incorrectly, to King Louis XIV (1638–1715), especially since he did pronounce another phrase on his deathbed that could be interpreted as meaning quite the opposite: "*Je meurs, mais l'État demeurera toujours*" [I am leaving (I die) but the state will always remain].

TABLE 1.2 Theories of sovereignty

	Source of power	*Organs in charge of exercising power*	*Political regime*
Royal sovereignty Bodin *The Six Books of the Republic* 1576	God	King	Absolute monarchy of divine right
Popular sovereignty Rousseau *On the Social Contract* 1762	The People *Each citizen has a fraction of sovereignty*	Popular Assembly consisting of the citizens or their delegates	Direct democracy or, at the least, semi-direct democracy. Universal suffrage (citizens are equal, theory of the electorate-right). Specific and imperative mandate of the delegates. Examples in history and the present: Ancient city of Athens; 1793 French Constitution (never implemented); Swiss Cantons.
National sovereignty Sieyès *What is the Third Estate?* 1789	The Nation *The collective entity holds sovereignty which is indivisible*	National representatives who can be embodied in a National Assembly, a King, or a President of the Republic	Representative regime whether monarchical or republican depending on the type of representatives. Suffrage not necessarily universal (theory of the electorate-function). General and representative mandate of the representatives. Examples in history: 1791, 1830, and 1875 French Constitutions.

Enlightenment philosophers proposed that this source should be the people or the nation, on the practical level, the 1789 revolutionaries oscillated between the two approaches.[40]

Popular sovereignty v national sovereignty. Rousseau introduced the concept of *popular sovereignty* in the eighteenth century, which contrasts with national sovereignty.[41] Popular sovereignty posits that only the people hold sovereign power. Rousseau's definition of the people encompasses all the citizens within a country. Each citizen, under the terms set out in the social contract, has an equal entitlement to sovereignty and the right to engage in shaping the expression of the general will, including the adoption of the constitution and laws.

40 During the period known as the Enlightenment, certain thinkers, including Montesquieu, expressed the belief that the King could play a role in the exercise of political authority, albeit with certain limits, within a constitutional monarchy system.

41 Jean-Jacques Rousseau, *The Social Contract* (*Du Contrat Social* 1762).

Sovereignty was considered as necessarily indivisible, as the general will can solely emanate from the people.

The implementation of the theory of popular sovereignty had several implications. Firstly, the power must be exercised through a representative assembly of the people. In principle, this assembly should directly govern the affairs of the state, similar to what was practised under the Greek city-state in Athens, although it is generally done through delegates for practical reasons. Either way, whether via an assembly of citizens or an assembly of delegates, a *popular assembly* entrusts specific responsibilities, notably executive, to organs (i.e., government, commission, or committee) that are accountable to it. Secondly, since the direct exercise of popular sovereignty via direct democracy is a challenge for obvious practical reasons (i.e., size of the territory and of the population, complexity of the decisions to make etc.), the preferred form of government is through delegates. Therefore, the delegates exercise power on behalf of the citizens while reserving the possibility for them to exercise power directly in referendums, for example; in that case, we talk about a semi-direct democracy. The mandate that the citizens give to their delegates is necessarily imperative: being accountable to the citizens, delegates must abide by their instructions. The possibility of popular revocation exists, though, whereby citizens may revoke any of their delegates. Besides, the popular mandate is specific since delegates only commit to do what the citizens tell them to do on their behalf and in lieu of their direct participation. In other words, delegates, or deputies, of the people cannot be the citizens' representatives; they are only their "commissioners" according to Rousseau. Thirdly, those delegates are elected following the theory of the electorate-right (*électorat-droit*). Based on the premise of the equality of all citizens whereby each one of them holds a fraction of sovereignty, each citizen has *a right* to express their will. Universal suffrage logically follows suit because no citizen is more entitled than another citizen in the matter of deciding who can exercise power on their behalf. Interestingly, Rousseau conceived of the law as expressing the *general* will, even though the law is obviously the result of a *majority* vote. According to Rousseau, this was so because the minority, by not voting like the majority, are considered as having "erred" in their decision by not having perceived the "general will."

The theory of *national sovereignty* was developed during the eighteenth century, notably by Sieyès[42] drawing from the work of Montesquieu.[43] For moderate revolutionaries, resorting to national sovereignty was a way to curtail the absolute power of the monarch—and a way to dissociate the person of the King from the embodiment of political power—without, however, entrusting the people with such power. Moderate revolutionaries, unlike Rousseau, did not trust the people, whose lack of civic instruction and of a sense of moderation could jeopardize the transition from absolute monarchy to the intended new way of governing the affairs of the state. Resorting to the abstract legal fiction of the nation allowed the establishment of a permanent political power, the exercise of which could be detached from the person of the King. Under the theory of national sovereignty, the nation was therefore the only source of political power.

The theory of national sovereignty had several implications. Firstly, the nation, as the source of political power, displays several features. As an abstract and collective entity, the nation is indivisible and distinct from the people it represents. The nation brings together the

42 Sieyès, *What is the Third Estate?* (*Qu'est-ce que le Tiers-État ?* 1789).

43 Montesquieu, *The Spirit of the Laws* (*De l'Esprit des Lois* 1748)

whole community of past, existing, and future individuals who, living on the same territory, share a common past, a common culture, and common values, and plan a common future.[44] Accordingly, those individuals who belong to the said community (i.e., the nationals) and those who are destined to join it (i.e., by acquisition of the nationality) are part of the nation. Under Sieyès's theory, the nation has legal personality with the attributions of sovereignty, namely unity, indivisibility, inalienability, and imprescriptibility—the nation's sovereignty cannot be taken away nor delegated, unless for a limited period to the representatives of the nation. Secondly, since the nation is an abstract entity, the way for citizens to be heard is through their representatives. National representatives are individuals entitled to act and speak on behalf of the nation. As such, these individuals should have some awareness of the history and the current situation of the nation. They must have some kind of vision for its future in order to act in its superior interest, that is, above contingencies and sectional preferences. Therefore, the nation is represented by deputies in a national assembly and by an executive body, the latter being a president in the context of a republic, or a monarch in the context of a constitutional monarchy. The theory of national sovereignty advocates a principle of separation of powers which can accommodate either a republic or a monarchy. This last form of government was largely supported by the theorists of national sovereignty since it was regarded as the best guarantee of the continuity of the nation, in a hereditary monarchy in particular. This was, for example, the regime envisaged under the 1791 Constitution. Thirdly, the regime under national sovereignty being representative, the citizens who are elected to office are accountable to the nation only. They cannot be accountable to the instructions or directives of their electorate; their mandate is thus *representative* as opposed to *imperative*. Moreover, their mandate is general because the deputies represent the entire nation, and not the electorate of their constituencies. Contrary to the theory of popular sovereignty whereby everybody, holding a fraction of the sovereignty, has a right to vote and be heard via delegates, the theory of national sovereignty is concerned with what is best for the nation. It follows that not everybody is entitled to vote, but only the most enlightened part of the electorate. Voting is therefore not a right but a function under the idea of the electorate-function (*électorat-fonction*). The electorate-function does not prevent the granting of the right to vote to all national citizens (universal suffrage), but, most of the time in history, the right to vote was limited to a part of the electorate (restricted suffrage) according to criteria relating to capacity (capacity suffrage) and/or wealth (census suffrage). Capacity suffrage was when the function of the electorate was limited by reason of education. This was the case, for example, under the 1795 Constitution which article 2 provided: "*Les jeunes gens ne peuvent être inscrits sur les registres civiques, s'ils ne prouvent qu'ils sachent lire et écrire, et exercer une profession mécanique.*"[45] Census (or censitary) suffrage was so called because of the *cens*, which was a tax imposed on the electorate: only those who could afford to pay such tax were entitled to vote. The amount of the tax could be adjusted depending on the desirability of the size of the electorate. The 1791 Constitution, for example, mentioned that to be an active

44 This was the object of an interesting debate when Alsace-Lorraine was ceded to Germany by the Treaty of Frankfurt in 1871. Deputies elected in the constituencies concerned presented their resignation to the president of the National Assembly. Their resignation was refused in the first place because it was considered that these deputies represented the whole nation and not these two specific departments. The debate then moved on to discuss whether these departments belonged to the French nation despite being under the jurisdiction of another state.

45 "Young (male) people cannot be registered in the civic register if they do not prove that they know how to read and write and exercise a mechanical profession."

voter, one had to pay a direct contribution equivalent to at least three days of work. Until the nineteenth century, census suffrage overlapped with capacity suffrage, given that education was reserved to the upper classes. However, if restricted suffrage is, in theory, compatible with national sovereignty, its conciliation with the democratic principle in modern times was problematic, hence the generalisation of universal suffrage.

From 1789 onwards, France experienced the two theories of national sovereignty and of popular sovereignty in succession. As regards the former, article 3 of the 1789 Declaration of the Rights of Man and of the Citizen states, for example, that: "The principle of all sovereignty lies primarily in the Nation. No other body or individual may exercise any authority which does not expressly proceed from the Nation." As regards the latter, examples include the (unapplied) 1793 Constitution directly inspired from Rousseau's ideas, the 1795 Constitution, and the 1848 Constitution under the Second Republic, as well as the first draft of the 1946 Constitution, which was rejected by referendum. However, the implementation of the theory of popular sovereignty may result in a despotic form of power, which was the case of the dictatorial regime under the French Terror (1793–1794). In between these experimentations, there were also periods of a return to royal sovereignty, with significant consequences regarding the size and composition of the electorate. This was the case under the reign of Louis XVIII with the 1814 Constitutional Charter and under the reign of his brother Charles X, who was crowned "King of France" in Reims Cathedral following the old *Ancien Régime* tradition. Louis-Philippe, from the cousin branch of the Orléans, then re-established national sovereignty under the 1830 Charter and acceded to the throne as the representative of the nation under the symbolic title of "King of the French." The ensuing drift towards "imperial sovereignty" was the *fait* of Napoleon I (1804) and his nephew Napoleon III (1852) under their respective authoritarian regimes.[46]

This debate has become somewhat outdated. Article 3 of the current French Constitution is rooted in the practice of the two theories. According to paragraph one of article 3, the Constitution affirms that: "*National* sovereignty belongs to *the people* who shall exercise it through their representatives or by way of referendum (emphasis added)."[47] While the French approach, like in most pluralist democracies, predominantly relies on national sovereignty, it also allows for the direct participation of citizens through referendums.

Constitution and Hierarchy of Norms

> « *Le respect de la Constitution est non un risque mais un devoir.* »[48]

Strictly defined, the constitution is a set of rules that determine the status of those who govern and their relationships with those who are governed. As the highest norm in the state, the constitution determines the conditions of the exercise of state power and of the elaboration of other norms.[49] As such, the constitution lays down rules about the form of the state, the organisation

46 For more detail on the historical developments, see Chapter 2 on the history of French constitutional law.

47 In addition to article 3, article 27 paragraph one of the Constitution prohibits any imperative mandate: "Any imperative mandate shall be null and void."

48 Pierre Mazeaud, former president of the Constitutional Council (2004–2007) [Respect for the Constitution is not a risk but a duty].

49 Norms can be described as legally binding rules, which have a general and impersonal character. These rules aim at organising and regulating life in society by imposing obligations and limitations, while also granting and safeguarding rights and freedoms.

of powers, and the working relationships between institutions in order to guarantee the rights and freedoms of the citizens. The constitution is as much a legal document as it is a political document. As a legal document, the constitution represents the legitimate source of power determining the limits of the rule of law. As a political document, the constitution expresses a global political project for those who accept. In that sense, the constitution is formed by the fundamental laws that a group of individuals impose upon themselves as the basis of their political project with a view to guaranteeing their fundamental freedoms and ensuring their peaceful coexistence (see Box 1.1 on Conceptions of the constitution).

This section explores in more detail the concept of a constitution and explores the process of drafting, adopting, and amending it. Furthermore, as the supreme governing document, the constitution holds a paramount position within the hierarchy of norms. We will also examine the unique role that the constitution plays with respect to other norms, particularly laws.

The notion of constitution

In order to enhance our understanding of the concept of constitution, it is helpful to consider a couple of key distinctions. Firstly, we can differentiate between the material constitution, which pertains to the tangible elements of a constitution, and the formal constitution, which refers to the procedural aspects. Secondly, we can distinguish between the written constitution, which is explicitly documented, and the non-written constitution, which relies on customary practices and unwritten conventions.[50] These distinctions are examined in turn in this subsection.

Material v formal constitution. A *material* approach to the constitution considers the content of constitutional norms rather than the form or process of their adoption. Understood as such, the content of the constitution refers to all the fundamental rules, written or not, which relate to the exercise of power. Such rules generally concern the form of the state, their institutional setup, and the fundamental principles governing the relationships between the state and its citizens. For example, article 16 of the 1789 Declaration illustrates this conception of the constitution as follows: "Any society in which the protection of rights is not guaranteed, nor the separation of powers ensured shall have no constitution." Under the material conception of the constitution, all democratic states necessarily have a constitution. The other approach is that of the *formal* constitution, which is concerned with the legal process of adoption of constitutional norms by a specific body or organ (e.g., a constituent assembly), and/or according to a specific procedure (e.g., referendum). The specific body and procedure set these norms apart from the other norms; as such, these norms are constitutional in nature and do not form part of the body of norms adopted under the ordinary legislative process. Under such a conception, the UK, for example, would have to be regarded as having no constitution since there is no specific organ or procedure other than the adoption of an Act of Parliament under the ordinary legislative procedure for all norms, including for the fundamental norms. Under such a conception, constitutional norms are then superior to ordinary norms (i.e., the constitution is superior to

50 French constitutional law also traditionally distinguishes between the flexible constitution and the rigid, or entrenched, constitution (see below).

the law), such superiority being ensured by the mechanism of (constitutional) judicial review, further examined below.

Written v unwritten constitution. *Written* constitutions are nowadays the most common form of constitutions. Such constitutions generally contain several articles, often preceded by a preamble, and they sometimes include a catalogue of rights. They are elaborated by the constituent power, that is, the sovereign power or its representatives. Written constitutions offer the advantage of "setting in stone" the social contract by ensuring the durability and coherency of constitutional norms and principles, including those on rights and freedoms. Written constitutions have a stronger symbolic and legal value in this respect. Experience tells us that many written constitutions have emerged in the aftermath of some major political or legal disturbance or other disruptive event, such as the creation of a new state following the achievement of independence or following the creation of a new legal order after a revolution or a war. Examples include the 1787 US Constitution,[51] which was the product of the embryonic USA severing their links with Britain, and the 1791 French Constitution as the first achievement of the National Assembly during the 1789 Revolution after throwing away the *Ancien Régime*.[52] Other examples include the 1937 Constitution of the Republic of Ireland, which consolidated the regime of the newly independent state,[53] and the 1949 Constitution of the Federal Republic of Germany, implemented after the Second World War. *Unwritten* constitutions, on the other hand, refer to the customary form of constitutions which aggregate an ensemble of diverse rules relating to the organisation and the functioning of the institutions. These rules can be written or unwritten (e.g., constitutional conventions) but share the common feature of having acquired legal binding force due to their constant and uninterrupted application over a length of time. These rules are flexible in the sense that they can be amended like ordinary laws, without any particular procedure or formality (e.g., the requirement of a super majority vote in Parliament). The downside of unwritten constitutional rules is that they bear less solemnity and clarity than written ones. Very few countries are now regarded as having a customary constitution, the best example being the UK.[54] As non-codified, the UK Constitution can be found in various unwritten (conventions, practices, or customs) and written (statutes, judicial decisions) sources. As not entrenched, it can be modified through ordinary parliamentary

51 The US Constitution was drafted in 1787, ratified in 1788, and entered into force in 1789.

52 For more detail on the 1791 Constitution, see Chapter 2 on the history of French constitutional law.

53 Ireland acquired its independence in 1922 as the Irish Free State after the War of Independence (1919–1921). This significant event was marked by the signing of the Anglo-Irish Treaty on 6 December 1921, which granted Ireland the status of a self-governing Dominion. Subsequently, in the aftermath of the Civil War (1922–1923) and the establishment of the country's institutional framework, the 1937 Constitution was adopted.

54 The example of Israel is interesting too. Israel is recognised for not having a formal written constitution. Instead, Israel's constitutional framework relies on a set of basic laws that govern government structures and safeguard fundamental rights. In a significant ruling on 9 November 1995, the Israeli Supreme Court, in the *United Mizrahi Bank v Migdal Cooperative Village* case, declared that these fundamental laws can be considered the country's constitution. See also the more recent judgement of the Israeli Supreme Court sitting as the High Court of Justice in *Movement for Quality Government in Israel v the Knesset* issued on 1 January 2024, in which the Court settled the question of its authority to strike down fundamental laws if and when certain conditions are met.

legislation or indeed through judicial decision or a change in political practice. An interesting definition of the UK Constitution is the following:

> the set of laws, rules and practices that create the basic institutions of the state, and its components and related parts, and stipulate the powers of those institutions and the relationships between the different institutions and between those institutions and the individual.[55]

However, the distinction between written and unwritten constitutions could be more nuanced as all national constitutions are in some way written, and all of them are sustained by uncodified constitutional norms. A better distinction among constitutions is whether they consist of a single written document or many separate written documents.[56]

To sum up, under modern constitutionalism, the concept of a democratic state's constitution is envisioned in the following manner: it serves as a symbolic, foundational act that establishes the state's identity and embodies a political project; it provides the basis of political authority, delineating the central (and potentially regional) systems of governance while also imposing constraints on state power; and it serves as a framework for defining the interactions between the state and its citizens, safeguarding their rights and freedoms.

Drafting, adopting, and amending the constitution

Carefully drafted and adopted through an often-complex process, the constitution is designed to provide a certain level of stability to the state. The constitution is also a living document that is destined to develop alongside the evolving landscape of politics and society. This subsection introduces the reader to the main points about the process of drafting and adopting the constitution, as well as the methods by which it can be modified.

Drafting and adopting the constitution. The constitution is drafted by the constituent power (*pouvoir constituant*).[57] The original (or primary) constituent power (*pouvoir constituant originaire*) is distinct from the derived (or instituted) constituent power (*pouvoir constituant dérivé*). While the former oversees the creation of a new constitution, the latter is in charge of partially amending it. In other words, the derived constituent power deals with the subsequent amendments to the constitution that has been adopted, in the first place, by the primary constituent power. The idea of the unity of the sovereign constituent power capable of both adopting and amending the constitution can also be defended. The adoption of a new constitution occurs on the occasion of, for example, the establishment of a new state (e.g., USA in 1787) or an overhaul of a political regime accompanied by a revolution (e.g., France in 1789). Leaders of the provisional regime generally take charge of constitutional drafting. For that matter, their power is unconditional, so that they can establish a new legal order

55 House of Lords Select Committee on the Constitution, *Reviewing the Constitution* (First Report of Session 2001–2002), HL 11, July 2001, [20]. See also *R (Miller) v Secretary of State for Exiting the European Union* [2016] EWHC 2768 (Admin), [18].

56 For an explanation of this key point, see Richard Albert, "Multi-Textual Constitutions" (2023) 109 *Virginia Law Review* 1629.

57 There is no reference to such constituent power as regards the unwritten or customary constitution, which, by definition, is established and evolves over time without any particular procedure.

without any constraints, legal or otherwise. The constitution may be elaborated through a democratic process, whereby the citizens are fully associated with the process, or through a non-democratic process, whereby an authoritarian power elaborates the constitution without the people's involvement. Examples for the latter come from French history. The 1814 Charter epitomised the authoritarian way of adopting a constitution when Louis XVIII unilaterally "granted" the Charter to its people without involving national representatives, hence the idea of a "granted charter" (*charte octroyée*). The 1830 Charter was adopted with a little more involvement from national representation since it was the result of a pact between Louis-Philippe and the deputies, but there was still limited involvement of the people, hence the idea of a negotiated charter (*charte négociée*).[58] Under the democratic mode of elaboration of the constitution, the constituent power belongs to the sovereign people. The constituent power generally acts through an elected constituent assembly whose task is to elaborate the new constitution as well as, should the assembly be also entrusted with legislative powers, adopt new laws, so that arrangements can be made to set up the future government. The people may themselves exercise the constituent power when they vote in a referendum on the draft constitution elaborated by the constituent assembly or by the executive power—in that case, when people are only associated at certain stages of the adoption process, the process is still regarded as democratic, but to a lesser degree. For example, the adoption of the 1958 French Constitution was not entirely democratic since the writing of the first draft was achieved by the executive (i.e., the De Gaulle Government) assisted by an expert committee (i.e., *comité consultatif constitutionnel*), thus leaving the people to approve the final text by referendum at the very end of the process.[59] The same is true as regards the 1937 Irish Constitution, which was drafted by governmental experts, notably the Legal Advisor to the Department of External Affairs under the supervision of De Valera, then minister for External Affairs.[60] Nevertheless, after being approved by the Oireachtas (Irish Parliament), the framers of the 1937 Constitution decided that it would be enacted by the people instead of an elected body, hence the adoption of the Plebiscite (Draft Constitution) Act 1937, which mandated the holding of a referendum on the draft constitution.

Amending the constitution. The constitution evolves as society changes. This necessity for change needs to be anticipated, and the amendment to the constitution procedure is logically inscribed in the original text. Contrary to the original constituent power, which is unlimited, the derived constituent power, though still regarded as an expression of sovereignty, is constrained by the constitutional amendment provision. The amendment provision lays down the conditions and procedure of amendment, that is, the organ entitled to put an amendment proposal forward (i.e., the government, Parliament, the people, or the states in a federal system), the organ competent to adopt the amendment proposal (i.e., the parliamentary assemblies, congress of the two assemblies, ad hoc assembly, or committee), the voting requirements (i.e., time frame,

58 For more detail, see Chapter 2 on the history of French constitutional law.

59 For more detail, see Chapter 3 on historical and legal foundations of the Fifth Republic.

60 Father John Charles McQuaid, later Archbishop of Dublin, contributed to the drafting process about religious, educational, family, and social welfare issues. The Protestant Church was also consulted on the draft Irish Constitution. Additionally, the draft was submitted to the Vatican for examination.

majority rules etc.), and the requirements for the promulgation of the final text (i.e., adoption by Parliament, by popular referendum, or ratification by the states in a federal system).

Amending the constitution can be difficult depending on the level of entrenchment of its provisions. A constitution is regarded as *flexible* when it can be amended in the same way as ordinary law. In that case, being no different in nature from an ordinary legislative instrument, the constitution can be amended in the same way. This renders the possibility of judicial review of the law superfluous since the constitution is of the same rank as the law in the legal system. An example is the customary non-written constitution of the UK.[61] On the other hand, a constitution is said to be *rigid* when it necessitates a special body and/or procedure for its amendment. This means that the constitution has a special nature, distinct from the law. This makes it possible to review the conformity of the law as regards the constitution, hereby ensuring constitutional supremacy in the legal system. The entrenchment of the constitution arguably eschews easy, often frequent, and hasty amendments, thus ensuring a certain stability. Yet, the downside of too rigid a constitution is that amendment requirements may be so difficult that they block any possible change, even when much needed. The upshot is that other means, often violent and radical because they are outside of the normal amendment process, will be used to change the constitution. A good illustration is the demise of the 1848 French Constitution. When Louis Napoleon Bonaparte (nephew of Napoleon) sought to amend the Constitution because he knew that he could not be re-elected after his four-year mandate, he also knew that the three-quarter super majority as laid down in the Constitution would be very difficult to obtain from the deputies. So, he did away with this by simply organising a coup which put an end to the regime!

There is a great variety of amendment procedures. Most constitutions provide for some limitations either as regards to *when* the constitution can be amended or to *what* provisions can be amended. Regarding the moment of the constitutional amendment, the aim here is to ensure that the constitution, when it enters into force, is implemented for a minimum of time without interruption to consolidate the newly established regime and allow the institutions to work. It can also be the case that the constitution cannot be amended during certain crises (e.g., presidential interim, state of siege, war etc.). For example, the 1831 Belgian Constitution prohibits constitutional revision in times of war (article 196). The 1958 French Constitution provides that constitutional revision is prohibited when the President of the Republic is prevented from exercising his/her duties (article 7) or when there is a threat to the integrity of the territory such as, for example, an invasion from external forces (article 89 paragraph four). Such provisions are obviously a reaction to what had happened during the Second World War when Nazi Germany occupied France from 1940 to 1944, with a similar provision in place in the post-war 1946 Constitution. Regarding the object of the constitutional amendment, the constitution may explicitly provide that some of its provisions *cannot* be amended. For example, the Constitutional Law of 25 February 1875, as part of the package of constitutional laws forming the Constitution of the Third Republic, contained a provision prohibiting the amendment of the republican form of government (i.e., a return to the monarchy)—though this was not respected by the Vichy Government, which granted full powers to Marshal Pétain under

61 The 1814 Charter and 1830 Charter, mentioned above, are noteworthy instances of what is commonly referred to as flexible constitutions, even though they were written. These constitutions notably lacked any provisions regarding their amendment or modification.

the Law of 10 July 1940. Another example is in the 1949 German Basic Law, which prohibits any revision related to the federal organisation of the state and the participation of the *Länder* in the federal decision-making process as well as to the principles laid down under articles 1 to 20 on fundamental rights (article 79 paragraph 3). However, these limits can always be circumvented. Indeed, the constituent power is the sovereign power that is, in theory, always entitled to undo, either by legal or illegal means (e.g., coup, revolution), what has been done. In other words, no rule, even constitutional, is intangible. The counterargument is the idea of supra-constitutionality, which postulates the existence of superior unamendable principles contained in the constitution and that cannot be changed.[62]

The amendment procedure contains several steps. The first step is the decision to initiate the amendment procedure. The right of initiative generally belongs to the government as the best-placed organ to foresee a need for constitutional change. A constitutional amendment can also be initiated by members of Parliament who, as representatives of the people, can also be involved in the modification of the fundamental text. The initiative can come from both Houses of Parliament, or one of them, generally the one representing the people (i.e., the lower House). The initiative can also come from the people by means of a petition which must be signed by a minimum number of citizens (e.g., 100,000 signatures are required to initiate a constitutional amendment in Switzerland).[63] Once the constitutional text is drafted, the second step is the discussion and the adoption of the draft amendment. The adoption of the amendment can be made according to several scenarios: adoption either by the Houses of Parliament[64] or by a specially elected assembly (e.g., solution adopted in the USA under the Convention to Propose Amendments to the US Constitution, or Article V Convention); or submission of the draft amendment for approval by the people via referendum.

Supremacy of the constitution, hierarchy of norms, and constitutional review

The exercise of political power within a state necessitates the existence of norms that are enacted by public authorities and that bind the citizens. Several questions arise concerning these coercive norms and their effect on individuals. How are these norms organised in the domestic legal system, and do they all have the same legally binding force? Which norms take precedence over others? How are conflicts between these norms resolved? What if these norms are not respectful of the rights and freedoms of citizens? What if political power abuses its prerogatives? Answers to these questions have been addressed through a concept known as *constitutionalism*.

Constitutionalism is a political theory which emerged, in its modern acceptation, in the nineteenth century and which offers "a series of principles arguments for the limitation of

62 The concept of supra-constitutionality, which was first introduced in German law, is acknowledged in the constitutions of Austria, India, Italy, and South Africa, among others. However, its application is a topic of debate in various other jurisdictions. See, for example, Yaniv Roznai, *Unconstitutional Constitutional Amendments: The Limits of Amendment Powers* (OUP 2017), which presents a comprehensive exploration of this contentious issue.

63 Article 139 of the 1999 Swiss Federal Constitution on Popular Initiative for Partial Revision of the Federal Constitution, paragraph 1: "100 000 citizens entitled to vote may propose partial revision of the Federal Constitution."

64 It can be one House of Parliament, generally the Lower House, whose members are directly elected by the people, or both Houses of Parliament as is, for example, the case in France with the Congress. The Congress is the gathering in one "constitutional assembly" of the deputies of the National Assembly and the senators of the Senate.

political power in general and of government's sway over citizens in particular."[65] The development of constitutionalism over the course of the last two centuries has shown how these limitations and underlying principles are embodied in the institutions and practices of the modern constitutional state. In liberal political regimes, "[c]onstitutions have therefore been presented as the centre piece in the strategy for the limitation of power." [66] Under constitutionalism, government action is thus constrained by limits posed by the constitution and the respect of individual rights and of the rule of law (*État de droit*). The state, as created by law, is subject to these limits. For these limits to be efficient, the executive and legislative powers must respect the limits laid down in the constitution when enacting norms within their sphere of competence. This has necessarily two implications: firstly, the different kinds of norms are articulated around a hierarchy in which constitutional norms are placed at the top; secondly, the guarantee of the constitution's supremacy is realised under a system of constitutional justice entrusted with courts (and not with the political branch of power) via the mechanism of judicial (constitutional) review (*contrôle de constitutionnalité*). This subsection succinctly presents the main tenets of the hierarchy of norms and of constitutional review.[67]

The hierarchy of norms. Because different norms coexist in the legal system, it is necessary to organise these norms in a certain way. This is done by attributing to these norms a validity, or legal binding force, in a structured hierarchical system. The validity, or legal binding force, attributed to each norm depends on the object of the norm, that is, the nature of the rule that it enacts (material criterion), the body that has enacted the norm (organic criterion), and the mode of elaboration of the norm (formal criterion). The working principle of the hierarchy is that inferior norms must conform to superior norms—this is, in its broadest sense, the meaning of *the principle of legality*. The constitution, through which the sovereign people have determined the fundamental rules aimed at protecting their rights and freedoms, sits at the top of the hierarchy of norms. As such, the constitution is said to be supreme over other norms (*principle of supremacy, or primacy*). Infra-constitutional norms must therefore be compatible with the constitution—this is the meaning of *the principle of constitutionality. The principle of the hierarchy of norms* was developed by Kelsen in his work *The Pure Theory of Law (1934).*[68] Kelsen viewed the categorisation of legal norms as a classification of these norms based on their value under the authority of the most fundamental norm of all, namely the constitution (*Grundnorm*). Kelsen's theory is based on the concepts of validity and conformity: in order to be valid, any norm must conform to the norm directly superior to it; in cases where an inferior

65 Dario Castiglione, "The Political Theory of the Constitution" (1996) 44 (3) *Political Studies* 417.

66 Ibid.

67 These themes of constitutional justice and constitutional review are examined in more detail in the context of the French Fifth Republic under Chapter 6 on constitutional justice and rights protection.

68 Hans Kelsen, Austrian jurist (1881–1973). See the two references to his main piece, *Introduction to the Problems of Legal Theory: A Translation of the First Edition of the* Reine Rechtslehre *or Pure Theory of Law* (Bonnie Litschewski Paulson Stanley L Paulson tr, Clarendon Press 1992), and *Pure Theory of Law* (Max Knight tr, University of California Press 1967).

norm does not conform to the superior norm, it is regarded as invalid and should be reformed or annulled.

Articulation between norms of domestic law, international law, and European law. The pyramidal paradigm, as devised by Kelsen, finds its limits when it comes to incorporating extra-domestic norms. Indeed, the place of international law and European law in the domestic hierarchy of norms is not as straightforward as it seems. Foreign norms are best accommodated in a system which puts plurality and horizontality to the fore. The starting point here is the principle of pacta sunt servanda, which requires that states comply with the provisions of signed and ratified international treaties and conventions. However, the articulation between international law and domestic law depends on how each state interprets the relationship between the two legal orders, domestic and international. Two approaches have been proposed in that regard, namely the monist approach as advocated by Kelsen, and the dualist approach as advocated by Triepel and Anzilotti.[69]

A problematic issue has been the relationship between international law (EU law in particular), on the one hand, and the domestic constitution, on the other hand. The ICJ (former PCIJ) clearly decided in favour of the primacy of international law over domestic constitutions,[70] as the CJEU did concerning EU law vis-à-vis the constitutions of the member states.[71] A number of member states have recognised the primacy of international law such as, for example, the Netherlands. Qualified by the doctrine as moderately monist (or monistic), the Dutch legal system is indeed relatively open towards international law. The 1983 *Grondwet* declares that the government shall promote the development of the international legal order (article 90). Treaties that have become binding for the state automatically constitute part of the legal order of those parts of the Kingdom to which they apply. Approval by Parliament is not a requirement in those cases where such an approval is not a conditio sine qua non for becoming a party to the treaty. Publicity is also not a requirement for internal legal force. However, provisions of treaties may only be applied by courts and be given precedence over conflicting domestic law after they have been duly made public (articles 93 and 94). Besides, "[a]ny provision of a treaty that conflicts with the Dutch Constitution or which leads to conflicts with it may be approved by the Houses of the States General only if at least two-thirds of the votes cast are in favour" (article 91).[72]

69 Heinrich Triepel (1868–1946), German jurist and legal philosopher; Dionisio Anzilotti (1867–1950), Italian jurist and judge at the Permanent Court of International Justice.

70 *Treatment of Polish Nationals and Other Persons of Polish Origin or Speech in the Danzig Territory* (Advisory Opinion including the text of the declaration by Baron Rolin-Jaequemyns) [1932] PCIJ A/B 44.

71 *Flaminio Costa v ENEL* (Case 6/64), EU:C:1964:66, 15 July 1964; *Internationale Handelsgesellschaft (Solange I)* (Case C-11/70), EU:C:1970:114, 17 December 1970; *Stefano Melloni v Ministerio Fiscal* (Case C-399/11), EU:C:2013:107, 26 February 2013. See also *The Minister for Justice and Equality and Commissioner of the Garda Síochána* (Case C-378/17), EU:C:2018:979, 4 December 2018.

72 The first two paragraphs of article 91 read as follows: "1. The Kingdom shall not be bound by treaties, nor shall such treaties be denounced without the prior approval of the States General. The cases in which approval is not required shall be specified by Act of Parliament. 2. The manner in which approval shall be granted shall be laid down by Act of Parliament, which may provide for the possibility of tacit approval."

Concerning EU law, member states have recognised its primacy on the condition that it respects fundamental rights and freedoms as guaranteed under domestic constitutional law.[73] The position of the CJEU is different in that it allows for the recognition of a "reserve of fundamentality," which protects fundamental values as guaranteed under the domestic constitution.[74] This paradigm shift from a hierarchical approach to a combinatory approach is based on the equivalence of rights protection between the international and domestic legal systems that allows their articulation in a multi-layered legal order.[75] More generally, in the context of globalisation, internationalisation, and Europeanisation of law, such a shift appears better suited to an horizontal approach that takes into account the various sources, levels, and authorities (be they political, judicial, or regulatory) involved in the enactment of legal norms.

Constitutional review. The constitution, which guarantees the rights and freedoms of citizens and defines the limits of the exercise of political power, is supreme to ordinary law and sits at the top of the hierarchy of legal norms. Any law, as voted by Parliament, must conform to the constitution. However, the existence of the constitution does not suffice in itself; a mechanism aimed at guaranteeing the supremacy of the constitution must be put in place. This is the raison d'être of constitutional review, or control of constitutionality, defined as "the power of a court to determine the constitutionality of legislation enacted by Parliament, as a means to check and limit the exercise of power by those in charge."[76] Although constitutional review is now well established and widespread,[77] its raison d'être did not immediately make complete sense, especially in jurisdictions with a long tradition of "legicentrism," or sovereignty of the law, such as France. Indeed, one interrogation was whether it was ever legitimate to review the law since the law is supposed to be the expression of the general will. It was counter-argued that the constitution, especially as the fundamental text of the nation, is the expression of the general will too, and in that respect, the law, as enacted by Parliament, should conform to it. Also, because constitutional provisions are generally phrased in general terms and, as such, open to interpretation, they may clash with principles and norms contained in the law, especially

73 See, for example, Constitutional Court (Italy), Decision No 170 of 8 June 1984, *S.p.a. Granital v Amministrazione delle Finanze dello Stato*; and Constitutional Court (Spain), Decision on the Treaty establishing a Constitution for Europe (13 December 2004), complemented by Constitutional Court Judgment No 26/2014 of 13 February 2014.

74 See *Omega Spielhallen und Automatenaufstellungs-GmbH v Oberbürgermeisterin der Bundesstadt Bonn* (Case C-36/02), EU:C:2004:614, 14 October 2004.

75 For this approach, see, in the EU context, *Yassin Abdullah Kadi and Al Barakaat International Foundation v Council of the European Union and Commission of the European Communities* (Joined Cases C-402/05 P and C-415/05 P), EU:C:2008:461, 3 September 2008; and in the ECHR context, *Bosphorus Hava Yolları Turizm ve Ticaret Anonim Şirketi (Bosphorus Airways) v Ireland* [GC], App No 45036/98, 30 June 2005.

76 Marie-Luce Paris, "Setting the Scene: Elements of Constitutional Theory and Methodology of the Research" in John Bell & Marie-Luce Paris (eds), *Rights-Based Constitutional Review: Constitutional Courts in a Changing Landscape* (Edward Elgar 2016) 1–26, 2–3.

77 Constitutional review is "now generally accepted as an essential or desirable feature of a liberal constitutional democracy" and has become a "global phenomenon" according to Chen and Poiares Maduro. See Albert H Y Chen & Miguel Poiares Maduro, "The Judiciary and Constitutional Review" in Mark Tushnet, Thomas Fleiner & Cheryl Saunders, *Routledge Handbook of Constitutional Law* (Routledge 2013) 100–101.

regarding fundamental freedoms. Therefore, it makes sense to provide for a review of the law as regards the constitution.

In theory, constitutional review can be entrusted with a political organ or with a judicial organ. In legal systems where constitutional review is entrusted with a political organ, members of such an organ are not, by definition, independent from it. Still, such a *political review* system is a priori legitimate since it gives the political branch of power the means to undo what it has (wrongly) done according to the theory of self-limitation. It is also regarded as legitimate to involve a political organ, Parliament or another body, whose members are appointed by political authorities, as fully respectful of the democratic and separation of powers principles preventing any interference from the other powers with the legislative power. The French example shows that constitutional review of a political nature prevailed for most of its modern constitutional history, from the 1795 Constitution (Parliament) till the 1946 Constitution (constitutional committee, composed of ten members elected by Parliament). It is only under the current Constitution that a constitutional review of a judicial nature is established.[78] However, review exercised by a political organ is rare since it is likely to lack the legitimacy associated with an independent and objective review. Constitutional review has been best realised when entrusted with a judicial organ, namely the courts, independent from the political power. *Constitutional judicial review* (i.e., review of the conformity of the laws with the constitution)[79] is what efficiently guarantees the respect of the rule of law—that is, a system where state authorities are, as much as its citizens, subject to legal norms under the control of independent courts whose role it is to protect fundamental freedoms. Constitutional courts exercise their review on the basis of legal arguments and according to judicial proceedings. Their decisions are legally binding on domestic courts and other public authorities because constitutional rulings have the authority of res judicata (*autorité de la chose jugée*). In other words, judicial review exemplifies noteworthy attributes of efficiency and objectivity, and is competency based. This explains the prevailing prominence of judicial review as the predominant method of constitutional review in contemporary liberal democracies.[80]

Most liberal democracies have established a mechanism of judicial constitutional review, which is outlined to varying degrees in the constitution itself. The terms governing this review process depend on how certain key questions are addressed. These questions include: which norms are open to review, which courts are responsible for conducting the review, and how and when the judicial constitutional review can be carried out.

First of all, norms susceptible to review are primarily ordinary laws. As Kelsen explained, the protection of the constitution means, in the first place, "the protection of the legality of the norms immediately subordinated to the constitution, that is essentially the constitutionality of

78 Marie-Luce Paris, "The French System of Rights-Based Review: From Exceptionalism to Parochial Constitutionalism" in John Bell & Marie-Luce Paris (eds), *Rights-Based Constitutional Review: Constitutional Courts in a Changing Landscape* (Edward Elgar 2016) 302–345. See also Chapter 6 on constitutional justice and rights protection.

79 Judicial review also concerns the examination of executive actions, potentially resulting in the invalidation of such actions or in questioning the authority responsible for carrying them out, such as in impeachment proceedings. However, in this context, judicial review primarily pertains to the scrutiny of laws.

80 Marie-Luce Paris, "Setting the Scene: Elements of Constitutional Theory and Methodology of the Research" in John Bell & Marie-Luce Paris (eds), *Rights-Based Constitutional Review: Constitutional Courts in a Changing Landscape* (Edward Elgar 2016) 1–26.

laws."[81] However, other norms than laws are susceptible to constitutional review, such as treaties and international conventions, organic laws, rules of procedure of the Houses of Parliament, regulatory measures, acts of local government bodies, and judicial decisions. Expanding the range of norms susceptible to constitutional review correlatively allows the expansion of the protection of rights and freedoms guaranteed under the constitution. In Germany, for example, the protection of individual rights and freedoms means that any act of a public authority can be judicially reviewed by the Federal Constitutional Court. The case of constitutional laws (i.e., amendments to the constitution) is specific. Should the domestic system accept the theory of supra-constitutionality, a number of constitutional provisions are literally intangible and cannot be amended; as such, they are not susceptible to judicial review.[82]

Constitutional courts exercise their review by reference to the provisions contained in the constitution and by reference to several principles of constitutional value. These constitutional principles can be found in texts such as preambles, charters, declarations, and bills of rights attached to the constitution, and even in judicial decisions. The common denominator for these texts, be they contained in the constitution[83] or in an annex to it,[84] is that they expressly protect fundamental rights and freedoms. Constitutional provisions relating to the sharing of competences between public powers (horizontal approach),[85] and between the different levels of power (vertical approach),[86] are also particularly protected by the constitutional court. Also, in a number of jurisdictions, the constitutional court has progressively extended the scope of constitutional review to encompass norms outside of the domestic legal system such as duly ratified international treaties and conventions, thus exercising what is called "control of conventionality" (i.e., constitutional review of the conformity of international provisions with the constitution).[87] In cases where such control is not expressly recognised under the constitution, the constitutional court nevertheless takes these international norms into account and

81 Hans Kelsen, "La garantie juridictionnelle de la Constitution" (1928) *Revue du Droit Public* 197.

82 See, for example, Federal Constitutional Court (Germany), Decision of 15 December 1970, 2 BvF 1/69 et al., BVerfGE 30, 1 in the electronic eavesdropping case in relation to the amendment of article 13 of the Basic Law (inviolability of the home); and Supreme Court (India), Decision *Kesavananda Bharati v State of Kerala*, (1973) 4 SCC 225, in which the Indian Supreme Court held that although no part of the Constitution, including fundamental rights, was beyond the Parliament's amending power, the "basic structure of the Constitution could not be abrogated even by a constitutional amendment." See also the French decisions in decision No 92-312 of 2 September 1992, *Traité sur l'Union européenne*, Rec. 76, and decision No 2003-469 DC of 26 March 2003, *Révision constitutionnelle relative à l'organisation décentralisée de la République*, Rec. 293, in which the Constitutional Council declares that it was not competent to review constitutional laws as they are regarded as expressions of the sovereign constituent power be they adopted by Congress or by referendum.

83 For instance, the provisions on fundamental rights and freedoms are contained in the first provisions of the constitution in Germany and Italy, and at the end of the constitution in Latvia and the USA.

84 For instance, the provisions on fundamental rights and freedoms are contained in an ensemble of texts annexed to the 1958 Constitution, namely the 1789 Declaration, the Preamble to the 1946 Constitution, and the 2004 Charter on the Environment. The 1958 Constitution lacks an explicit list of fundamental principles, except for acknowledging the significance of the principle of equality and individual freedom.

85 Constitutional review aims at protecting the sharing of competence between Parliament and government in, for example, France, Spain, Russia, and Senegal.

86 Constitutional review aims at protecting the sharing of competence between the federal state and the states in, for example, Germany, the USA, Russia, and South Africa, or between the state and its regions, provinces, or other autonomous entities in, for example, Portugal, Italy, and Spain.

87 For example, in Poland and Austria, as opposed to France (see below).

interprets constitutional provisions in the light of such norms, either spontaneously or because the constitution expressly requires such an interpretation.

In terms of the type of courts exercising constitutional review, two models have emerged. These models have been adapted, with variants, by most of the jurisdictions worldwide. The first model is the so-called American model. Such a model, which appeared in the USA based on the 1803 seminal decision in *Marbury v Madison*,[88] is based on a decentralised, or diffused, judicial review exercised by ordinary judges under the supervision of a supreme court. This model has been adopted, to a varying extent, by Japan, Ireland, and a few countries in South America such as Argentina, Brazil, and Mexico. The second model is the so-called European model devised on the basis of Kelsen's theory and put into place in the 1920 Austrian Constitution. The Kelsenian model is based on a centralised, or concentrated, judicial review exercised by a special court, called a constitutional court. This model has spread greatly, firstly in Austria and Germany, and then in most European countries, including in Eastern and Central Europe. Such model has also inspired a number of African countries such as Benin, Côte d'Ivoire, and Senegal. The double issue of decentralised/centralised review, and supreme court/constitutional court, has been decisive in the way each jurisdiction has organised constitutional review in its legal system.

In a system of centralised review, judicial review of issues of constitutionality is exclusively conferred upon a judicial body (a court or equivalent body), although such a body may also act in other capacities such as an advisory body or as an electoral judge. An issue of constitutionality may be referred to such a court either directly, by the relevant authorities or by the citizens, or indirectly, by ordinary judges who, faced with such an issue during proceedings, decide to refer the issue as a preliminary question. The specialised court entrusted with centralised review sits apart from the other courts in the court-system and is independent from other public powers. This is the model adopted by most European states. A constitutional court generally comprises between nine and twenty members, chosen by election or by appointment, for a mandate of between six and twelve years, and according to a procedure involving, depending on each jurisdiction, a number of public authorities (i.e., the Head of State, the government, Parliament, the judiciary).

On the contrary, in a system of decentralised constitutional review, any judge, at any level of the court-system, has the power to review the conformity of the law with the constitution. The highest court in the domestic order is entrusted with the task of ensuring the consistency and unity of the body of judicial decisions on constitutionality rendered at the lower level. In a decentralised review system, the review is conferred upon a supreme court placed, as evident, at the top of the court system. Such a court is the court of last resort when judicial decisions of lower ordinary courts are referred to it, as is commonly the case worldwide (e.g., Brazil, Canada, Japan, India, Israel). In a few jurisdictions, the supreme court is also entrusted with the task of reviewing issues of constitutionality (e.g., USA, Mexico). In some jurisdictions, a supreme court can coexist with a constitutional court which is solely competent with reviewing issues of constitutionality. This is the case, for example, in Spain, Portugal, Latvia, Russia, and Cameroon.

Other aspects of judicial constitutional review relate to access to constitutional justice, as well as to the nature and effects of the judicial decision. In terms of access to constitutional

88 *Marbury v Madison*, 5 U.S. (1 Cranch) 137 (1803).

justice, access is either restricted or open. A restricted access (i.e., restricted referral or *saisine fermée*) means that the initiative of judicial review proceedings is limited, generally to the public authorities such as the Head of State, the government, members of Parliament, or the public prosecutor. On the contrary, an open access (i.e., open referral or *saisine ouverte*) means that the initiative of judicial review proceedings is widely accessible to litigants. In the former system, referral is necessarily motivated by political considerations. If the authority initiating the proceedings is of the same political hue as the party in power, the authority in question will likely not refer an issue of constitutionality affecting the law that they just voted for; in other words, referral by political authorities is only truly efficient and democratic if, firstly, the reviewing body is truly independent (for example, if the reviewing body maintains its case law policy after a change in political power), and, secondly, if the referral is available to members of the opposition (e.g., 1974 constitutional reform in France opening access to constitutional justice to 60 deputies or 60 senators in addition to the initiative being opened to the President of the Republic, the Prime Minister, the president of the National Assembly, and the president of the Senate). In the latter system, that of an open referral system, citizens can refer an issue of constitutionality to the constitutional court either directly or indirectly. If citizens are allowed to refer an issue of constitutionality directly to the constitutional court in order to protect their individual rights and freedoms, strict conditions generally exist to curtail any floodgate of claims. Such a system exists, for instance, in Germany, Spain, Austria, Belgium, Slovakia, and Brazil. Referral by citizens themselves is obviously the most democratic way, and, under such a system, any litigant may challenge the constitutionality of a law which is susceptible to affect his/her interests, or his/her rights should the citizen have a legitimate interest to do so (i.e., the law applicable to him/her is susceptible to be unconstitutional). Because of the risk of floodgate of cases, such a direct referral system generally involves a filter mechanism that requires the exhaustion of all other available judicial remedies. Under an indirect referral system, citizens cannot directly access the constitutional court but can instead raise an issue of constitutionality in the course of ordinary court proceedings where the dispute can then be referred to the constitutional court. In very rare instances, the judicial system does not allow citizens to access the constitutional court at all.[89]

The question of when the issue of constitutionality can be raised before the constitutional court has also to be specified. Laws may be judicially reviewed *before* their promulgation under the so-called ex-ante (or a priori) review,[90] or *after* their promulgation and their entry into force (i.e., once they are applied) under the so-called ex-post (or a posteriori) review.[91] The advantage of ex-ante review is that it ensures immunity to the laws in question since these cannot be later challenged, thus guaranteeing some stability to the citizens and public authorities abiding by constitutionally compliant laws. The weakness of such a review is that it is not a systematic review since it depends on the decision to refer the issue of constitutionality in the first place. Should a law not be referred, such an enacted law may subsequently prove to be unconstitutional. Under the ex-post review, should a law be found unconstitutional, it will be declared null and void with retroactive effect. The retroactive effect may, under certain cir-

89 It is also possible to provide for the right of the constitutional court to refer an issue of constitutionality ex officio, that is, of its own motion.

90 This type of review is necessarily by way of main action (*par voie d'action*).

91 This type of review can be triggered by way of main action or by way of exception (*par voie d'exception*).

cumstances, notably because of legal certainty concerns, require adjustments to maintain the acquired rights. There is generally a strong advantage in combining both systems of ex-ante and ex-post judicial review.[92]

Any chosen system of judicial review relates to the type of outcome that the review is supposed to achieve, whether it is to annul the law in question (review by action, or *contrôle par voie d'action*) or to declare the law inapplicable in the case at hand (review by exception, or *contrôle par voie d'exception*). In the former case, the sole motivation of the litigant is to have the alleged unconstitutionality of the law objectively recognised with all the related consequences. In other words, this is an *abstract* form of review, not linked to any particular case, and bearing a general and absolute effect. This type of review is widely used in Europe and generally goes hand in hand with restricted access to the constitutional court. In the latter case, the aim of judicial review proceedings is to prevent the allegedly unconstitutional law from being applied to the litigant. Because his/her case before the ordinary judge depends on the outcome of the judicial review decision, the litigant is not interested in the application of this law to other pending or future cases. In other words, this is a *concrete* form of review that is subjectively linked to the defence of a particular litigant. This type of incidental review is usually associated with wider access to the constitutional court whereby the litigant claims, during proceedings before domestic courts, that the law susceptible to be applied to him/her should not be applied in his/her case because of its alleged unconstitutionality. The ordinary judge is thus perfectly entitled to set aside the law in this case. However, the law in question is still in force and susceptible to be applied in other cases unless this is changed, either by the supreme court declaring the law unconstitutional, or by Parliament passing new legislation. This form of review is the one used in the American system[93] and, by extension and with slightly different modalities, in Canada and Australia, as well as in other common law-inspired jurisdictions such as Ireland. The two forms of review, by way of action and by way of exception, may coexist in one system (e.g., Germany, Italy).

The constitutional ruling on the issue of constitutionality has an erga omnes effect, meaning that the decision has a general effect towards all public authorities and parties to the case. In that sense, the decision of the constitutional judge has the authority of res judicata (i.e., the adjudicated matter is not susceptible to further litigation between the same parties). Should the law in question be found unconstitutional, the law will be declared null and void, either with retroactive effect or only for the future depending on the domestic arrangements in place. In the case of a review by exception, the constitutional ruling has an inter partes effect, meaning that the unconstitutional law in question is inapplicable as regards the parties to the case only, under the *relative* res judicata effect. Although the law in question does not disappear from the domestic legal order, other courts will, however, be reluctant to apply such a law to other instances.

The classical distinction between the American and European (or Kelsenian) models has been eroded over time, for the different models and techniques of judicial constitutional review have been combined in different shapes and to different degrees in the various jurisdictions of the world. Ex-post judicial review, based on the American model, has spread all over

92 See the French example in Chapter 6 on constitutional justice and rights protection.

93 Since the famous 1803 *Marbury v Madison* decision of the Supreme Court, although this was applied before at state level.

Europe, including in France. The American model has, in turn, been inspired by features of the European model, such as in practice the erga omnes effect of the constitutional ruling. The 1996 Constitution of South Africa is a good example of a mixed system whereby ordinary judges operate a review of constitutionality on the American model but whose decisions must be upheld by the constitutional court. Judicial review in Irish law is another example of a hybrid system. While the Irish legal system emerged from the British system, judicial review represents one of the key areas of divergence with the Commonwealth system (characterised as a weak form of constitutional review) and is closer to the American system in some respects, save that the Irish courts have the express power to invalidate a law as unconstitutional under article 34.3.2°.[94]

BOX 1.1 CONCEPTIONS OF THE CONSTITUTION

The **political** constitution (Aristotle, Hauriou, Schmitt) considers an institutional approach centred on the state and the organisation of state power, that is, the working of the government and its institutions in a setup allowing for the participation of the citizens.

Key concepts: state, democracy, separation of powers, government.

The **social** constitution (Hauriou) considers a social approach centred on the citizens and the protection of their political, social, and economic rights in a particular organised social group.

Key concepts: society, liberalism, individual, private sphere v state.

The **normative** constitution (Kelsen) refers to a formal approach of the constitution centred on its place in the legal order as the highest-placed norm whose validity must be enforced via a mechanism of judicial review aimed at guaranteeing rights and freedoms, as laid down in the constitution.

Key concepts: supreme norm, constituent power, legality, judicial (constitutional) review, fundamental freedoms.

Democracy and the Rule of Law

> « *La démocratie, c'est 'le gouvernement du peuple, par le peuple, pour le peuple.'* »[95]

Democracy, originating from the ideals of the Enlightenment era, typically signifies the victory of legality over arbitrariness. Pluralist democracy is founded on the fundamental principle of liberty, which forms the bedrock of the social, institutional, and political structures within a society. Liberty, in essence, refers to the freedom bestowed upon individuals, placing them at the heart of society and enabling them to act, move, and express their opinions freely.

94 Séamus Ó Tuama, "Judicial Review under the Irish Constitution: More American than Commonwealth" (2008) 12 (2) *Electronic Journal of Comparative Law.*

95 Abraham Lincoln (1809–1865), President of the USA (1861–1865) [Democracy is "the government of the people, by the people, for the people"].

This notion gives rise to the concept of *individual* freedoms. In a pluralist democracy, sovereignty rests with the people, who are comprised of individuals coming together. Each individual exercises their sovereignty through elected representatives, freely chosen via the principle of universal suffrage. Therefore, democracy entails the active involvement of individuals in wielding political authority, primarily through the mechanism of elections.

This section delves into the origins and modern characteristics of democracy. It explores specific developments related to citizens' participation in elections and to the organisation of representative democracy. Additionally, it includes insights on the concept of the rule of law.

The origins of democracy

Democracy, derived from the Greek words *dēmos* (people) and *kratia* (power or rule), refers to a political system in which the people hold the ultimate authority. In ancient Greece, this form of political regime was based on three key principles, namely equality before the law, the equal participation of all citizens in public affairs, and freedom of expression. However, it is important to note that despite these principles, certain segments of the population, including women, slaves, and aliens, were excluded from participation. Only a small percentage, ranging between 5% and 10% of the city's population, were considered eligible citizens with the right to engage in public life during that time. Greek philosophers such as Herodotus, Plato, and Aristotle recognised democracy as one among several political regimes described during that era. Thus, democracy, characterised by power being vested in the people, stood in contrast to other forms of political regimes where power resided in the hands of a single ruler (monarchy with a single ruler, or tyranny with a single *authoritarian* ruler), a select few (oligarchy), or a privileged group with wealth (aristocracy).

Modern characteristics of democracy

After a prolonged period of feudal and absolute monarchy, modern political regimes have once again embraced the principle of democracy. This principle was initially conceptualised by Enlightenment philosophers. In its contemporary interpretation, democracy refers to a system of governance based on popular sovereignty. According to Rousseau, it encompasses *the principles of freedom and equality of all citizens before the law.* A democratic regime operates on the premise that the law represents the "expression of the general will," which is determined through voting by the electorate and accepted by the citizens as binding. In essence, democracy can be defined as "government of the people, by the people, for the people," as eloquently expressed by President Lincoln in his Gettysburg speech in 1863 and reiterated in article 2 of the French Constitution. True democratic regimes emerged in the mid-nineteenth century in western industrialised societies and gradually spread to other regions of the world. For instance, Southern Europe witnessed a transition to democracy in the 1970s, followed by Latin America in the late 1980s. Sub-Saharan Africa experienced a similar transition in the 1990s, while Eastern Europe underwent significant changes after the dissolution of the Soviet Union in 1991. However, despite the widespread adoption of democratic principles, satisfactory implementation is limited to only a few countries worldwide. According to the *Democracy Index* 2022, out of the 166 countries evaluated, only 72 meet the criteria for a democratic regime. This includes 24 countries with a fully democratic regime and 48 countries with a flawed democratic regime. In contrast, 95 countries are classified as operating under a hybrid or authoritarian regime. In other words, approximately 43% of the world's population reside in countries with a democratic regime.[96]

Modern democracy also encompasses the principles of *pluralism and liberalism*. These principles entail the conduct of regular and free elections, universal suffrage (with the principle of "one voice, one vote"), the presence of multiple political parties offering genuine choices among different political ideologies, and the protection of the rights of the opposition through various means. Political liberalism further emphasises that citizens should have the freedom to make political choices, thereby encompassing the exercise of freedom of thought, expression, and assembly.

In addition to the aforementioned essential characteristics, democracy has flourished due to various factors. These include the advancement of education, the establishment of a free press, and the assurance of individual and collective freedoms. Education has played a crucial role in enabling citizens to comprehend the significance of their involvement in the political process and to exercise their right to vote effectively. The development of a free press has facilitated the exchange of diverse political opinions by providing a platform for pluralist information. This has, in turn, encouraged the formation of public opinion. Ensuring individual and collective freedoms, particularly through mechanisms of judicial review, has been pivotal in fostering citizens' political awareness. Citizens are confident that their rights, such as their right to freedom of assembly and association, including the right to enter a trade union and the right to strike, as well as the right to property ownership, are safeguarded allowing them to freely express their ideas. Furthermore, the improvement in living standards has allowed individuals to prioritise political engagement over basic survival tasks. Additionally, the progressive structuring of political parties has contributed to a clearer understanding of the political landscape, offering distinct trends in domestic politics. These factors have collectively contributed to the emergence of mature democratic regimes.

Citizens' participation in politics. Historically, the origin of political power was believed to be bestowed by a divine entity. It was believed that God selected individuals to rule under the monarchy based on divine right. However, during the Enlightenment period in the eighteenth century, philosophers and intellectuals challenged this notion and introduced a new perspective. They proposed that political power actually originates from the citizens themselves, who are recognised as the ultimate authority. This concept gave rise to two political theories, namely that of national sovereignty and that of popular sovereignty. Under the idea of national sovereignty, the power lies within the collective identity of the nation as a whole. This theory suggests that the citizens, as a unified entity, hold the authority to determine the course of political decisions. On the other hand, popular sovereignty emphasises the importance of individual citizens and their participation in the exercise of political power. It suggests that every citizen has the right to directly engage in the political process and influence decision-making. Citizens have the opportunity to participate in politics either by directly involving themselves in the exercise of political power or by engaging in representative democracy. In direct participation, citizens

96 The *Democracy Index* is issued by the Economist Intelligence Unit of The Economist Group. It is based on 60 indicators, grouped into five categories: electoral process and pluralism, civil liberties, functioning of government, political participation, and political culture. The *Democracy Index* for 2022 is accessible at <https://www.eiu.com/n/campaigns/democracy-index-2022/>.

play an active role in shaping political decisions and policies, expressing their opinions, and contributing to the governance of their society. On the other hand, representative democracy allows citizens to elect individuals who will represent their interests and make decisions on their behalf.

In a system of *direct democracy*, citizens actively participate in the decision-making process by voting on laws, making treaties, appointing civil servants, and administering justice. This means that citizens are responsible for all legislative, executive, and judicial functions. However, implementing direct democracy in its purest form is practically unfeasible due to various obvious reasons. This form of governance was only possible in small communities such as the ancient Greek cities, where citizens themselves managed public affairs in the open public forum known as the *agora*. Direct democracy, although considered a "political curiosity,"[97] is still practised today on a smaller scale in certain Swiss cantons, such as Glarus and Appenzell Innerrhoden, as well as in small towns where popular assemblies, known as *Landsgemeinde*, decide on local political matters. However, the majority of modern political systems are representative democracies, which may incorporate certain elements of direct democracy.

In a *representative democracy*, the responsibility of exercising political power is given to elected representatives, who form a smaller group of individuals entrusted with the task of deliberating and making decisions on political matters on behalf of the citizens. This particular form of democracy assumes the presence of well-informed citizens who actively engage in public affairs and exercise their voting rights to elect leaders whom they can identify with and trust. While representative democracy is primarily based on majority voting, which reflects the collective will of the people (i.e., the expression of "the general will"), it also ensures the protection of minority interests. Some even argue that democracy is not solely about majority rule, but rather about safeguarding the rights and interests of the minority.[98] Another characteristic of representative democracy is the recognition that the people themselves may not possess the necessary skills or knowledge to govern effectively, thus entrusting politicians to act on their behalf. In this type of democracy, citizens participate in universal suffrage to elect representatives to Parliament, who in turn appoint the government. In certain systems, citizens have the opportunity to elect both the representatives in Parliament and the Head of the Executive through universal suffrage. For example, in France, the French people have directly elected deputies in the National Assembly as well as the President of the Republic since 1962. This arrangement further enhances the legitimacy and prestige of both the legislative and executive branches of power.[99]

The concept of so-called "semi-direct" democracy incorporates certain aspects of direct democracy within a representative form of government. This primarily involves utilising referendums as a means to involve the public in the decision-making process by seeking their input on significant national issues. Technically speaking, a referendum allows citizens to cast their vote on a particular text or question. Referendums can take various forms: a *ratification* referendum seeks people's approval for a text that has already been voted on by Parliament; a *constituent* referendum poses a constitutional question to the public; a *legislative* referendum asks a question pertaining to legislation; a *mandatory* referendum is required for certain

97 Pauline Türk, *Principes fondamentaux du droit constitutionnel* (Gualino 2018) 110.
98 As famously coined by Albert Camus, French philosopher and writer (1913–1960).
99 See Chapter 4 on the institutions of the Fifth Republic.

matters that can only be decided through a referendum (such as an amendment to the Irish Constitution); and a *non-mandatory* referendum is conducted when a reform could have been discussed and decided by Parliament, but is instead put to a public vote (such as an amendment to the French Constitution). A referendum can turn into a plebiscite when it is employed to seek popular support and consolidate personal power. Historical examples of this include the extensive use of plebiscites by both Napoleon Bonaparte and Napoleon III. Referendums are widely practised in western democracies, with a few exceptions. For instance, Germany abstains from their use due to historical reasons, as the Nazi regime attained power with popular approval. Similarly, the USA generally avoids referendums, except in certain states. In the UK, the tradition has also been to rely on an ultra-representative political system based on parliamentary sovereignty. However, in the past decade, there have been three notable exceptions: the Alternative Vote referendum in 2011, the Scottish independence referendum in 2014, and the infamous Brexit referendum in 2016, which determined the UK's exit from the EU.

There are several mechanisms available to facilitate active participation of citizens in the process of decision-making.[100] These mechanisms include mini-publics, popular assemblies where decisions can be reached through a show of hands, and popular revocations or recall elections that empower voters to remove elected officials from office before their term ends. Moreover, the right of petition grants citizens the ability to present questions for public approval or propose legislation. Additionally, there are other popular initiatives that allow citizens to directly contribute to the decision-making process. It is important to acknowledge that these techniques can be combined, for instance, by utilising both the right of petition and referendums to support popular initiatives aimed at adopting legislative or constitutional provisions.[101]

Representative democracy. Representative democracy is the prevailing political system in most western democracies today. Such a form of government is compatible with both a monarchical system and a republican system. It is important to note that the presence of a monarchy or a republic does not automatically determine whether a political regime is democratic.[102] In a monarchy, the ruler (such as a King, Queen, Prince, or Princess) derives their political authority from divine origins (such as the concept of a monarchy ordained by a higher power, or a monarchy of divine right based on the sacrament of the King) or hereditary succession.[103] Monarchies typically involve the passing down of power through generations, although there have been exceptions in the form of elective monarchies throughout history. Monarchies can be either absolute or limited in terms of their power. In a limited or constitutional monarchy, the monarch's authority is defined by a constitution and is carried out within the boundaries set by the government and the prerogatives of Parliament. The monarch is just

100 Mechanisms other than universal suffrage can of course be used for regular elections, referendums, and any popular consultation.

101 See, for example, article 75 of the Italian Constitution, which indicates the initiative of 500,000 citizen petitioners for a referendum aimed at abrogating legislation or part thereof.

102 See, for example, the authoritarian regime of the People's Republic of China, to be compared with the liberal regimes of the constitutional monarchies in Spain, Sweden, and the UK.

103 Initially, the establishment of monarchy as a political system was not subjected to criticism, primarily because it was believed to provide a certain degree of political stability. However, over time, the concept of monarchy began to be viewed as potentially dangerous, as it had a tendency to transform into oppressive or despotic regimes.

one representative of the sovereign nation, alongside elected assemblies, within a system that separates powers.[104] In a parliamentary monarchy, the government is appointed by the monarch but remains accountable to Parliament. The government holds the actual political power, while the monarch's role is primarily symbolic and ceremonial. Examples of parliamentary monarchies include the UK, Belgium, and Spain. Thus, a constitutional monarchy can indeed coexist with representative democracy.

The republican system stands in stark contrast to the monarchy as it places political authority in the hands of the people rather than the King. Within a republic, power is bestowed upon elected representatives who act on behalf of the citizens. Depending on the chosen ideologies, a republic can embody various forms such as being "popular" (reflecting the will of the people), democratic, socialist, or liberal. Consequently, representative democracy can manifest as either a republic (e.g., France, Ireland, Italy, USA) or a monarchy (e.g., Belgium, Spain, Sweden, UK) where the elected representatives actively participate in the political decision-making process.

The system of representative democracy necessitates the presence of parliamentary assemblies, political parties, and a functional electoral system.[105] Representatives, elected through the principle of universal suffrage, are given the responsibility of exercising state power by serving in Parliament.[106] Parliament, therefore, serves as the national political institution responsible for representing citizens, voting on laws, imposing taxes, and scrutinising government actions. Parliament is typically composed of one or two chambers (or houses, or assemblies), with the two-house legislature (known as a bicameral Parliament) being the most prevalent arrangement. Members of the Lower House are directly elected by the people, while members of the Upper House are elected through indirect means. The Upper House generally holds less authority compared to the Lower House, resulting in an "unequal bicameralism" situation, as seen in the French Fifth Republic regime, for example. However, there are also political systems where both Houses of Parliament possess equal powers, referred to as "equal bicameralism" as observed in the current Italian regime. In Italy, both the House of Deputies and the Senate enjoy similar powers, allowing them to overthrow the government or impede the passage of laws, significantly impeding government actions.[107]

The existence of a second House of Parliament in a state can be justified based on its history and sociology. This leads to the existence of different types of bicameralism. A typology can be used to distinguish between these types, which include federal, territorial, aristocratic, republican, and sociological bicameralism. *Federal bicameralism* involves the participation of federated states in the constituent and legislative powers of a main federal parliamentary assembly. Examples of this type include the US Senate, German *Bundesrat*, and Indian *Rajya Sabha* or Council of States. *Territorial bicameralism* aims to represent different territories, such as local authorities, provinces, or regions, in decentralised states. Examples of this type can be found in

104 Montesquieu and Constant advocated for such a regime for the stability of state power, the King embodying the "neutral" supreme power in opposition to the "active" power of ministers in government.

105 Specific principles about political parties and elections under French law are dealt with under Chapter 5 on political parties, elections, and referendums.

106 Other elected representatives at national level may be the Head of State such as, for instance, the French President of the Republic.

107 A reform aimed at decreasing the powers of the Senate failed in 2016. The object of the reform was to differentiate between two legislative procedures; one of them—the unicameral procedure—would have made the role of the Senate mostly consultative.

the Senate of Spain, Italy, and Gabon. *Aristocratic bicameralism* represents a specific faction of the population, such as the nobility or the clergy, whose role is to advise the monarch. The House of Lords in the UK before 2009 and the *Chambre des Pairs* in France from 1814 to 1848 are examples of this type. *Republican bicameralism* generally refers to a conservative House of Parliament that appears more conservative than the Lower House. Its purpose is to balance the political forces within the parliamentary system. The *Conseil des Anciens* in France in 1795 and the Senate in Italy today are examples of this type. Lastly, *sociological bicameralism* is based on the representation of various social, economic, or cultural groups, such as associations, trade unions, professional bodies, religious organisations, or ethnic groups. The *Seanad* in Ireland, National Council in Slovenia, and Senate in Mauritania are examples of this type.[108]

Political parties play a vital role in the functioning of democracy. In a healthy democracy, political debates should not be diluted, and consensus should not be easily achieved. It is regular elections that inject new life into political affairs, compelling parties to assert their distinct characteristics and formulate a comprehensive government agenda. Another dynamic element in politics, and therefore in democracy, is the rise of new political forces driven by the aspirations of citizens. These emerging parties possess the ability to challenge the established order, often advocating for more specific or sectoral viewpoints. Western democracies, such as France, have witnessed the flourishing of numerous political parties, with an astonishing count of 75 or more main formations.[109] Some of these parties are centred around a single theme, such as the Animalist Party (*Parti animaliste*) founded in 2016, which bases its ideology on anti-speciesism. The regulations governing political parties' fundraising practices and their interactions with the media during electoral campaigns, including the use of various communication channels and opinion polls, all contribute to a well-functioning democracy. These rules, along with other regulatory frameworks, aim to ensure fairness among candidates and impartiality from both the administration and the media.[110]

Representative democracy can have unintended consequences in two ways. Firstly, there is potential for a disconnect between the rulers and the governed, between the government and the people. This can occur when elected members of Parliament fail to fulfil their electoral promises. However, measures have been implemented to address this issue. For instance, in the Fifth Republic, the decision to directly elect the President of the Republic in 1962 aimed to establish a closer connection between the French people and the primary political institution of the regime. Additionally, the introduction of judicial constitutional review of laws has helped restore the bond between power and the people, safeguarding their rights. This was further reinforced by the 2008 constitutional amendment, which extended the review to include ex-post assessment. Secondly, there is a genuine risk of the political elite appropriating power, particularly when supported by a formidable administration resembling a technocracy, as well as influential media.

The existing crisis faced by representative democracy serves as evidence for two significant phenomena. It is undeniably true that the original model of representative democracy is now outdated. Taking on the commendable task of "reimagining democracy"[111] involves

108 Pauline Türk, *Principes fondamentaux du droit constitutionnel* (Gualino 2018) 116.

109 At present, the political landscape in France comprises over 500 political parties, varying in their level of prominence and recognition.

110 This is also detailed further below in Chapter 5 in respect of French law.

111 David Farrell and Jane Suiter, *Reimagining Democracy* (Cornell University Press 2019).

re-evaluating the relationship between those who govern and those who are governed, ensuring that citizens feel more engaged and valued within their democratic system. This task necessitates adapting or even reinventing the democratic process to include additional stakeholders beyond the people and their representatives, such as civil society, courts, and various institutional and administrative bodies with legitimate representation. Despite its shortcomings, democracy remains the most preferable form of political regime among the available options.[112]

In the present circumstances, deliberative democracy and participatory democracy have emerged as innovative concepts to revitalise the idea of democracy. *Deliberative democracy* emphasises the importance of public opinion and highlights that continuous exchanges in the public sphere will enlighten the government and validate its decisions. Under this system, democracy is not solely reliant on decisions made exclusively by the majority in government, but also stems from open and contentious discussions facilitated by an active civil society.[113] Similarly, *participatory democracy* promotes the establishment of various platforms outside the traditional parliamentary representation. Public consultations, general assemblies, citizen panels, petitions, local committees, public inquiries, impact assessments, referendums, and popular initiatives are among the tools used in participatory democracy. This form of democracy does not reflect a lack of trust in citizens' engagement with public affairs but is rather a concerted effort to regain their interest in politics and reinvigorate their involvement in the decision-making process. In other words, participatory democracy complements representative democracy and does not aim to replace it. However, these novel democratic approaches face the risk of being influenced or controlled by powerful interest groups and lobbies. Consequently, it is crucial to carefully consider the framework and procedures governing these democratic mechanisms.[114]

The rule of law

The concept of the rule of law has its origins in western political thought, particularly in England. One notable definition, provided by Dicey, states: "It [the rule of law] means, in the first place, the absolute supremacy or predominance of regular law as opposed to the influence of arbitrary power, and excludes the existence of arbitrariness, of prerogative, or even of wide discretionary authority on the part of the government."[115] Today, the rule of law has evolved into a broader concept that comprises multiple interpretations that range from its role in limiting the arbitrary exercise of state power, to its function in defining the attributes necessary for attaining a just society that upholds various ideals and values, such as human rights. Therefore, the rule of law is a somewhat allusive concept whose content continues to be a topic of debate

112 As adapted from a quote attributed to Winston Churchill: "Many forms of Government have been tried and will be tried in this world of sin and woe. No one pretends that democracy is perfect or all-wise. Indeed, it has been said that democracy is the worst form of government except all those other forms that have been tried from time to time" (House of Commons, 11 November 1947).

113 For the philosophical theory behind deliberative democracy, see Jürgen Habermas, *The Structural Transformation of the Public Sphere* (MIT Press, 1962, trans. 1989 by Thomas Burger and Frederick Lawrence).

114 For more detail on these points concerning the citizens' assemblies, see Marthe Fatin-Rouge Stefanini & Xavier Magnon (eds), *Les Assemblées citoyennes : nouvelle utopie démocratique ?* Confluence des Droits (DICE Publications 2022).

115 A V Dicey, *Introduction to the Study of the Law of the Constitution* (3rd edn, Macillan and Co 1889) 189.

and, to some extent, controversy. What is certain is that the rule of law is a cornerstone of democratic governance that ought to be preserved in the face of current difficult challenges.[116]

The rule of law and democracy are mutually reinforcing principles (see Table 1.3 Features of the rule of law and democracy). Democracy cannot thrive without the rule of law, as it ensures that the will of the people is exercised within a framework that upholds individual rights and protects against arbitrary actions. Similarly, the rule of law relies on democracy to ensure its legitimacy and responsiveness to societal needs. Consequently, the interplay between the rule of law and democracy is three-fold: firstly, the rule of law ensures the supremacy of law over arbitrary decision-making; secondly, the rule of law promotes equal treatment and protection of citizens; and thirdly, the rule of law establishes legal frameworks that safeguard individual rights and freedoms. In that perspective, this interplay between the two concepts can be further described in the following terms. Democracy promotes *government accountability* by providing opportunities for citizens to elect their representatives and hold them responsible for their actions. The rule of law reinforces this accountability by establishing clear legal mechanisms to investigate and address any abuses of power. Constitutional law further strengthens accountability by delineating the powers and limitations of government institutions. Also, *the principle of legality*, a fundamental aspect of the rule of law, requires that laws be clear, predictable, and applied prospectively. Democracy ensures that laws are enacted through transparent and participatory processes, reflecting the will of the people. Constitutional law provides a framework for interpreting and applying laws consistently, promoting legal certainty and fairness. Lastly, both the rule of law and democracy play crucial roles in *safeguarding individual rights*. Constitutional law serves as a framework for protecting these rights, ensuring that they are not violated by either the government or other citizens. The rule of law guarantees that everyone is equal before the law, irrespective of their social or political standing, while democracy provides mechanisms for individuals to participate in shaping the laws that govern them. Therefore, by upholding individual rights, ensuring government accountability, and promoting the principle of legality, both the rule of law and democracy foster stability, equality, and progress.

The rule of law is a fundamental principle in French law. French law incorporates several key principles that underpin the rule of law such as legal certainty, equality before the law, procedural fairness, separation of powers, and judicial independence. This polysemic nature of the term explains why, in the French language, the rule of law may be translated by several expressions such as "*État de droit*," "*prééminence du droit*," "*primauté du droit*," or even "*principe de légalité*."[117] *Legal certainty* means that the law must be clear, precise, and accessible to all individuals, ensuring that they are aware of their rights and obligations. French law is primarily based on codified laws, which are written statutes enacted by the legislature. This provides legal certainty and ensures that laws are applied uniformly across the country. According to the principle of *equality*, all individuals are entitled to equal treatment under the law, without any discrimination based on factors such as race, gender, or social status. The principle of

116 For instance, see Stanley Greenstein, "Preserving the Rule of Law in the Era of Artificial Intelligence (AI)" (2022) 30 *Artificial Intelligence Law* 291.

117 Laurent Pech, "The Rule of Law" in Paul Craig & Gráinne de Búrca (eds), *The Evolution of EU Law* (3rd edn, OUP 2021) 307, 310–311. For a discussion of the rule of law in the EU context, see also, Laurent Pech, "The Rule of Law as a Well-Established and Well-Defined Principle of EU Law" (2022) 14 *Hague Journal on the Rule Law* 107, and Laurent Pech, "The European Union's Rule of Law Crisis: From Rule of Law to Rule of Lawlessness in Europe?" (2003) 70 *Irish Jurist* 10.

procedural fairness requires that legal procedures must be fair and impartial, guaranteeing a fair trial and due process for all parties involved. It is in application of these two principles, equality and procedural fairness, that French law ensures that individuals have equal access to justice, regardless of their financial means. Legal aid is available to those who cannot afford legal representation, ensuring that everyone can seek redress and have their cases heard in court. The French legal system adheres to the principle of *separation of powers*, ensuring that the legislative, executive, and judicial branches operate independently of each other. As for *judicial independence*, this means that judges must be impartial, free from any external influence or pressure. This guarantees that decisions are made solely on the basis of the law and evidence presented. Also, the French legal system includes a mechanism for judicial review, allowing courts to review the constitutionality of laws. This ensures that laws comply with constitutional principles and do not infringe upon individual rights (see Table 1.3 Features of democracy and the rule of law).

TABLE 1.3 Features of democracy and the rule of law

Key features of:	
Democracy	**Rule of Law**
■ Separation of powers	■ Equality before the law
■ Free and fair elections	■ Legal certainty
■ Protection of human rights	■ Accessible and impartial courts

Separation of Powers and Systems of Government

> « *Pour qu'on ne puisse abuser du pouvoir, il faut que, par la disposition des choses, le pouvoir arrête le pouvoir.* »[118]

The principle of separation of powers serves as a foundational principle in political organisation. Its objective is to organise the various branches of power into distinct levels and entities, thereby ensuring government stability and safeguarding individual freedoms. Initially conceived as a direct response to the oppressive nature of absolute monarchy, this principle originated from the comprehensive theories put forth by Montesquieu. Over time, this principle has evolved into a significant driving factor behind the establishment of major democratic political systems worldwide.

This section serves as an introduction to the principle of separation of powers, elucidating its significance in comprehending the various types of governmental systems.

118 Charles Louis de Secondat, Baron de La Brède et de Montesquieu [Montesquieu] (1689–1765), French judge, writer, historian, and political philosopher [So that power cannot be abused, it is necessary that, through the arrangement of things, power stops power].

The principle of separation of powers

Observing that "every man with power is inclined to abuse it,"[119] Montesquieu developed the theory of separation of powers. The theory posits that the main functions of the state should not be concentrated in the hands of a single person or entity. The following subsection discusses the origins and principles underlying the separation of powers, outlining the three distinct branches of power, namely the legislative, executive, and judicial branches.

Origins of the separation of powers. The origins of the separation of powers can be traced back to ancient Greek and Roman political theories, particularly those put forth by Aristotle. However, it was during the Enlightenment era that this theory was fully developed by influential thinkers such as Locke and Montesquieu.[120] Montesquieu, in his renowned work *The Spirit of the Laws* (1748), extensively studied the English Constitution and Locke's ideas published in *Civil Government* to formulate his own theory (see Box 1.2 Montesquieu's theory).[121] Montesquieu not only conceptualised the separation of powers but also provided a comprehensive analysis and description of these powers and their functioning. His fundamental premise was rather straightforward: when an individual or an institution possesses an excessive concentration of state powers, it poses a threat to the freedom of individuals. To counter this, Montesquieu advocated for the limitation of power (or self-restraint) and the division of powers among different independent bodies, for "power stops power" ("*le pouvoir arrête le pouvoir*"). However, it is crucial to note that Montesquieu's theory emphasises the interdependence of these powers rather than their isolation. In other words, the various powers, such as the judiciary and the executive, must collaborate and work together. For instance, the judicial power requires the assistance of the executive power to enforce its decisions effectively. Ultimately, Montesquieu's theory aimed to establish a balanced form of government that would safeguard individuals, who were not yet considered citizens during that time, from the oppressive rule of a monarch.[122]

The tenets of the separation of powers. Separation of powers encompasses the idea that distinct functions and organs exist within a governing system. Montesquieu proposed an approach to differentiate between the legislative, executive, and judicial *functions*, which has gained universal recognition and is still utilised to explain the division of governmental powers. The separation of *organs* of the state means that each organ, responsible for one of the aforementioned functions, operates independently in terms of its composition and role. Despite its appellation, the principle of separation of powers is founded on the balance and the

119 The full quote reads: "*C'est une expérience éternelle que tout homme qui a du pouvoir est porté à en abuser*" [It is an eternal experience that every man who has power is inclined to abuse it] (Charles de Secondat, Baron de Montesquieu, *L'Esprit des Lois* [The Spirit of the Laws] (1748), Book XI, Chapter IV).

120 Prior to these groundbreaking theoretical works, the principle of separation of powers had already been put into practice in Great Britain starting from the thirteenth century, when the sovereign was compelled to share his powers with parliamentary assemblies.

121 The full title of the work is *Two Treatises of Government: In the Former, The False Principles, and Foundation of Sir Robert Filmer, and His Followers, Are Detected and Overthrown. The Latter Is an Essay Concerning The True Original, Extent, and End of Civil Government* (published 1689, dated 1690).

122 Montesquieu, hailing from an aristocratic background and a supporter of the monarchy, did not actively resist the monarchy. Nonetheless, he held a deep admiration for the British monarchy, which, during that time, demonstrated a remarkable degree of restraint in the face of absolutism.

collaboration between powers. As Montesquieu expressed it, powers must work together (*aller de concert*), meaning that the authority to make decisions and act (*faculté de statuer*) can be counterbalanced by the authority of another power to oppose or veto (*faculté d'empêcher*). This principle, akin to the concept of sovereignty, has played a crucial role in shaping the constitutionalist movement that emerged during the eighteenth and nineteenth centuries, leading to the adoption of numerous written constitutions.[123] Constitutions serve the purpose of organising political authority and safeguarding public freedoms by explicitly defining the roles of different power entities. Therefore, the separation of powers is not only an essential element of a constitution but also a fundamental aspect of its objective. This principle is an indispensable condition for democracy and can be compatible with both republican and monarchical forms of government. However, it is inherently incompatible with a system where powers are muddled or confused.[124]

The legislative power. The legislative power is the authority given to representative assemblies to make, modify, and repeal laws, as well as to approve the budget. In the past, the democratic legitimacy of legislative bodies, specifically the Lower House of Parliament, granted them supremacy over executive bodies. However, towards the end of the nineteenth century, there was a gradual shift in the balance of power from legislative bodies to executive bodies due to changes in the functions of these legislative bodies. First, the executive gained control over the legislative function of lawmaking (i.e., its deliberative function), while Parliament's role transformed into that of a think tank where discussions and proposals were generated. Secondly, the budgetary and financial power of the legislative assemblies decreased, particularly in matters of expenditure. Thirdly, the decreasing power of parliamentary assemblies can also be attributed to the transfer or devolution of powers and competencies to other decision-making centres, whether at local level with local government, or at European level with the transfer of sovereign competences to the EU, which they willingly agreed to relinquish. Presently, the primary role of legislative assemblies is to scrutinise and evaluate government policies.

The executive power. The executive power is responsible for carrying out the laws enacted by Parliament and for making day-to-day decisions, including in emergency situations. The executive power has undergone significant changes over time. Originally considered a secondary power, it has now become more prominent due to various transformations that have occurred within the state. In addition to being subject to legislative oversight in a parliamentary system, the executive branch possesses several additional powers. Firstly, it holds the regulatory

123 See, for example, article 16 of the French 1789 Declaration of the Rights of Man and of the Citizen: "Any society in which the protection of rights is not guaranteed, nor the separation of powers ensured shall have no constitution."

124 In a regime of confusion of powers, it is conceivable for a single individual to wield all three powers, backed by the military, the populace, and/or the Parliament, effectively resulting in a dictatorship. This can be exemplified by historical instances such as the French First Empire (1804–1814) during Napoleon the First's reign, or the Vichy regime (1940–1944) under Marshal Pétain's leadership.

Alternatively, the powers can be concentrated within a single legislative body, supported by a subordinate executive organ, creating what is known as an assembly regime. Instances of such a regime include the 1792 Convention during the period of Terror in France, or the 1793 Convention under the *Montagnarde* Constitution, although the latter was never implemented.

power, exemplified by provisions such as articles 34 and 37 of the 1958 French Constitution. Secondly, it has control over the armed forces, being responsible for defending against external aggression, internal conflicts, and maintaining public order. Lastly, the executive wields power over the public administration. This last power has proved to be a decisive tool in the implementation of government policies. However, it has also presented challenges, particularly in cases where a sizable public administration sector is affected by significant inertia. In such instances, the power of the public administration can become a formidable force of resistance.

The judicial power. The role of the judiciary is to oversee criminal cases and settle disputes between individuals, as well as between individuals and the government. By ensuring robust judicial independence, the majority of western democracies have effectively separated political influence from the judiciary, which acts as a vital protection against the arbitrariness of power. Nonetheless, in certain countries, detaching these connections has proven to be more challenging.[125]

Montesquieu's theory has been subject to diverse interpretations, particularly in the UK, France, the USA, and several other jurisdictions. Two distinct approaches have emerged from these interpretations. The *horizontal* approach emphasises the separation of governmental powers within the same level of authority. On the other hand, the *vertical* approach emphasises the separation between various tiers of governance, such as federal and state levels in a federal state, or local and central levels in a decentralised unitary state.[126]

Overall, achieving and maintaining a strict separation of powers is rarely seen in practice. What holds more significance is the level of collaboration observed among these distinct powers, which is prevalent in pluralist democratic regimes. This collaboration enables the classification of political systems into different categories.

BOX 1.2 MONTESQUIEU'S THEORY

☛ The Spirit of the Laws, 1748

"In every government there are three sorts of power: the legislative; the executive in respect to things dependent on the law of nations; and the executive in regard to matters that depend on the civil law.

By virtue of the first, the prince or magistrate enacts temporary or perpetual laws, and amends or abrogates those that have been already enacted. By the second, he makes peace or war, sends or receives embassies, establishes the public security, and provides against invasions. By the third, he punishes criminals, or determines the disputes that arise between

125 France, for example, has repeatedly experienced instances where the executive branch exerts its influence over judicial members, a phenomenon that has been widely observed. Additionally, the French administrative courts maintain a strong connection with the administration, both in terms of their structure and intellectual interactions. However, it is worth noting that the administrative judges do not hesitate to declare administrative acts as invalid.

126 See, for instance, the perspective of the Founding Fathers in the USA, who viewed federalism as a means of guaranteeing the separation of powers. Tocqueville, on the other hand, regarded local administration and intermediary institutions within civil society as essential safeguards to limit the authority of the government.

individuals. The latter we shall call the judiciary power, and the other simply the executive power of the state.

The political liberty of the subject is a tranquillity of mind arising from the opinion each person has of his safety. In order to have this liberty, it is requisite the government be so constituted as one man need not be afraid of another.

When the legislative and executive powers are united in the same person, or in the same body of magistrates, there can be no liberty; because apprehensions may arise, lest the same monarch or senate should enact tyrannical laws, to execute them in a tyrannical manner.

Again, there is no liberty, if the judiciary power be not separated from the legislative and executive. Were it joined with the legislative, the life and liberty of the subject would be exposed to arbitrary control; for the judge would be then the legislator. Were it joined to the executive power, the judge might behave with violence and oppression...

In what a situation must the poor subject be in those republics! The same body of magistrates are possessed, as executors of the laws, of the whole power they have given themselves in quality of legislators. They may plunder the state by their general determinations; and as they have likewise the judiciary power in their hands, every private citizen may be ruined by their particular decisions."

Book XI, Chapter VI (excerpts)

The different types of political systems

The character of a political system can be determined by how much it upholds the concept of separation of powers within its institutions. It is crucial to distinguish between political systems that neglect the principle of separation of powers and instead foster a confusion of powers, and those that actively adhere to this principle.

Regime of confusion of powers. Regimes characterised by a confusion of powers are often compared to autocratic systems and typically feature a single-party system with no opposition, such as civil or military dictatorships, as well as socialist regimes.

The Marxist regime epitomises an authoritarian regime of confusion of powers because it concentrates power in the hands of a single party, the Communist Party.[127] This regime

127 Another type of government that involves a confusion of powers is known as the "assembly regime" (*régime d'assemblée*). In this type of regime, the parliamentary assembly or assemblies hold dominance over the other branches of power, particularly the executive branch. Initially, this regime is not considered authoritarian, as it theoretically preserves freedom and pluralism. The confusion of powers occurs in favour of the assembly or assemblies, which are delegated by the people as the true holders of sovereignty. Consequently, the executive branch is perceived as a power derived from the legislature and entirely reliant on it. However, historical practice has demonstrated that the executive branch swiftly regains its central role and marginalises the relevant assembly or assemblies over time. A prime example of such a regime is the one established during the Convention in France from 1792 to 1795, which ultimately paved the way for a brutal dictatorship under the authority of Robespierre. Despite the Convention (legislature) electing a Council (executive) known as the Committee of Public Salvation, this Committee gradually rejected the dominance of the Convention and eventually established a destructive and ill-fated dictatorship.

originates from the Marxist-Leninist ideology, which emerged as a response to capitalism. Marxism-Leninism is built upon the recognition that capitalism enables the exploitation of a subordinate class (known as the proletariat) by a dominant class (known as the bourgeoisie). The state serves as a repressive tool for enforcing this domination. Theoretically, the transition towards communism unfolds in several stages: first, through class struggle, the state is overthrown; secondly, the dictatorship of the proletariat is established, leading to the subjugation of the bourgeoisie; thirdly, a period of violent transformation of society occurs, resulting in the abolition of social classes; fourthly, the economy is socialised, and the state gradually fades away. This confusion of powers is indispensable for achieving a classless society. In such a society, the state governs a homogeneous community of people, rendering any division of power and functions redundant—consequently, pluralism loses its significance. The single-party system operates on the principles of democratic centralism. The individual is rendered powerless against a state entirely controlled by the dominant single party, with no recourse to any independent authority for the protection of their rights. Furthermore, the concepts of law, the rule of law, and the legal system are solely regarded from a formal standpoint with deep mistrust as, according to Marxist theory, law and the legal system are instruments utilised by the bourgeoisie to uphold their privileges.

Nevertheless, the practical application of communism has consistently strayed from its original theoretical principles. In such regimes, rather than disappearing, the state has grown remarkably influential. Additionally, the economic collapse and downfall of the former USSR have dealt a strong blow to this ideology. Presently, the remaining strongholds of Marxism are found in countries such as China (although it embraces certain liberal practices), Cuba, Vietnam, and North Korea.

Regime of separation of powers. The principle of separation of powers is a fundamental aspect of governance in democratic regimes. Regimes of separation of powers are characterised by pluralism, which means they encompass a wide range of opinions and allow for the existence of opposition. Additionally, they uphold liberal values, ensuring the protection of individual liberties and promoting economic liberalism. From an institutional perspective, democracies are built upon the principle of separating and balancing powers.[128] The extent to which powers are separated, and the level of collaboration between them, ultimately determine the nature of the political regime. Some regimes adopt a flexible approach to the separation of powers, as seen in the parliamentary system. Conversely, others adhere to a more rigid separation of powers, such as the presidential system.[129]

The *parliamentary regime* emerged in England towards the close of the eighteenth century. This regime's widespread adoption across Europe, and subsequently in France during the nineteenth century, coincided with the gradual but inevitable decline of monarchy and

128 Except in the case of an assembly regime as seen above.

129 There are also *mixed* regimes that combine features of the parliamentary regime and features of the presidential regime. France is a prime example of a mixed regime that blends elements from both parliamentary and presidential regimes. In this unique political structure, the President is elected through direct and universal suffrage, showcasing a presidential characteristic. Additionally, the government is held accountable to the National Assembly, reflecting the principle of responsibility, and the President holds the power to dissolve the National Assembly, representing parliamentary traits. For more details, see Chapter 3 on historical and legal foundations of the Fifth Republic, and Chapter 4 on the institutions of the Fifth Republic.

the concurrent advancement of representative institutions. It was only through the expansion of suffrage and the subsequent implementation of universal suffrage that the parliamentary system truly attained a democratic character. In the following analysis, we shall delve into the progression of this regime and explore its present-day characteristics.

Initially, during the era of monarchy, the parliamentary regime operated under a *dualist* framework. This meant that the government had a dual responsibility to both the assembly and the monarch (or Head of State in non-monarchical regimes). The purpose of this arrangement was to ensure that the throne was not an empty seat ("*le trône n'est pas un fauteuil vide*"), symbolising the importance of the monarchy.[130] However, this dual responsibility posed challenges whenever there was a disagreement between the parliamentary majority and the Head of State. As a result, this system was eventually abandoned in favour of the *monist* parliamentary system that we have today. In a monist parliamentary regime, the King or monarch reigns but does not govern ("*le roi règne mais ne gouverne pas*").[131] This type of regime is characterised by two significant aspects. Firstly, the executive power is transferred to the Head of Government. In other words, the acts or decisions made by the Head of State must be approved or endorsed by the Head of Government and the relevant ministers. Therefore, the true holder of the executive power lies with the Head of Government. Secondly, the government is solely accountable to the assembly or Parliament.

The parliamentary regime can also be characterised by three key aspects. Firstly, the government is formed from Parliament, specifically by the majority of elected members who have been chosen through direct universal suffrage. Consequently, the government exercises the full extent of its executive power and is responsible for shaping and implementing national policies. The government is collectively accountable for the decisions it makes. Secondly, the role of the Head of State is often purely ceremonial and detached from the political arena. As a result, s/he is not held accountable for political decisions. Although s/he possesses the authority to appoint the Head of Government, his/her choice is limited as s/he is generally required to choose the leader of the parliamentary majority. Additionally, the relationship between the government and parliament is characterised by cooperation. The government, whose legitimacy relies on the support of the parliamentary majority, necessitates their backing to effectively carry out its actions. This collaborative dynamic is most evident in the legislative process, where both the executive and legislative branches hold the power to propose legislation, and the government is closely involved in the entire procedure.

Alongside collaboration, mechanisms are in place to address political tensions and crises. Firstly, the Prime Minister has the ability to assume responsibility for his/her government's actions or policies. This involves exerting pressure on the majority by threatening to resign if they refuse to vote in favour of a specific law. Conversely, members of Parliament can also initiate the government's accountability by passing a motion of censure, which, if successful,

130 François Guizot (1787–1874), Prime Minister of France (1847–1848) during the July Monarchy (1830–1848), statesman and historian. Because such a dualist regime was first experienced under the reign of Louis-Philippe of Orléans (1830–1848), it was referred to as the Orléanist parliamentary regime in French and continental parlance. Currently, there are only a limited number of dualist parliamentary regimes in existence. See, for example, articles 111 and 133 of the 1975 Constitution of Portugal, and article 52 of the 2001 Constitution of Senegal.

131 Adolphe Thiers (1797–1877), President of the Republic (1871–1873), stateman and historian. Thiers was the first President of the Third Republic (1870–1940). Thiers and Guizot had diametrically opposed views on the role of the monarch in the parliamentary system.

would require the government to resign. Finally, the Prime Minister has the option to proactively dissolve the assembly, which is elected through direct universal suffrage. This action serves as a precautionary measure to signal the majority about its insufficient backing for the government. To ensure governmental stability, the implementation of these measures, such as a vote of confidence, motion of censure or vote of no confidence, and dissolution, is typically subject to strict regulations. For instance, an absolute majority may be necessary to pass a motion of censure.

The parliamentary system of government has undergone a unique evolution, particularly in situations where a dominant party or coalition seizes control over both the executive and legislative branches of powers. This scenario becomes plausible due to the fact that elected candidates from general elections align themselves with their respective political parties in Parliament, rendering them reliant on and obedient to the directives issued by their own party. Consequently, depending on whether the system is based on a two-party or multi-party system, the parliamentary majority inevitably materialises to serve the interests of a particular party or a coalition that typically forms post-elections. The appointment of the Head of Government by the Head of State, as well as the formation of the government, are contingent upon the majority composition within Parliament, thereby binding them to the interests and preferences of the prevailing majority. Furthermore, given that the parliamentary majority consistently lends support to the government's actions, the conventional means of exerting pressure, such as votes of confidence and dissolution, hold minimal significance in this context. Political crises that arise typically stem from disagreements or conflicts within the majority party or coalition.

The evolution of the parliamentary regime has witnessed numerous shortcomings and excesses that have been detrimental to both the executive and Parliament. One major issue is the disproportionate influence that Parliament holds over the executive, leading to what is commonly referred to as the "*régime d'assemblée*." In this type of regime, Parliament utilises and abuses its power to pressure and scrutinise ministers, which ultimately results in governmental instability when Parliament repeatedly passes votes of no confidence.[132] Conversely, there has been a more recent phenomenon where the executive excessively influences Parliament. This phenomenon has impacted several contemporary regimes, including Germany, France, Spain, and the UK. It is primarily driven by the diminishing role of Parliament in modern democracies, which is a consequence of externalising its responsibilities under the pressure of European integration and the imposition of norms by Brussels. Additionally, there is an increasing reliance of the central government on local government in various areas of competence. Furthermore, the establishment of stable majorities in parliamentary regimes, where the ruling government aligns with its supporters in Parliament, has resulted in Parliament becoming less significant in decision-making processes. As a result, it is imperative to provide

132 One notable instance of this phenomenon can be observed in the context of the French Third Republic (1875–1940). Following the political crisis of 1877, the dissolution of Parliament became a challenging endeavour, thereby eliminating any constraints or risks for Parliament to endorse governmental actions under a regime centred around parliamentary sovereignty. A similar situation occurred in the Italian parliamentary system until 1993, where the presence of a multiparty system and proportional representation facilitated the formation of political coalitions driven by partisan interests, often at the expense of maintaining governmental stability.

Parliament with robust mechanisms for scrutinising and evaluating public policies, as well as acknowledging the contributions of opposition members.[133]

To curtail the excesses of parliamentarism, the parliamentary regime has undergone a process of "rationalisation"[134] through the implementation of legal and political measures to prevent the abuse of certain political practices. This rationalisation primarily involves the establishment of a stringent regulatory framework governing the collaboration between various branches of power. It particularly focuses on two aspects: the utilisation of a vote of no confidence by Parliament to hold the government accountable, and the exercise of the executive's authority to dissolve Parliament.

The emergence of the *presidential* regime can be traced back to the adoption of the American Constitution in 1787. Primarily an experiment within the context of the USA,[135] it aimed to establish a distinct form of governance. However, attempts to replicate the American model in Latin America and Africa proved unsuccessful, resulting in a distorted version of presidentialism that centred around the President's authority. The distinguishing feature of the presidential regime lies in the separation of its institutions and functions. The executive function, typically entrusted to a President, is separate from the legislative function performed by assemblies. The legitimacy of both the executive and legislative powers derives from their election through universal suffrage, thereby gaining the support of the general public.[136]

A "strict" separation of powers has two main implications. Firstly, it implies that the President possesses complete executive authority, making the President the driving force behind political decisions. The President's appointed Secretaries, particularly the Secretary of State who handles foreign affairs, are not ministers but rather personal collaborators accountable solely to the President. They do not constitute a collective government that shares responsibility with the President. Conversely, the President is not permitted to interfere in the legislative decision-making process and lacks the right to propose new laws. Secondly, the mechanisms of pressure commonly found in parliamentary regimes are absent in presidential regimes. Congress, entrusted with legislative and budgetary powers, holds a monopoly on the initiation of legislation.[137] The President cannot dissolve Congress, and Congress lacks the ability to politically hold the President accountable or challenge their actions. The President can only be held responsible for criminal offenses.[138] In essence, the President and Congress must coexist until the completion of their respective terms.

133 This situation is typical of the parliamentary regime in the UK where the government runs the political scene, amounting to a "dictatorship of the Cabinet."

134 The expression of "rationalisation" was coined by constitutionalist Mirkin-Getzevich (or Mirsky) at the beginning of the twentieth century.

135 Walter Bagehot reportedly introduced the term "presidential regime" in 1867 as a comparison to the familiar parliamentary regime. The characteristics of a presidential regime can be traced back to various French regimes, such as the constitutional monarchy of 1791, the *Directoire* of 1795, and the Republic of 1848, even though none of these regimes were actually led by a president. Tragically, all these regimes ended violently due to their failure to adapt the system to a less dogmatic and less rigid interpretation and implementation.

136 The legitimacy of the Head of State, whether s/he is a monarch, president, or head of government, stems from his/her election rather than from the Parliament. This aspect is crucial for ensuring his/her independence and autonomy.

137 In a presidential regime, Parliament can, in theory, feature one or two houses.

138 See the impeachment procedure in the USA.

However, relations between these two powers do exist as a certain level of collaboration is necessary in practice. Each power possesses a "veto power" over the other, meaning they have the ability to block decisions made by the opposing power. For example, the Head of State holds a legislative veto that can suspend decisions. Similarly, Congress holds the power to scrutinise, through committee investigations, the procedure of approving top appointments in the government, and the approval of treaties, among others. Due to the absence of a conflict-resolution mechanism at the institutional level, the President and Congress must engage in constant negotiation and dialogue in order to avoid impasses, particularly when the President faces a hostile majority.

While still valid, at least in pedagogical terms, the classical distinction between parliamentary and presidential regimes has been called into question due to the evolution of these "models" in different parts of the world. It is questionable whether one can still talk about a presidential model. The concept of a presidential model is now debatable, as it is primarily associated with the USA where it has found its greatest success. However, despite the initial intention of a strict separation of powers, American political practice has demonstrated that powers actually collaborate in a balanced manner. Similarly, there is no universally accepted standard model for a parliamentary regime. Unlike the US presidential regime, which is closely identified with a specific jurisdiction, the parliamentary model is known for its diverse and successful adaptations across various jurisdictions.

In addition, the parliamentary system relies less on a confrontational relationship between the executive and the legislature, where they act as opposing powers, and more on a convergence of interests between those in power (such as the government and its majority in Parliament). The real counter-power rests in the hands of the opposition. In other words, modern parliamentary regimes are better characterised by a government that is supported by its majority in facing the opposition (or a shadow government in the British system), rather than an executive directly facing Parliament. Therefore, it is critically important to formally acknowledge the rights of opposition parties, ensuring their protection and enabling them to serve as a credible alternative to the ruling government. Overall, the distinction between parliamentary and presidential regimes does not account for the diverse range of intermediary experiences found in mixed, presidentialist, or semi-presidential regimes that define certain political systems.

Towards a renewed approach to separation of powers. The growing importance of the judicial power, the advancement of judicial review, the ongoing continuous of decentralisation, the progress in European integration, and the increasing development of independent administrative authorities all contribute to the curtailment of governmental power. Serving as diverse counter-powers, these elements taken together foster a renewed perspective on the principle of separation of powers. Indeed, in recent years scholars such as Carolan have put forth new theories about the separation of powers that challenge long-held assumptions, offering fresh perspectives on governance.[139] Carolan's theory centres on embracing the dynamic nature of powers and highlighting the interdependence between different branches of powers. By adopting a flexible understanding of the separation of powers, governments can overcome bureaucratic hurdles and expedite decision-making processes. Essentially, through collaboration and cooperation,

139 Eoin Carolan, *The New Separation of Powers: A Theory for the Modern State* (OUP 2009).

governments can enhance efficiency, strengthen accountability, and respond more effectively to societal challenges. While criticisms exist, careful implementation and necessary safeguards can mitigate potential risks. As we navigate an ever-changing world, these theories proposing a revised approach to the principle of separation of powers act as a compass towards more adaptable and resilient democratic systems.

SELECTED FURTHER READINGS

Bruce **Ackerman**, "New Separation of Powers" (2000) 113 (3) *Harvard Law Review* 633

Jean-Bernard **Auby**, *La globalisation, le droit et l'État* (3rd edn, LGDJ 2020)

________________, *La décentralisation et le droit* (LGDJ 2006)

André **Bächtiger** et alii (eds), *The Oxford Handbook of Deliberative Democracy* (OUP 2018)

Denis **Baranger** & Christine Murray, "Systems of Government" in Mark Tushnet et alii (eds), *Routledge Handbook of Constitutional Law* (Routledge 2013) 73

Michaël **Bardin** et alii, *La démocratie connectée : Ambitions, enjeux et réalité* (DICE Éditions 2018)

Olivier **Beaud**, *Théorie de la fédération* (2nd edn, PUF 2009)

__________, *La puissance de l'État* (PUF 1994)

Denis **de Béchillon**, *Hiérarchie des normes et hiérarchie des fonctions normatives de l'État* (Economica 1996)

Richard **Bellamy**, *Political Constitutionalism: A Republican Defence of the Constitutionality of Democracy* (CUP 2007)

Tom **Bingham**, *The Rule of Law* (Penguin Books 2011)

Loïc **Blondiaux** & Bernard Manin (eds), *Le tournant délibératif de la démocratie* (Presses de Sciences Po 2021)

Georges **Burdeau**, *La démocratie* (Seuil 1978)

______________, *L'État* (Seuil 1970)

Eoin **Carolan**, *The New Separation of Powers: A Theory for the Modern State* (OUP 2009)

René **Carré de Malberg**, *Contribution à la théorie générale de l'État* (Sirey 1920–1922, Dalloz 2003)

Edoardo **Celeste**, *Digital Constitutionalism: The Role of the Internet Bill of Rights* (Routledge 2023)

Albert H Y **Chen** & Miguel Poiares Maduro, "The Judiciary and Constitutional Review" in Mark Tushnet et alii (eds), *Routledge Handbook of Constitutional Law* (Routledge 2013) 97

Stephen **Coleman**, Anna Przybylska & Yves Sintomer (eds), *Deliberation and Democracy: Innovative Processes and Institutions* (Peter Lang 2016)

Noel **Cox**, *Constitutional Paradigms and the Stability of States* (Routledge 2012)

Paul **Craig**, "Democracy" in Roger Masterman & Robert Schütze (eds), *The Cambridge Companion to Comparative Constitutional Law* (CUP 2019) 201

Jon **Elster**, *Deliberative Democracy* (CUP 1998)

David **Farrell** & Jane Suiter, *Reimagining Democracy* (Cornell University Press 2019)

James S **Fishkin**, *When the People are Thinking: Revitalizing our Politics through Public Deliberation* (OUP 2018)

_____________, *When the People Speak: Deliberative Democracy and Public Consultation* (OUP 2011)

Günter **Frankenberg**, "Democracy" in Michel Rosenfeld & András Sajó (eds), *The Oxford Handbook on Comparative Constitutional Law* (OUP 2012) 250

Jürgen **Habermas**, *Droit et démocratie : Entre faits et normes* (Christian Bouchindhomme & Rainer Rochlitz tr, Gallimard 1997)

Arnaud **Haquet**, *Le concept de souveraineté en droit constitutionnel français* (PUF 2004)

David **Held**, *Models of Democracy* (3rd edn, Stanford University Press 2006)

Luc **Heuschling**, *État de droit, Rechtsstaat, Rule of Law* (Dalloz 2002)

Aileen **Kavanagh**, "The Constitutional Separation of Powers" in David Dyzenhaus & Malcolm Thornburn (eds), *Philosophical Foundations of Constitutional Law* (OUP 2016)

Hans **Kelsen**, *La démocratie, sa nature, sa valeur* (Charles Eisenmann tr, Dalloz 2004)

__________, *General Theory of Law and State* (Russell & Russell 1945)

Bill **Kissane**, *New Beginnings: Constitutionalism and Democracy in Modern Ireland* (UCD Press 2011)

Louis **Le Fur**, *État fédéral et confédération d'États* [1896] (Éditions Panthéon-Assas 2000)

Peter **Lindseth**, *Power and Legitimacy: Reconciling Europe and the Nation-State* (OUP 2010)
Charles de Secondat, Baron de **Montesquieu**, *De l'Esprit des lois* [1748] (Laurent Versini ed, Gallimard 1995, Tomes I & II)
____________________, *The Spirit of the Laws* [1748] (Anne M Cohler, Basia Carolyn Miller & Harold Samuel Stone, tr and eds, CUP 1989)
Philip **Pettit**, *On the People's Terms: A Republican Theory and Model of Democracy* (CUP 2012)
Pouvoirs, *La constitution*, No 187 (Seuil 2023)
_______, *Que peut l'État ?* No 177 (Seuil 2021)
_______, *La démocratie participative*, No 175 (Seuil 2020)
_______, *La séparation des pouvoirs*, No 143 (Seuil 2012)
_______, *La souveraineté*, No 67 (PUF 1993)
Richard **Rawlings**, Peter Leyland & Alison Young, *Sovereignty and the Law: Domestic, European and International Perspectives* (OUP 2013)
Yaniv **Roznai**, *Unconstitutional Constitutional Amendments: The Limits of Amendment Powers* (OUP 2017)
Jean-Jacques **Rousseau**, *Du contrat social* [1762] (Bruno Bernardi ed, Flammarion 2012)
____________________, *On the Social Contract* [1762] (G D H Cole tr, 1789, Penguin Books 1968)
Carl **Schmitt**, *Parlementarisme et démocratie* (Seuil 1988)
Jean **Terrel**, *Les théories du pacte social : Droit naturel, souveraineté et contrat de Bodin à Rousseau* (Seuil 2001)
Michel **Troper**, *La théorie du droit, le droit, l'État* (PUF 2001)
_____________, *Pour une théorie juridique de l'État* (PUF 1994)
_____________, *La séparation des pouvoirs et l'histoire constitutionnelle française* (LGDJ 1973)
Pauline **Türk** & Christian Vallar, *La souveraineté numérique : Le concept, les enjeux* (Mare & Martin 2018)
Frank **Vibert**, *The Rise of the Unelected: Democracy and the New Separation of Powers* (CUP 2007)

2

HISTORY OF FRENCH CONSTITUTIONAL LAW

To comprehend the present, one must be aware of the past. Political regimes are often a response to the actions of previous regimes. The current political regime in France is no exception, as it is a complex amalgamation of both positive and negative reactions to a long line of constitutional and institutional experiments. Even the *Ancien Régime* (Old Regime, as in pre-revolutionary time) bequeathed important influential elements. However, the year 1789 is generally considered the defining moment in French constitutional history. From that point onward, most of the subsequent political regimes were based on a constitution, which was not the case under the monarchy. Legal historians and constitutionalists hold various views on how to divide up the different stages of French constitutional history. This chapter is divided into two main parts, preceded by a brief examination of the *Ancien Régime*. The first part examines the experimentation with the separation of powers in the aftermath of the 1789 Revolution (1789–1870), which led, as explored in the second part, to the progressive establishment of the parliamentary regime under the Republic (1870–1958).

Although there was an organised polity under the *Ancien Régime*, which had a customary constitution embedded within the fundamental laws of the Kingdom, there was no constitution in the modern sense. This means that there was no set of rules and principles that governed the relationship between the government and its citizens. The 1789 Revolution brought about a significant departure from previous political tenets in this regard. While the 1789 Revolution caused great upheaval and trauma in French society, it also marked a new beginning towards the establishment of institutional and constitutional principles that are still relevant today. Over time, these principles emerged and developed at varying rates. These principles included concepts such as sovereignty, the separation of powers, the enactment of a bill of rights, the primacy of the constitution, and the right of suffrage. This is so because France has experimented with an unusually high number of constitutional texts, especially in the first century following the revolutionary period. The aftermath of the 1789 Revolution triggered a quest for

DOI: 10.4324/9781003268871-3

a consensus-based and efficient regime, which took time to formulate as various constitutional issues needed to be addressed and resolved. These issues primarily revolved around the right to vote, the type of political system in place at the time, whether it be a monarchy, an empire, or a republic, as well as the relationships between the executive and legislative branches of power. French constitutional history may be divided into four main identifiable periods:[1] The initial period, spanning from 1789 to 1875, focuses on the aftermath of the 1789 Revolution and the various attempts made to establish a stable governing system. The second period encompasses the lengthy era of the Third Republic, which lasted from 1875 to 1940 and saw the installation of the parliamentary regime, albeit with many defects including that of governmental instability. In contrast, the third period encompasses the relatively short duration of the Fourth Republic, spanning from 1946 to 1958. During this period, there was a mitigated attempt to rationalise the rules of the parliamentary regime. Lastly, the fourth period delves into the current political regime in France, known as the Fifth Republic, which has been in place since 1958 and is now the longest-running regime in the country's history.

Details about historical developments concerning the origins, unfolding, and consequences of political, social, and economic events, as well as the involvement of key figures involved in these events, are kept to a minimum. These historical developments hold significance solely to the extent that they elucidate *constitutional* developments.[2]

Ancien Régime (before 1789)

> « *[Louis XIV] est Dieu. Il faut attendre sa volonté avec soumission, et tout espérer de sa justice et de sa bonté, sans impatience, afin d'en avoir plus de mérite.* »[3]

Monarchy is an integral part of France's history. For 14 centuries, 81 monarchs succeeded one another on the throne. Initially feudal, then becoming absolute and later constitutional, the French monarchy enjoyed exceptional longevity and relative continuity. The sovereigns, from the Merovingians to the Capetian Louis VII, were bestowed with the title of "King of the Franks." Towards the end of the twelfth century, Philippe Auguste became the first monarch in a long lineage to bear the title of "King of France." The hereditary and sacred character of the sovereign elevated the King of France as the central figure in political life and the pivotal point around which society revolved (see Table 2.1 Chronology of French monarchical dynasties).

Under article 16 of the of the 1789 Declaration, "[a]ny society in which the protection of rights is not guaranteed, nor the separation of powers ensured shall have no constitution." It would follow that, under such an approach reflecting the tenets of liberal constitutionalism, the *Ancien Régime* had no constitution. However, this assertion is open to debate. Regardless of how archaic or authoritarian a political system may be, it operates under a set of rules

1 See, for example, Pierre Bodineau & Michel Verpeaux, *Histoire constitutionnelle de la France* (6th edn, PUF 2020) on the artificial character of these divisions.

2 These historical developments partly draw from Marie-Luce Paris, *Constitutional Law in France*, International Encyclopaedia of Laws (2nd edn, Wolters Kluwer 2024) 23–33 (paras 2–23).

3 Anne Marie Louise d'Orléans, Duchess of Montpensier (1627–1693), granddaughter of Henry IV and niece of Louis XIII, named "Granddaughter of France" (*Petite Fille de France*) [[Louis XIV] is God. We must await his will with submission, and hope for everything from his justice and goodness, without impatience, in order to have more merit].

that essentially "constitutes" that particular regime. This was certainly the case with the former French monarchy prior to 1789. The monarchy adhered to the Fundamental Laws of the Kingdom, known as *Les Lois Fondamentales du Royaume*. The laws in question expressly concerned the sovereign (including its monarchical character, the principles of the Crown's inalienability and continuity, and the nationality of the sovereign). They also addressed matters of hereditary rules and the inheritance of the Crown (such as the Salic Law, which dictated that only first-born males could succeed to the throne), as well as the principle of sovereignty (such as the requirement for the King to be Catholic) and its limitations (such as the inalienability of the royal domain). In many respects, these fundamental laws were deeply ingrained in the political system since they were more difficult to change than the other laws of the Kingdom. Under the so-called "Constitution of the Monarchy," the Laws of the King, which could be amended by the King himself without any specific procedure, were distinct from the Fundamental Laws of the Kingdom. The latter were considered as eternal laws that were unchangeable under any circumstances. Therefore, although not in the modern sense of the term, the French Monarchy did possess a constitution.[4]

Experimentation with regimes of separation of powers (1789–1870)

> « *Les Français ont fait en 1789 le plus grand effort auquel se soit jamais livré aucun peuple.* »[5]

1789 ushered in a revolutionary period which saw significant transformations in the political and institutional order of France. Overall, the century following the 1789 Revolution is marked by three traits: firstly, the acceptance, or rejection, by successive political regimes of the principles posed in 1789; secondly, the fact that the English and American systems of government were a constant source of inspiration for the drafters of the various French constitutional texts; and thirdly, the numerous attempts to restore the monarchy which resulted in the republican regime not being installed until the last quarter of the nineteenth century. It is important to note that the 1789 Revolution was both an inspiration of the finest principles of a new democracy and an awful warning of what can happen when idealism goes wrong. According to Davidson:

> From a philosophical and existential point of view, the French Revolution has long been justly celebrated as one the greatest sources of inspiration for republican and liberal ideals, the foundation story of the French Republic and French republicanism and in some ways the foundation story of democracy in a continental Europe.
>
> But from a hard-headed, operational perspective, one must conclude that the French Revolution was, for at least the next hundred years, a deep and damaging failure. The Revolutionaries succeeded in pushing over the *ancien régime*, but they did not succeed in setting up a durable alternative system of government, even in theory.[6]

4 For these developments, see Frédéric Rouvillois, *Droit constitutionnel : La Vème République* (4th edn, Flammarion 2014) 105 et seq.

5 Alexis De Tocqueville (1805–1859), French politician and political philosopher [In 1789 the French made the greatest effort that any people has ever made].

6 Ian Davidson, *The French Revolution: From Enlightenment to Tyranny* (Profile Books 2016) 244.

TABLE 2.1 Chronology of French monarchical dynasties

Dynasty	*Dates*	*Years of reign*	*Number of rulers*	*Notable rulers*
MEROVINGIANS	481–752	271	33 kings	**Clovis** (481–511), first king of the Franks
CAROLINGIANS	751–987	235	14 kings (including four emperors)	**Pepin the Short** (751–768) **Charles the Great** [Charlemagne] (768–814, emperor from 800)
CAPETIANS (direct lineage)	987–1328	341	15 kings (including one posthumous)	**Hugh Capet** (987–996) **Philip August** (1180–1223) **Louis IX** [Saint Louis] (1226–1270) **Philip IV the Fair** (1285–1314) Philip IV's daughter Isabel married Edward II, King of England *Edward III, King of England and pretender to the throne of France*
VALOIS	1328–1589	261	13 kings	**Philip VI of Valois** (1328–1350) **Francois the First** (1515–1547) **Henry III** (1574–1589)
BOURBONS	1589–1792	203	Six kings (before the 1789 Revolution)	**Henry IV** (1589–1610) **Louis XIV the Great** (1643–1715) **Louis XV** (1715–1774) **Louis XVI** (1774–1792) **Louis XVIII** (1814–1824) **Charles X** (1824–1830) **Louis-Philip the First** (1830–1848), King of the French, last king to rule France
	(1814–1848 post-Revolution restoration)			

The break with the absolute monarchy was achieved with the *coup d'état* by the Third Estate on 17 June 1789. The National Constituent Assembly, which convened on the occasion, issued two foundational acts, namely the Declaration of the Rights of Man and of the Citizen of 26 August 1789 and the Constitution of 3 September 1791. Inspired by the ideas of the Enlightenment as well as by the English and American experiences of bills of rights, the 1789 Declaration was drafted in just three months by some of the brightest and most ambitious of France's growing enlightened bourgeoisie (*bourgeoisie éclairée*). The 1789 Declaration proclaimed the existence of natural and fundamental rights applicable to all men [*sic*] and citizens at all times and in the whole of society, hence its universal scope. Encapsulating the ideas of liberalism and individualism of the time, the 1789 Declaration was to become the archetype of all subsequent rights declarations worldwide. Today, the 1789 Declaration forms an integral part of the Preamble to the Constitution. As such, it is regarded as positive law and can be used as a norm of reference to review the constitutionality of laws in judicial review proceedings. As for the 1791 Constitution, it was inspired by the US Constitution of 1787. It consecrated the principle of national sovereignty and installed a presidential regime with a strict separation of powers endowing the King, in charge of the executive power, with a suspensive legislative veto that could last up to six years.

Following the abolition of the monarchy on 20 September 1792 and the death sentence of Louis XVI on 21 January 1793, a new period of turmoil ensued. Two other constitutions followed suit. The Constitution of 24 June 1793 (Year I of the First Republic), although never applied, contained interesting features, such as the principle of popular sovereignty and the introduction, for the first time in French constitutional history, of direct universal suffrage. The revolutionary government and the "Reign of Terror" under the dictatorship of Robespierre were the immediate unfortunate events that followed the establishment of the First Republic. The Constitution of 22 August 1795 (Year III of the First Republic) was drafted by the survivors of the Terror and, as such, was strongly marked by a fear of the return to a dictatorial regime, hence its emphasis on an absolute separation of powers. The 1795 Constitution also introduced the notion of bicameralism. However, unable to collaborate because of the strict separation of powers, the institutions were constantly fighting each other. This regime ended with the *coup d'état* of Napoléon Bonaparte on 9 November 1799 (18 Brumaire of Year VIII).[7]

The period between 1799 and 1848 is characterised by a dictatorship of the executive power, with two distinct periods: the first period (1799–1814) under the Consulate and then the First Empire is the reign of Napoléon Bonaparte, and the second period (1814–1848) marks the return of the monarchy to power with Louis XVIII and then Charles X. The Constitution of 13 December 1799 (22 Frimaire Year VIII) is tailor-made to the needs of Napoléon Bonaparte, who established a Consulate based on the dictatorship of the executive power. The prominent role afforded to the First Consul was matched by the neutralisation of the Legislature, which was deprived of the power of legislative initiative. Progressively, the Consulate evolved towards a fully fledged authoritarian regime with the establishment of the Consulate for life (Constitution of 2 August 1802) and of the First Empire a couple of years later (Constitution of 18 May 1804). Overall, the Napoleonic regime featured the traits of a dictatorship, internally, with increased policing powers and drastic limitations on freedoms, as well as externally, with a string of conquest wars. However, the military defeat of Napoléon at Waterloo in 1815 swept away the regime, despite his efforts to legitimise the regime. Despite this swift turn of events, the Consulate and the First Empire left a significant legacy in terms of institutional and legal instruments, many of which are still in existence today.

7 The Revolutionary Calendar (also called the Republican Calendar) began on 22 September 1792 (1 Vendémiaire Year I), the day after the proclamation of the Republic in France. Contrary to the Gregorian Calendar used before, it was a solar calendar. It was created by the National Convention in 1793, during the French Revolution, to erase all references to the monarchy (then abolished a year earlier) and to Christianity. Months and days were renamed and/or renumbered, and weeks were replaced by decades (i.e., blocks of ten days in each month). Napoléon Bonaparte decided to abandon it in 1806 with just a short rehabilitation in 1871 by the revolutionary government of the Paris Commune.

The return to a monarchy in 1814 was possible due to the support of several European allies, namely Austria, England, Prussia, and Russia. The Bourbon Restoration (*Restauration*) started off when Louis XVIII, brother of Louis XVI and Charles X, and grandson of Louis XV (House of Bourbon), granted a constitutional Charter to his people (Charter of 4 June 1814). The 1814 Charter maintained a number of principles from the 1789 Revolution, concerning the protection of individual freedoms in particular. It also laid down the foundations of the parliamentary regime. The King, who had been in exile in the UK, took inspiration from the English system with, for instance, the establishment of a bicameral Parliament (i.e., House of Peers and House of Deputies) and a rudimentary parliamentary scrutiny with the introduction, for the first time, of the right of dissolution. However, the major defect of the 1814 Charter was the lack of government accountability. The revolutionary days of 1830 ensued, provoked by the much less apt politically, and successor of Louis XVIII, namely his brother Charles X.

The July Monarchy started with the ascent of Louis-Philippe I (House of Orléans) to power. The Charter of 1830 represented a compromise between the monarch and Parliament which afforded more powers to the latter, notably via the right of legislative initiative. The 18 years of Louis-Philippe's reign allowed the parliamentary system to take root. However, the increasing intrusion of the monarch in public affairs, especially after 1840, prevented its normal development. In the troubled context of economic and social upheaval throughout Europe at the time, a revolt began in 1848. After the fall of Louis-Philippe, a temporary government proclaimed the (Second) Republic on 24 February 1848. The government decided to elect, by universal suffrage, a Constituent Assembly, which produced, during an insurrectional climate, the Constitution of 4 November 1848. The drafters of the 1848 Constitution took inspiration from, among others, the US Constitution of 1787. The 1848 Constitution enshrined the principle of direct universal suffrage and a strict separation of powers. However, this last feature was responsible for the downfall of the regime as public powers were unable to resolve their conflicts in the absence of a right to dissolution of Parliament and of a mechanism of government accountability. In the meantime, the Prince-President Louis-Napoléon Bonaparte, nephew of Napoléon Bonaparte, did not manage to get rid of the ban imposing that the President of the Republic could not be re-elected right away. He then decided to obtain by force what he could not obtain by constitutional means. His *coup d'état* of 2 December 1851 allowed Louis-Napoléon Bonaparte to draft the Constitution of 14 January 1852. Despite its republican character and adherence to the main 1789 tenets, the 1852 Constitution re-established the institutions of the Empire under the reign of Napoléon III. This regime later evolved towards a more parliamentary one. However, the Second Empire ended with the defeat of France against Prussia, at Sedan, on 1–2 September 1870.

This section aims to shed light on the various attempts made by France to establish a suitable political regime in the period following the Revolution. During this time, there was immense uncertainty and confusion as the nation sought to determine a viable structure of governance, ultimately leading to the abandonment of the monarchy and the establishment of a parliamentary regime.

Looking for a suitable political regime: Between separation and confusion of powers (1791–1813)

This subsection delves into the period encompassing the 1789 Revolution and its immediate aftermath and the regimes that witnessed the arrival of Napoleon Bonaparte to power under the Consulate and the First Empire.

The revolutionary period (1789–1799). The *coup d'état* of the Third Estate on 17 June 1789 broke with the old regime. The gathering of the Third Estate in a national assembly resulted in the adoption of two foundational texts, namely the 1789 Declaration of the Rights of Man and of the Citizen adopted on 26 August 1789, and the 1791 Monarchical Constitution enacted on 3 September 1791. *The 1789 Declaration* expressed the ideals of progress and individualism of the enlightened bourgeoisie of the time. It was also meant to have a universal value in that it proclaimed the existence of natural rights and fundamental principles which ought to apply to every individual, as well as govern the relationships between individuals in any society. In other words, the 1789 Declaration aimed at individuals and citizens of all times and all countries. The inspiration for the 1789 Declaration stemmed from the ideas of the Enlightenment as well as from the English experience of charters and bills of rights. The 1789 Declaration is now included in the Preamble to the 1958 Constitution and, as such, forms part of French positive law. It acts as one of the texts of reference against which to test the constitutionality of laws in judicial review proceedings. *The 1791 Constitution was* inspired by the 1787 US Constitution. The 1791 Constitution proclaimed that sovereignty belonged to the nation. It also marked the first attempt to establish a strict separation of powers whereby the executive and legislative functions were clearly distinct and were represented by independent organs under a constitutional monarchy. Entrusted with the legislative power, the National Assembly (or *Corps Législatif*) consisted of a unique house whose legitimacy was based on election.[8] Executive power was held by King Louis XVI, who exercised it as the legitimate hereditary power. However, the interactions between institutional powers were limited and the different branches of powers did not enjoy means of pressure over one another, except for the suspensive right of veto in the hands of the King. Such veto was the way for the King to block the decrees from becoming laws with royal assent. Those features were precisely what caused the downfall of the regime. Political tensions between the King and the National Assembly mounted, resulting in a political crisis. While the King was accused of colluding with foreign hostile powers, the National Assembly pressed to adopt a series of decrees concerning members of the aristocracy who had fled abroad to escape the new regime. These measures also concerned those members of the clergy who refused to swear allegiance to the ideals of the revolution (the so-called "refractory priests"). The crisis clearly could not be resolved through dialogue and institutional mechanisms. The people's rebellion that ensued provoked the demise of the King on 10 August 1792.[9] A provisional council allowed the return of a Convention whose members were elected by universal suffrage on 20 September 1792. The Convention decided on the abolition of the monarchy and the establishment of the Republic on 21 September 1792.

The two other constitutions that followed illustrate further attempts at establishing some form of separation of powers. Different principles were experimented with under the so-called

8 During that period, the right to vote was restricted to those active citizens who possessed the means to meet a specific taxation requirement, referred to as the *cens* in French. This system, known as *censitaire suffrage*, was based on the theory of the electorate-function (i.e., the participation of the citizens in democratic life is to elect their representatives).

9 Louis XVI attempted to flee France but was apprehended at Varennes-en-Argonne in the northeast of the country on the night of 20 June 1791. Subsequently, he and his family were imprisoned in Paris. He was later guillotined on 21 January 1793.

Constitution Montagnarde[10] of 24 June 1793 such as, and for the first time in French constitutional history, the establishment of direct universal suffrage, albeit still reserved to males who paid a certain amount of tax at the time. The 1793 Constitution also consecrated a number of new rights (i.e., *droits-créances*, economic and social rights). Inspired by Rousseau's ideas, the 1793 Constitution organised a semi-direct democracy based on popular sovereignty, as opposed to national sovereignty which was entrenched under the previous 1791 Constitution.[11] The government rested on a unique popular assembly which was to delegate the day-to-day execution of governmental functions to a subordinated executive council. Despite marking Year One of the Republic and having been largely approved by the people by referendum, the 1793 Constitution was never applied. What happened instead was that the Convention in charge of the revolutionary government took exceptional measures to maintain order and ensure the so-called *Salut public*. By concentrating the legislative, executive, and judicial functions in its hands, the regime quickly slid towards a confusion of powers. Dramatic political events ensued. In a bid to save the *idéaux de la Révolution* at all costs, the most radical leaders, among them Robespierre (1758–1794), led the country to a "Reign of Terror" (5 September 1793–27 July 1794).

Written by the survivors of the Terror, the so-called *Constitution Thermidorienne* of 22 August 1795 (of 5 Fructidor of Year III under the new republican calendar) was based on a strict separation of powers. This strict separation of powers was regarded as a bulwark against the excesses of the previous period. The moderate bourgeois deputies who presided over this enterprise of reconstruction sought primarily to establish a stable form of government. They were dealing with the void left by the demise of the monarchy and the traumatising events of the Terror. The commission that was in charge consisted of 11 members, among them the famous Cambacérès and Sieyès. The executive power, contrary to the 1791 Constitution when it was exercised by the King, was to be exercised by a *Directoire* of five *Directeurs*, who collectively acted as the Head of State and were assisted by ministers. The same concern of dividing up power led to the introduction, for the first time in French constitutional history, of the principle of bicameralism. The two Houses of Parliament could not sit in the same room, though, and were meant to act as respective counter-powers to each other in order to balance the actions of Parliament. The *Conseil des Cinq Cents* was an assembly of junior deputies (over 30 years old) entrusted with the right of legislative initiative, whereas the *Conseil des Anciens* acted as an assembly with supposedly more wisdom grouping married men, or male widowers, of over 40 years of age and entrusted with the power to debate, albeit without amending power, the laws and vote on them. The strict separation of powers aimed at avoiding a direct confrontation between the executive and legislative powers. Once again, the rigidity of the institutional framework proved problematic in the face of the chaotic events of the time. The 1795 Constitution did not provide for any mechanism of dialogue or interaction between the powers (i.e., no right of dissolution of Parliament, no ministerial accountability to Parliament, no sharing of the right of legislative initiative, no access of *Directoire* members to Parliament, no veto power). Moreover, the attempts by each side to destabilise the other multiplied during

10 The term *montagne* (mountain) referred to a place in the National Assembly, situated at the higher section of the room, where the deputies sat, as opposed to those who stood in the lower section. Among those seated on the *montagne*, known as the *Montagnards*, were representatives with diverse political inclinations. For example, the *Girondins* were known to be more moderate in comparison to the *Jacobins*.

11 The people were associated with the political process by way of referendum and popular veto.

the period. On 9 November 1799 (or 18 Brumaire Year VIII), Napoleon Bonaparte, empowered by his numerous military victories, successfully orchestrated a *coup d'état*. This event truly marked the end of the revolutionary era. From then on, the executive power went from strength to strength until it culminated in another dictatorship, this time under the rule of one man: Napoleon.

1799–1813 The Consulate, the First Empire, and the confusion of powers in the hands of Napoleon. With the Constitution of 22 Frimaire of Year VIII (13 December 1799), Napoleon Bonaparte tailored his own regime. This regime established the dictatorship of the executive and of the first Consul in particular, the two other consuls having only an advisory role. Institutionally, it meant that the legislative power was dispersed among different organs with weakened powers, notably depriving them of the power of legislative initiative.[12] The judiciary was also submitted to the executive power. Under the Constitution of Year X (4 August 1802), Napoleon Bonaparte arranged for his immovability through the instatement of the consulate for life. A further step was reached when a new *senatus-consulte*, approved by a plebiscite, transformed the Life Consulate regime into an imperial hereditary regime under the Constitution of Year XII (18 May 1804). Bearing the title of "Emperor of the French," Napoleon I ruled by concentrating all the political power in his hands: as the head of the executive, he promulgated laws and the *senates-consulte*; he presided over the Senate and the Council of State; he validated the acts of the Legislative Body; and he also appointed the top members of the judiciary and the president of the third legislative body, the *Tribunat*.[13] Although Napoleon Bonaparte wanted to maintain the appearance of a democracy, the regime bore all the hallmarks of a dictatorship with strict repression and limitations of freedoms at home, and wars abroad. *Democratic caesarism* ("*césarisme démocratique*") is the expression that qualifies such a political approach which purports to combine authoritarianism and popular legitimacy. In this regard, the organisation of his coronation in the Notre Dame de Paris cathedral on 2 December 1804 is an interesting move of Napoleon to legitimise his power and firmly establish the Empire (and his dynasty) in the French political landscape as well as, almost certainly, in the minds of the French people. This was arguably a paragon of successful propaganda. Despite the overall negative impact of the Napoleonic reign, the regime left a number of long-lasting features and institutions such as, for instance, the administrative organisation of France, the institution of the prefect, and the establishment of the Council of State, the Senate, the Court of Auditors, and the *Banque de France*. Another legacy is of course the Napoleonic Code, or Civil Code, which outlived all the other less glorious moments, as described by Napoleon himself: "Waterloo

12 In addition to the *Sénat* and *Corps Législatif*, the legislative power consisted of a *Tribunat* comprising 100 members whose primary responsibility was to engage in debates on laws, although they were not granted any power to make amendments. The regime's dictatorial nature is further showcased through the utilisation of the system called "*listes de confiance*." This system aimed at undermining the impact of universal suffrage by dividing the elected representatives into three tiers. Initially, the local lists were formed from which the local representatives were chosen, and then one-tenth of its members could proceed to elect the second tier at the department level. Similarly, the third tier was elected at the national level using the same process. This system was based on the belief articulated by Sieyès that "the power comes from the top [but] trust comes from the bottom."

13 The *Tribunat* was dismantled in 1807 under pressure from the Emperor, who was worried about the emergence of dissident forces.

will erase the memory of so many victories. What will live eternally is my Code Civil."[14] It is well known how the string of Napoleon's glorious military victories was overshadowed by a few resounding defeats.[15] The Waterloo defeat in 1815, combined with the defections of his supporters and the weariness of the French people, led to the fall of Napoleon. Stripping him of his power, the Senate decided to send Napoleon into exile, in the first instance on the island of Elba.

Accepting the parliamentary regime: The final twitches of the monarchy (1814–1870)

This subsection explores the next phase of French constitutional history, which witnessed the gradual acceptance of the parliamentary system following the last remnants of the monarchy. During this period, relatively concise constitutional texts allowed for a certain degree of flexibility in political practices. Within the progressively liberal context of the nineteenth century, this flexibility proved favourable to the establishment of a robust parliamentary system. After an authoritarian stint under the Second Empire, the parliamentary regime is regarded to have taken root and prospered towards the conclusion of the nineteenth century.

1814–1848 From the Restoration to the experiment of the separation of powers. After the turmoil of the Napoleonic era, the French people saw the return of Louis XVII, Louis XVI's brother, as a path to some stability and peace for the country. Accepted by the French people, the King was also supported by his allies in Prussia, Russia, Austria, and of course the UK, where he had been in exile. However, the Constitution that the King bestowed on the people (i.e., the constitutional Charter of 4 June 1814) was in fact imposed by the monarch without popular consultation, as illustrated by the following excerpt: "We have voluntarily, and by the free exercise of our royal authority, granted, and indeed do grant, have made concession and have grant to our subjects … the following Constitutional Charter." Institutionally speaking, the *1814 Charter* was the result of a compromise between the *acquis* of the 1789 Revolution (i.e., guarantee of civil and political rights, principle of separation of powers, elected House of Deputies) and the restoration of the monarchy (i.e., royal sovereignty of the King as "King of France," restricted suffrage, right of dissolution and right of legislative initiative in the hands of the King).[16] Nevertheless, the 1814 Charter laid down the first bases of the parliamentary regime with a bicameral parliament comprising an upper house and a lower house, and an element of parliamentary scrutiny. While the 1814 Charter was not completely explicit concerning the relations between the different powers, it instated a regime flexible enough to allow the development of parliamentary institutional practices on the model of the British monarchy. For example, the ministers started to form a collective Cabinet (or "Ministry") with a leader at their

14 As quoted in Marie-Luce Paris, "Still Alive? Some Observations about the Two-Hundred Years of Existence of the French Code Civil 1804" (2005) 12 *Irish Journal of European Law* 72, 97.

15 Napoleonic victories are the following: Marengo (1800); Austerlitz (1805); Jena (1806); Friedland (1807); and Wagram (1809). Napoleonic defeats are the following: Trafalgar (1805); Berezina (1812); and Waterloo (1815).

16 The operation of the 1814 Charter faced a disruption in what came to be known as the Hundred Days period (*Les Cent Jours*), spanning March to July 1815. During this time, Napoleon made a brief comeback to power after escaping from the island of Elba. However, this reinstatement was short-lived, as Napoleon was ultimately banished to the remote island of St Helena in the South Atlantic Ocean.

head as the President of the Council, who liaised between the deputies and the King, viewed as a "neutral power." Also, the House of Deputies started to exercise some form of scrutiny of the actions of the Ministry, notably during legislative debates on the budget. Lastly, from 1821, the practice emerged of the King's Address, whereby the King would address the deputies at the start of the opening of Parliament. This was followed by a vote by the deputies in support of the action of the Ministry, hereby leading to an early form of political accountability of the government before Parliament.

The accession of Charles X to the throne, after the death of his brother Louis XVIII, marked a halt in the development of new liberal ideas mixing revolutionary *acquis* and parliamentary principles. Louis XVIII was very sick towards the end of his life, unable to walk due to gout. He knew very well that his whimsical and disinterested brother was not predisposed to hold power according to the new rules, except to re-establish an absolute monarchical power, hence the image of a succession between the "King without legs" and the "King without a head." Charles X overtly despised the newly established mutual relationship between the Ministry and the House of Deputies, and in general the liberal ideas imposed on the monarchy. He provoked a political crisis by appointing an ultra-royalist as President of the Council at the head of the Cabinet, despite the liberal majority of the House of Deputies. Bluntly ignoring the principle that the Cabinet must have the confidence of the parliamentary majority, as reminded by the said majority in its "Address of the 221 [221 deputies of the majority]," the King threatened to dissolve the House of Deputies in May 1830. The King then took another series of decisions, including the actual dissolution, the censure of the press, and news restrictions on the right to vote, that contributed to escalating the crisis and led to a popular revolt—the armed insurgency of the Three Glorious Days (27–29 July 1830), eventually forcing Charles X into exile.

The *1830 Charter* represents another, albeit more successful, attempt to reconcile liberal principles with the monarchy. The new King, Louis-Philippe, Duke of Orleans,[17] agreed to compromise and to act as the "King of the French" [instead of the "King of France"]. The 1830 Charter is almost a copy of the 1814 Charter albeit with some changes, including the recognition of the principle of national sovereignty (as well as the use of the tricolour flag as a powerful symbol of a monarchical regime espousing the revolutionary heritage). The relative success of what was known as the *July Monarchy* is however due to a further shift towards political liberalism that eventually allowed the parliamentary regime to truly take root. Notable changes included a right of legislative initiative shared between the King and Parliament, better national representation based on a more liberal approach to the right of suffrage, and an increased protection of the freedom of the press. More importantly, institutional practice contributed to improving the operation of key parliamentary mechanisms between the executive and legislative branches, notably the regular use (by the King) of the right of dissolution and the acceptance of the principle of government accountability. In addition to the address seen above, new mechanisms emerged such as the motion of confidence at the initiative of the Cabinet, the technique of "interpellation," which was the practice of questions to the government, and the establishment of investigative committees. The interpellation corresponded to the developmental phase of the parliamentary regime whereby members of Parliament could call on the

17 Louis-Philippe was not a direct descendant of Louis XIV; he was the cousin of the three previous reigning Kings (i.e., brothers Louis XVI, Louis XVIII, and Charles X). Louis-Philippe was a direct descendant of Philippe of Orléans, Louis XIV's brother.

ministers to provide explanations on particular policy decisions or on the budget. Should they not be satisfied with the answers, members of Parliament could organise a vote of no confidence, possibly resulting in the resignation of the government.

Overall, the relatively long reign of Louis-Philippe I (1830–1848), as the last reigning King, allowed the development of the parliamentary regime in France. However, the King's growing involvement in political life, especially his dualist (or Orleanist) conception of the parliamentary regime, caused increasing frustration among the Republicans. According to the dualist conception of the regime, the government was accountable to *two* entities, namely Parliament and the King—the throne indeed not being regarded as "an empty seat" and necessarily implying a political role of the monarch. The opposite view, that of the monist approach, considered the accountability principle as going *one* way only, that is, between a government that is accountable to its majority in Parliament—in application of the adage "the King reigns but does not govern." However, the context of economic hardship and social crisis across Europe got the better of the regime, which ended with the revolutionary period of 1848.[18]

1848–1870 The difficult road to the parliamentary regime. During this period, two further constitutions were adopted before France switched again to an imperial regime for the second time in its history. The *Constitution of 4 November 1848* followed the proclamation of the Second Republic on 24 February and 23 April 1848. The constituent assembly focused as much on guaranteeing the stability of the regime by empowering the institutions (i.e., Head of State and Parliament) with real popular legitimacy as on rekindling the revolutionary spirit and liberal ideas. That certainly represented a challenge in a historical context which witnessed the concomitant emergence of socialism. This resulted in a regime of strict separation of powers, directly inspired by the American regime. However, this rigid conception of the separation of powers allowing for no collaborative solutions between the executive and legislative branches of power (i.e., no right of dissolution of the National Assembly and no government accountability before Parliament) was, as previously, the direct cause of the downfall of the regime. When Louis Napoleon Bonaparte, Napoleon's nephew, was elected as the first President of the Second Republic on 10 December 1848, the political class, Republicans and Conservatives alike, were sure that they could handle this "moron."[19] Events proved them wrong and clashes soon emerged between the two legitimate powers, namely the President of the Republic, Louis Napoleon Bonaparte, and the National Assembly. Once again, the various disagreements were rooted in the inability of the different political forces to agree on the fundamental turn that the French political regime ought to take. Once again, the most habile politician of the time, playing on all his opponents' weaknesses, managed to reach absolute power. Specifically, Louis Napoleon Bonaparte took advantage of an unpopular reform voted by Parliament on the restriction of the right of suffrage[20] to dissolve the National Assembly and to legitimise, on a *coup d'état*

18 The direct cause of the first rebellious outburst was a move towards universal suffrage led by the Republicans that weakened the parliamentary majority held tight until then under a restricted right of suffrage.

19 The words were from Thiers. Louis Napoleon Bonaparte was elected with 75% of the votes after the first round. So, moron or not, he certainly had popular legitimacy.

20 The right of universal suffrage was proclaimed on 5 March 1848.

on 2 December 1851,[21] his ten-year mandate as Head of State under the so-called "Decennial Republic" (*La République décennale*).

The *Constitution of 14 January 1852,* which founded this particular form of Republic, marked a return to the imperial regime while, at the same time, maintaining the principles of the 1789 Revolution. From there, the slide towards a more personalised regime ensued. The Empire was reinstated on 7 November 1852, and Louis Napoleon Bonaparte took the name of Napoleon III with the official proclamation of the Second Empire on 2 December 1852. Institutionally speaking, the regime was the application of the 1852 Constitution, the institution of the Emperor replacing the one of the President of the Republic. Whereas the first years were marked by authoritarianism, the regime soon evolved towards a parliamentary form of government when Napoleon III realised that he had to compromise with the different political forces, notably the Orleanists. Among the liberal measures that Napoleon III took were the re-establishment of the address in reply to the Emperor's speech, the recognition of the role of the President of the Council (of ministers), the principle of publicity of parliamentary debates, an enhanced amending power for members of the Legislative Body, the restoration of bicameralism with the re-establishment of the Senate, and the sharing of the right of legislative initiative between the Emperor and the Legislative Body. However, the consolidation of the parliamentary regime was cut short by the defeat of France against Prussia in Sedan on 1 September 1870. This marked the end of the Second Empire and the start of another Republic on 4 September 1870.

Establishment of the parliamentary regime under the Republic (1870–1958)

> « *Je suis en république, et pour roi j'ai moi-même* ».[22]

The parliamentary system came into existence during the restoration period and the reign of Louis Philippe. However, it flourished and evolved significantly during the Third Republic and became firmly established in the Fourth Republic. Nevertheless, both the Third and Fourth Republics displayed a fundamental imbalance in favour of Parliament, leading to a persistent and ultimately baneful governmental instability.

The parliamentary regime under the Third Republic (1875–1940)

This subsection explains the genesis of the Third Republic and presents its institutions and the practice of the regime.

Genesis of the Third Republic. The Third Republic was sandwiched between two wars—in fact, two defeats—the 1870 defeat against Prussia, and the 1940 surrender to Nazi Germany. The Third Republic represents, however, the longest regime in French constitutional history despite the significant perils that marked this period, the trauma of the First World War in

21 The date was symbolic since it referred to the anniversary of his uncle's coronation on 2 December 1804 and his victory in Austerlitz on 2 December 1805.

22 Victor Hugo (1802–1885), French novelist and politician [I am in a republic, and for king I have myself].

particular.[23] On the external front, the capitulation of Napoléon III on 4 September 1870 led to the conclusion of the Treaty of Frankfurt on 10 May 1871, which ended the Franco-Prussian war and re-established peace between the two countries. The treaty also organised the secession to Prussia of the Alsace-Lorraine region. Internally, the breakdown of the Second Empire and the pressing influence of socialist movements led to social unrest. The events of the Paris Commune (*Commune de Paris*) saw the installation of a radical socialist and revolutionary government that ruled Paris for several months in 1871. Order was progressively restored but the process was long and chaotic, first under a national defence government (comprising such illustrious figures as Trochu, Gambetta, and Ferry). Notwithstanding, the government managed to ensure the continuity of the state and to conduct the policy of the nation before a new constitution could be adopted. The difficulties mainly lay in the opposition between the Monarchists and the Republicans, as well as in internal divisions on the monarchist side. While the Republicans were in favour of reprising hostilities with Prussia, the Monarchists were eager to make peace and to stabilise the domestic situation—the latter largely winning the elections in the new national constituent assembly in February 1871. The Monarchists, who were in favour of establishing a constitutional monarchy, fought over who to place on the throne: either the Count of Paris, Louis Philippe's heir, for the Orleanists, or the Count of Chambord, the legitimist heir, descendant of the Bourbon branch, for the so-called "Legitimists." The Orleanists were in tune with the liberal ideas of the time. Although sufficiently strong politically to ascend to power, the Legitimists were impeded by the hard line taken by the Count of Chambord in the so-called "war of the flags" incident in July 1871: symbolically refusing to accept the tricolour flag, the Count wanted to re-establish the white flag of the monarchy. The ensuing period, between 1871 and 1875, saw the adoption of a series of constitutional laws which contributed to clarifying the situation. The role of Head of State was first attributed to the Republican Adolphe Thiers, who was then replaced by the Monarchist Marshal Patrice de Mac Mahon. This was done in order to keep open the possibility of reverting to a monarchical regime, as confirmed by the choice of Mac Mahon to appoint a royalist, the Count of Broglie, to the post of President of the Council of Ministers. The restoration of the monarchy never happened because, as mentioned above, of the conservative stance taken by the pretender to the throne, the Count of Chambord, who eventually died without a descendant. A string of temporary constitutional laws, representing a much-needed compromise between the Monarchists and the Republicans after a period of deep trouble, were adopted during this transition period. These constitutional laws led to the more definitive set of constitutional laws of 1875, which formally established the Third Republic.

The first of these temporary constitutional laws was the *Constitution Rivet*, adopted on 31 August 1871. The Constitution Rivet assigned the official title of "President of the Republic" to the Head of the executive branch. His functions consisted in the right to promulgate laws and ensure their implementation.[24] The President of the Republic had the right to appoint ministers whose role was to assist him. One feature of this constitutional law resided in the politi-

23 During the course of four years, the casualties incurred in the First World War were staggering, with an estimated 6,000 soldiers losing their lives every day. Among the nations embroiled in the conflict, France suffered the most profound impact in terms of combat-related fatalities with 1.45 million soldiers who perished or went missing, alongside a total of 1.9 million injured military personnel. This toll accounted for roughly 30% of the country's active male population at that time.

24 The pronoun "he" is used here. The Third Republic is part of history, and there was no female President of the Third Republic. Women could neither vote nor be elected.

cal accountability of the President and ministers to the Assembly of elected representatives with the practice of the ministerial countersignature. Such a practice meant that all acts of the President had to be countersigned by the relevant minister(s) since the President was politically unaccountable. The Constitution Rivet was partially amended by a second temporary constitutional law, the so-called *Constitution de Broglie*, adopted on 13 March 1873. The Constitution de Broglie mainly aimed at limiting the intervention of the then President of the Republic, Thiers, in the Assembly. Thiers was a skilful politician and an excellent orator. In order to limit his influence—that is, the influence of the executive power over Parliament—the principle of his responsibility before the National Assembly was established. Also, his access to the National Assembly was made procedurally difficult, under what was called, at the time, the "Chinese ceremonial." In the face of all these difficulties, Thiers ended up resigning from his position. The third temporary constitutional law was called the *Loi du Septennat*. Adopted on 20 November 1873, the Loi du Septennat established a compromise between the two monarchic dynasties, namely the Orleanists and the Legitimists. This compromise referred to the dispute between the two pretenders to the throne and consisted, in the eventuality of a return to the monarchy, in giving to the Count of Chambord, the Legitimist pretender, the throne as the future Henri V. Since the Count of Chambord did not have any descendants, the heir to the throne would have to come from the Legitimist dynasty. However, the Count of Chambord's steady refusal to accept the tricolour flag, which reflected his desire to re-establish an absolute monarchy, aborted the compromise. Parliament eventually decided to establish a provisional regency of seven years for the sole benefit of Marshal Patrice de Mac Mahon, Duke of Magenta. Mac Mahon was conferred the executive power intuitu personae until the coming of a King. Nonetheless, the personal seven-year term of office was changed to an impersonal seven-year term after the vote—by a very narrow majority of 353 votes in favour and 352 votes against—on the so-called *Wallon Amendment* on 30 January 1875. Under the new amendment, the President of the Republic was to be elected at an absolute majority of the votes cast by both the Senate and the House of Deputies convened in a National Assembly for a term of seven years. The Wallon Amendment was significant since, by institutionalising the presidential function, it changed the nature of the regime and officially (re-)established the Republic.[25]

Following on the preceding laws, another set of constitutional laws were adopted, namely the constitutional law of 24 February 1875 relating to the organisation of the Senate,[26] the constitutional law of 25 February 1875 relating to the organisation of public powers,[27] and the constitutional law of 16 July 1875 relating to the relationships between public powers.[28] This ensemble formed the basis of the Third Republic constitution, known as the *1875 Constitution*. The 1875 Constitution was founded on the core principles of universal suffrage, separation of powers, government accountability, and bicameralism. As a result of a compromise between the Republicans and the moderate Monarchists, these laws were concise, without any mention

25 Symbolically, the Wallon Amendment was one of the first constitutional provisions to be abrogated by the Vichy Laws in July 1940.

26 Due to its composition, the Senate could potentially lead to the restoration of the monarchy.

27 The organisation of public powers featured a bicameral Parliament and a two-headed executive (i.e., the President of the Republic and the Council of Ministers, both accountable to Parliament).

28 In that regard, the constitutional law of 16 July 1875 basically posed the various mechanisms and rules of a parliamentary system.

of fundamental principles; they merely aimed at laying down the rules organising the functioning of public powers. These laws were also easily amendable.

The institutions of the Third Republic. The Third Republic was a parliamentary regime. A two-headed executive, a bicameral Parliament, and classical parliamentary mechanisms thus characterised the regime. The executive consisted of the (indefinitely re-eligible) President of the Republic and of ministers. The former was granted important powers such as the power to appoint ministers, the right of legislative initiative, and the right of dissolution of the House of Deputies with the approbation of the Senate. However, these presidential powers were only formal. This was due to two correlated principles: the President needed a ministerial countersignature for all his acts, and he was politically unaccountable. As for the government, it acted as a collegial body whose members were, as laid down for the first time in the 1975 Constitution, jointly accountable to Parliament.[29] The institution of the President of the Council (of ministers) had no textual basis (yet), although customary practice increasingly gave prominence to the role. The legislature consisted of the two Houses of Parliament with equal powers. This "perfect bicameralism" (*bicaméralisme parfait*) meant that both Houses of Parliament were granted fully fledged legislative power which comprised the right of legislative initiative and whereby laws had to be voted in identical terms by both Houses. Both Houses also had the power, under different conditions, to hold the government accountable—save for finance and budgetary bills, which had to be tabled and voted upon by the House of Deputies in the first place. The House of Deputies comprised between 500 and 600 members elected for a four-year term by universal direct suffrage in a two-round, first-past-the-post system. The 300 members of the Senate were elected by indirect universal suffrage for a nine-year renewable term (with 75 of them, irremovable, elected by the National Assembly). The Senate represented a rather conservative assembly stemming from the countryside and small towns, although it still defended the republican values of the regime. The relationship between the executive and the legislature was supposed to be balanced, based on the two reciprocal means of pressure of the parliamentary regime, namely the principle of political accountability of the government before both Houses of Parliament, on the one hand, and the right of dissolution of the House of Deputies in the hands of the President, on the other hand.

The practice of the regime. The regime of the Third Republic, although long in duration, was unsuccessful in many respects. Initially, even though it clearly functioned as a parliamentary regime, it failed to define its true nature. However, this uncertainty was eventually dissipated with a memorable political crisis in 1877. This crisis involved the dissolution of the House of Deputies by the President of the Republic. Consequently, the 1877 dissolution discredited the utilisation of dissolution as a key parliamentary mechanism for a long time, thereby contributing to an imbalance within the regime. In general terms, the Third Republic operated as a dysfunctional parliamentary system, marked by persistent governmental instability that

29 The relevant provisions of the law of 25 February 1875 aimed at the collegial accountability of the Cabinet for the decisions of general policy taken by the government as well as at the individual responsibility of each minister for their personal acts.

precipitated the downfall of the regime. These occurrences will be elaborated on in subsequent paragraphs.

On 16 May 1877, the then President of the Republic, Marshal Patrice de Mac Mahon, accused the President of the Council, Jules Simon, of undue concessions in favour of the Republicans. What had happened is that, after the legislative elections of 1876, Simon enjoyed the strong support of the House of Deputies, composed of a majority of Republicans. Refusing to appoint a President of the Council from the ranks of the Republicans, Mac Mahon appointed Albert de Broglie, a notorious Monarchist. Facing strong opposition from the deputies,[30] Mac Mahon then dissolved the Lower House on 25 June 1876, with the approbation of the Senate. However, the Republicans prevailed again during the following legislative elections in 1877, as well as during the senatorial elections of December 1877.[31] As a consequence, Mac Mahon resigned on 30 January 1879 and was replaced by Jules Grévy, who declared that he would never "fight the national will as expressed by Parliament." This interpretation of the 1975 Constitution was later branded as the *Constitution Grévy.*

The 1877 crisis revealed the confrontation between the two conceptions of the parliamentary regime: on the one hand, a monist conception whereby the government is accountable to the House of Deputies only, as advocated by the Republicans; on the other hand, a dualist conception whereby the government is held to account both to the House of Deputies *and* to the President of the Republic, as advocated by Mac Mahon. The underlying reason for keeping a strong role in the hands of the President was that it was envisaged that the monarchy could be restored with a monarch as the Head of State. The consequences of the 1877 crisis contributed to clarifying the ambiguities surrounding the nature of the regime. Firstly, it signalled the definitive installation of a monist type of parliamentary regime as well as of a republican form of government.[32] Secondly, the use, and even abuse,[33] of the right of dissolution resulted in such a parliamentary tool being discredited. From then on, dissolution was perceived as an unacceptable threat to Parliament. The ensuing perverse effect was a progressive submission of the government to Parliament in a so-called *régime d'assemblée.*

The Third Republic experienced more than a hundred governments between 1875 and 1940, of which eight were dismissed because of a vote of no confidence by the Senate.[34] The chronic governmental instability was due to a combination of factors. In the first place, the weakening

30 The Republicans, led by Gambetta, reminded Mac Mahon of the fundamental principle of the parliamentary system through their influential "*Manifeste des 363.*" This declaration emphasised that the government's authority stemmed from the support of the parliamentary majority.

31 Majorities in both the House of Deputies and the Senate were republican by early 1879.

32 There were very few constitutional amendments implemented during the Third Republic. One notable amendment, introduced through the Law of 14 August 1884, brought about several changes concerning the secularisation of institutions. Notably, this amendment firmly established that the republican form of government could not be altered, effectively eliminating any possibility of restoring a monarchy. Two other rules were adopted. Firstly, it was decreed that individuals descended from royal families were ineligible to hold the position of President of the Republic. Secondly, the previously immutable status of senators was lifted, allowing individuals from diverse political affiliations, beyond just the Monarchists, to join their ranks. Another significant constitutional revision involved the symbolic relocation of the capital from Versailles to Paris.

33 Mac Mahon made another attempt at announcing a dissolution in October 1877 but failed to secure the consent of the Senate on this subsequent occasion.

34 While the Senate, indirectly elected, was not threatened by the dissolution, it could nevertheless use its power to hold the government accountable.

of the President of the Republic—whose role was to "*inaugurer les chrysanthèmes*"[35]—was correlated with the reinforcement of the role of the President of the Council. However, the President of the Council had no real legal recognition until the adoption of a law in 1934. For the first time, the institution of the President of the Council was officially recognised, endowing him with the necessary administrative and budgetary means to carry out his role. Moreover, while the President of the Council was the holder of the executive power, he was under constant pressure because the majority in Parliament could turn against him.

Indeed, several factors made it difficult to resist a vote of no confidence by Parliament. The first factor was that the procedure to hold the government accountable before Parliament was not regulated, and Parliament had many ways to oust a government such as the interpellation followed by a vote of no confidence, the refusal to vote on a confidence vote, or the refusal to vote on the installation of the appointed government These ways could be used spontaneously, at the initiative of a member of Parliament or of a minister (without prior discussion within the Council of Ministers), and with no delay between the decision to proceed to hold government accountable and the vote of confidence in Parliament, all this rendering the procedure quick and easy. Also, no special qualified majority was required for the vote of confidence, a relative majority being sufficient to throw a whole government out. The second factor was that the government could be held accountable before both Houses of Parliament, therefore increasing the chances of such an occurrence. Also, the absence of incompatibility between ministerial and parliamentary mandates played a role in governmental instability since members of Parliament always tried to throw out the government in the hope of becoming ministers in the new one. The third factor lay in the fundamental imbalance created by the non-use, since the 1877 crisis, of the right of dissolution. The deprivation of such a key means of pressure vis-à-vis Parliament contributed de facto to a dependence of the government vis-à-vis the legislature. Lastly, the fourth factor had to do with the political landscape of the time. While existing political parties were adopting proper structures, new political forces) emerged. The Radical Party was created in 1901, the *SFIO* (future Socialists) in 1905, and the Communist Party in 1920. Such multipartyism caused difficulty in terms of forming strong majorities since successive governments were in fact based on fragile political alliances and coalitions. Yet, there was an appearance of coherence and duration under the Clémenceau Government (1917–1920), which was appointed to deal with the throes of the First World War, and also under the Blum Government (1936–1938), which led the country under a left-wing coalition during the *Front Populaire* years.

Despite a number of measures to mitigate such defects (e.g., adoption of decree-laws allowing the government to intervene in the legislative area), the regime of the Third Republic could not be cured—all this happening in the context of a series of political scandals. The regime therefore plunged into a context of growing anti-parliamentarism, worsened by the rise of extremism. On the positive side, though, the Third Republic was also the regime which contributed to consecrating the main republican values and freedoms such as freedom of association and assembly, freedom of the press, freedom of religion, trade-union rights, and the principle of secularism. The Third Republic also advanced social and economic rights such as the right to free education, the right to a limited number of working hours (i.e., 40 hours a week), to pay rises, to the first ever paid annual leave, as well as the development of cultural and sports

35 President Poincaré described ironically the Constitution of the Third Republic in the following manner: "Article 1: The President [of the Republic] has every right. Article 2: He does not exercise any."

activities. Last, but not least, the Third Republic contributed to overcoming the trauma of the Great War. Nonetheless, too preoccupied by the turmoil of internal affairs, French leaders did not fully appreciate the danger of the rise of Nazism. On 3 September 1939, France, along with the UK, declared war on Germany after the invasion of Poland on 1 September 1939, and that was the start of the Second World War.

The Third Republic came to an end after the German invasion of France (also of the Netherlands, Belgium, and Luxembourg) after the *Bataille de France* (May–June 1940), which resulted in the resignation of the President of the Council, Paul Reynaud, who was replaced by Marshal Pétain.[36] Pétain signed the armistice on 22 June 1940 and started a regime of collaboration with the occupying forces. The Constitutional Law of 10 July 1940 endowed Pétain and his Government, based in the town of Vichy (*Gouvernement de Vichy*), with full powers to draft a new constitution. The new text primarily guaranteed the values of "work, family, and homeland" (*travail, famille, patrie*). The Vichy Government attributed all powers, executive, legislative, and judicial, to President Pétain and abrogated all pre-existing constitutional texts. The Vichy Government substituted the Republic with the French (metropolitan) State and negated all protection of individual rights and freedoms. Concomitantly, the Government of Free France (*Gouvernement de la France libre*) was being installed on the initiative of General De Gaulle. On 18 June 1940, while exiled in London, De Gaulle appealed to his compatriots to continue the fight against the occupier by joining the Free French Forces (*Forces françaises libres*). Broadcast to France on the BBC, the so-called "Appeal of 18 June" was the first speech made by De Gaulle when he arrived in London in 1940. It is generally regarded as marking the beginning of the French resistance movement although it was not heard by many French people. During the victorious Campaign of France resulting in the entire liberation of the country (*Libération*, 1944–1946),[37] the provisional Government of the French Republic reinstalled the republican legality and declared null and void all acts taken under the Vichy Government. Constitutionally speaking, the 1940 Constitutional Law was in fact invalid since it had not respected the normal procedure for constitutional amendment. The Vichy Government, instead of the National Assembly, proceeded to amend the constitutional texts and also infringed one of the fundamental tenets of the French regime, namely its republican nature. Hence the provision of the first article of the Ordinance of 9 August 1944 relating to the restoration of republican legality on the continental territory: "The form of the Government of France is and remains the Republic. In law, it has not ceased to exist."

The parliamentary regime under the Fourth Republic (1946–1958)

As in the previous subsection, this subsection explains the genesis of the Fourth Republic and presents its institutions and practice.

36 By 1942, the totality of French mainland territory was occupied by the Germans.

37 The US, British, and Canadian army forces took part in the liberation of France, joined by the Free French Forces, notably led by Marshal de Lattre de Tassigny and General Leclerc. The liberation of France was achieved in several stages, namely the liberation of Corsica (October 1943), the landing in Normandy (5–6 June 1944, 2 million soldiers), the landing in Provence (15–16 August 1944, 500,000 soldiers), and the liberation of Paris (August 1944).

Genesis of the Fourth Republic. The Fourth Republic was established after the Second World War. Despite a few attempts at rationalisation, the regime failed to function properly and crumbled after just 12 years of existence. In many respects, it marked a return to the regime of the previous Republic. After he launched his appeal on 18 June 1940, De Gaulle established the Government of Free France (*Gouvernement de la France libre*), which aimed at safeguarding the honour of the Republic and at organising the Resistance movement from London in the first instance, and then from Algiers. On 3 June 1944, the French Committee for the National Liberation, derived from the Government of Free France, became the first temporary government of the French Republic. As an extension of the Government of Algiers, the subsequent provisional Government of the French Republic (*Gouvernement provisoire de la République française*) established its headquarters in Paris in August 1944, following the liberation of the capital. The provisional Government of the French Republic did not conform with the legality of the Third Republic, nor with that of Vichy, but derived its legitimacy from the Resistance movement. This temporary government gave the French people the following alternative: either to re-establish the regime of the Third Republic, or to vote for a national constituent assembly that would be granted the power to draft a new constitution. The French people decided in favour of the latter in a referendum on 21 October 1945.[38]

A second temporary government was established in accordance with the Constitutional Law of 2 November 1945. Also adopted by referendum, the 1945 Constitutional Law granted limited powers to the national constituent assembly with the imperative to prepare a draft constitution within seven months and to submit it to a referendum. It also provided for the interim organisation of public authorities. In the end, the divergences between De Gaulle, who advocated for a strong executive power, and the Socialists and Communists proved irreconcilable. This steered De Gaulle to resign in January 1946.[39] A first constitutional draft, elaborated in April 1946, was rejected by the French people on 5 May 1946 for political and institutional reasons. Politically, the constitution reignited the fear of communist influence (i.e., fear of the "red constitution") because it was elaborated by Socialists and Communists who had the majority in the constituent assembly. Institutionally, this first constitutional project was based on the principle of a single legislative assembly elected through universal suffrage which left very little power to the executive and reignited the fear of domination of the parliamentary assembly, an inefficient model that was distrusted by most French people. A new constituent assembly was then elected in the summer of 1946 in which the political balance was slightly less favourable to the leftist parties. The French people subsequently approved, albeit with almost a third abstaining, a toned-down constitution which came into force on 27 October 1946.

The institutions of the Fourth Republic. The Fourth Republic featured a legislative assembly and an executive power holding a non-predominant position. The executive power was composed of the President of the Republic and, for the first time recognised under the

38 The referendum allowed French women to exercise their right to vote for the first time, a right which had been granted by the Ordinance of 21 April 1944 on the organisation of public authorities in France after the liberation. The last section of the population to be deprived of their right to vote was the military. Members of the military were eventually granted this right in 1945.

39 Later in the year, De Gaulle exposed his vision of the restoration of the power of the state in the so-called Bayeux Speech delivered on 16 June 1946 while the second constituent assembly was still working on a second draft. See also Chapter 3 on historical and legal foundations of the Fifth Republic.

constitution,[40] the President of the Council of Ministers. The President was, like under the Third Republic, elected for seven years (re-eligible only once) by indirect universal suffrage by Parliament. Endowed with only formal powers, he no longer had the power of legislative initiative nor the right of dissolution of Parliament.[41] Politically unaccountable, the President had to submit all his acts to the countersignature of the President of the Council or the relevant ministers. However, the power to appoint the President of the Council allowed him to enjoy a certain amount of strategic power.[42] The President of the Council, whose appointment by the President had to be approved by the National Assembly, was the real holder of the executive power. As the Head of Government, the President of the Council had the power to appoint (and dismiss) the ministers, according to the procedure of the so-called *double investiture*. Under such a procedure, the President of the Council was approved by the National Assembly, in the first place, and then approved together with his government, in the second place. As head of the Cabinet, the President of the Council was in charge of guiding and conducting the policy of the nation and taking responsibility for it. The legislature consisted of the National Assembly, which succeeded the House of Deputies, and of the Council of the Republic, which succeeded the Senate. This time, the Houses of Parliament had unequal powers (i.e., *bicaméralisme imparfait*). Members of the National Assembly were elected by direct universal suffrage for a period of seven years, although the choice of electoral mode (i.e., proportional representation within the department) prevented the establishment of stable majorities, especially from the mid-1950s when the Communist Party turned against the regime. The National Assembly was clearly the central institution of the regime. It was endowed with full legislative powers as well as the power to scrutinise government action. This meant that the National Assembly had the right of legislative initiative and the exclusive right to vote on the law. Such power was significant at a time when the law was the central norm, supreme (i.e., not susceptible to judicial review), and with unlimited scope (i.e., capable of regulating any area), giving rise to the so-called "legicentrism." No power of judicial review existed as such under the Fourth Republic despite the existence of a constitutional committee. The constitutional committee was a political institution merely in charge of ensuring that no constitutional amendment was necessary after the adoption of a law; it had no power to declare a law unconstitutional. In practice, the constitutional committee rendered one decision only, in 1948. The Council of the Republic, like the Senate under the Third Republic, represented the conservative trends of the countryside and small towns. Its political powers were greatly diminished since the last word belonged to the National Assembly in terms of law-making.[43] Also, the government

40 Article 45 of the 1946 Constitution.

41 The pronoun "he" is used here. The Fourth Republic is part of history and there was no female President of the Republic of the Fourth Republic. Women could neither vote nor be elected. The same was true as regards the President of the Council.

42 Despite a rather toned-down institutional function, the role of the President of the Republic was occupied by two strong personalities, namely Vincent Auriol and René Coty. Auriol strived to exert a determining political influence on partisan conflicts and fully used the powers at his disposal to that effect (i.e., request for a new deliberation of the law, president of the Superior Council of the Judiciary, choice of the President of the Council etc.). Albeit less influential, Coty played a crucial role at two key political moments: firstly, when he imposed Guy Mollet as the President of the Council in 1956, and secondly, when he threatened to resign if De Gaulle was not returned to power when the 1958 crisis broke.

43 The Council of the Republic was initially conceived as a "think tank" (i.e., *chambre de réflexion*). It became a fully fledged parliamentary House only after the 1954 constitutional amendment.

was no longer accountable before the Council of the Republic, which was no longer able to scrutinise the actions of the executive. The powers common to both Houses of Parliament were the election of the President and the designation of the members of the constitutional committee. In addition to the National Assembly and the Council of the Republic, also established were an Economic Council endowed with an advisory role and, France still being a colonial Empire at the time, an Assembly of the French Union, composed of the delegates and representatives of the territories in mainland France as well as of the overseas territories and associated states.

The practice of the regime. The Fourth Republic attempted to rationalise the parliamentary regime inherited from the previous Republic. For example, the 1946 Constitution imposed specific rules concerning the dissolution of the National Assembly to allay the fear of an inappropriate dissolution, which was a reaction to the 1877 episode. The objective was to make recourse to dissolution more difficult. Therefore, the decision to dissolve taken by the President of the Republic was to be at the request of the President of the Council, who could not resort to it within 18 months of the legislative elections. Also, stricter rules were established concerning the decision to hold a vote of no confidence in order to avoid untimely governmental resignations. New conditions were also put in place regarding the vote of no confidence itself. The motion of censure had to be voted upon one day after it was tabled. This was to allow the government to gather support and deputies to think twice before making their decision. The no confidence vote was won at an absolute majority of the votes cast. No motion of censure was ever adopted under these conditions. The vote of confidence, aimed at obtaining the support or confidence of the National Assembly, regarding the general policy or a specific text, was submitted to the same strict conditions as the motion of censure.

Despite these attempts to rationalise parliamentary techniques, the Fourth Republic never proved to be a satisfactory regime. Once again, it degenerated into a regime marked by governmental instability (i.e., 24 different governments over 12 years of existence).[44] The reasons were mainly political, due to the persistence of a fierce partisanship that was detrimental to national interests, misappropriate use of parliamentary procedures, and, correlatively, difficult use of the right of dissolution. Concerning the first reason on partisanship, the difficulty stemmed from the disaggregation, a few years after the war, of tripartism. De Gaulle established his own political party in April 1947, the *Rassemblement du Peuple français*, and the Communists were excluded from the Ramadier Government in May 1947 as a direct consequence of the confrontation between the western bloc and the Communist bloc in the Cold War. This, plus the introduction of some proportional representation in the mode of suffrage, made it quite difficult to obtain a solid majority in Parliament. Concerning the second reason on the wrong use of parliamentary procedures, the precedent created by the President of the Council, the socialist Ramadier, totally ruined the efficiency of the appointment procedure of the government laid down in the 1946 Constitution. While his nomination

44 The only constitutional amendment of the 1946 Constitution was made by the Law of 7 December 1954 in order to rationalise the *double investiture* procedure, with two changes. Firstly, the approval of the appointment of the President of the Council and his government were made in one go before the National Assembly, hereby making the installation of the government much quicker. Secondly, the approval by the National Assembly had to be voted by a relative majority of the votes cast, meaning that abstention played in favour of the government.

had been approved by an absolute majority by the National Assembly, Ramadier decided on his own initiative, and against the advice of President Auriol, to present himself a second time (i.e., *double investiture*) together with his Cabinet to be approved by the Assembly. But such a second phase in the investiture procedure, which was not provided for under the 1946 Constitution, made the whole exercise dangerous because it could be decided by a relative majority of the Assembly, hereby potentially leading to weak partisan coalitions. Another issue was the deleterious effect of a potential motion of censure. The successive governments never really waited to be called out in cases where such a motion was put to the vote; and, as a matter of fact, no motion of censure was ever adopted under the Fourth Republic. What the successive governments tended to do was to resign before this happened when they felt threatened by a simple majority of hostile votes or even by a waning parliamentary majority. Another diversion of the procedures on government accountability is to be found in the so-called practice of the "calibrated vote" (*vote calibré*). The practice consisted in members of the National Assembly deliberately choosing to express their distrust of government by voting at an absolute majority of the votes cast, or by a simple majority vote. According to this practice, the deputies would agree, after consultation of the political groups, to vote by just the number of votes that was necessary to put the government in the minority. Without a strong majority to implement its programme, while at the same time being unable to dissolve the National Assembly, the government was thus forced to resign. Of the 24 governments of the Fourth Republic, only five were dismissed according to constitutional rules; the others were dismissed by the practice of "calibrated vote." The third reason for governmental instability is closely related to the previous two: since governments tended to go spontaneously (i.e., outside the context of a genuine political crisis), the conditions to use the right of dissolution were never really met nor used. This explains why there was only one dissolution under the Fourth Republic in 1955, with a gap of nearly a century since the last one in 1877. The 1955 dissolution was initiated by the President of the Republic, Coty, at the request of the President the Council of Ministers, Faure, for tactical reasons.

Overall, the regime was characterised by a trivialisation of government accountability, further complicated by the difficulty in utilising the right to dissolve the National Assembly. The use of delegated legislation, despite its prohibition under the 1946 Constitution, was also a factor which contributed to perverting the regime. The use of such delegated legislation proved problematic for two reasons: firstly, it was extensively employed through framework laws (known as *lois-cadres*) instead of allowing Parliament to define the limits of government actions; and secondly, it involved the use of decree-laws (referred to as *décrets-lois*) which effectively granted the government the authority to intervene in legislative matters.

Ultimately, the downfall of the Fourth Republic can be attributed to its warped operation. Additionally, it was unable to overcome the strenuous context of the decolonisation wars. While the Mendès France Government (1954–1955) brought, with the hardness associated with war, the Indochina conflict (1946–1954) to a close through the Geneva Agreement in 1954, the Algerian War (1954–1962) tested the regime to its limits. The Algerian independence movement resulted in a civil war that posed a threat to the French regime. A faction of the French military, stationed in Algiers, opposed the idea of independence and rebelled against the government. This unrest led to the creation of a committee of public safety (*comité de salut public*) in May 1958. Because the situation had spiralled out of control, President

Coty made the decision to recall De Gaulle. On 29 May 1958, De Gaulle was appointed President of the Council, receiving approval from the National Assembly under pressure from Coty. Over the next few days, De Gaulle was granted full powers and tasked with finding a resolution to the Algerian crisis. He successfully tackled this challenge by implementing a new regime.

In conclusion, France's constitutional experience is incomparable. From monarchy to empire and eventually to a republic, the French have tried almost everything. They have explored various political and institutional possibilities, experimenting with a presidential regime and later adopting a modified form of parliamentary system during a period dominated by assemblies. They have experienced collective leadership as well as a two-headed executive. The country has also witnessed the proclamation and temporary abandonment of universal suffrage, only to embrace it again later. Examining French history through the lens of its constitutional development reveals the challenges in finding stability amidst turmoil, and the difficulty in distinguishing between events shaped by circumstance and those influenced by individuals' intentions. In other words, it is a captivating account that illustrates the evolution of the country's system of government and the construction of its democracy (see Table 2.2 and Figure 2.1 on political regimes of France since 1789).

There is no agreement as to how many constitutions France has actually experienced. Fourteen seems to be the number, including three during the revolutionary period, three during the Consulate and the Empire, two charters, the Hundred Days Constitution of 1815, and the Constitutions of 1848, 1852, 1875, 1946, and 1958. However, this count includes a couple of constitutions that were never put into effect, such as the Constitution of 1793, or were only in force for a very brief period, such as the Constitution of 1815. Additionally, this tally overlooks the intervals when no constitutional text was in effect, such as the revolutionary government from 1793 to 1794, the provisional governments of 1848 and 1870, and the Vichy regime of 1940, despite its annulment in law.

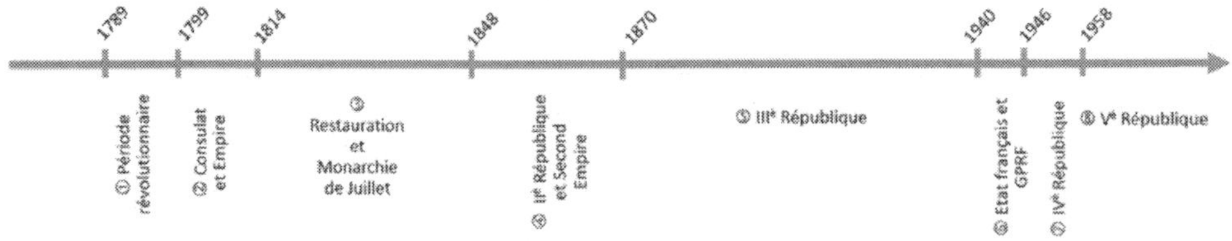

FIGURE 2.1 Political regimes of France since 1789

TABLE 2.2 A summary of the political regimes of France since 1789

Type of regime	*Corresponding constitutions & other constitutional texts*
① **1789–1799**	Constitution of 3 September 1791
Abolition of the monarchy and	Proclamation of the Convention of 20 September 1792
founding of the First Republic	Constitution of 24 June 1793
Directory (*Directoire*)	Constitution of 22 August 1795 (5 Fructidor Year III)
② **1799–1814**	Constitution of 13 December 1790 (22 Frimaire Year VIII)
Consulate (*Consulat*)	Senatus-consultum of 18 May 1804 (28 Floréal Year XII)
Empire	
③ **1814–1848**	Constitutional Charter of 4 June 1814
Restoration	Constitutional Charter of 14 August 1830
July Monarchy	
④ **1848–1870**	Constitution of 4 November 1848
Second Republic	Constitution of 14 January 1852
Second Empire	Senatus-consultum of 7 November 1852
⑤ **1870–1940**	Resolution of 17 February 1871
Third Republic	Law of 31 August 1871 (*Rivet Constitution*)
	Law of 13 March 1873 (*De Broglie Constitution*)
	Constitutional Laws of 24 February, 25 February, and 16 July 1875
⑥ **1940–1946**	Constitutional Law of 10 July 1940 (*Vichy regime*)
French State (*État français*)	Order of 9 August 1944 (*Gaullist regime*)
Provisional Government of the French Republic (*Gouvernement provisoire de la République française*)	Constitutional Law of 2 November 1945
⑦ **1946–1958**	Constitution of 27 October 1946
Fourth Republic	
⑧ **1958–present**	Constitution of 4 October 1958
Fifth Republic	

SELECTED FURTHER READINGS

Pierre **Bodineau** & Michel Verpeaux, *Histoire constitutionnelle de la France* (6th edn, PUF 2020)

Jeannette **Bougrab**, *Aux origines de la Constitution de la IVe République* (Dalloz 2002)

Paul **Bouju** & Henri Dubois, *La Troisième République : 1870–1940* (PUF 2000)

Jean-Félix de **Bujadoux**, *La "Constitution de la III° République"* (LGDJ 2014)

René **Cassin**, "Un coup d'État. La soi-disant constitution de Vichy" (December 1940/January 1941) 1 (2&3) *La France libre* 162 & 252

Dominique **Chagnollaud**, *Histoire constitutionnelle et politique de la France : 1789–1958* (Dalloz 2011)

Jean-Jacques **Chevallier** et alii, *Histoire de la Ve République (1958–2015)* (16th edn, Dalloz 2017)

Gérard **Conac**, Marc Debene & Gérard Teboul (eds), *La Déclaration des droits de l'Homme et du citoyen de 1789* (Economica 1993)

___________, Xavier Prétot & Gérard Teboul (eds), *Le préambule de la Constitution de 1946* (Dalloz 2001)

Ian **Davidson**, *The French Revolution: From Enlightenment to Tyranny* (Profile Books 2016)

Maurice **Duverger**, *Les Constitutions de la France* (14th edn, PUF 2004)

Patrick **Facon**, *La IV République, 1944–1958 : De la Libération au 13 mai* (Pygmalion 1997)

Éric **Gasparini** & Éric Gojosso, *Cours d'introduction historique au droit et d'histoire des institutions* (12th edn, Gualino 2022)

Pascal **Jan**, *Les Constitutions de la France, 1791–1814 : Le temps des expériences (vol 1), Les Constitutions de la France, 1814–1958 : L'établissement du régime parlementaire (vol 2)* (LGDJ 2016)

La Documentation Française, Volume I *Des origines de la loi constitutionnelle du 3 juin 1958 à l'avant-projet du 29 juillet 1958, 1987*; Volume II *Le Comité consultatif constitutionnel : De l'avant-projet du 29 juillet 1958 au projet du 21 août 1958, 1988*; Volume III *Du Conseil d'État au référendum : 20 août–28 septembre 1958, 1991*; Volume IV *Commentaires sur la Constitution (1958–1959)*, 2001.

Alain **Laquièze**, *Les origines du régime parlementaire en France (1814–1848)* (PUF 2002)

Mathieu **Martial**, *Histoire des institutions avant 1789* (2nd edn, LexisNexis 2022)

Marcel **Morabito**, *Histoire constitutionnelle de la France (1789–1958)* (17th edn, LGDJ 2022)

Marie-Luce **Paris**, "Still Alive? Some Observations about the Two-Hundred Years of Existence of the French Code Civil 1804" (2005) 12 *Irish Journal of European Law* 72

Pouvoirs, *1789–1989 Histoire constitutionnelle*, No 50 (PUF 1989)

Stéphanie **Rials**, *Textes constitutionnels français* (PUF 2014)

François **Saint-Bonnet** & Yves Sassier, *Histoire des institutions avant 1789* (7th edn, LGDJ 2022)

Michel **Troper**, *La séparation des pouvoirs et l'histoire constitutionnelle française* (LGDJ 2014)

___________ & Lucien Jaume (eds), *1789 et l'invention de la Constitution* (Bruylant LGDJ 1994)

Serge **Velley**, *Histoire constitutionnelle française de 1789 à nos jours* (3rd edn, Ellipses 2009)

Pierre **Villard** & Louis-Augustin Barrière, *Histoire des institutions publiques de la France de 1789 à nos jours* (11th edn, Dalloz 2020)

PART II
The Fifth Republic

Part II constitutes the main part of this book. It examines the Fifth Republic, which is the current political regime of France. The chapters within this part successively unravel the roots of the French constitutional regime from a historical and legal perspective in Chapter 3, highlight the institutions of the Fifth Republic in Chapter 4, supplemented by insights into political parties, electoral processes, and referendums in Chapter 5. Furthermore, it explores the realm of constitutional justice and the system of rights protection in Chapter 6. Collectively, these chapters paint a comprehensive picture of the current political landscape in France.

DOI: 10.4324/9781003268871-4

3

HISTORICAL AND LEGAL FOUNDATIONS OF THE FIFTH REPUBLIC

The Fifth Republic is the political system currently in force in France. It came into effect with the adoption of the Constitution on 4 October 1958 (hereafter the Constitution), which set the foundation for a parliamentary regime. However, over the course of its 60-plus years of existence, this regime has transformed into a hybrid or mixed system with elements of a presidential regime. To fully grasp the main characteristics and evolution of the Fifth Republic, this chapter delves into its origins and sources of inspiration.[1]

Origins and Sources of Inspiration

> « *D'emblée, la Vème République se trouve placée sous le signe de la rupture et de la continuité.* »[2]

The Fifth Republic was born out of a specific historical context linked to the instability of the previous Republics and the pressing events of the Algerian War. The collapse of the Fourth Republic and, concomitantly, the return of De Gaulle to power led to the adoption of the Constitution in 1958. This section explains how the Constitution was adopted and what is the spirit that supports it.

The adoption of the Constitution of 4 October 1958

The return of De Gaulle to power occurred in the context of the Algerian crisis. What was first qualified as the "Algerian events," but eventually acknowledged as the "Algerian War," had

1 These developments partly draw from Marie-Luce Paris, *Constitutional Law in France*, International Encyclopaedia of Laws (2nd edn, Wolters Kluwer 2024) 33–44 (paras 24–53).

2 Frédéric Rouvillois, *Droit constitutionnel : La Vème République* (4th edn, Flammarion 2014) 31 [From the outset, the Fifth Republic was characterised by both a break from the past and a seamless continuation of certain aspects].

DOI: 10.4324/9781003268871-5

been unfolding since 1954 when a group of Algerian separatists formed the National Liberation Front and engaged in an open conflict with the French army. This subsection explains the unfolding of the Algerian events, ultimately leading to the enactment of the Constitution in 1958. Furthermore, it examines the various influences that shaped the Constitution.

The Algerian War and the return of De Gaulle to power. After the fall of the Gaillard Government in April 1958, a new government presided by Pflimlin was formed. The Pflimlin Government was supposedly more open than its predecessor to finding an acceptable solution to the Algerian troubles. The earlier trigger to this governmental crisis was a specific event that took place at the border between Tunisia and Algeria, namely the bombing of the small village of Sakiet Sidi Youssef in February 1958 that killed many civilians. The bombing was decided by the French military forces as a reprisal for the actions of the Algerian National Liberation Front. This event provoked a major diplomatic incident with Tunisia. In addition to international repercussions, it led to an internal crisis within the French Government.[3] As Pflimlin was waiting to obtain confirmation of his nomination as the new President of the Council, the situation further degenerated on 13 May 1958 when a number of civilians and military, in favour of maintaining Algeria in the French Republic, stormed the government headquarters in Algiers and provoked an uprising. The rioters were led by General Massu, a supporter of De Gaulle but strongly committed to maintaining Algeria as part of France. Massu's determination to impose a change of policy kind of swarmed everywhere, including to Corsica. The fact that Corsica joined the insurrection was significant at the time because it meant that the crisis could potentially reach mainland France and trigger a civil war in the country. The military coup thus called for an immediate response by the French Government, leading to intense negotiations primarily led by De Gaulle. Immediately positioning himself at the centre of the negotiations, De Gaulle declared, on 15 May 1958, that he was "ready to assume the powers of the Republic" and added, on 27 May, that he had started "the process required to establish a regular republican power in order to ensure the unity and the independence of the country."[4] Despite having the support of the majority in Parliament, the Pflimlin Government resigned on 28 May. President Coty had then no other choice than to call back "the most famous of the French" ("*le plus illustre des Français*"). Coty's support for De Gaulle's return to power was evident since Coty had indicated that he would resign if this was not accepted by the National Assembly. On 1 June 1958,[5] De Gaulle, approved by the National Assembly,[6] became the new Head of Government (and would be the last of the Fourth Republic). All political parties were represented in the new government, bar the Communists. The De Gaulle Government comprised only members of the old regime, most of them Socialists and excluding the Communists. There was also a representative from Africa, Félix Houphouët-Boigny, future President of the Ivory Coast, whose support for a smooth decolonising transition with

3 Jacques Valette, "The Bombing of Sakhiet Sidi Youssef in 1958 and the Complexity of the Algerian War" (2009) 233 (1) *Guerres mondiales et conflits contemporains* 37.

4 This was pure bluff from De Gaulle, who was looking to coax the military as well as nudge the Pflimlin Government to resign.

5 The indication of the dates is significant here since it reveals the rapidity of the unfolding events.

6 The vote was 329 in favour and 224 against.

the "*ensemble français*" appealed to De Gaulle. The return of De Gaulle to power reportedly meant a return to law and order.[7]

The constitutional law of 3 June 1958 and the adoption of the 1958 Constitution. By adopting the constitutional law of 3 June 1958, the French Parliament granted the government the authority to issue ordinances in order to restore domestic order.[8] However, this deviated from the standard procedure for amending the Constitution as laid out in the 1946 Constitution, as the 1958 Laws also bestowed the De Gaulle Government with the power to modify the Constitution itself. This transfer of powers was not absolute, though, because of the still recent episode of the controversial transfer of powers to Pétain in 1940. While the comparison between the transfers of powers in 1940 and 1958 may be historically open to debate,[9] the transfer of power to De Gaulle in 1958 was subject to several conditions, both in terms of content and procedural requirements.

In terms of substantive conditions, De Gaulle committed to respecting five principles of government in the exercise of political power, namely to guarantee the right of universal suffrage as the sole source of sovereignty, to respect the separation between the executive and the legislative powers, to respect the principle of responsible government, to guarantee the independence of the judiciary, and to provide for the organisation of new relationships with the associated peoples of the overseas territories.

In terms of formal commitments, De Gaulle accepted to follow three procedural steps concerning the drafting and final approval of the constitutional text: firstly, he committed to obtain the approval of a consultative committee composed of two-thirds of members of Parliament; secondly, he agreed to consult the Council of State before submitting the constitutional draft to the Council of Ministers; and, thirdly, he made it clear that the approved text was to be put to a referendum. The detailed stages of the process were the following. A preliminary draft was produced by the government within a working group comprising members of the Council of State, working under the authority of Debré, the minister for Justice. The draft was discussed and revised by a joint ministerial committee comprising state ministers (i.e., the main leaders of the Fourth Republic), the minister for Justice, and the vice-president of the Council of State (Cassin). The draft was then approved by a Cabinet Council chaired by De Gaulle in July 1958. The approved draft was submitted to the Advisory Constitutional Committee comprising 39 members, including 26 members of Parliament and 13 personalities appointed by the government, among them a law professor (Waline).[10] Finally, after the advisory opinion of the Council of State obtained at the end of August 1958, the text was approved by the Council of Ministers on 3 September 1958.

7 Frédéric Rouvillois, *Droit constitutionnel : La Vème République* (4th edn, Flammarion 2014) 38.

8 Constitutional Law of 3 June 1958 providing for a transitional derogation from the provisions of article 90 of the [1946] Constitution and providing for a referendum, as complemented by Law No 58-520 of 3 June 1958 relating to the full powers [granted to the De Gaulle Government for a duration of six months].

9 The 1940 delegation of powers was quite vague and only required the Pétain Government to guarantee rights as regards work, family, and the country, the infamous official motto "*Travail, Famille, Patrie*." One may note the irony of asking members of Parliament to proceed to give another delegation of the constituent power, this time to De Gaulle, just a few years after the very same members of Parliament had been vilified for giving their approval to Pétain.

10 The debates of the Advisory Constitutional Committee were never fully made public, except for the parts that were later published by the *Documentation Française*.

The entire process of drafting and implementing a new regime took a mere four months (3 June 1958–4 October 1958). This is notably short when compared to the significantly longer time frames required for the adoption of the 1875 Constitutional Laws and the 1946 Constitution. However, this is hardly surprising since the drafting of the Constitution was conducted secretly within government and expert committees, whereas the previous constitutions were extensively debated in Parliament.[11] On 4 September 1958, De Gaulle formally presented the constitutional project to the French people in a public address at the Place de la République in Paris.[12] He proclaimed:

> The French nation will flourish or perish depending on whether or not the state will have enough strength, consistency, prestige, to lead it where it needs to go.

De Gaulle had always made it clear that, if he were to come back, it would be to install a new regime or, at least, a regime devoid of the defects of the previous ones. Still, the referendum campaign revealed the many factions that opposed the constitutional draft, namely the Communist Party, the far left, the far right, and part of the Socialists. Among the dissenting voices were Mendès France and Mitterrand, on the left, and Poujade, on the right. The referendum on the Constitution was of course connoted as a plebiscite for or against De Gaulle. However, the French people massively approved the text on 28 September 1958. The participation rate was 85%. The "Yes" vote represented 79.25%, at 80.1% in mainland France and even higher in Algeria (96.5%) and all the overseas departments (93%).[13] The Constitution was then promulgated on 4 October 1958 by Coty, as Head of State, with the countersignature of De Gaulle, as Head of Government. A span of four months was necessary for the installation of the new institutions, which the government did by way of ordinances and several organic laws.[14] The two-round first-past-the-post electoral system was used for the legislative elections of November 1958. The elections were won by the Union for the New Republic (*Union pour la Nouvelle République* or *UNR*), a political party established to support De Gaulle's actions and to federate moderate political factions around him. In December 1958, De Gaulle won the presidential election against two left-wing candidates with 78.5% of the votes cast in his favour. He became the first President of the Fifth Republic.[15]

The sources of inspiration of the 1958 Constitution. The sources of inspiration of the Constitution are diverse. They stem from its main instigator, De Gaulle, and from other key figures. In his speech delivered in the town of Bayeux on 16 June 1946, De Gaulle had given the outline of the type of constitution that he thought was needed for France at the

11 This also explains why, contrary to a well-established rule in republican regimes, the debates and *travaux préparatoires* of the draft Constitution were not immediately and fully officially published.

12 The date and place are symbolic as they marked the anniversary of the proclamation of the Republic on 4 September 1870.

13 The vote held for the overseas territories held a deeper significance beyond the Constitution itself. It encompassed the decision of whether to maintain their connection with France and the French Community. Only Guinea chose to depart from its French ties by voting "No" and became independent thereafter.

14 The government passed quite a number of these ordinances—nearly 300—that went far beyond the organic laws.

15 On whether the Constitution adopted in 1958 actually established the Fifth Republic, see Christophe Chabrot, "Ceci n'est pas une Vème République" (2010) 82 (2) *Revue française de droit constitutionnel* 257.

time (see Box 3.1 The 1946 Bayeux Speech).[16] In reaction to the absolutism of Parliament and the general weaknesses of the previous regimes, De Gaulle considered that it was critical to strengthen the role of the executive power. The President of the Republic ought to fulfil such a role by acting as the "arbiter" between public powers. It also meant that the President of the Republic was to be regarded as a kind of "outsider" detached from political manoeuvring and endowed with the task of representing the continuity of the regime. On this point, De Gaulle was quite inclined to adopt the US model of presidential regime, as was Debré for a while. The idea never took root, though, and the leaders felt that they could not commit to such a radical step. Passing from a fairly rooted parliamentary tradition to a presidential regime would also have been interpreted by the left as a "Bonapartist" move from De Gaulle, too hard to swallow for the Socialists whose support De Gaulle needed.[17] Nevertheless, the drafters did not depart from the vision of a strong executive at the helm of a strong state. This basic tenet was eventually translated into several constitutional provisions entrusting the Head of State with significant powers. This would translate into, for example in normal times, the right of the President of the Republic to dissolve the National Assembly, and, in times of crisis, the doctrine of emergency powers, later embodied under article 16 of the Constitution on exceptional powers. Other instigators of the 1958 Constitution provided inputs of a more technical nature. For example, Debré, a close ally of De Gaulle, refined the organisation of parliamentary work and put it under the direction of the government. Debré also imposed his ideas as regards the legislative and regulatory powers whose demarcation would be entrusted to the newly created Constitutional Council. As for former Presidents of the Council, notably Mollet and Pfimlin, who both later became ministers under De Gaulle's presidency, they contributed to the reform of government responsibility and of delegated legislation.

The result was a text of compromise. While a compromise has the advantage of accommodating a number of views, it is also problematic because it meant that the constitutional text was susceptible to several interpretations. While De Gaulle managed to incorporate most of his conceptions on the role of the Head of State, and Debré most of his on rationalised parliamentarism, some vagueness about the Constitution has remained to date. This vagueness concerns primarily the articulation between the parliamentary nature of the regime and its "strong state" dimension. This concerns in particular two sets of relationships, namely the relationship between the two heads of the executive (i.e., the President of the Republic and the Prime Minister), on the one hand, and the relationship between the executive power and the legislative power, on the other hand. Moreover, the mode of designation of the President of the Republic and the composition of the Senate were still in debate and remained open matters at the time. The first years of the regime, under the Debré Government (January 1959–April 1962) up until the end of the first Pompidou Government (April–November 1962), shaped what can be termed

16 The famous speeches of De Gaulle are Bayeux Speech, 16 June 1946; Epinal Speech, 29 September 1946; Strasbourg Speech, 7 April 1947; *Place de la République* Speech, 4 September 1958.

17 The President of the Republic was indirectly elected at the time by an electoral college comprising approximately 80,000 voters. The idea of a President elected by direct universal suffrage was considered with great caution, primarily due to the influential presence of the Communist Party within the political arena at that time. Furthermore, implementing such a direct election would have involved voters from the Franco-African community. The reform of the designation of the President of the Republic is addressed in Chapter 4 on the institutions of the Fifth Republic. The subject of the presidential election itself is discussed in Chapter 5 on political parties, elections, and referendums.

the "classical configuration" of the Fifth Republic.[18] Several constitutional amendments as well as constitutional practice have subsequently clarified some of the ambiguities surrounding the Constitution, hereby contributing to a better grasp of its interpretation.

BOX 3.1 THE 1946 BAYEUX SPEECH

☛ "In our glorious and mutilated Normandy, Bayeux and its surroundings witnessed one of the greatest events in history. We testify that [these events] were worthy. It is here that, four years after the initial disaster for France and the Allies, the final victory of the Allies and of France began, it is here that the effort of those who had never yielded and around whom, from 18 June 1940, the national instinct has rallied and the French power has reformed, drew its decisive justification from events.

At the same time, it is here that, on the soil of the ancestors, the State reappeared. The legitimate State because it rested on the interest and the sentiment of the nation (...).

It is true that public powers are only valid in fact and in law if they are in line with the country's best interests, if they are based on the confident support of citizens. When it comes to institutions, building on anything else would be building on sand. It would be a risk of seeing the edifice collapse once again during one of those crises to which, by the nature of things, our country is so often exposed.

This is why, once the salvation of the State was assured in the victory won, and national unity maintained, the urgent and essential task above all was the establishment of new French institutions (...).

There is, moreover, for us, a question of life or death, in the world and in the century we live in, where the position, the independence and even the existence of our country and our French Union are indeed at stake.

Certainly, it is of the very essence of democracy that opinions are expressed and that they strive through suffrage to guide public action and legislation. But also, all the principles and all the experiences require that the public powers—legislative, executive, judicial—be clearly separated and strongly balanced, and that above political contingencies be established a national arbitration which asserts continuity in the middle of combinations (...).

It is therefore from the Head of State, placed above the [political] parties, elected by a college which includes Parliament, but much broader and composed in such a way as to make him the president of the French Union at the same time as that of the [French] Republic, that the executive power must emanate.

Let us be lucid and strong enough to give ourselves and to observe rules for the life of our nation which tend to bring us together when, relentlessly, we are inclined to divide ourselves! Our entire history is the alternation of the immense pains of a dispersed people, and the fruitful greatness of a free nation grouped under the aegis of a strong State."

De Gaulle, 16 June 1946, Bayeux (excerpts)

18 Frédéric Rouvillois, *Droit constitutionnel : La Vème République* (4th edn, Flammarion 2014) 50.

The spirit of the Constitution of 4 October 1958

De Gaulle coined the famous phrase about what it is that a constitution covers, namely "a spirit, institutions, and practice."[19] While subsequent chapters address the institutions and constitutional practice of the Fifth Republic, it is important to briefly touch upon the essence or "spirit" of the Constitution. The main goal of the constituent power was to establish an effective system that would stand the test of time. However, the practical application of the constitution has continuously tested the fundamental principles of the Fifth Republic. This subsection deals with these two points, namely the efficacy and durability of the Constitution, as well as instances where its spirit has been transgressed.

Efficacy and durability of the Constitution. The spirit of a constitution, in its Gaullist interpretation, relates to the "guiding idea, the driving principle, animator and organiser of a rule or a system [or constitution]."[20] Besides, the spirit of such rule, system, or constitution, only exists in so far as the instigator of the said rule, system, or constitution—the constituent power in this case—has a determined, coherent, and unambiguous project in mind.[21] In the case of the Fifth Republic, De Gaulle described its spirit "as arising from the necessity to ensure the efficacy, stability and accountability of public powers,"[22] all traits that were missing under the previous regimes. De Gaulle also had strong ideas as regards the legislative power, which, in his opinion, ought not be influenced too much by political parties. For De Gaulle, power was not about partisanship but about the nation, thus implying that the Head of State, elected by the people, would be the only source and holder of such power. De Gaulle had articulated these ideas in his 1946 Bayeux Speech, thus prefiguring the constitutional principles that he would put in place in 1958. These constitutional principles were reaffirmed on different occasions up until De Gaulle left power in 1969. Another consideration was to ensure continuity with the symbols and principles that were in force under the previous regimes. However, as practice will prove, this will contrast with ways in which to implement these in the new regime. According to Debré, the task of the constituent power was, at the time, "to try rebuild a power without which there is no state, no democracy, that is, in our situation, no France nor Republic."[23] Still, adhering to the spirit of the Constitution was not, by any means, a way to rigidify it, for, if a constitution is to last, it must evolve. The evolution of a constitution may occur in conformity with its spirit. For example, the 1962 constitutional amendment that changed the mode of designation of the President of the Republic from indirect to direct universal suffrage was certainly made in conformity with the spirit of the Constitution.[24] Because the President of the Republic is the guardian of constitutional principles, s/he is the key figure of the French

19 De Gaulle, Press Conference of 31 January 1964 in *Discours et messages* (Plon 1970) 168.

20 Frédéric Rouvillois, *Droit constitutionnel : La Vème République* (4th edn, Flammarion 2014) 10.

21 Ibid 10–11.

22 Ibid 13.

23 As cited in Frédéric Rouvillois, *Droit constitutionnel : La Vème République* (4th edn, Flammarion 2014) 47.

24 Ibid 17.

political regime and should be in a position to ensure its smooth running and, in principle, prevent any setback.

The spirit transgressed, or discontent about the Fifth Republic. Discontent with the regime of the Fifth Republic appeared early on and has not disappeared, far from it. The spirit of the Constitution has gradually been denatured by institutional practice, thus breaking the peculiar logic of the regime and provoking a "*malaise dans la Constitution.*"[25] Institutional practice, in particular the phenomenon of cohabitation and the increasing importance of judicial review, has arguably damaged the logic of the regime. Cohabitation in particular has been the "most radical transgression of the spirit of the Fifth Republic."[26] Cohabitation allows the President of the Republic whose majority has lost the general elections to stay in place, which is in contradiction with the idea of a continuity, in the power line, between the majority in Parliament, the President of the Republic, and the Prime Minister appointed by the President. Cohabitation has resulted in installing an executive dyarchy (i.e., President and Prime Minister of different political hues) in which the Head of State, who is supposed to be the strong figurehead of the state, is de facto dispossessed of his/her powers. Besides, the centre of political power switches back to Parliament, the National Assembly in particular, and makes political parties the masters of the political game, which is exactly what De Gaulle had sought to avoid. As for the increasing importance of judicial review, this mainly concerns the increased role of the Constitutional Council.[27] The Council reviews, including at the initiative of members of Parliament, the conformity of laws to the Constitution and to its Preamble. This type of constitutional review amounts to placing political matters under the scrutiny of a non-elected body that has the power to interpret the Constitution. Still, the Council is not, constitutionally speaking, the "guardian of the Constitution"—the President is (article 5 paragraph one of the Constitution).[28] Making an analogy with the development of the role of the Council of State, one may question this type of "legal coup" (*coup d'état juridique*) as regards the spirit of the Constitution, however beneficial such a development might be for the rule of law.[29]

There are other explanations for the transgression of the spirit of the Constitution. These lie in the frequency of constitutional amendments, on the one hand, and on the encroachments on several principles, on the other hand, all having contributed to altering the original institutional balance of the Constitution. While it is agreed that a constitution must evolve, a constitution should also represent an element of stability in the institutional setup. The acceleration of constitutional amendments since the early 1990s has somehow undermined such

25 Ibid 18 et seq.

26 Ibid 20. Cohabitation is addressed in Chapter 4 on the institutions of the Fifth Republic.

27 Ibid 21. Rouvillois also highlights the establishment of the Court of Justice of the Republic competent to adjudicate the criminal actions committed by government officials. Additionally, provisions pertaining to the responsibility of the President of the Republic (articles 67 and 68 of the Constitution) were introduced. These measures indicate a shift towards a judicial approach in the realm of politics, or a judicialisation of political life. While this may be seen as positive, it contradicts the principle of political responsibility embedded within the institutions of the Fifth Republic. Furthermore, it disregards the distinction between political and non-political matters, despite their inherent differences in nature and concerns.

28 Article 5 paragraph one of the Constitution: "The President of the Republic shall ensure respect for this Constitution. He shall ensure, under his arbitration, the normal operation of public powers as well as the continuity of the State..."

29 Frédéric Rouvillois, *Droit constitutionnel : La Vème République* (4th edn, Flammarion 2014) 20.

stability. If only these constitutional amendments had been necessary to improve the visibility and clarity of constitutional principles, but that has not always been the case. For example, the amendments concerning the Superior Council of the Judiciary or the Court of Justice of the Republic were adopted hastily without really settling the matter. Besides, most of the constitutional amendments were adopted by Congress, a special formation of Parliament, and not by referendum, which questions the power of the French people over their basic law. As rightly put by Rouvillois, constitutional amendments are not regarded as the ultimate stage towards restoring stability anymore. Rather, they have somehow become steps towards an "unknown path."[30] Some of these amendments merely reacted to a Constitutional Council ruling as a way to bypass legal obstacles, while other proposed amendments stand as examples of pure political opportunism. For example, the attempt by Macron to introduce the guarantee of "the protection of the environment and biological diversity" and the fight "against climate change" in article 1 of the Constitution, on the basis of the recommendations made by the Citizens' Convention on Climate (October 2019–June 2020), has been regarded as useless. The constitutional amendment was supposed to be adopted by referendum in 2021 but was subsequently dropped due to various contingencies. All in all, the successive amendments of the Constitution, even the marginal ones, have substantially contributed to eroding its prestige, even more so in a context where the sovereignty of the State is challenged both by internal (i.e., decentralisation) and external forces (i.e., Europeanisation) that have also involved their lot of constitutional amendments. In that context, how can the state still be strong? That can indeed be considered as negating the spirit of the Constitution.

The increased criticism of the regime comes, in the first place, from the citizens. The spirit of the Constitution partly lay in the promise of resorting to "participatory democracy" with elements of direct democracy such as the referendum. However, in contrast with Ireland for example, the referendum has never been extensively used under the Fifth Republic, hereby depriving the French people of the possibility of exercising their constituent power. The exercise of power rests in partisan politics and is backed by a number of non-elected technocratic and judicial bodies. Besides, citizens have become disillusioned with their government and their representatives in Parliament as demonstrated by a strong abstentionist trend in most elections and referendums.[31] However, there has also been in recent years a demand to reconnect the French people with their civic duties and with political life, sometimes in a quite radical form. For example, the claim to establish a referendum at the initiative of the citizens (*référendum d'initiative citoyenne* or *RIC*) was emblematic of the Yellow Vests movement, which erupted in November 2018 in a context of extreme political tension and general social discontent.[32] The establishment of two citizens' assemblies, namely the Citizens' Convention on Climate (October 2019–June 2020) and the Citizens' Convention on the End of Life (December 2022–April 2023), were the government's response to address claims for more citizen participation. It remains to be seen how, in the long term, these innovative experiences of deliberative

30 Ibid 22.

31 One good example is the 2000 referendum concerning the extension of the presidential term to five years, where an overwhelming 70% of individuals abstained from participating.

32 The Yellow Vests protests erupted in November 2018 and ended in March 2020. This marked the initial stage of the movement. Then, in September 2020, the second phase of protests recommenced. The initial lockdown imposed due to the Covid-19 pandemic temporarily halted the protests, which sporadically resumed thereafter.

democracy will be perceived by the citizens and if they usefully complement representative democracy.

Criticism of the Fifth Republic also emerges from within the government itself. Members of the government have played a significant role in reshaping the balance of power through constitutional amendments and political practices. It is not a matter of saying that this has been good or bad, but rather to highlight how they have altered the original balance envisioned by the framers of the Constitution. The fact remains that such criticism has progressively gained more traction from both ends of the political spectrum, prompting legitimate considerations regarding the potential replacement of the current regime with a new Republic.

While the adoption of a Sixth Republic might still be seen as a distant possibility, the existence of a debate surrounding it is undeniable.[33] This debate revolves around two main options: the first being a steadfast commitment to a parliamentary system, and the second being the adoption of a genuine presidential system, which would involve abandoning the Prime Minister's office, the principle of government accountability to Parliament, and the ability to dissolve the National Assembly. However, what has prevailed until now is the "theory of the two interpretations of the Constitution," wherein the Constitution can be understood through either a presidentialist lens or a parliamentary one. Nevertheless, given the intricacies of the political decision-making process, the reconfiguration of political parties beyond traditional left–right divisions, and the overall evolution of politics, this current state of affairs may no longer be deemed satisfactory.

Main Features and Evolution of the Regime

> *« Un des caractères essentiels de la Constitution de la Vème République, c'est qu'elle donne une tête à l'État. »*[34]

When examining the key features of the Fifth Republic, one might be inclined to draw comparisons between the current regime and its historical counterparts by considering the various political systems that have existed in France since 1789. For example, an analogy can be drawn between the Fifth Republic and the Consulate regime or the Orleanist regime. The Consulate serves as a fitting comparison due to the implicit pre-eminence it affords to the instigator of the Constitution. In a way, one could rephrase the famous quote "What's in the Constitution [of the Consulate]? There is Bonaparte" and apply it to the Fifth Republic by asking, "What's in the 1958 Constitution? There is De Gaulle." The Orleanist regime can also serve as an apt comparison because of the parallel between the Monarch/Prime Minister dynamic, represented by King Louis-Philippe and Prime Minister Guizot at that time, and the current dual leadership system of the President of the Republic/Prime Minister. This parallel refers to the two sources of legitimacy, namely the Gaullist legitimacy and the democratic legitimacy.

The reality is that the regime instituted by the Constitution of the Fifth Republic cannot be compared to anything previously in place. The regime is without precedent in French constitutional history, and it does not fit any, parliamentary or presidential, category.[35] As

33 Julie Benetti, "Le mythe de la sixième République" (2018) 166 (3) *Pouvoirs* 139.

34 De Gaulle (1890–1970), President of the Republic (1958–1965; 1965–1969) [One of the essential characteristics of the Constitution of the Fifth Republic is that it gives a head to the state].

35 Jean-Jacques Chevallier et alii, *Histoire de la Ve République (1958–2015)* (15th edn, Dalloz 2015) 40.

straightforwardly put by De Gaulle at the time: "Let's say, if you want our Constitution to be parliamentary and presidential at the same time … ."[36] Such a statement made sense because of the two-fold underlying concern at the time. Firstly, the presidential traits were supposed to allow a tailored regime suited to the historical figure that was De Gaulle.[37] Secondly, it was important to envisage a functioning regime in the longer term. This meant that the regime should function without completely relying on its main instigator and should be able to offer a more normal kind of parliamentary regime at some point. In any case, the Constitution represents a new approach to the parliamentary regime. While strict limits are defined vis-à-vis the legislative power, the regime contributes to reinforcing the autonomy and scope of action of the executive power.

The principles of the Fifth Republic

The Fifth Republic is based on several key principles that can be categorised into two types: the foundational principles of the state and the principles governing government.[38] The foundational principles, found in the preamble of the Constitution and its first title on sovereignty, have been inherited from previous constitutions, indicating a sense of continuity with the previous regimes. On the other hand, the principles governing the government mark a distinct departure from the practices of the previous regimes.

Foundational principles of the state. Any regime is built on certain principles and values, and the Fifth Republic is no exception. Traditional republican values of the previous regimes were reprised through the reaffirmation of the protection of human rights, on the one hand, and the promotion of the republican social order, on the other hand. The 1958 Preamble proclaims the attachment of the French people to human rights and to the principle of national sovereignty as defined in the 1789 Declaration, the preamble to the 1946 Constitution (1946 Preamble), and the 2004 Charter for the Environment (2004 Charter).[39] In addition to the 1958 Preamble, the first article of the Constitution defines the essential characteristics of the French state: "France is an indivisible, secular, democratic and social Republic. [The Republic] shall ensure the equality of all citizens under the law regardless of origin, race or religion."[40] The following developments

36 De Gaulle, Press Conference, 11 April 1961 as cited in Jean-Jacques Chevallier et alii, *Histoire de la Ve République (1958–2015)* (15th edn, Dalloz 2015) 41.

37 A contingent element was that De Gaulle was about to deal with immediate pressing issues, notably the Algerian crisis.

38 This division borrows from Robert Debbasch, *Droit constitutionnel* (13th edn, LexisNexis 2021).

39 The 2004 Charter was added by Constitutional Law No 2005-205 of 1 March 2005 on the Charter for the Environment.

40 The rest of the provision reads as follows: "[The Republic] shall respect all beliefs. Its organisation is decentralised. The law shall promote equal access for women and men to electoral mandates and elective functions, as well as equal access to professional and social responsibilities."

examine, in turn, the principle of respect for human rights, the principle of indivisibility of the Republic, and the democratic and social features of the Republic.

Respect for human rights, including environmental rights. The protection of human rights has been a foundational value ever since the 1789 Declaration,[41] a value reprised by all subsequent republican regimes. The effective constitutional value of the 1789 Declaration was recognised much later, though, when constitutional judicial review eventually emerged under the Fifth Republic (see below). The 1789 Declaration protects several principles such as the principle of national sovereignty; the principle of the separation of powers; the democratic and protective character of the law, as well as its binding force; the principle of equal taxation of citizens based on their capabilities; the equal access of citizens to public employment; and the principle of accountability of public administration. The 1789 Declaration also guarantees seminal rights including the right to liberty, the right to equality (i.e., equality before the law), the right to property, freedom of opinion, freedom of expression, and freedom of religion. All these principles, rights, and freedoms contributed to putting an end to the exercise of arbitrary power. The 1946 Preamble reaffirms the 1789 principles as well as the so-called the "Fundamental Principles recognised by the Laws of the Republic" (*principes fondamentaux reconnus par les lois de la République*). It also proclaims new principles called "Principles of Law Particularly Necessary to Our Time" (*principes particulièrement nécessaires à notre temps*) such as the principle of equality between men and women, the right to asylum, the right to a livelihood, trade-union rights, the right to strike, the right to health, the right to instruction and culture etc. The content of all these principles has been progressively defined by the Constitutional Council's case law (see below). The attachment of the French regime to environmental rights is affirmed under the 2004 Charter, whose provisions have constitutional value under the 1958 Preamble. The 2004 Charter's thrust is that the future of humankind is indissociable from its natural habitat and that the preservation of the environment is as much a goal to attain as are the other fundamental interests of the nation. According to the 2004 Charter, public policies must promote sustainable development and protect biological diversity against certain harmful production and consumption modes, as well as against the excessive exploitation of natural resources. The 2004 Charter also contains provisions on the precautionary principle that must guide public policy actions and guard against any unnecessary risk to the environment. Lastly, the 2004 Charter promotes the necessity to provide education about the environment. Overall, the 2004 Charter inspires the actions of France at both European and international levels.

The principle of indivisibility of the Republic. Since 1789, the principle of indivisibility of the Republic has been a traditional principle of French constitutional law. It holds constitutional value and is enshrined in the first article of the current Constitution. Rooted in the historical notion of national sovereignty, this principle carries dual significance.

41 The 1791 Constitution recognised the constitutional value of the 1789 Declaration. However, this was short-lived. Besides, this would have been limited due to the absence of constitutional review at the time.

Firstly, the principle is attached to the *territory* of the Republic.[42] By stating that the French Republic is indivisible, the Constitution affirms the unitary character of the state. The French territory, comprising mainland France and the nearby islands including Corsica, cannot be divided or dismembered. Local authorities cannot be granted normative powers which are normally attributed to the legislature by the Constitution, save under the specific limits authorised by decentralisation and territorial administration. The unity of the legislative power over the territory of the Republic, and the powers attributed to Parliament and the government, must be preserved.[43] Moreover, although "the law can lay down the conditions for the autonomy of the administration of local authorities, it is subject to preserving the prerogatives of the central state."[44] The Constitutional Council specified that these prerogatives cannot be restricted or deprived of effect, even temporarily.[45] However, indivisibility and decentralisation are not incompatible, and France has a long tradition of de-concentration and decentralisation as shown by the organisation of local administration and local government. On the basis of the process of devolution and empowerment of local authorities initiated in 1982, the major 2003 constitutional amendment qualified the unitary form of the state by allowing for the decentralised organisation of the Republic in the following terms: "France is an indivisible, secular, democratic and social Republic. [The Republic] shall ensure the equality of all citizens under the law regardless of origin, race or religion. [The Republic] shall respect all beliefs. *Its organisation is decentralised* (emphasis added)."[46] Decentralisation, as a constitutional principle, does not challenge the unity of the Republic because decentralisation is still clearly different from federalism.

Secondly, the principle of indivisibility is linked to the French *people*. It follows that any dissociation of the people into specific communities, whether locally based or ethnicity based, cannot be envisaged.[47] In other words, the French people are "a unit incapable of any subdivision by law."[48] Moreover, the principle of indivisibility of the Republic is opposed to the recognition of collective rights to a group as defined by a community of origin, culture, language, or belief. This was decided in relation to the 1999 European Charter for Regional or Minority Languages, which was regarded as incompatible with the Constitution in two respects: firstly, by conferring specific rights on "groups of speakers" of regional or minority languages, within "territories" in which these languages are practised, the 1999 Charter undermines the constitutional principles of indivisibility of the Republic and of the French people, as well as of equality before the law. Secondly, the provisions of the 1999 Charter are also regarded as

42 The territorial organisation of France is quite intricate, as it relies on multiple tiers of local authorities that possess diverse and distinct powers. For more details on the territorial organisation of France, see Marie-Luce Paris, *Constitutional Law in France*, International Encyclopaedia of Laws (2nd edn, Wolters Kluwer 2024) 35–36 (paras 31–33), and 181–220 (paras 320–399).

43 Decision No 91-290 DC of 9 May 1991 *Loi portant statut de la collectivité territoriale de Corse*, pt 15.

44 Decision No 82-137 DC of 25 February 1982 *Loi relative aux droits et libertés des communes, des départements et des régions*, pt 4.

45 Ibid.

46 The rest of the provision reads as follows: "The law shall promote equal access for women and men to electoral mandates and elective functions, as well as equal access to professional and social responsibilities."

47 Decision No 2007-557 DC of 15 November 2007 *Loi relative à la maîtrise de l'immigration, à l'intégration et à l'asile* in which the Constitutional Council ruled on the unconstitutionality of a provision of the law on immigration authorising the collection of data on the ethnic origin and race of individuals.

48 Decision No 91-290 DC of 9 May 1991 *Loi portant statut de la collectivité territoriale de Corse*, pt 11.

contrary to article 2 of the Constitution on the French language in that they tend to recognise a right to use a language other than French not only in "private life" but also in "public life."[49] This explains why the 1999 Charter, while signed by France, has not been ratified yet. The French Republic recognises and protects rights only as regards citizens and not groups. In that regard, the principle of indivisibility is indissociable from the principle of equality of all citizens before the law without any distinction based on origin, race, or religion (article 1 of the Constitution). In other words, the constitutionally protected principle of indivisibility of its territory and of its population allows France to deal with any discrimination based on ethnic, racial, or religious grounds.

The principle of secularism (*laïcité*). France is a secular country, meaning that it does not establish any link between political power and any religious power whatsoever. Although its origin hails from various landmarks since the 1789 Revolution, the principle of secularism is generally regarded as embodied, although not mentioned expressly, in the Law of 9 December 1905 concerning the separation of Church and State (see Figure 3.1 French laicity: A timeline).[50] Often controversial in its application because often misunderstood, the thrust of secularism *à la française* or laicity (*laïcité*)[51] lies in four main legal principles: the principle of separation of state and religion; the principle of neutrality of the state; the principle of freedom of conscience; and the principle of equality and non-discrimination.[52] Laicity is indeed primarily a legal concept, distinct from any philosophical or political conception that can be proposed or advocated. In its 2004 report, the Council of State gave the following definition that best encapsulates the idea of laicity:

> [t]he principle of laicity is three-fold, namely the principles of neutrality of the state, of freedom of religion, and of respect of pluralism.[53]

These principles, albeit differently termed in our examination, are developed below. The principle of separation of state and religion means that public authority is not based on religion (anymore). However, laicity is not secularisation of society but secularisation of the political sphere where state decisions are taken on the basis of accessible and universal considerations

49 Decision No 99-412 DC of 15 June 1999 *Charte européenne des langues régionales ou minoritaires*. Only the objectives and general principles set out in the 1999 Charter in its preamble and in its part II were found unconstitutional. The other commitments of practical scope entered into by France in part III of the Charter relating to education, justice, administrative authorities and public services, the media, cultural activities and facilities, economic and social life, and cross-border exchanges, were ruled compatible with the Constitution.

50 Law of 9 December 1905 concerning the separation of Church and State.

51 The word *laïcité* comes from the Latin *laicus*, which means "common" or "ordinary." The Greek origin is *laikos*, meaning "that does not belong to the clergy," hence as opposed to *clericos*, the cleric or man of the church. The word "secular" is also used. It means the ordinary man who lives in the century and is hence not associated with the scholarly religious domain. The separation between the secular (or temporal) and spiritual realms holds significant importance within the Christian faith, as reflected in the biblical verse ("Render unto Caesar the things that are Caesar's, and unto God the things that are God's").

52 For more details on the principle of laicity, see Marie-Luce Paris, *Constitutional Law in France*, International Encyclopaedia of Laws (2nd edn, Wolters Kluwer 2024) 319 (paras 603–604); also Mathilde Philip-Gay, *Droit de la laïcité* (Ellipses 2016).

53 Conseil d'État, *Un siècle de laïcité*, Études et documents du Conseil d'État, No 54 (La Documentation française 2004).

and not considerations grounded in religious ones. In other words, laicity does not mean that political power rejects, despises, or is indifferent to, religion. Rather, laicity means that the exercise of political power is exercised by the nation and cannot be conferred and exercised on behalf of any religion. Linked to this is the principle of neutrality of the state which guarantees the neutrality of public authorities vis-à-vis religion. The principle of neutrality applies to all employees in the administration and in schools. Again, this does not go as far as imposing neutrality in the public sphere since public manifestation of religious, and non-religious, beliefs are allowed. On the contrary, neutrality *protects* the free manifestation of worship, within the limits of the law. In that sense, both principles (i.e., separation of church and state, and neutrality) do not imply that religion is irremediably confined to the private sphere. The principle of freedom of conscience is a fundamental human right. It is not a right that is granted by a particular political authority. Such a right means that the law guarantees freedom *to believe* as well as freedom *not to believe*; being a promoter of laicity does not mean to advocate for atheism. It also means freedom to change religion for a political regime which simply tolerates other creeds and may not tolerate atheism or apostasy (i.e., to abandon or renunciate one's religious beliefs). Besides, the state must protect the rights and freedoms of the citizens in their relationship with religion. Religious practice must be done freely. The state ensures that religious organisations do not take advantage of religion to submit or enslave individuals because, for a religion to be worthy of respect and protection, it must respect and protect the believers.[54] As part of its mission to protect public order, the state has the duty to condemn individuals or groups of individuals (i.e., cults) who abuse others' human dignity or commit offences covered by the legislation on cults and sects (e.g., non-assistance to a person in danger, sequestration, violence, theft etc.).[55] The principle of equality prohibits any preferential treatment in favour of one particular religion. Correlatively, such a prohibition entails the prohibition of the recognition of an official religion as well as the prohibition to discriminate against a particular religion. In that sense, as understood under both principles (i.e., freedom of conscience and equality), laicity goes beyond simple religious tolerance. In a state under a regime of religious tolerance, favouring one religion over another is allowed; under a laicity regime, this is not allowed. Besides, laicity refers to the principle of equality of all citizens before the law without distinction based on religious grounds. The neutral and independent stance vis-à-vis religion allows the state to treat all citizens equally whatever their religion. These four principles constitute the legal notion of laicity whatever the non-legal conceptions that can otherwise be advocated are, whether advocating a more flexible conception of laicity or a stricter approach to laicity (see Box 3.2 Sarkozy speech on laicity).

The domestic sources of the principle of laicity do not all refer expressly to the word "*laïcité*" as mentioned above. The first category of sources aims at protecting freedom of religion. They include article 10 of the 1789 Declaration ensuring that everyone is entitled to hold opinions, including religious, without interference, provided their manifestation does not disturb the public order as established by law; article 1 of the 1905 Law guaranteeing freedom of conscience and the free exercise of worship within the restrictions enacted in

54 The problem of the cults and their prohibition is different obviously, but some religious practices may fall under the category of illegal cult practices.

55 Law No 2001-504 of 12 June 2001 aimed at strengthening the prevention and repression of sectarian movements that undermine human rights and fundamental freedoms. The 2001 Law sanctions more strictly cult movements when human rights and fundamental freedoms are at stake.

the interest of public order; and paragraphs one (enjoyment of inalienable and sacred rights without distinction based on race, religion, or creed), five (prohibition of discrimination in work and employment by reason of origin, opinions, or beliefs), and sixteen (enjoyment in France and its overseas territories of equal rights and duties without distinction of race or religion) of the Preamble to the 1946 Constitution. This is complemented, at international level, by article 9 of the ECHR, which protects freedom of thought, conscience, and religion. The second category of sources governs the relationships between church and state as firstly affirmed under article 2 of the 1905 Law, according to which the French Republic does not recognise, pay, or subsidise any religion. This is complemented by a couple of other laws which aim at accommodating the relationship between the state and the Catholic Church.[56] The first article to the current Constitution obviously confirms the relationship by defining the French Republic as secular. The third category of sources specifically addresses the issue of laicity at school. The first laws are sourced under the Third Republic with the so-called *Jules Ferry Laws*. This pair of laws on primary school made public school education free and compulsory and, generally, contributed to secularising the public education system.[57] This is complemented by paragraph thirteen of the Preamble to the 1946 Constitution, which reminds us that the provision of free and secular public education at all levels is one of the duties of the state. The 2004 Law on the prohibition of ostentatious religious signs or clothing in public primary and secondary schools, and the 2021 Law aimed at fighting against separatism, including in education, are recent markers of laicity.[58]

These sources are complemented by a number of soft law measures such as administrative orders (e.g., the 2012 Blanquer circular),[59] as well as by seminal cases by the highest domestic courts (e.g., the 2012 decision of the Constitutional Council about the application of laicity to the Protestant churches in Alsace-Moselle).[60] The role of customs is also important in this area as it is grounded in deep historical usages which justify traditional practices rooted in religion (e.g., the ringing of church bells) and local customs. The French regime of laicity accommodates indeed a number of exceptions due to historical and geographical reasons. The notable exception in metropolitan France concerns the regime in

56 Law of 2 January 1907 concerning the public exercise of worship; and Law of 28 March 1907 relating to public meetings.

57 Law of 16 June 1881 establishing free primary education in public schools; and Law of 28 March 1882 on the organisation of primary education.

58 Law No 2004-228 of 15 March 2004 governing, in application of the principle of secularism, the wearing of signs or clothing indicating religious affiliation in public schools, colleges and high schools; Law No 2021-1109 of 24 August 2021 confirming respect for the principles of the Republic. The 2010 Law prohibiting the concealment of the face in the public space is not about education but rather about societal and public order concerns. See Law No 2010-1192 of 11 October 2010 prohibiting the concealment of the face in public space.

59 Circular No 2012-056 of 27 March 2012 (excerpt): "It is recommended to recall in the [school] rules of procedure that the principles of secular education and neutrality of the public service are fully applicable within public schools. These principles make it possible in particular to prevent the parents of pupils or any other intervening party from manifesting, by their clothing or their words, their religious, political or philosophical convictions when they accompany the pupils on school outings and trips."

60 Decision No 2012-297 QPC of 21 February 2013 *Association pour la promotion et l'expansion de la laïcité [Traitement des pasteurs des églises consistoriales dans les départements du Bas-Rhin, du Haut-Rhin et de la Moselle]*. Seminal decisions of the Court of Cassation and of the Council of State also intervened about, for instance, the wearing of religious clothing in private companies, and the prohibition of public financing of religious denominations and its application, respectively.

force in Alsace-Moselle, which is a derogatory regime where the principle of separation between church and state does not apply. The 1905 Law was passed when the departments of Bas-Rhin, Haut-Rhin, and Moselle were annexed by the German Empire. When Alsace-Moselle became French again in 1918, it was decided that it would retain its local laws and still be governed by the pre-1870 regime (i.e., before the German annexation), which is the 1802 Concordat.[61] This explains why in these three departments, unlike in other French departments, denominational religious education is provided in public schools for the four recognised faiths, namely the Catholic faith, Judaism, and the Protestant Lutheran faith and Reformed Protestant faith. The other exceptions concern the French overseas territories. In Guadeloupe, Martinique, Réunion, Saint-Barthélemy, and Saint-Martin, a regime very similar to the 1905 Law on the separation of church and state and of the 1907 Law concerning the public exercise of worship was established by a 1911 Decree. This was repealed by the 2021 Law on separatism, which makes the 1905 and 1907 laws fully applicable to these territories. In the other overseas territories, namely French Guyana, French Polynesia, Mayotte, New Caledonia, Saint-Pierre and Miquelon, Wallis and Futuna, and the French Southern and Antarctica Lands (*Terres Australes et Antarctiques Françaises* or *TAAF*), however, these laws do not apply but are governed by a specific worship regime reflecting various legal and historical developments, mainly under the 1939 Mandel Decrees-Laws.[62]

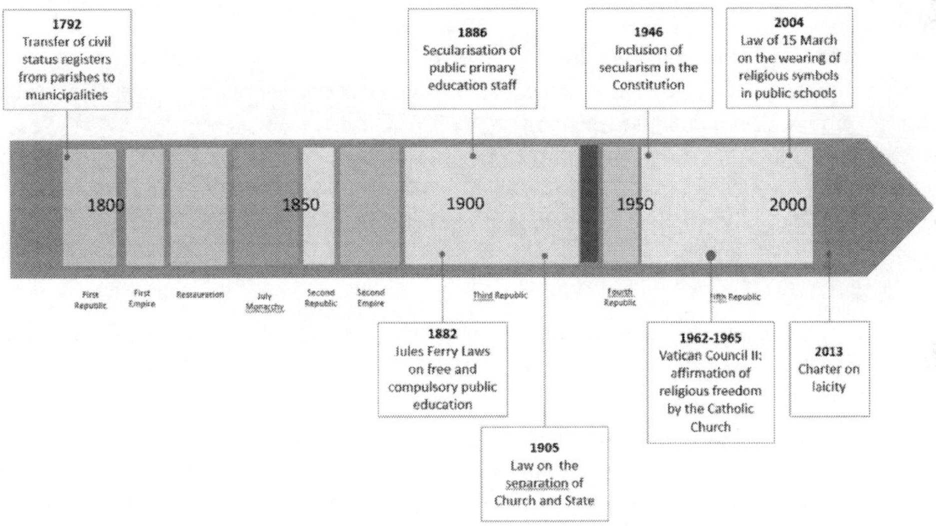

FIGURE 3.1 French laicity: A timeline

61 Law of 1 June 1924 implementing French civil legislation in the departments of Bas-Rhin, Haut-Rhin, and Moselle.

62 Decree of 16 January 1939 establishing overseas boards of directors of religious missions; and Decree of 6 December 1939 relating to the boards of directors of religious missions in the colonies. For more details on the derogatory regimes, see Circular of 25 August 2011 on regulations of worship overseas; and Mathilde Philip-Gay, *Droit de la laïcité* (Ellipses 2016) 101–124.

BOX 3.2 SARKOZY SPEECH ON LAICITY

"Where are we with secularism (*laïcité*)?

I will not reuse the term "positive secularism" so as not to fuel unnecessary controversy. However, I strongly believe that secularism does not entail outright rejection of all religions or religious sentiments. Instead, it upholds the principle of neutrality and the principle of respect. Secularism is respect for all opinions and all beliefs. When Jules Ferry wrote to the teachers, he told them:

'When proposing to students a precept, any maxim, ask yourself if there is a single honest man you know who could be offended by what you are going to say. Ask yourself if a father, I say just one [father], present in your class and listening to you, could in good faith refuse his assent to what he hears us say. If so, refrain from saying so.'

Who can forget the challenges that arose during the introduction of the separation of Church and State? However, should we persist in engaging in a battle that no longer holds any justification? We are not threatened by clericalism. Instead, our concern lies with a form of intolerance which stigmatises all religious affiliation. I say this thinking in particular of French people of Muslim faith. We must ensure that we do not misdirect our efforts. Within the [French Republic], the Muslim religion deserves just as much respect as any other religion.

The issue with the burka is not a religious problem. It is a problem of women's freedom and dignity. [The burka] is not a religious sign, it is a sign of enslavement, it is a sign of degradation.

I want to say it solemnly, the burka is not welcome in France. We cannot accept in our country women prisoners behind a fence, cut off from all social life, deprived of all identity. This is not our idea of the dignity of women."

Sarkozy, 22 June 2009, Parliament meeting in Congress, Versailles (excerpts)

Vie publique website <https://www.vie-publique.fr/discours/175696-declaration-de-m-nicolas-sarkozy-president-de-la-republique-devant-le>

The democratic and social features of the Republic. France is a democratic and social Republic. The *democratic* character means, in the first place, that the Fifth Republic is based on the rule of law. In the French context, the rule of law primarily refers to core principles of the republican order. These principles are: the recognition of the right to universal suffrage, which has been a postulate of French republicanism since 1848; the respect for public freedoms and fundamental rights; the principle of "government of the people, by the people, and for the people" (article 2 of the Constitution); the principle of national sovereignty (article 3 of the Constitution); and the express recognition of political parties and groups which contribute to the expression of suffrage (article 4 of the Constitution). As part of the 1789 heritage, national sovereignty belongs to the French people, thus allowing the two approaches to sovereignty, namely national sovereignty (via parliamentary representation) and popular sovereignty (via direct expression of democracy such as the referendum). The power of the state proceeds from the nation, that is, the body of French citizens (article 3 of the 1789 Declaration and article 3 of the Constitution). The concepts of nation and citizenship are fundamental *acquis* of the 1789 Revolution, linking citizenship to nationality. Citizenship acquired its full meaning and application only after the inhabitants of the colonies, and later women, were allowed to vote, respectively by the decrees of 1848 establishing universal male suffrage and abolishing slavery in the colonies, and by Ordinance of 26 April 1944 allowing women to vote for the first time in the municipal elections of April 1945.[63] Citizenship involves certain rights such as civic rights, including the right to vote and to stand for election. As for nationality, it may be attributed or obtained in different ways (i.e., filiation/parentage, birth in France, marriage to a French spouse, naturalisation) and is regulated by law under the Nationality Code.[64] Nationality law is part of civil law, and disputes are brought before ordinary courts. All French nationals are regarded as citizens as long as they enjoy their civil and political rights, with particular situations concerning citizens of the EU and citizens of New Caledonia. On the contrary, people who do not possess French nationality (and stateless persons) are regarded as foreigners who are, as a matter of principle, not entitled to vote in domestic elections. An exception concerns EU citizens residing on French territory who are entitled to vote in European elections and local domestic elections as required under the citizenship provisions of the EU treaties (article 39 of the EU Charter on Fundamental Rights, article 20 of the TFEU).

Respect for the rule of law also refers to the separation of powers, which has been a key component of French constitutional principles since the 1789 Declaration. Under article 16 of the 1789 Declaration, "any society in which the guarantee of rights is not guaranteed, nor the separation of powers determined, has no constitution." The separation of powers principle is the necessary condition to the limitation of political power: the mutual control exercised by the three branches of government—namely the legislative branch, the executive branch, and the judicial branch—protects individuals from infringements against their rights and from abuses by the rulers. The implementation of separation of powers was not always satisfactory in practice, and adjustments were made over the years under successive French regimes. A too strict separation of powers led, for example, to the paralysis of the institutions during the *Directoire* period (1795–1799), and under the Second Republic (1848–1851), where the conflict between the executive and the legislature ended in a *coup d'état*. Rather than a strict separation, a system of flexible separation, where the different branches of powers collaborate in order to guarantee the regular functioning of public authorities, gradually developed. Such collaboration means that the executive power can intervene in the drafting of laws and, conversely, that the legislative power can intervene in regulatory functions. Under the Fifth Republic, the power of the President of the Republic to dissolve the National Assembly, the possibility for the legislative power to overthrow the government, and the submission of public prosecutors to the hierarchical authority of the government are all manifestations of a flexible approach to the separation of powers principle.

In addition, the separation of powers principle had specific consequences in the French legal system, for indeed, historically, ordinary judges could not interfere in government affairs. Courts were deprived of the jurisdiction to deal with disputes concerning the administration

63 The right to vote is examined under Chapter 5 on political parties, elections, and referendums.

64 The Nationality Code was enacted by Ordinance No 45-2441 of 19 October 1945 on the French Nationality Code and overhauled by Law No 93-933 of 22 July 1993 reforming the law of nationality, as amended several times since. For more details on French nationality law, see Marie-Luce Paris, *Constitutional Law in France*, International Encyclopaedia of Laws (2nd edn, Wolters Kluwer 2024) 221–234 (paras 401–433).

under the Law of 16 and 24 August 1790 on judicial organisation.[65] Overall, due regard to the separation of powers principle combined with a profound distrust of judges meant that the acts of the legislature and of the executive were not susceptible to judicial review. Simply said, ordinary courts did not have sufficient legitimacy to judge acts emanating from authorities proceeding from universal suffrage and acting in the name of the general interest. Aggrieved individuals had to bring their case before the administration itself, up to ministerial level. This was the so-called "minister-judge system" whereby the administration was judge and party at the same time. The establishment of administrative courts, namely the Council of State by the Constitution of Year VIII (1799), and the departmental prefectural councils by the Law of 28 *Pluviôse* Year VIII (17 February 1800) concerning the division of the French territory and the administration, and the subsequent development of administrative law, modified this situation.[66] From then on, administrative acts could be challenged before a separate set of courts, namely the administrative courts. As a result, the "French conception of the separation of powers"[67] has become associated with a dual judicial order, namely the ordinary judicial order (*ordre judiciaire*), with the Court of Cassation (*Cour de cassation*) at its top, and the administrative judicial order (*ordre administratif*), with the Council of State (*Conseil d'État*) at its top. The development of a constitutional court came about more recently with the establishment of the Constitutional Council (*Conseil constitutionnel*) under the Fifth Republic. Originally a body with a limited power of review, the Constitutional Council has developed into a constitutional court akin to other European constitutional courts. While the Council of State is empowered to judicially review the legality of *regulatory acts*, the Constitutional Council has the power to review the conformity of *laws* with the Constitution. Constitutional judicial review can intervene before laws are promulgated (ex-ante review), or after laws are promulgated (ex-post review).[68]

France is also a *social* Republic. The meaning of the social character of the French Republic is somewhat elusive. In essence, it means that the French democratic regime is associated with a specific project of society aimed at ensuring the collective cohesion of all individuals and groups of individuals. In other words, the Republic is not fully achieved unless it features a minimum of social content. This is also an *acquis* of the 1789 Revolution. The National Constituent Assembly (1789–1791) proclaimed at the time that "every man at birth is entitled to protection and help from humanity [*sic*]," thereby establishing a close association between the promotion of human rights and the recognition of social rights. This idea was consecrated by subsequent regimes, notably under the legislation of the Third Republic and, mostly, by the recognition of economic and social rights as enshrined in the 1946 Preamble. For some, the realisation of the social character of the Republic translates into the development of a branch of law dedicated to the protection of social rights (i.e., *droit social*), as well as into the development of the public

65 This was complemented by Decree of 16 *Fructidor* Year III (2 September 1795), which prohibited the courts from hearing acts of administration, and cancels all procedures and judgments made in this regard.

66 Notably the Law of 24 May 1872 reorganising the Council of State, which allowed the Council of State to become a fully fledged administrative court deciding without interference from the executive in a so-called system of "delegated justice" (*justice déléguée*). See also the *Cadot* Case of 13 December 1889, in which the Council of State abandoned the system of the minister-judge.

67 Decision No 86-224 DC of 23 January 1987 *Loi transférant à la juridiction judiciaire le contentieux des décisions du Conseil de la concurrence*, pt 15.

68 The French court-system and constitutional review are dealt with under Chapter 6 on constitutional justice and protection of rights.

service and the promotion of a social policy based on solidarity.[69] Other principles manifest the social character of the Republic such as the fraternity principle based on citizenship, the equality of opportunity provided for by the schools of the Republic, the social interventionism of the state, the pursuit of the common good, as well as the national solidarity recognised not only between the citizens but also between the different parts of the territory of the Republic.

The Constitution definitively laid the foundation for a democratic Republic, which was further strengthened by the election of the President of the Republic by universal suffrage. Nonetheless, the democratic basis of the Republic, grounded in the principle of national sovereignty, has become less evident due to the transfer of numerous competences and powers to the EU.[70]

Principles of government. The Fifth Republic, in comparison to its predecessor Republics, embodies a distinctive political system in two significant ways. Firstly, it restores the importance of executive power. Secondly, it streamlines the parliamentary system, seeking to make it more efficient and logical, known as the rationalisation of the parliamentary system. These interwoven elements have played a vital role in shaping the constitutional framework of the Fifth Republic.

The restoration of the executive power. Under the Fifth Republic, the executive power is characterised by its independence and its duality. Firstly, regarding the independence of the executive power, the concern was to break away from parliamentary absolutism. The way it was done was to make the government proceed directly from the Head of State, so that there could be no subordination of the executive to the legislature.[71] Concretely, this resulted in a number of constitutional mechanisms such as the appointment of the Prime Minister by the President of the Republic (article 8 paragraph one of the Constitution), and the affirmation of an autonomous regulatory power reserved to the executive and distinct from the area of the law (article 37 of the Constitution). Secondly, the Constitution reaffirmed the governmental dyarchy formed by the President of the Republic and the Prime Minister (formerly President of the Council under the previous regimes). Although the Prime Minister is endowed with important prerogatives, the main one being to direct the action of the government (article 21 of the Constitution), such a dyarchy has not resisted political practice which has seen the rise of the President of the Republic as the figurehead of the dyarchy. In the relationship between the Head of State and the Head of Government, the evolution of the regime shows that the balance has resolutely tipped in favour of the former due to the appointment power and the decision-making power in the hands of the President, as widely interpreted and used by De Gaulle (see below). De Gaulle got away with such a generous interpretation of his powers thanks to his historical aura and to the legitimacy he acquired from the French people from 1962 when he was directly elected by universal suffrage. The only moments of true dyarchy occurred during

69 Michel Borgetto & Robert Lafore, *La mise en œuvre de la République sociale : Contribution à l'étude de la question démocratique en France* (PUF 2000).

70 Robert Debbasch, *Droit constitutionnel* (13th edn, LexisNexis 2021) 124.

71 The proposal was even to establish a form of dualist parliamentary regime, although it was eventually defined as monist under the Constitution.

the so-called cohabitation periods in the 1980s and 1990s when the President was of a different political orientation than that of the parliamentary majority and the government.[72]

The rationalisation of the parliamentary system. The Constitution organises the powers of Parliament as well as its relationship with the government. The whole point of the Constitution was to place the executive power at the centre of gravity of political power. While slightly rebalancing the balance of power in favour of Parliament, the 2008 constitutional amendment has not resulted in drastically changing the original balance of a strong executive facing a diminished legislature. Concerning the organisation of Parliament, the main development has concerned the incompatibility between the parliamentary mandate and a ministerial office (article 23 of the Constitution). Despite being an essential feature of the separation of powers principle,[73] the impossibility for a member of Parliament to be a member of government was not respected under the previous Republics and was in fact the main cause of their instability. This was so because members of Parliament could put a vote of non-confidence against the government in place with the hope of getting a ministerial post in the subsequently formed government. There is nothing like this under the Fifth Republic, where a deputy or senator who enters government must resign from his/her parliamentary mandate and be substituted in his/her role by an alternative member of Parliament. Since the 2008 constitutional amendment, such a substitution is temporary, and the member of Parliament resumes his/her role when s/he leaves the government. The choice of a temporary interruption of the parliamentary mandate has been regarded as essential to entice members of Parliament into taking up a ministerial role while, at the same time, facilitating governmental reshuffles when the President of the Republic and the Prime Minister must decide fairly quickly on how to reorganise their majority.

Concerning the powers of Parliament, the main novelties introduced in the Constitution concern the limitation of the area of the law and the attribution of an autonomous regulatory power to the government. Before 1958, the law was seen as the expression of the general will and of national sovereignty. In accordance with the principle of parliamentary sovereignty, the law was regarded as the supreme norm whose field of application was unlimited and which could not be judicially reviewed. The government was entitled to a regulatory power only in so far as Parliament did not exercise its power over the particular area concerned or, on the contrary, when Parliament requested the executive power to take the necessary executive measures in the legislative area in question. The Constitution put an end to the supremacy of the law by, firstly, delimiting its field of action and, secondly, by subjecting its validity to the respect of the Constitution via judicial review.[74] Article 34 of the Constitution confers competence upon Parliament in all the key areas that are necessary for governing the country.

72 The three periods of cohabitation were as follows: 1986–1988: François Mitterrand (President) and Jacques Chirac (Prime Minister); 1993–1995: François Mitterrand (President) and Édouard Balladur (Prime Minister); 1997–2002: Jacques Chirac (President) and Lionel Jospin (Prime Minister). For more details, see Marie-Luce Paris, *Constitutional Law in France*, International Encyclopaedia of Laws (2nd edn, Wolters Kluwer 2024) 42 (paras 47–48).

73 The incompatibility between the parliamentary mandate and a ministerial office featured, as a constitutional principle, in the 1791 Constitution, the 1795 (Year III) Constitution, and the 1848 and 1852 constitutions.

74 In addition to losing its supremacy (or sovereignty), the law has also lost its homogeneity as a norm in the sense that there are now various types of laws that do not have the same legal value (i.e., constitutional laws, referendum laws, organic laws, ordinary laws, laws of the land).

Therefore, the law determines the *rules* relating to areas such as civil rights and fundamental freedoms; freedom, pluralism, and the independence of the media; limitations on citizens' rights and property by reason of national defence; the nationality, status, and capacity of natural persons, and matrimonial regimes; the determination of criminal offences and the penalties applicable to them, criminal procedure, the establishment of new orders in the court-system, and the status of judges; as well as tax and currency regimes. The law also determines the *fundamental principles* as regards matters such as the general organisation of the national defence; the free administration of local authorities, powers, and resources; education; the protection of the environment; property rights; and employment law, trade-union law, and the social security regime. New areas of legislative competence may be added to this list by an organic law. Additionally, other constitutional provisions confer power upon the legislature such as article 35 on the declaration of war, article 53 on the ratification of international treaties by law, article 66 on the role of the judiciary as guardian of individual liberty within the limits prescribed by law, and article 72 on the power of the legislature concerning local authorities and local government.

Any area of competence that does not fall within the confines of article 34 of the Constitution falls within the regulatory power of the government under article 37—that being the real shift in the conferral principle of the normative power under the Fifth Republic. Such autonomous regulatory power, that is, the power of the executive to adopt norms in areas not covered by the legislative power, is protected against encroachments by the legislature by several constitutional mechanisms such as the "delegalisation" mechanism (article 37 paragraph two of the Constitution) and the "inadmissibility" mechanism (article 41 of the Constitution). In addition to the limitation of the area of the law, and the recognition of a residual regulatory power, the power to issue ordinances is another shift brought about under the Fifth Republic. The government may seek, for the implementation of its programme, approval from Parliament to take by way of ordinances, and for a limited duration, acts that are normally within the legislature's remit (article 38 of the Constitution). Such ordinances are adopted within the Council of Ministers after receiving the opinion of the Council of State. The advantage of ordinances is their efficiency because they allow the government to take measures swiftly on a pressing issue instead of going through the lengthy process of enacting a government bill through Parliament. Accessorily, members of Parliament may also find the enactment of ordinances quite convenient since the responsibility for their adoption is attached to the government and not to them. This may be worthwhile, especially when the text adopted proves to be unpopular.[75]

Regarding the relationship between Parliament and the government, and as a reaction to the excesses of the previous regimes, the regime of the Fifth Republic incorporates constitutional mechanisms to foster a positive relationship through a more stringent regulation of ministerial accountability procedures, as well as granting the government a role in the legislative process.[76]

75 The powers of Parliament are dealt with under Chapter 4 on the institutions of the Fifth Republic.

76 The relationships between Parliament and the government are examined in Chapter 4 on the institutions of the Fifth Republic.

The evolution of the Fifth Republic

The Fifth Republic has undergone drastic changes since its establishment in 1958. These changes have been influenced both by the extensive experience gained over the course of nearly 70 years, as well as the numerous amendments made to the Constitution. To fully comprehend these changes, it is necessary to delve into the initial system of governance that the 1958 constituents originally put in place and contrast it with the one that it has become today.

The practice of the 1958 Constitution. Constitutional practice under the Fifth Republic has revealed that, contrary to the previous regimes, the government has always been in a position to count on a parliamentary majority. The occurrence of what has been called the "*fait majoritaire*" is due to a shift from multipartyism, which characterised previous regimes, to bipartisanship, which has seen contemporary political life structured around the two main political trends of the right and of the left. Such transformation is itself due to changes in the voting system of the legislative elections (i.e., from proportional representation to a first-past-the-post in two rounds election system) and in the mode of election of the President of the Republic (i.e., from an indirect election to a direct election by universal suffrage from 1962). Under such a system, the continuity of political power is as follows: the presidential election determines the leader of the country, the President of the Republic, who rules with his/her Prime Minister and government as supported by a majority in Parliament as the outcome of legislative elections. However, because of this "*double ancrage démocratique*"[77] (i.e., the democratic legitimacy of directly elected deputies and the democratic legitimacy of the directly elected President), the Fifth Republic has given rise to two possible practices of the regime.[78]

The first practice arises when the President of the Republic is of the same political hue as the majority in Parliament, which corresponds to the normal functioning of the regime. Because of the perfect alignment between the political hue of the President of the Republic, the government, and the majority in Parliament (the so-called "*fait majoritaire parfait*"), the President benefits fully from the prominence of his/her role. The second practice arises when there is a discordance in results in the two elections, legislative and presidential, which return a different majority. In that case, the political alignment of majorities is disrupted (the so-called "*fait majoritaire imparfait*"). Such political configuration has led to the phenomenon of *cohabitation*, whereby the President of the Republic is bound to appoint—and thus, "cohabitate," as in "exercises the executive power together with"—a Prime Minister reflecting the majority in Parliament,[79] that majority not being of the same political hue as that of the President. There have been three periods of cohabitation under the Fifth Republic so far: 1986–1988: François Mitterrand (President/left) and Jacques Chirac (Prime Minister/right); 1993–1995: François Mitterrand (President/left) and Édouard Balladur (Prime Minister/right); 1997–2002: Jacques Chirac (President/right) and Lionel Jospin (Prime Minister/left). The cohabitation represents an abnormal functioning of the regime, although arguably one which is more in line with its parliamentary nature. Without changing this state of affairs, the concordance of the presidential

77 Ferdinand Mélin-Soucramanien & Pierre Pactet, *Droit constitutionnel* (39th edn, Sirey 2021) 385.

78 See also Chapter 5 on political parties, elections, and referendums.

79 Although the Prime Minister needs to be from the victorious political party in the legislative elections, s/he does not necessarily need to be its leader.

term of office with that of the parliamentary mandate into a five-year mandate for both, with, correlatively, a coincidence of both elections, was an attempt to reduce the risk of cohabitation. The change from a seven-year to a five-year presidential term was indeed meant to reduce, albeit without eliminating completely, the probability that the French people would vote for a completely different majority a few weeks apart. Besides, other factors can intervene and disrupt the sequence of presidential/legislative elections. One of them is the dissolution of the National Assembly decided by the President, albeit provoking a snap election is a risky political move. Also, presidential elections may be called earlier than planned when the presidential mandate is cut short due to the (mostly unlikely) occurrence of impeachment, resignation, or death of the President. In whatever configuration of the regime—under its normal functioning or under cohabitation—the President has mostly assumed the prominence conferred upon him/her. However, periods of cohabitation certainly allowed the Prime Minister to also benefit from the prominence of his/her own role.[80]

Whatever the combination has been—*fait majoritaire parfait* or *fait majoritaire imparfait*, the executive power has relied on the indispensable support of the majority in Parliament. This denotes the paradox on which the regime is based: the President of the Republic, who is the figurehead of the regime, is not in fact endowed with significant powers in normal times, as opposed to times of crisis when s/he enjoys much more far-reaching powers (e.g., exceptional powers). The power of the President therefore depends much on the parliamentary majority with the risk, as explained above, that the said majority may differ from the presidential political hue. Under the normal functioning of the regime, the President holds the real power, not so much by virtue of the powers conferred upon him/her by the Constitution, but rather thanks to the political supports s/he gets from the Prime Minister and his/her government as supported by the parliamentary majority.[81] Such pre-eminence is in line with the intention of the 1958 drafters. This, however, makes the President an ambivalent figure of the regime. As the democratically elected "*élu national*," the President should act as the President of all French people. As the Head of State, s/he embodies the unity of the nation, represents France, and defends French interests abroad. In other words, the President cannot represent his/her own political party only and must elevate himself/herself above party politics. This is challenging for a President who won his/her election thanks to partisan support and is imbued with the ideas (and sometimes ideology) of his/her political family. It is submitted that "*un Président qui gouverne*"[82] is hardly the President of all French people, only maybe in a legal and abstract sense, but certainly not in practice.[83] Under the abnormal functioning of the regime that is cohabitation, the Prime Minister holds the real power by virtue of the constitutional text. Because s/he is not dependent on the President in that situation, the Prime Minister can exercise his/her leadership in directing the action of the government. Correlatively, and although still the guardian of the institutions and endowed with significant prerogatives in the areas of foreign affairs and defence, the President, with no majority support, is relegated to the background. Among the levers of action that the President can contemplate in such a situation, the dissolution of the National

80 See also Chapter 5 on political parties, elections, and referendums.

81 Clearly, the extent of the power exercised by the President of the Republic is contingent upon the manner in which it is exerted. In that regard, the President's approach to governance plays a significant role.

82 Jean-Baptiste de Montvalon, "Le 'président qui gouverne', casse-tête constitutionnel", *Le Monde*, 12 September 2007.

83 Ferdinand Mélin-Soucramanien & Pierre Pactet, *Droit constitutionnel* (39th edn, Sirey 2021) 391 et seq.

Assembly is a difficult one; likewise, the resignation of the President is not an option, not so much because of the reluctance of the President himself/herself, but because of the reluctance of members of Parliament of the presidential party who would have no interest in the resignation of their leader and, on the contrary, would like to maintain him/her in power. The analysis that prevailed until a few years ago was that cohabitation would be less likely to occur, albeit still possible. It has been suggested that a coincidence of the majorities would prevail, resulting undoubtedly in a presidentialisation of the regime.[84] However, the scenario of an absorption of the different political forces into a marked centrist trend ("*l'extrême centre*"), as has occurred under the current Macron presidency, was not envisaged. But such a situation is likely to render the possibility of a cohabitation moot because the political forces are not opposed anymore except, obviously, at the extremes of the political spectrum. However, the paradox mentioned above is one that was imposed on the 1958 drafters as inherited from French constitutional history, that is, how to set up a proper parliamentary regime without its defects while giving a real "head" to the state. Hence the near impossibility to really change the nature of the regime, as exemplified by the thwarted attempt to redefine the relationship between the President of the Republic and the Prime Minister under the Sarkozy presidency, for example.[85]

Different approaches have been proposed to describe the evolution of the regime with various landmarks and breaking points.[86] One such approach, for example, identifies three main phases divided up into six periods: a first phase is qualified as "constitutional orthodoxy" and distinguishes the Gaullist period (1958–1969) and the post-Gaullist period (1969–1981); a second phase, that of a "democratic window," comprises the two seven-year mandates of Mitterrand (1981–1995) and the first mandate of Chirac's contrasted presidencies (1995–2002); a third phase of "institutional dysfunction" starts when the presidential mandate was changed from a seven-year term to a five-year term, that is, from the second mandate of Chirac (2002–2007) and which also comprises the last three presidencies, namely the "hyper-presidency" of Sarkozy (2007–2012), the "normal presidency" of Hollande (2012–2017), and the "Jupiterian presidency" of Macron (2017–present). These periods are briefly described in the developments below.

The Gaullist period is marked by the "*volontarisme gaullien*," the 1962 constitutional amendment on the election of the President of the Republic by direct universal suffrage, and the emergence of clear majorities of government. De Gaulle's role during the Second World War combined with strong personality traits conferred on him a certain aura in French post-war society. Regarded as the Founding Father of the Constitution, De Gaulle certainly left an indelible mark on the regime. He emphatically and significantly declared at the time that all sources

84 Ibid 394 et seq.

85 The 2008 constitutional amendment was introduced with the aim of rebalancing the exercise of political power in favour of Parliament. It achieved some degree of success, albeit limited. Nevertheless, the suggested redefinition of the dynamics between the two executive heads, which involved significant revisions to articles 5, 20, and 21 of the Constitution as put forth by the Balladur Committee, did not find acceptance in the ultimate version of the text.

86 For example, Hugues Portelli & Thomas Ehrhard, *Droit constitutionnel* (14th edn, Dalloz 2021) 176–182. Portelli & Ehrhard distinguish the three following periods: from the Gaullist model to the presidential power (1958–1981); the gradual return to parliamentarism (1981–2002); and the presidentialist impact of the five-year presidential mandate (2002–present).

of power derived from the Head of State.[87] Yet, despite claiming his readiness to exercise fully the presidential power, De Gaulle showed moderation in this regard (perhaps putting aside the implementation of the exceptional powers, between April and September 1961, during the Algerian War). In other words, while De Gaulle fully embraced his role, he did so within the confines of the constitutional powers conferred upon him, unlike some of his successors who pushed these confines beyond what had originally been envisaged.

After De Gaulle, the regime functioned in its original form under Pompidou's and Giscard d'Estaing's presidencies, at least from an institutional perspective. Presidential pre-eminence was still regarded as the cornerstone of the regime. In terms of constitutional amendments, some minor changes were made. The only significant amendment of this period was the 1974 constitutional amendment on the extension of the right to bring constitutional review proceedings before the Constitutional Council, which was extended to 60 deputies or 60 senators.[88] Matters were, however, different on the political plane. A right-wing majority was deeply affected by internal tensions, as best illustrated by the election of Giscard d'Estaing in 1974, who came from a minority party (*Les Républicains Indépendants*) he had created, within the majority presidential party of *Union pour la Nouvelle République*.[89] Such a weakened right-wing majority thus left an opportune political space for the left-wing opposition, which had progressively managed to rally the electorate in its favour.

The election of the Socialist Mitterrand in May 1981 represented the "*alternance politique*" after 23 years of uninterrupted right-wing governance. The two seven-year terms of Mitterrand were marked by the domination of the Socialist Party. However, this was not a continuous domination, as attested by episodes of cohabitation. This was due to a certain instability of the electorate, which, on two occasions, voted to oust the left-wing majority. The complete shift in majority in 1981 (i.e., from right-wing dominance to left-wing dominance) was only political though. Institutionally speaking, the regime functioned, at least until 1986, and again from 1988 to 1993 (i.e., outside of the cohabitation periods), normally, that is, according to the orthodoxy of the 1958 drafters. The continuity displayed under Mitterrand's presidency was not obvious though, given the amount of criticism that Mitterrand, and the Socialists in general, had previously launched against the Fifth Republic.[90] However, once in power, Mitterrand saw the advantages of the regime and exploited them to the fullest to such a point that the presidential pre-eminence reached a quasi-state of monarchical governance with a reinforcement of the state machinery.[91] In any case, the Senate, under a right-wing majority, would have opposed any constitutional amendment aimed at overhauling the institutional balance of the regime. Several constitutional amendments were adopted at the end of the Mitterrand's presidency though. These amendments related to the European integration project after the adoption of the 1992 Treaty of Maastricht. Other amendments were about more technical constitutional

87 General Charles De Gaulle, 31 January 1964, Press Conference, Élysée Palace, Paris (excerpt): "This is why the spirit of the new Constitution consists, while keeping a legislative Parliament [*sic*], in ensuring that power no longer rests with partisanship, but that [power] proceeds directly from the people, which implies that the head of the state, elected by the nation, be its source and holder."

88 For more details, see Chapter 6 on constitutional justice and rights protection.

89 Subsequently, in 1976, Prime Minister Chirac's resignation transpired, primarily driven by his strained association with Giscard d'Estaing, with both vying for dominance of the right-wing leadership.

90 François Mitterrand, *Le coup d'état permanent* (Plon 1964). In this groundbreaking book, Mitterrand denounced the exercise of personal power by De Gaulle.

91 Ferdinand Mélin-Soucramanien & Pierre Pactet, *Droit constitutionnel* (39th edn, Sirey 2021) 399.

revisions relating, among others, to the Court of Justice of the Republic, the Superior Council of the Judiciary, and the right to asylum.[92]

Chirac's presidency was not homogenous and underwent different phases. The first phase (1995–1997) corresponded to the return of majorities, presidential and parliamentary, after a period of cohabitation under the previous presidency. However, the dissolution of the National Assembly in 1997 broke this continuity. The 1997 dissolution was atypical in the sense that it was more a tactical move by Chirac than a real threat against a reticent majority. Chirac's idea was to provoke a snap election to avoid the concomitance of the 1998 legislative elections (as well as with the highly sensitive progressive implementation of the euro at the time) and the 1999 European elections. However, the 1997 dissolution did not produce the expected result. Held in late May and early June, the 1997 legislative elections following the dissolution saw a shift in the electorate from the right to the left. This was due largely to a growing disappointment of the right-wing electorate as regards persistent internal divisions in the party as well as insufficient ideological lines, and failure to respect a number of electoral promises. In that context, the left-wing coalition successfully won the elections, therefore marking the start of a second phase in the presidency under another period of cohabitation (1997–2002). The real power was thus transferred to the Socialist Prime Minister Jospin, who governed with a multi-party left-wing coalition ("*gauche plurielle*"). From a constitutional perspective, this third cohabitation was characterised by a multitude of proposals for constitutional amendment at the instigation of the Prime Minister and agreed on by the President. The last phase of Chirac's presidency (2002–2007) was more troubled. It started with the infamous 2002 presidential election, which saw the defeat of Jospin in the first round and put Jean-Marie Le Pen in the second round. Chirac won the election by a landslide of 82% of the votes cast thanks to the "*sursaut républicain*." Further constitutional amendments were passed including the 2003 amendment on the decentralised organisation of the Republic and the 2005 amendment, which appended the 2004 Charter for the Environment to the Constitution. The events of 2005 (i.e., the decisive rejection by the French people of the 2005 Treaty establishing a Constitution for Europe on 29 May 2005, and the ensuing appointment of a new Prime Minister, De Villepin, on 31 May 2005) gave rise to a somewhat paradoxical institutional crisis. While, on paper, the regime was back to its normal functioning (i.e., coincidence of majorities), an important rift arose in the relationship between the political power and the French people. Many French people completely lost confidence in their government, not only because of the unfortunate European referendum result, but also because of a series of internal disturbances, notably the November 2005 suburban riots, which triggered the state of emergency for the first time in relation to events in metropolitan France. This was compounded by general social unrest linked to some unpopular economic measures, notably the "first job contract" (*contrat première embauche*) in March 2006, as well as a string of political scandals (i.e., Clearstream, EADS). The national representation seemed to be completely cut off from its popular base, and the President was left with a narrow margin of action to resolve the crisis. It made the last leg of Chirac's mandate

92 During that period, two more significant constitutional proposals were formulated with the intention of modifying several provisions of the Constitution. The first proposal was about the Constitutional Council, the judiciary, and the High Court, while the second proposal focused on the organisation of public authorities and aimed at amending the 1958 Preamble, article 1, and Title I of the Constitution. Unfortunately, these proposals were presented shortly before the 1993 legislative elections, which resulted in a shift in the political majority. Consequently, these revisions were unable to come to fruition.

extremely difficult to handle, although the President managed to push through several constitutional amendments in 2007 relating to the electorate of New Caledonia, the criminal liability regime of the President of the Republic, and the prohibition of the death penalty at all times. Overall, Chirac was the President who amended the Constitution the most (i.e., 14 constitutional laws adopted between 1995 and 2007), which is fairly paradoxical for a political figure of Gaullist heritage.

What also marked Chirac's presidency was the 2002 constitutional reform, which had a significant impact on the institutional balance of the Fifth Republic. This reform, which reduced the presidential term from seven to five years, was just as important as the 1962 reform that introduced direct election of the President. By increasing the frequency of important political elections, such as presidential and legislative elections every five years, this reform naturally transformed the regime into a "presidential government" by consolidating political power in the hands of the President. This phenomenon has continued to evolve in various ways under subsequent presidencies and appears to have intensified during Macron's tenure.[93]

Sarkozy's presidency arguably represents a step further in changing the approach to the regime by considerably reinforcing the weight of the "presidential government." This was done in the 2008 constitutional amendment, which aimed at clarifying the role of the President of the Republic and that of the Prime Minister, and their relationships. Even though the idea of a hierarchisation between the President, as the sole head of the executive, and the Prime Minister, as a simple executant, via rewording articles 5 and 20 was abandoned, other modifications of the Constitution have arguably contributed to changing (denaturing?) the role of the President, such as, among others, the prohibition to hold two consecutive presidential mandates, the stricter control imposed on the President's appointment power and on the exercise of the exceptional powers, and the ousting of the President from the chair of the Superior Council of the Judiciary. Such changes can be regarded as diminishing the pre-eminent role of the Head of State because s/he does not seem to be above political contingencies anymore, but rather more directly involved in day-to-day politics. This is what De Gaulle was reluctant about, given his dislike of Parliament and of partisan disputes. Most of all, the practice of the regime by Sarkozy resulted in a de facto absorption of the governmental functions by the President. Sarkozy did not hesitate to call for the support of the parliamentary majority, thereby relegating his ministers, and his Prime Minister in particular, to the role of mere collaborators charged with endorsing his actions. Another revealing mark of a break with the original republican logic of the regime is to be found in the modification of the right of message. While, pursuant to the separation of powers principle, the President cannot access Parliament and may only deliver messages, the President is authorised, since the 2008 constitutional amendment, to address Parliament convened as the Congress (i.e., both Houses of Parliament sitting in Versailles). The President's statement may be followed by a debate but without a vote.[94] This period can arguably be interpreted as a change towards a monist type of parliamentary regime, short of a presidential type of regime, that is, a regime where the governmental functions are not carried out by the Prime Minister and his/her government accountable before Parliament, but rather a regime where the President is accountable before the people. This type

93 Ferdinand Mélin-Soucramanien & Pierre Pactet, *Droit constitutionnel* (39th edn, Sirey 2021) 402.

94 This possibility of addressing Parliament in Congress was used for the first time by Sarkozy when he delivered his speech on the challenges and priorities of government policy on 22 June 2009.

of regime is not theoretically off the point and was envisaged by, for example, scholars such as Prélot and Capitant in the immediate aftermath of the Second World War.[95] All in all, the 2008 constitutional amendment is the most substantial revision of the Constitution that has ever been made of the Fifth Republic to date.

By contrast, Hollande's presidency is characterised by efforts to bring the regime back to its normal functioning as originally intended.[96] It should be remembered that such normal functioning relates to the parliamentary nature of the regime with, however, the original features of the election of the President of the Republic by direct universal suffrage and his endowment with significant powers. Ironically, since Hollande wanted to leave the imprint of his "normal" presidency, he never managed to push through a series of constitutional amendments that were instigated under his leadership, marking his mandate with a kind of "constitutional impotence." A first series of amendments in 2013 concerned long-awaited but previously unsuccessful reforms such as the reform of the status of the President of the Republic, the demise of the Court of Justice of the Republic, the incompatibilities regime of members of the government, and the ousting of the former Presidents from the membership of the Constitutional Council. Another series of reforms was the attempt to entrench provisions relating to the state of emergency and to the withdrawal of French nationality in the Constitution, proposed in 2016 after the tragic Islamist terrorist attacks of November 2015. These unsuccessful attempts on the constitutional front, compounded with a string of electoral setbacks, led to the unusual situation under the Fifth Republic of an outgoing President who decided not to run for his re-election.

After an unprecedented presidential campaign, Macron was elected President of the Republic on 14 May 2017 beating Marine Le Pen, the candidate of the far-right party.[97] The 2017 presidential election saw the defeat of the two traditional political forces of the country, namely the Republicans and the Socialists, projecting to the forefront a new centrist political force the ideological positioning of which is still, to this day, to be defined. Yet, a consequential high abstention rate (i.e., 57.35%) tainted the results of the following 2017 legislative elections, which returned a very strong majority in the National Assembly in favour of the presidential party, *La République en Marche !*. However, this could also be interpreted as a sensible political move of the electorate understanding that the real centre of political power henceforth revolves around the President and not Parliament. Other signs have shown this trend of an aggregation of political action around the President such as, for example, the worrying commitment of *La République en Marche !* candidates to vote, at the start of their parliamentary mandate, on a number of bills instigated by Macron without any precise knowledge of their actual content, which was thereby in complete contravention of the prohibition of the imperative mandate imposed on members of Parliament. Another example is the use of the right of message by Macron. Instead of using it as a tool to inform Parliament about specific issues, Macron somehow modelled such a right on the American State of the Union Address when he delivered an address in Congress at the start of his first mandate on 3 July 2007 in order to

95 As cited in Ferdinand Mélin-Soucramanien & Pierre Pactet, *Droit constitutionnel* (39th edn, Sirey 2021) 405.

96 Hollande invoked the idea of a "normal" President when he announced his candidacy for the 2012 presidential election. Unfortunately, this choice of words was highly ill-advised and Hollande went on to face relentless ridicule. From an institutional standpoint, the President of the Republic is anything but a normal individual.

97 Macron had never held any electoral mandate before he was elected President of the Republic. He was previously the Deputy Secretary General to the President of the Republic under President Hollande (2012–2014) and Hollande's minister for the Economy, Industry and Digital Affairs (2014–2016).

present the priorities of his future actions. Fast-forward to the end of his first mandate and his re-election in 2022, albeit with a high abstention rate,[98] and Macron has found himself in the same kind of predicament as his predecessor concerning constitutional reforms. A major constitutional amendment aimed at renewing democracy failed under the Philippe Government (2017–2020).[99] It is true that a series of unfortunate events and political setbacks plagued Macron's first mandate (i.e., the Benalla scandal in the summer of 2018, the Yellow Vests movement from November 2018, Covid-19 from March 2020, and the war in Ukraine from February 2022). Macron's second mandate saw a very quick waning of the "*état de grâce*" after his re-election (again, against Le Pen). The latest turmoil were the protests from January 2023 provoked by the reform of the pension system. If the necessary, and eventually adopted, reform represents a minimal political victory for Macron, it was clumsily brought about by the government. With now a relative majority in the National Assembly and a relatively hostile Senate dominated by the opposition, any political move represents a challenge for the presidential side. There is a striking contrast between the exaltation of an omnipresent presidential function and a form of powerlessness, even resignation, of the institution. What is more worrying is the political discourse of Macron, who is seemingly unable to get a clear message across about the political strategy and vision for France in the face of mounting difficulties (i.e., public deficit and debt, climate change challenges, insecurity and riots, uncontrolled immigration, the energy policy etc.).

The revision of the 1958 Constitution. The evolution of the Constitution is also due to the adoption of numerous amendments, 24 in total so far (see Box 3.3 Constitutional amendments to the 1958 Constitution). Constitutional amendments are governed by article 89 of the Constitution, even though article 11 was also used for this purpose.[100] Article 89 is the unique provision of Title XVI on "The Revision," which sets the limits of the amending power as well as providing for the amendment procedure. In terms of limits, the first limit concerns the circumstances of the amendment process. Constitutional amendments cannot be "instituted or carried out when the integrity of the national territory is impaired." Adopted in response to the July 1940 amendment marking the fall of the Third Republic, this limit aims at making it impossible to change the Constitution under pressure of an invading power.[101] Article 89 also sets a substantive limit to the amending power which concerns the republican form of the government that cannot be changed. However, the constituent has the power to remove or modify the provisions which contain such limitations, thus rendering them very contingent. In

98 For more details on the results of the presidential election, see Chapter 5 on political parties, elections, and referendums.

99 See Edouard Philippe & Nicole Belloubet, *Projet de loi constitutionnelle pour un renouveau de la vie démocratique*, No 2203, National Assembly, 29 August 2019, accessible at <https://www.assemblee-nationale.fr/dyn/15/textes/l15b2203_projet-loi>. The 2019 bill is a second iteration of a previous bill aimed at establishing "a more representative, responsible, and efficient democracy" presented in May 2018.

100 These developments partly draw from Marie-Luce Paris, *Constitutional Law in France*, International Encyclopaedia of Laws (2nd edn, Wolters Kluwer 2024) 58–60 (paras 74–80).

101 In addition to this limit set under article 89 of the Constitution, article 7 prohibits any constitutional amendments "during the vacancy of the office of the President of the Republic or during the period elapsing between the official declaration of the permanent incapacity of the President of the Republic and the election of his successor." Constitutional amendments are also impossible when the President of the Republic exercises the exceptional powers under article 16. See Decision No 81-132 DC of 16 January 1982 *Loi de nationalisation* (*Nationalisation*).

terms of the amending procedure, there are several steps, from the initiative to the enactment of the amendment. The initiative to amend the Constitution belongs to the President of the Republic on a proposal of the Prime Minister, who can put forward a "*projet de révision*," as well as to members of Parliament who can put forward a "*proposition de révision*." Politically, the real instigator of the amendment is the President himself/herself, except in a scenario of cohabitation where the Prime Minister "reclaims" his/her right to submit a proposal independently of what the President wants. However, in such a scenario, each can block the initiative of the other. In the case of a parliamentary initiative, any member of Parliament may table a constitutional bill, but s/he must be supported by his/her House, the National Assembly, or the Senate, which must vote on a resolution for this purpose. However, no constitutional amendment on the initiative of members of Parliament has been successful so far because the government can prevent such an initiative, especially coming from the opposition. Conversely, there is no point for a member of Parliament in the majority in tabling a constitutional bill on his/her own since s/he can turn to the government to instigate and support it.

Amendments to the Constitution are carried out through a two-stage procedure. In the first stage, a bill to amend the Constitution must be voted, by a simple majority, in identical terms by both Houses of Parliament. In contrast to the legislative procedure, the last word cannot be given to the National Assembly when it comes to amending the Constitution, thus conferring a de facto veto power upon the Senate, which can oppose constitutional amendments by not voting on them as it did on several occasions such as, for instance, on the amendment proposed by Mitterrand on the establishment of constitutional review by way of exception in 1990. The second stage depends on the authority that has initiated the amending proposal. Where a bill has been introduced by a member of Parliament, the constitutional amendment must be approved by a referendum, the President of the Republic having no choice in that case. Conversely, where a bill has been introduced at the initiative of the executive, the President has the choice between two routes, namely the referendum route and the parliamentary route. In cases where the President chooses not to resort to a referendum, s/he may choose the alternative and convene Parliament in Congress (i.e., the two Houses sitting together). The Congress must then adopt the constitutional amendment by a three-fifths majority of the votes cast. Only once, in 2000, regarding the amendment to the term of office of the President from seven to five years, was the amendment procedure carried out by a referendum.[102] The only other time the referendum route was taken was in relation to the constitutional referendum of 29 May 2005 on the 2005 Treaty establishing a Constitution for Europe. The decisive rejection by the French people (54.7% of "No" votes) rendered the constitutional amendment without object and stopped the ratification process of the 2005 Treaty altogether. This explains why the parliamentary route, rather than recourse to popular approval, has generally been considered as the safer option by French Presidents.

Aside from article 89, two constitutional amendments were carried out on the basis of article 11 of the Constitution. The first was a referendum that took place on 28 October 1962, regarding the direct suffrage of the President of the Republic by universal vote, which was approved.

102 Constitutional referendum of 24 September 2000 on the five-year presidential mandate (73.21% "Yes"; 26.79% "No"); Constitutional Law No 2000-964 of 2 October 2000 relating to the duration of the mandate of the President of the Republic.

The second referendum, held on 27 April 1969, focused on the reform of the Senate and the establishment of regional entities. However, this proposition was rejected.

A hybrid regime. The Constitution marks a real break with previous regimes. However, the nature of the regime is mixed and, to an extent, ambiguous. The regime borrows from both the parliamentary regime and the presidential regime. There is indeed a major contradiction between the mechanisms of the parliamentary regime that the constituents wished to establish, and the active role entrusted to the President of the Republic by virtue of the Constitution and embodied by De Gaulle. In short, the Fifth Republic is atypical in nature, neither presidential nor parliamentary, hence the various terms attributed to the French regime from "hybrid" to "mixed," or "semi-presidential." The parliamentary traits mostly result from the type of regime that the constituents sought to establish. This was all the more significant to ensure a filiation with the Fourth Republic and forget the somewhat hazardous origins of the Fifth Republic regime after the "coup" of 13 May 1958. Mechanisms such as the principle of government responsibility, the collaboration of the government with Parliament on the legislative level, and the right of dissolution of the National Assembly (though by the President of the Republic) are all typical of a parliamentary regime. These characteristics also derive from the practice of the regime, particularly in a period of cohabitation where a disowned President remains in place but is relegated behind the Prime Minister and the government acting as the real centre of political power. As Debré put it:

> "The government wanted to renovate the parliamentary system. I would even be tempted to say that the government wanted to establish it because, for many reasons, the Republic has never succeeded in doing so."[103]

As for the presidential traits, those are found not in the constitutional text itself but rather result from practice as attached to the historical legitimacy of De Gaulle, reinforced by his election by direct universal suffrage from 1962. These traits are reflected in the pre-eminence of the President. Other expressions have been used to describe the prominent place occupied by the President in the regime such as the omnipresence, or omnipotence, of the President, or, in the case of Sarkozy, his "hyper-presidency," or, in the case of Macron, his "Jupiterian" style of presidency.[104] The executive proceeds from the President, who has the power to set the broad guidelines of the nation's policy. The conferring of such effective political powers, including the "*pouvoirs propres*" of the President, is what distinguishes the regime of the Fifth Republic from the previous ones as it operates a complete break from the republican tradition and its most consistent constitutional law principles since the beginnings of the Third Republic.

103 Michel Debré Speech, 27 August 1958, Council of State, Paris. The famous speech delivered by Debré before the Council of State comprised three parts: the first part on "Giving to France a parliamentary regime"; the second part on "Creating a Community [with overseas territories]"; and the third part about "The President of the Republic," as the keystone of the regime.

104 Regarding Sarkozy, commentators and media bestowed upon him the epithet of "hyper-president." Conversely, Macron himself chose to characterise his presidency during October 2016 in a specific manner. Drawing inspiration from Greek mythology, he aimed to embody the style of the god Jupiter, surpassing the other deities. Macron considered that it was a clever approach to differentiate his leadership style from the "normal" presidency of Hollande.

Despite facing criticism from Mendès France and Mitterrand, the Constitution has stood the test of time and became France's second longest-serving regime in October 2023.[105] The institutions of the Fifth Republic have proven their flexibility allowing, for example, periods of cohabitation on three occasions. However, certain underlying dysfunctions and a lack of overall institutional coherence, such as the unusually prominent role of the President and its relationship with that of the Prime Minister, raise questions about the future of the Fifth Republic. The possibility of comprehensive institutional reforms or even the establishment of a Sixth Republic remains open.

BOX 3.3 CONSTITUTIONAL AMENDMENTS TO THE 1958 CONSTITUTION[106]

1. Constitutional Law No 60-525 of 4 June 1960 *États de la Communauté* [States of the Community]
2. Constitutional Law No 62-1292 of 6 November 1962 *Élection du Président de la République au suffrage universel* [Election of the President of the Republic by universal suffrage]
3. Constitutional Law No 63-1327 of 30 December 1963 *Session parlementaire* [Parliamentary session]
4. Constitutional Law No 74-904 of 29 October 1974 *Possibilité pour 60 députés ou 60 sénateurs de déférer une loi au Conseil constitutionnel* [Possibility for 60 deputies or 60 senators to refer a law to the Constitutional Council]
5. Constitutional Law No 76-527 of 18 June 1976 *Intérim de la Présidence de la République* [Interim Presidency of the Republic]
6. Constitutional Law No 92-554 of 25 June 1992 *Dispositions permettant de ratifier le traité de Maastricht* [Provisions allowing ratification of the Maastricht Treaty]
7. Constitutional Law No 93-952 of 27 July 1993 *Cour de justice de la République* [Court of Justice of the Republic]
8. Constitutional Law No 93-1256 of 25 Novembre 1993 *Droit d'asile* [Right of asylum]
9. Constitutional Law No 95-880 of 4 August 1995 *Session parlementaire unique ; aménagement des immunités parlementaires ; et élargissement des possibilités de recours au référendum* [Single parliamentary session; adjustment of parliamentary immunities; and expansion of the possibilities of recourse to referendum]
10. Constitutional Law No 96-138 of 22 February 1996 *Loi de financement de la sécurité sociale* [Social security financing law]
11. Constitutional Law No 98-610 of 20 July 1998 *Avenir de la Nouvelle-Calédonie* [Future of New Caledonia]
12. Constitutional Law No 99-49 of 25 January 1999 *Traité d'Amsterdam* [Treaty of Amsterdam]
13. Constitutional Law No 99-568 of 8 July 1999 *Cour Pénale Internationale* [International Criminal Court]

105 After the Third Republic, which lasted 70 years (1870–1940).

106 The text following the date of the constitutional law is not the official name of the law but indicates the area of law that was amended by it.

14. Constitutional Law No 99-569 of 8 July 1999 *Égalité entre les femmes et les hommes* [Equality between women and men]
15. Constitutional Law No 2000-964 of 2 October 2000 *Durée du mandat du Président de la République* [Duration of the mandate of the President of the Republic]
16. Constitutional Law No 2003-267 of 25 March 2003 *Mandat d'arrêt européen* [European Arrest Warrant]
17. Constitutional Law No 2003-276 of 28 March 2003 *Organisation décentralisée de la République* [Decentralised organisation of the Republic]
18. Constitutional Law No 2005-204 of 1 March 2005 *Traité établissant une Constitution pour l'Europe* [Treaty establishing a Constitution for Europe]
19. Constitutional Law No 2005-205 of 1 March 2005 *Charte de l'environnement* [Charter for the Environment]
20. Constitutional Law No 2007-237 of 23 February 2007 *Corps électoral de la Nouvelle-Calédonie* [Electoral body of New Caledonia]
21. Constitutional Law No 2007-238 of 23 February 2007 *Responsabilité du Président de la République* [Responsibility of the President of the Republic]
22. Constitutional Law No 2007-239 of 23 February 2007 *Interdiction de la peine de mort* [Prohibition of the death penalty]
23. Constitutional Law No 2008-103 of 4 February 2008 *modifiant le titre XV de la Constitution-Traité de Lisbonne* [amending Title XV of the Constitution-Treaty of Lisbon]
24. Constitutional Law No 2008-724 of 23 July 2008 *de modernisation des institutions de la V République* [Modernisation of the institutions of the Fifth Republic]
25. Constitutional Law No 2024-200 of 8 March 2024 *relative à la liberté de recourir à l'interruption volontaire de grossesse* [Freedom to resort to voluntary termination of pregnancy]

SELECTED FURTHER READINGS

Jean **Baubérot**, *Histoire de la laïcité en France* (8th edn, PUF 2021)

Olivier **Beaud**, Les mutations de la Ve République ou comment modifier une Constitution écrite, *Pouvoirs* No 99 (2001/4) 19

John **Bell**, Sophie Boyron & Simon Whittaker, *Principles of French Law* (2nd edn, Oxford University Press 2008)

Julie **Benetti**, "Le mythe de la sixième République" (2018) 3 (166) *Pouvoirs* 139

__________ (ed.), *Les collectivités territoriales et le principe d'égalité* (L'Harmattan 2016)

__________ et alii, *Révision de la Constitution : Mode d'emploi* (Dalloz 2017)

Michel **Borgetto** & Robert Lafore, *La mise en œuvre de la République sociale : Contribution à l'étude de la question démocratique en France* (PUF 2000)

René **Carré de Malberg**, *Contribution à la théorie générale de l'État* (Sirey 1920–1922, rééd Dalloz 2003)

Eoin **Daly**, "The Indivisibility of the French Republic as Political Theory and Constitutional Doctrine" (2015) 11 *European Constitutional Law Review* 458

________, "Ostentation and Republican Civility: Notes from the French Face-Veiling Debates" (2015) 14 (3) *European Journal of Political Theory* 298

________, "Reframing the Universalist Republic. Legal Pluralism in the French Periphery" (2015) 24 (4) *Social & Legal Studies* 531

________, "Public Funding of Religions in French Law: The Role of the Council of State in the Politics of Constitutional Secularism" (2014) 3 *Oxford Journal of Law and Religion* 103

La Documentation Française, Volume I *Des origines de la loi constitutionnelle du 3 juin 1958 à l'avant-projet du 29 juillet 1958, 1987*; Volume II *Le Comité consultatif constitutionnel : De l'avant-projet du 29 juillet 1958 au projet du 21 août 1958, 1988*; Volume III *Du Conseil d'État au référendum : 20 août–28 septembre 1958, 1991*; Volume IV *Commentaires sur la Constitution (1958–1959), 2001*
Maurice **Duverger**, *Le système politique français* (PUF 1996)
Bertrand **Faure**, *Droit des collectivités territoriales* (6th edn, Dalloz 2021)
_____________ & Antoinette Hastings-Marchadier (eds), *La décentralisation à la française* (LGDJ 2015)
Jean **Gicquel**, "Variations sur la présidence normale de François Hollande" in *L'État, le Droit, le Politique: Mélanges en l'honneur de Jean-Claude Colliard* (Dalloz 2014) 305
Didier **Guignard** (ed.), *40ème anniversaire des lois de décentralisation 1982–2022* (LexisNexis 2023)
Guy **Haarscher**, *La laïcité* (7th edn, PUF 2021)
Alain **Laquièze**, "Le modèle du régime présidentiel sous la Ve République" (2006) *Droits* 45
Florence **Lerique** (ed.), *Les fondements de l'administration territorialisée* (L'Harmattan 2023)
Jean **Massot**, *Alternance et cohabitation sous la Cinquième République* (La Documentation française 1997)
Michel **Miaille**, *La laïcité* (4th ed., Dalloz 2020)
Jean **Morange**, *La laïcité dans la République : Garantie ou menace pour les libertés ?* (LGDJ 2023)
Alexis **Niepceron**, *La place des régions dans la décentralisation française* (L'Harmattan 2017)
Marie-Luce **Paris**, "Popular Sovereignty and the Use of the Referendum: Comparative Perspectives with Reference to France" in Eoin Carolan (ed.), *75 years of the Irish Constitution: Past, Present and Future* (Bloomsbury Professional 2012) 279
Mathilde **Philip-Gay**, *Droit de la laïcité* (Ellipses 2016)
Philippe **Raynaud**, *L'esprit de la Ve République : L'histoire, le régime, le système* (Perrin 2017)
Dominique **Schnapper**, *De la démocratie en France : République, nation, laïcité* (Odile Jacob 2017)
Michel Verpeaux (ed.), "Révision de la Constitution : La Ve République rénovée ? À propos de la loi constitutionnelle du 23 juillet 2008" (2008) *Juris-Classeur Périodique*
_____________ et alii, *Les collectivités territoriales et la décentralisation* (12th edn, La Documentation française 2021)
Patrick **Weil** (ed.), *Politiques de la laïcité au XXème siècle* (PUF 2007)
Patrick **Weil** & Nicolas Truong, *Le sens de la République* (Grasset 2015)
Jean-Claude **Zarka**, *L'essentiel du droit des collectivités territoriales* (Gualino 2023)

4

THE INSTITUTIONS OF THE FIFTH REPUBLIC

The institutions of the Fifth Republic have been in place for 65 years, which is almost as long as the institutions of the Third Republic, which lasted for 70 years. The longevity of this political system was not initially anticipated. In fact, the Fifth Republic faced significant criticism as it was seen as being too reliant on its inspirational figure and first President, De Gaulle. However, the regime has endured, primarily due to the adaptability of its institutions. These institutions comprise, in the first place, the President of the Republic as the figurehead of the regime. Understanding the overall structure and the dominance of the executive branch over the legislature requires, in the second place, examining the government, Parliament, and their interrelationships. Other institutions such as, among others, the Economic, Social and Environmental Council, the Council of State, the Court of Auditors, and the independent administrative authorities complete the overview of the institutions of the Fifth Republic in this chapter.[1]

The President of the Republic

« *Il y a deux organes inutiles: la prostate et le Président de la République.* »[2]

The President of the Republic occupies a pre-eminent position in the Constitution (see Figure 4.1 Presidents of the Fifth Republic). Title II of the Constitution dedicated to the office of the President of the Republic (articles 5 to 19) features in second place, immediately after Title I dedicated to sovereignty (articles 2 to 4). This represents a break from the republican tradition

1 These developments partly draw from Marie-Luce Paris et alii, *Constitutional Law in France*, International Encyclopaedia of Laws (Wolters Kluwer 2019) 95–176 (paras 141–320).

2 Georges Clémenceau (1841–1929), French Prime Minister (1906–1909; 1917–1920) [There are two useless organs: the prostate and the President of the Republic].

DOI: 10.4324/9781003268871-6

where Parliament had traditionally occupied such pre-eminence. The 1958 drafters, De Gaulle and Debré in particular, sought to put in place a "republican monarch."[3] However, their respective conceptions of such an idea were not identical.[4] Debré saw the figure of the "republican monarch" as a way to reconcile a strong Head of State with the peculiarities of the French political system of a parliamentary nature under the long-lasting Third Republic. In 1940, France was defeated because of, among other factors, the weaknesses of its institutions, its executive power in particular. Debré observed that the only two western powers that resisted during the Second World War were the UK and the USA—the UK where the Head of State is a proper hereditary monarch, and the USA where the Head of State is elected by the people—thus making these systems the only possible constitutional models to draw inspiration from. Obviously, none of these models could be reproduced as such in the French post-war regime: not the UK model for obvious historical reasons; not the US model due to the unlikelihood, should the French President be elected by universal suffrage, of obtaining a majority of the votes, in which case the elected President would not represent the majority of the French people, making the situation politically unacceptable. As a result, for Debré, the "only chance for French democracy [was] the so-called republican monarch."[5] De Gaulle's inclination towards the monarchical approach can be explained differently, for reasons due to his own family roots and tradition, and to his approach to power and politics. For De Gaulle, the state, like the army, cannot function without a single undisputable leader. A leader is, by definition, in a position to solve major issues and, ultimately, takes the most important decisions for the country. In other words, there needs to be a "head at the helm of the state" in order to ensure adequate decision-making and ensuing action—such is, for De Gaulle, the prerequisite of an efficient leadership. The difference in perspective between Debré and De Gaulle was therefore a subtle one: the former saw the "republican monarch" as an impartial figure above party politics and detached from the acting powers that are the government and Parliament, derived from the idea of "a monarch who reigns but does not rule," while the latter saw the "republican monarch" as an active and powerful figure. Debré's conception was encapsulated in the well-known metaphor that he used to describe the President as the "*clé de voûte*"[6] or keystone of the institutional system. The Constitution somehow embodies this double influence, one drawn from the liberal idea of a constitutional monarch from Debré's inspiration, on the one hand, and one drawn from the idea of an active monarch under the Gaullist conception, on the other hand.

Understanding the status and powers of the President of the Republic requires recognising the crucial impact of this dual influence. In the following developments, we delve into an analysis of the President's status and powers, tracing their origins. This is followed by developments about the President in action.

3 Maurice Duverger, *La monarchie républicaine, ou comment les démocraties se donnent des rois* (Robert Laffont 1974).

4 For a detailed discussion of this aspect, see Frédéric Rouvillois, *Droit constitutionnel : La Vème République* (4th edn, Flammarion 2014) 141–144.

5 As cited in Frédéric Rouvillois, *Droit constitutionnel : La Vème République* (4th edn, Flammarion 2014) 141.

6 Michel Debré Speech, 27 August 1958, Council of State, Paris (excerpt). The famous speech delivered by Debré before the Council of State comprised three parts: the first part about "Giving to France a parliamentary regime"; the second part on "Creating a Community [with overseas territories]"; and the third part about "The President of the Republic" as the keystone of the regime.

Charles **De Gaulle** (1958–1965; 1965–1969 after direct election)	two terms
Georges **Pompidou** (1969–1974)	
Valéry **Giscard d'Estaing** (1974–1981)	
François **Mitterrand** (1981–1988; 1988–1995)	two terms
Jacques **Chirac** (1995–2002; 2002–2007)	two terms
Nicolas **Sarkozy** (2007–2012)	
François **Hollande** (2012–2017)	
Emmanuel **Macron** (2017–2022; 2022–present)	two terms

FIGURE 4.1 Presidents of the Fifth Republic

The status of the President of the Republic

The President of the Republic is the figurehead of French politics, blending monarchical traditions with republican values. As the foremost public figure, the President is bestowed with the highest civil and military honours at official ceremonies.[7] Over time, the President has emerged as the central institution of the Fifth Republic.[8] Consequently, any proposals to alter the process of appointment, duration of tenure, or level of accountability have sparked extensive debates. Several significant constitutional amendments have been enacted to address these issues, including revisions pertaining to the election of the President and the length of his/her term in office.

The presidential election. The President of the Republic is elected for a five-year term which can be renewed only once. The elective nature of the mandate plays a vital role in determining the President's authority and legitimacy. The modalities of the presidential election are examined below in Chapter 5 on political parties, elections, and referendums.

The presidential term of office. Originally, the President of the Republic was elected for a seven-year term, as this was the case under the previous Republics when the President had a rather neutral role. It was possible to consider the *septennat* (i.e., seven-year term of office) as a long term of office "necessary for a certain kind of vision and reflection on the evolution of

7 There is no specific law protecting the President of the Republic. The offence of insulting the Head of State was abolished in 2013, resulting in identical penalties applicable to any public servant, including police officer, firefighter, or judge (article 33 of the Criminal Code).

8 Moreover, based on legal provisions of uncertain origin (specifically, a document endorsed by the Prime Minister in 1985), former Presidents of the Republic are entitled to substantial privileges once they conclude their term in office. These privileges encompass the allocation of an official vehicle, complimentary housing and related amenities, along with specialised police protection. Additionally, former Presidents of the Republic are eligible to receive a lifelong salary as members of the Constitutional Council, provided that they actually sit on the Council.

the world,"[9] more germane to the role of President than a shorter term of office relevant to the day-to-day running of the country. However, this changed in 2000, when the *quinquennat* (i.e., five-year term of office) came into force.[10] This was to make it coincide with the five-year term of office of deputies elected to the National Assembly. One of the reasons for the reform—which had long been discussed before its adoption[11]—was to avoid cohabitation. However, while the concomitance of the presidential and parliamentary terms of office has reduced its probability, cohabitation is arguably still a possibility. This may be the case, for example, following dissolution of the National Assembly, or in the event of an unanticipated end of the presidential mandate (e.g., death, impeachment, or resignation). In 2008, another constitutional amendment was adopted limiting to two consecutive terms in office (i.e., ten years) the number of terms that the President can seek re-election for.[12] This raises the question of why it was not decided to limit re-election from the first term of office, hereby avoiding the President spending the last period of his/her first term campaigning for his/her re-election. Besides, no President of the Republic has ever sought to be re-elected a third time, which might be different with younger candidates such as Macron, who could seek re-election in 2032 (but not in 2027 as a third consecutive term is not possible).

The term of the presidency can be interrupted before the end of the five-year term under two sets of circumstances envisaged under constitutional provisions (article 7 paragraphs four to eight of the Constitution). The first circumstance pertains to the occurrence of a *vacancy* in the presidential position. Such a vacancy can be caused by the President's death,[13] resignation,[14] or removal from office, and these events are officially acknowledged by the Constitutional Council. The declaration of a vacancy is made upon the request of the government and requires a decisive majority vote from the Constitutional Council. The Council then determines whether the vacancy is temporary or permanent. In the latter scenario, the Council oversees the process for selecting a new President. It is mandatory for a presidential election to be held within a range of 20 to 35 days from the date of vacancy declaration.

Contrary to the situation of vacancy, other circumstances can also *prevent* the President from exercising his/her powers, whether such an impediment is permanent or temporary,[15] and

9 Jacques Chirac Speech, 14 July 1997, TV Interview addressing the Jospin Government's plans, the need to reduce the budget deficit, the President of the Republic's powers, and cohabitation.

10 Constitutional Law No 2000-964 of 2 October 2000 relating to the duration of the mandate of the President of the Republic. The constitutional amendment was adopted on 24 September 2000 by changing only one word (i.e., "*septennat*" to "*quinquennat*"). The reform was adopted by referendum by a large majority (73.21%), albeit amid great indifference (nearly 70% abstention). See Chapter 5 on political parties, elections, and referendums.

11 The opposition first called for a reduction of the presidential mandate in the 1960s as way to re-establish the balance between the President of the Republic and Parliament. This was in vain as long as De Gaulle was in power. De Gaulle's successor, Pompidou, renewed the call for a reform in the following decade (when he was already ill) by, interestingly, reverting the argument for a shorter term of office: while De Gaulle regarded the seven-year term as a guarantee of the superior democratic legitimacy of the President, Pompidou regarded it as excessive and putting the President at odds with Parliament since deputies were elected more frequently, therefore benefiting from a renewed democratic legitimacy at closer intervals than the President. There was indeed an implied ambiguity in the proposed reform that nobody was able to predict.

12 This reform was adopted without any difficulty by both Houses of Parliament and then Congress.

13 For instance, Pompidou died during his mandate, on 2 April 1974.

14 For instance, De Gaulle resigned before the end of his second mandate, on 28 April 1969.

15 If the impediment is permanent, the interim President cannot stay in power for more than 35 days from the announcement of the impediment to hold power. However, if the impediment is temporary, the interim presidency may continue for as long as required, while ensuring it does not exceed a reasonable duration. If the temporary

whether it is due to personal reasons or to reasons beyond his/her control. In the case of such events, the president of the Senate acts as the interim President of the Republic. The choice of the president of the Senate as the acting interim President is explained by legal and political reasons. Legally speaking, it would have been difficult to entrust the president of the National Assembly with such a role since the National Assembly could have been dissolved just before, or during, the interim. Politically speaking, the president of the Senate appears as less involved in day-to-day politics and more neutral than his/her counterpart in the National Assembly (or than the Prime Minister), thus better suited to ensuring the continuity of the state. If the president of the Senate happens to be incapacitated, the interim falls on the government. Tasked with the role of ensuring the "continuity of the state" in whatever circumstances, the interim President exercises all powers normally exercised by the President including the exceptional powers (see below). However, the interim President cannot exercise other significant powers such as deciding to hold a referendum or dissolve the National Assembly; also, the Constitution cannot be amended during the interim presidency, the government cannot be held accountable, and no motion of censure can be voted against the government, meaning that the government cannot be dismissed. The idea is that the interim President shall be endowed with the required power to avoid complete collapse of the state without, however, being facilitated in exercising power in a personalised way. The rules on interim presidency aim at crystallising the presidential office, making the interim President a fully fledged Head of State and maintaining the government in full operation. The issue of the interim presidency is more political than legal. During an interim presidency, the relationships between the interim President, on the one hand, and the Prime Minister and the majority, on the other hand, can be difficult to manage. A period of interim happened on two occasions under the Fifth Republic: once when De Gaulle resigned in 1969 (28 April–20 June 1969), and the other time because of the untimely passing of Pompidou in 1974 (2 April–27 May 1974). In both cases, the interim was held by Poher, president of the Senate at the time. The relationships between Poher and Prime Minister Couve de Murville during the 1969 interim were difficult.

Less serious than the interim situation is the situation that arises when the President is temporarily unable to fulfil his/her duties, such as being hospitalised or traveling abroad. In such circumstances, the Prime Minister undertakes the responsibility of representing the President during Council of Ministers meetings. This is done through a specific delegation and for a specific agenda.

Is the President of the Republic accountable? The accountability of the President of the Republic appears uncertain relative to the significance of his/her powers. In principle, the President is politically unaccountable and benefits from immunity in criminal proceedings. Firstly, as regards political accountability, the President is totally unaccountable during his/her term of office, certainly as regards Parliament and also as regards the nation. The principle of political unaccountability of the Head of State is due to the parliamentary nature of the regime.[16] Under the parliamentary regime, only the Prime Minister and the Cabinet are politically accountable

impediment persists unreasonably, the Constitutional Council will deem it a permanent impediment and formally declare it as such.

16 The principle is derived from the longstanding rule of the monarch's inviolability, and it continues to be relevant even after the President of the Republic has completed his/her term in office.

to Parliament. Under the French regime, the Prime Minister and his/her government, and not the Head of State, can be held politically accountable before the National Assembly and within the limits laid down under the Constitution (articles 49 and 50 of the Constitution). As a result, even a politically unpopular President stays in office until the end of his/her term. Macron, with a popularity rate of less than 30% at the time of writing, will stay until the end of his mandate (2027).[17] However, an unfavourable vote against a new presidential term can be perceived as testing the President and signalling that the people "dismiss" the President by their vote and sort of held him/her accountable for his/her political actions of the past term.

Furthermore, the President is not constitutionally obliged to resign from office after a negative referendum (even though this happened when De Gaulle left office in 1969 after losing the referendum about the regions and the Senate). Similarly, the President is not obligated to resign even if s/he loses his/her majority in the legislative elections, resulting in a cohabitation scenario. These circumstances introduce significant ambiguity and have prompted differing perspectives from various authors. Some authors have adopted a contrasting viewpoint, arguing that although the President is *theoretically* accountable to the people due to the institutional framework of the Fifth Republic, which places them at the forefront of the institutions, this accountability is greatly limited *in practice*.[18] The ambiguity stems from the fact that multiple successors of De Gaulle have asserted that their level of accountability aligns with their level of power. However, they have not consistently acted in accordance with the consequences of such declared accountability in specific situations. This highlights the need to address this issue. An illustrative example of the importance of addressing this matter is Sarkozy's position during the 2008 constitutional amendment. In July 2007, Sarkozy recognised that the proposed reform should centre around the principle of the Head of State's accountability, as he considered it to be "the central issue of the reform of the institutions of the Republic."[19] Neglecting this principle during the 1970s led to a gradual erosion of trust between the people and their leaders.

Secondly, as regards criminal immunity, the accountability regime is defined under Title IX of the Constitution on the High Court (articles 67 and 68 of the Constitution).[20] The President of the Republic is unaccountable for the acts accomplished in his/her capacity as President. S/he cannot be subject to any judicial proceedings, whether criminal, civil, or administrative. It means that the President cannot, during his/her term, be required to testify or be the subject of judicial proceedings, judicial investigations, or judicial prosecution before any French court or administrative authority (article 67 of the Constitution). The President is indeed no ordinary citizen and, as such, should be exempt from undue pressure while in office. While this is understandable under a regime with a weak Head of State, this is less so under the Fifth Republic, which affords significant powers to the President. However, the presidential immunity does not apply to acts committed outside of the exercise of presidential functions. Besides,

17 At the start of his first mandate in 2017, Macron was disapproved of by 31% of the French. Five years later, in 2022, this was 58%. In April 2023, one year after his re-election, this percentage stood at 72%. See *Cote de popularité d'Emmanuel Macron, Baromètre Politique Ipsos-Le Point*, accessible at <https://www.ipsos.com/fr-fr/cote-popularite-emmanuel-macron>.

18 René Capitant cited in Frédéric Rouvillois, *Droit constitutionnel : La Vème République* (4th edn, Flammarion 2014) 170–174.

19 Nicolas Sarkozy Speech, 12 July 2007, Épinal. The speech was about the role of the institutions of the Fifth Republic in the stability of French democracy and the creation of a reflection committee to adapt the institutions to the democratic requirements of the twenty-first century.

20 For more on the High Court, see below.

the presidential immunity ends one month after the President leaves office, at which point proceedings against him/her may be brought or resume before a court of law. Such immunity, which is total during the President's term of office, has been criticised. Some have invoked the textbook situation whereby a sitting President "kills his wife's lover"; however, in that case, it is likely that the act will not be regarded as linked to the presidential function and will indeed result in criminal prosecution before the assize court.

Two exceptions somehow mitigate the principle of presidential immunity, namely the possibility of removing the President of the Republic from office under the so-called "destitution procedure" (article 68 of the Constitution), on the one hand, and the possibility of bringing proceedings before the International Criminal Court of Justice (article 53-2 of the Constitution), on the other hand. Very similar to the US impeachment procedure, the destitution procedure aims at removing the President from office in cases of a serious breach of his/her duties that is manifestly incompatible with the exercise of the presidential function. However, it is not clear what kind of responsibility this procedure—which has never been applied so far—refers to, whether it is of a strictly political nature or of a criminal nature. In any case, the application of article 68 of the Constitution is likely to be limited to the most extreme cases of treason qualified as such by the High Court.[21] The vagueness of the facts likely to trigger the procedure is certainly unfortunate in this regard. Could one envisage destitution proceedings against Hollande and Macron concerning the accelerated demise of the French nuclear industry (i.e., closure of the nuclear plant in Fessenheim in 2020 etc.), which has de facto resulted in the country losing its energy autonomy?[22] The other exception to the principle of presidential immunity concerns the possibility of bringing international proceedings against the President for serious crimes such as genocide, war crimes, and crimes against humanity. Again, the gap between the theory (i.e., the enunciation of the constitutional principle of responsibility) and reality (i.e., ICC proceedings against a French President) must be noted. The likelihood of such proceedings is close to nil given the principle of state sovereignty. A former minister for Foreign Affairs acknowledged at the time that: "[the ICC] does not replace the States; the [ICC] intervenes in so far as national authorities are unable, or refuse, to bring to justice the individuals responsible for the most serious crimes."[23]

The powers of the President of the Republic

The President of the Republic "shall ensure the respect of [the] Constitution" and "under [her]/his arbitration, the normal operation of public powers as well as the continuity of the state." Additionally, the President of the Republic is "the guarantor of national independence, of the integrity of the territory, and of due respect for treaties" (article 5 of the Constitution). On the other hand, the government's role is to "determine and conduct the policy of the Nation"

21 The High Court is allotted a period of one month to deliberate and come to a decision regarding the removal of the President from his/her position. This decision is reached through a voting process, where a two-thirds majority of the court members is required. Voting is conducted confidentially and individually, without allowing proxy votes in this particular instance.

22 See Raphaël Schellenberger & Antoine Armand, *Rapport fait au nom de la Commission d'enquête visant à établir les raisons de la perte de souveraineté et d'indépendance énergétique de la France*, Report No 1028, National Assembly, 30 March 2023, accessible at <https://www.assemblee-nationale.fr/dyn/16/rapports/ceindener/l16b1028_rapport-enquete>.

23 Hubert Védrine cited in Frédéric Rouvillois, *Droit constitutionnel : La Vème République* (4th edn, Flammarion 2014) 168.

(article 20 of the Constitution). The Constitution grants the President of the Republic several powers. These powers are political powers (e.g., appointment of the Prime Minister), executive powers (e.g., promulgation of laws), and constitutional powers (e.g., respect of the Constitution and right of initiative to amend it). Powers are also conferred in relation to justice (e.g., right of individual pardon) and in the area of diplomacy and defence (e.g., power as Commander in Chief of the armed forces). These powers are outlined in further detail below.

The main innovation of the Constitution is the granting of specific powers that the President of the Republic exercises on his/her own, known as discretionary powers or *pouvoirs propres*. These powers differ from the ones the President shares with the government, referred to as shared powers or *pouvoirs partagés*. Under the Third and Fourth Republics, all acts of the President required the co-signature of the responsible minister, and the President was even prohibited from making any declaration without prior government approval. Consequently, the President's actions were subject to the control of the government, resulting in the Head of State's political irresponsibility. However, the Constitution of the Fifth Republic departs from this tradition by granting specific powers to the President that can be exercised without government oversight, meaning they no longer require the co-signature of the relevant minister(s). Under the current regime, the Prime Minister and the government have often been held accountable before the National Assembly for actions and decisions made without their involvement (sometimes even without prior knowledge). Nevertheless, the President's political lack of accountability persists, with the caveat mentioned previously.

The distinction between discretionary and shared powers is not as straightforward as it seems though. This is partly due to the practice of the regime under De Gaulle. He made sure early on to have a grip on reality regarding any major political decision, hereby contributing to somewhat changing the nature of the parliamentary regime that had been established in the first place. The action of the President manifests itself under other forms than legal acts and measures, though, such as, for instance, through attendance at meetings with foreign Heads of State and Heads of Government either in bilateral meetings or in the context of international high-ranking summits, or via visits in the country and abroad. Also, and this is another marker of De Gaulle's practice of the regime, the President manifests his/her role concretely by using press conferences and broadcasts, on a regular basis or on special occasions (i.e., major event, constitutional revision, crisis, war etc.), all acts that do not obviously require ministerial countersignature. De Gaulle had clearly understood the significance of his presence in the media as, in his words, the press conference was the "absolute weapon of the regime."[24]

The first cohabitation period (1986–1988) represented a departure from Gaullist practice. As matter of fact, the extent of the President's powers depends on the configuration of the regime, that is, whether the President has the support of a majority in Parliament or whether s/he "cohabitates" with a different majority (i.e., cohabitation). In the former situation, supposedly the "normal" functioning of the Fifth Republic, the President enjoys the maximum scope of his/her powers and dictates the choice of the Prime Minister, therefore the composition and action of the government. Indeed, when the majority in Parliament coincides with the presidential majority—which has been the case most of the time under the Fifth Republic—the

24 He added: "the French people have to see me and hear me, I have to hear them and see them (...) television and visits throughout the country give me such an opportunity." See Pierre Viansson-Ponté, *Les Gaullistes* (Paris 1963) 48, as cited in Frédéric Rouvillois, *Droit constitutionnel : La Vème République* (4th edn, Flammarion 2014) 176.

government is bound to apply the political programme championed by the President. In the latter situation, which is a period of cohabitation and represents a distortion of the normal functioning of the regime, the extent of the President's powers must comply with the strict reading of the Constitution whereby the government applies its programme with the support of the majority in Parliament.

Below, the subsequent content embarks on examining the powers vested in the President of the Republic, drawing a clear line between discretionary powers and powers that are jointly held with the government, with special emphasis on the Prime Minister.

The powers that the President exercises on his/her own. The President of the Republic is granted powers that s/he exercises independently, without the need for the approval of a government member. These *pouvoirs propres* are expressly outlined in the Constitution (article 19 of the Constitution). While significant, they are not the most frequently used by the President. These powers primarily pertain to the President's interactions with other constituted powers and authorities, such as the government, Parliament, the Constitutional Council, and the people. They include the exercise of exceptional powers in times of crisis. However, it is important to view these discretionary powers within the broader context of the President's role as an arbitrator and guardian of the Constitution (article 5 of the Constitution). In this regard, they aim to ensure respect for the Constitution, proper functioning of public institutions, protection of the state, preservation of national independence and territorial integrity, as well as adherence to international treaties. Therefore, the justification for and explanation of these discretionary powers can be found in article 5 of the Constitution.[25]

Firstly, as regards the government, the President of the Republic has the power to appoint the Prime Minister (article 8 paragraph one of the Constitution). The democratic legitimacy of the President acquired by his/her election by direct universal suffrage gives him/her a wide latitude in this choice. Since such an appointment is exercised freely, the chosen Prime Minister may not belong to Parliament.[26] However, this situation is called into question in the event of cohabitation where the President's room for manoeuvre is reduced since s/he is bound by the result of the legislative elections and must choose a Prime Minister who belongs to the newly elected parliamentary majority. In constitutional law terms, the President does not have the power to remove the Prime Minister from office but can only accept his/her resignation. However, the practice of the regime, barring periods of cohabitation,[27] has shown that the President has the political means to force a Prime Minister to resign.[28] Such "resignations" are therefore more akin to dismissals and can be brutal. For example, Edith Cresson, the first ever woman appointed as Prime Minister, was dismissed by Mitterrand after only 11 months in office (May 1991–April 1992). This leads us to question the meaning of a government reshuffle.

25 These powers are analysed under this tripartite division in some textbooks. See, for instance, Frédéric Rouvillois, *Droit constitutionnel : La Vème République* (4th edn, Flammarion 2014) 177 et seq.

26 Pompidou, originally professor of literature and bank manager, was appointed in 1962; Barre, professor of economics, was appointed in 1976; Cresson, local politician and member of the European Parliament, was appointed in 1991; Bérégovoy, local politician and former Minister, was appointed in 1992; De Villepin, diplomat, was appointed in 2005.

27 In case of a cohabitation, the Prime Minister is deemed "irremovable" as any dispute between him/her and the President of the Republic could result in a clash with the National Assembly, potentially leading to its dissolution.

28 The only voluntary resignation of a Prime Minister was the one presented by Chirac to Giscard d'Estaing in 1976.

Another power vis-à-vis the government is the power for the President to convene and chair the Council of Ministers, as well as approve its agenda as prepared by the General Secretariat of the government. The Council of Ministers takes place weekly, generally every Wednesday morning.

Secondly, as regards Parliament, the President of the Republic has the power to dissolve the National Assembly (article 12 of the Constitution).[29] While being a crucial mechanism of any parliamentary regime, the power of dissolution is a power that belongs to the Head of State under the Fifth Republic. Such a feature is not found neither in a classical parliamentary regime, in which the decision belongs to the Head of the Government, nor in a presidential regime, in which the President does not have the right to dissolve the National Assembly. Strictly defined under the Constitution, the discretionary power of dissolution is exercised after consultation of the Prime Minister and the presidents of both Houses of Parliament. The dissolution can be used at any moment, except within a year of a previous dissolution, in order to prevent instability.[30] The dissolution triggers legislative elections of the deputies of the National Assembly, elections which must be held within a time frame of 20 to 40 days. The newly elected National Assembly then convenes as of right. The power of dissolution, or the threat to resort to it, has been an essential tool for the stability of the regime. A dissolution has a double meaning. First of all, it represents a means of pressure that can force the National Assembly, and particularly the parliamentary majority, to give its support to the government. In addition, a dissolution may prevent and resolve crises; in that case, the President calls on the people's decision to renew the majority within the National Assembly in the face of a serious political predicament so that the institutions can function normally again. De Gaulle did dissolve on this ground on two occasions, firstly, in 1962 (Algerian War) and secondly, in 1968 (May 1968 strikes and riots). The other dissolutions of the Fifth Republic occurred for slightly different reasons. In 1981 and in 1988, Mitterrand dissolved the National Assembly at the start of his seven-year term in order to get a comfortable majority of deputies. The 1997 dissolution appears as the odd one out.[31] There was no real institutional or political crisis and Chirac enjoyed an overwhelming majority in the National Assembly. Chirac used the dissolution power for purely electoral reasons. He had announced that the dissolution was to "give the opportunity to the French people to decide on the political changes in the years to come"; this was in fact a tactical move to rekindle a parliamentary majority previously weakened by an internal conflict affecting right-wing leaders.[32] However, the electors did not understand the underlying reason and Chirac's decision proved to be a strategic failure: a left-wing majority returned to the National Assembly forcing him into a period of cohabitation with the Socialist Prime Minister Jospin. The 1997 dissolution also had the effect of casting aside the use of the procedure for a long time. There has been no dissolution since.

Pursuant to the separation of powers principle, the President of the Republic is not allowed to hold a seat in Parliament and is only permitted to communicate messages to the Houses of Parliament (article 18 of the Constitution). These messages can be conveyed through written

29 As the non-directly elected House of Parliament, the Senate cannot be dissolved.

30 Dissolution cannot occur either during the interim presidency or during the application of the exceptional powers under article 16 of the Constitution.

31 The 1997 dissolution is also explained under Chapter 3 on historical and legal foundations of the Fifth Republic.

32 The conflict was between Chirac and former Prime Minister Balladur (1993–1995), whose feud started when both ran for the 1995 presidential election.

means and, since the constitutional amendment of 2008, can also be delivered orally during a session of the Congress, wherein both Houses of Parliament assemble in Versailles. In such cases, the President's message may be followed by a debate, although no voting takes place. Under the Fifth Republic, most of these messages have been presented in written form, with only five instances in which they were read aloud to Parliament. The oral messages primarily revolve around political affairs, some of which encompass a general policy statement (e.g., Sarkozy in June 2009 and Macron in July 2018), while others mark the commencement of a new presidency (e.g., Macron in July 2017). In the aftermath of the Paris Islamist terrorist attacks on 13 November 2015, Hollande used the new procedure of delivering an oral message, which held great significance due to the traumatic nature of the events. Macron reverted to the written form on 25 February 2022 when he addressed the invasion of Ukraine by Russia.

Thirdly, the President of the Republic enjoys an appointment and a referral power vis-à-vis the Constitutional Council. The President appoints three of the Constitutional Council's members and chooses the Council's president. The appointment procedure is subject to approval by the parliamentary standing committee of each House of Parliament. A negative vote of three-fifths of committee members against a particular nominee will block the appointment. Inspired by the US system, the introduction of parliamentary approval has somewhat blurred the idea of *pouvoirs propres* since the two parliamentary standing committees have de facto acquired a right to veto these appointments. Also, the President has the power to make a referral to the Constitutional Council of a not-yet-ratified international agreement which is allegedly incompatible with the Constitution (article 54 of the Constitution) as well as of a voted but not-yet-promulgated law which is allegedly unconstitutional (article 61 paragraph two of the Constitution).[33]

Fourthly, the President of the Republic has the power to engage directly with the citizens through a legislative referendum (article 11 of the Constitution). Among the three types of national referendums (i.e., constituent referendum under article 89 of the Constitution, legislative referendum at the initiative of the President of the Republic, and legislative referendum of shared initiative, both under article 11 of the Constitution), only the legislative referendum is a discretionary power of the President.[34] The procedures and regulations pertaining to the article 11 referendum can be found in Chapter 5 on political parties, elections, and referendums.

The powers that the President of the Republic shares with the Prime Minister and the government. The so-called "shared powers" (*pouvoirs partagés*) are the powers of the President of the Republic that require the countersignature of the Prime Minister and, as appropriate, the countersignature of the ministers concerned. The Constitution delimits the extent of shared powers. The allocation rule is as follows: all acts of the President that are not regarded as discretionary powers are considered to fall within the scope of the shared powers (article 19 of the Constitution). In other words, whereas discretionary powers (i.e., articles 8

33 These powers are detailed under the Constitutional Council section in Chapter 6 on constitutional justice and rights protection.

34 The President of the Republic is also endowed with a referendum power concerning the accession of a new member state to the EU (article 88-5 of the Constitution). This implies that the Head of State is entitled to organise a public vote to seek the people's opinion on the approval of the treaty that facilitates the new country's accession. Nevertheless, nowadays, the parliamentary route is also available, rendering the referendum no longer the exclusive choice.

first paragraph one, 11, 12, 16, 18, 54, 56, and 61 of the Constitution) are regarded as conferred powers (*compétences d'attribution*), shared powers act as residual powers (*compétences de droit commun*). The countersignature requirement under the Fifth Republic has a different meaning than the one it had under the previous Republics. Whereas, under the Third and Fourth Republics, the countersignature of the President of the Council of Ministers was considered as a formal power since political power was in the hands of the Head of Government, the current regime endows the President of the Republic with real powers. As the figurehead of political power, thanks to his/her democratic legitimacy acquired by direct election and to the support of parliamentary majority, the President may, in certain cases, refuse to sign these acts. These shared powers mainly concern the day-to-day political life of the nation whether it involves the participation of the President in governmental action or his/her role in some aspects of the legislative or judicial process. These powers are detailed below.

The first shared power is an appointment power. The President of the Republic appoints, on a proposal from the Prime Minister, members of the government (article 8 paragraph two of the Constitution). The appointment of ministers is normally the result of a compromise between the President and the Prime Minister. However, the President often imposes his/her trusted collaborators in key government positions, notably in foreign affairs and defence, economy and finance, internal affairs, and justice, while being mindful of the balanced composition of the government. The government must indeed reflect the political parties of the presidential majority. Similarly, the resignation of ministers is, in theory, the result of a disagreement between the President and the Prime Minister; the resignation is formally proposed by the latter to the former, who puts an end to the functions of the minister concerned. Ministerial resignations can be the consequence of a critical attitude of the minister towards presidential policy such as, for example, the resignation of Chevènement, minister for Defence, under Mitterrand because of the President's decision to engage French troops in the 1991 Gulf War, or the (abrupt and televised) resignation of Hulot, minister for Ecological and Solidarity Transition, under Macron's first presidency in 2018 because of Hulot's perceived lack of control and autonomy in his actions. Resignations of ministers may also result from a variety of other reasons such as failure to declare properly their assets and various other conflicts of interest, which have been quite numerous under Macron's first presidency.

Another power of appointment of the President of the Republic shared with the government concerns the appointment of top civil servants and top military personnel of the state (article 13 paragraph two of the Constitution). This power must be read in conjunction with the power of the Prime Minister of also making civil and military appointments (article 21 paragraph one of the Constitution). However, the power of the Prime Minister is limited in scope, and it is the President who appoints to the highest positions. The top appointments are mandatory or discretionary. Mandatory appointments concern certain categories of the senior civil service (i.e., Council of State, Court of Auditors, judges of the judicial order, university professors, armed forces etc.) given the importance attached to these independent bodies. The leeway afforded to the President is also limited because these positions are filled based on strict competitive recruitment and because it concerns a high volume (circa 70,000) of appointments, which makes it difficult to examine each case in detail. As for discretionary appointments, these are made on a proposal of the Prime Minister with the agreement of the President and therefore involves consultation between the two. An issue has arisen as regards the politicisation of such appointments, notably when these appointments concern top civil servants or top managing directors of state companies (e.g., Airbus, Areva, Electricité de France, SNCF etc.).

Indeed, it has often occurred that, following a change of power, senior officials and leaders of such public bodies or companies were replaced by individuals closer to the new government's hue without this being necessarily justified. Some form of parliamentary control is now provided for, subject to the adoption of organic laws.[35] Before the President proceeds to the appointments, the relevant standing committee of each House of Parliament delivers an opinion on these "positions or functions because of their significance in respect of the guarantee of rights and freedoms or the economic and social life of the nation" (article 13 paragraph five of the Constitution).

Another type of power shared by the President of the Republic pertains to his/her participation in the normative power, which encompasses both the executive and legislative powers.

As regards the executive power, the President of the Republic signs two types of acts, namely ordinances and decrees deliberated within the Council of Ministers (article 13 paragraph one of the Constitution). Ordinances are regulatory acts whereby the government receives temporary legislative authority to achieve specified objectives in the field of law (article 38 of the Constitution). The power to sign ordinances by the President has been interpreted as a discretionary power since the Constitution sets no time limit in this regard, as opposed to the 15-day period imposed for the promulgation of laws. The President is thus not constitutionally obligated to sign ordinances, as is well illustrated by Mitterrand's refusal to sign ordinances on three occasions during the first cohabitation (1986–1988).[36] The only option left to the government in such a situation is to renounce using ordinances and to ask Parliament to legislate in this area. Decrees are defined as enforceable decisions of general scope (*décret règlementaire*) or of particular scope (*décret individuel*). Decrees are of two types: "implementing decrees" that specify the terms of application of a law, and "autonomous decrees" that deal with matters not falling within the scope of the law. Only the most important decrees (i.e., those deliberated in the Council of Ministers) are signed by the President of the Republic (article 13 paragraph one of the Constitution). The two other categories of decrees are "Council of State decrees" and "simple decrees." Council of State decrees are those deliberated within the Council of State when its consultation for an opinion is compulsory, and which are signed by the Prime Minister. Simple decrees are those simply issued by the Prime Minister and represent the most common mode of exercise of the regulatory power. Decrees are published in the Official Journal. Decrees can be imposed by a text, but most often it is the President who decides to include them in the deliberations of the Council of Ministers, thus interfering in the exercise of regulatory power. When the procedures required by the texts (e.g., signature of a decree taken in the Council of Ministers by the Head of State) are not respected, the decree can be annulled by the Council of State. The legal regime of decrees has been the object of a technical legal debate. The supreme administrative judge has ruled that any decree, which has been deliberated and signed within the Council of Ministers, can only be amended in a similar way, meaning that such a decree can only be amended by another decree deliberated on and signed in the Council of Ministers, making de facto the President of the Republic, who chairs the

35 This was introduced by the 2008 constitutional amendment. Since then, several organic laws were adopted. For example, a 2010 organic law lists 51 posts and functions that are submitted to the procedure in article 13 paragraph five including, for example, the CAO of Aéroports de Paris, the CAO of Météo France, and the governor of the Banque de France.

36 The ordinances in question concerned some key issues discussed at the time, such as issues relating to the privatisation of French companies, the delimitation of electoral constituencies, and working time arrangements.

Council of Ministers, the instigator of the decree in question.[37] This has had the critical result of considerably reducing the regulatory area of the Prime Minister while aggrandising that of the President, hereby confirming his/her pre-eminence in executive matters.

As regards the legislative power, the role of the President of the Republic is obviously limited pursuant to the separation of powers principle. His/her role is confined to promulgating laws (article 10 paragraph one of the Constitution). Promulgation of laws must occur within 15 days of their transmission to the government after their adoption by Parliament. By promulgating the law, the President recognises its legal existence and requests public authorities to abide by the voted law and enforce it. In other words, the law becomes enforceable, and, as soon as it is published in the Official Journal, this enforceability applies to all citizens. The decree of promulgation is also signed by the Prime Minister and the relevant ministers. The President is bound by the obligation to promulgate the law (*compétence liée*). However, the President is afforded some leeway because s/he is not obliged to rush to promulgate the law, thus leaving time for members of Parliament (generally the opposition gathering 60 signatures either from deputies or from senators) to make a referral to the Constitutional Council (article 61 paragraph two of the Constitution). Besides, should the President not be satisfied with the law or some of its provisions, s/he may, with the approval of the Prime Minister, request a further reading, in full or in part, of the law in question (article 10 paragraph two of the Constitution).[38] It is worth noting here the primary role of the Prime Minister in the relationship between the government and Parliament. The Prime Minister leads legislative initiatives and is at the heart of the law-making process since s/he is the one who decides which amendments will be tabled before Parliament on behalf of the government (article 44 of the Constitution). S/he takes the decision to convene a joint parliamentary committee in order to solve a disagreement between the two Houses of Parliament (article 45 of the Constitution) and decides to activate the responsibility of the government after deliberation in the Council of Ministers (article 49 of the Constitution). Like the President, the Prime Minister can refer a law to the Constitutional Council for judicial review (article 61 paragraph two of the Constitution).

A third category of shared powers relates to national defence and foreign affairs.[39] There is, however, a degree of overlap between the powers of the President of the Republic and the powers of the government in these areas. Through his/her role as guarantor of national independence, territorial integrity, and due respect for treaties (article 5 paragraph two of the Constitution), the President plays a leading role in national defence and foreign affairs. In relation to the armed forces, the President is the Commander in Chief of the armed forces and presides over the higher councils and committees for national defence (article 15 of the Constitution). However, the difficulty is to accord presidential power with that of the government, which has power over the armed forces (article 20 paragraph two of the Constitution), and with that of the Prime Minister, who has responsibility for national defence (article 21

37 CE, Ass., 10 September 1992, *Meyet*.

38 The possibility of a second reading has been passed down from past Republics. However, in the present regime, this practice holds minimal significance as the majority of laws originate from government bills that receive endorsement from the President of the Republic.

39 The President of the Republic also possesses the authority to officially appoint diplomats to serve as ambassadors in other countries. Additionally, the President has the privilege of accepting letters of accreditation from foreign countries for their respective ambassadors, as outlined in article 14 of the Constitution. As the leader responsible for foreign affairs, the President of the Republic represents his/her country's interests in the European Council.

of the Constitution). Besides, through the proposal and vote on military programming laws, Parliament and the government can influence defence policy choices. In reality, the President has pre-eminence in this area, even more so since the 1991 Gulf War when Mitterrand decided to commit French forces and was able to control the operations on the ground by presiding over a military staff council. However, the 2008 constitutional amendment introduced a degree of parliamentary control over the decision to send military troops abroad. The President must inform Parliament within three days of sending the troops. Parliament may debate, but not vote, on such a decision. Besides, any extension of a military intervention is subject to parliamentary approval, with the final word from the National Assembly, after four months of deployment (article 35 paragraphs two and three of the Constitution).[40] The only exception to the shared power, even in cases of cohabitation, and to parliamentary oversight is the power to resort to the use of nuclear weapons, which belongs exclusively to the President.[41]

Concerning powers in foreign affairs and diplomacy, the President is responsible for negotiating and ratifying international agreements and treaties and shall be informed of any negotiation leading to the conclusion of an international agreement not subject to ratification (article 52 of the Constitution). This reflects the primacy of the President in the conduct of foreign affairs and diplomacy. Successive Presidents have endeavoured to maintain their control over French foreign policy with certain constants, such as in relation to the policy on European integration or in relations with African countries. Such presidential pre-eminence is somewhat attenuated in times of cohabitation when the Prime Minister reclaims part of the executive leadership by taking part, for example, in state summits. In general terms, the President is in charge of foreign policy and, as such, sits in the European Council. However, there is a degree of overlap since the government, in charge of national policy, is also necessarily involved in international relations.

A fourth category of shared powers relates to judicial powers. The President of the Republic is responsible for ensuring the independence of the judiciary (article 64 of the Constitution). In that role, the President is assisted by the Superior Council of the Judiciary (*Conseil Supérieur de la Magistrature* or *CSM*). The question of the independence of the judiciary vis-à-vis the executive power is a recurrent issue in French politics. The 2008 constitutional amendment overhauled the constitutional provisions relating to the Superior Council of the Judiciary by notably ending the presidency of the Council by the President (article 65 of the Constitution). Membership of the Superior Council of the Judiciary was also amended, and it now comprises lawyers when the Council sits in formations relevant to sitting judges or prosecutors.[42] Another power in relation to justice is the power of pardon, which is granted to the President

40 The article 35 procedure was used to approve the following military deployments or external operations (*opérations extérieures* or *OPEX*): Afghanistan (September 2008); Chad, Central African Republic, Côte d'Ivoire, Lebanon, and Kosovo (January 2009); Libya (July 2011); and Mali (April 2013).

41 Decree No 64-46 of 14 January 1964 relating to strategic air forces. The strategic air forces are in fact the nuclear strike force. Although under the direct command of the President of the Republic, the Defence Council determines the mission, organisation, and rules of engagement for the strategic air forces. The fundamental principle of French defence policy is centred around nuclear deterrence, a concept initially defined and established by De Gaulle. For more details, see Marie-Luce Paris, "The President as Commander in Chief in a Comparative Constitutional Perspective under French and US Law" (2021) 59 (2) *The Military Law and Law of the War Review* 196.

42 For more details on the Superior Council of the Judiciary, see Chapter 6 on constitutional justice and rights protection.

and requires a ministerial countersignature (article 17 of the Constitution). This is a sovereign power, inherited from the monarchy. The power of pardon aims at neutralising the effects of a judicial sentence by suspending a criminal conviction or by exempting a convicted individual from penalties. This pardon only applies to individual convictions, and collective forms of pardon, which used to be allowed, are no longer acceptable.

Other shared powers relate to the referendum powers shared between the two heads of the executive, namely the President of the Republic and the Prime Minister. A first type of referendum concerns the European-related referendum (article 88-5 paragraph one of the Constitution). Any bill authorising the ratification of a treaty on the accession of a state to the EU must be approved by the French people in a referendum. While the government issues the bill authorising such a ratification, the decision to put it to a referendum is taken by the President. However, while the referendum route was initially the only possibility, the 2008 constitutional amendment opened the possibility of the parliamentary route (article 88-5 paragraph two of the Constitution). By voting on a motion adopted in identical terms in each House by a three-fifths majority, Parliament may authorise the adoption of the bill according to the constitutional amendment procedure (article 89 paragraph three of the Constitution). The other type of referendum concerns the power of the President, on a proposal submitted by the government (or on a joint proposal from both Houses of Parliament), to consult the people of an overseas territory on a question relating to the organisation, competences, or governance of that territory (article 72-4 paragraph two of the Constitution).[43]

Other powers of the President of the Republic relate to the Council of Ministers and to Parliament.[44] The President chairs Council of Ministers meetings (article 9 of the Constitution). In that capacity, the President convenes the weekly meetings of the Council of Ministers, determines the agenda, chairs the discussions, and has oversight of the minutes—in short, the President is in control of the organisation and conduct of this essential forum where s/he is in direct contact with the government. Vis-à-vis Parliament, the President may, at the request of the Prime Minister or at the request of the majority of deputies, order by decree that Parliament convenes for an extraordinary session (articles 29 and 30 of the Constitution). The power of the President is a "*compétence liée*," meaning that s/he is constitutionally bound to sign the decree opening the extraordinary session. However, the question of whether such power is legally binding can be posed since Presidents refused to convene Parliament on two occasions. In 1960, De Gaulle refused to convene Parliament in an extraordinary session despite the request of the majority in the National Assembly; and in 1987, Mitterrand, during the first cohabitation, rejected, via a press communiqué, a request from his Prime Minister Chirac to convene an extraordinary session of the Parliament on the status of the Renault car manufacturer, hereby confirming the discretionary nature of that power. Mitterrand did it again during the second cohabitation in 1993. This power to refuse to convene an extraordinary session of Parliament corresponds well to what can happen in periods of cohabitation when the President has limited political leverage in internal matters and is seeking other levers of action.

43 For more details on referendums, see Chapter 5 on political parties, elections, and referendums.

44 The President of the Republic is also endowed with honorary powers. When taking up his/her role, the President becomes the Grand Master of the National Order of the *Légion d'Honneur* and of the *Ordre National du Mérite* (National Order of Merit). S/he is also co-Prince of Andorra and honorary canon of the Basilica of St John Lateran in Rome. In all his/her roles, the French President of the Republic has protocol precedence.

The President of the Republic in action

Throughout the history of the Fifth Republic, successive French Presidents, with the backing of their parliamentary majority, have wielded a wide exercise of their power. The presidential pre-eminence is visible in the regular functioning of the Fifth Republic, with adjustments made during periods of cohabitation when the President finds himself/herself in opposition to the majority. In times of crisis, in contrast to ordinary circumstances, the President of the Republic possesses the ability to further expand his/her powers.

Exercise of presidential powers in normal times. Under the regular functioning of the Constitution, the government determines and conducts the policy of the nation (article 20 of the Constitution). However, practice has amply demonstrated that the President of the Republic also determines and conducts the policy of the nation. This has resulted in an unequal sharing of powers between the President and the government with a clear pre-eminence of the former over the latter. So, this begs the question of whether the competences of the President and the Prime Minister are really distinct or juxtaposed. As a matter of fact, both the President and the Prime Minister perform the same tasks, but not in the same way. The Head of State first determines the policy of the nation by setting out the main orientations and objectives of national policy. The Prime Minister and the government then intervene to implement the orientations as defined by the President. Much also depends on the personality of the President, who might be inclined to give more leeway to the government in those sensitive areas in order to avoid exposure or, on the contrary, decide to intervene in as many areas as s/he sees fit. De Gaulle, for example, and despite a grip on his majority, let the government govern. This can be compared to the "interventionist" style of Macron, who is involved in all matters, both externally and internally. One area of competence where this pre-eminence is particularly acute is the so-called "*domaine réservé*" or reserved area (of competence) in national defence and international affairs. Nonetheless, while the idea of a "*domaine réservé*" was prevalent during De Gaulle's presidency (1959–1969), it progressively lost its relevance in post-Gaullist times. This was confirmed by President Chirac in his speech of 14 July 1997 where he contended, at the time, that there was no presidential preserve but emphasised the particular role of the Head of State in preserving the role of France in the world, as well as maintaining the European and social *acquis*.[45]

Everything changes under a cohabitation, which occurs when the parliamentary majority resulting from the legislative elections differs from that of the President of the Republic. In that situation, the President can only appoint a Prime Minister from the new majority because, even though the President has discretion in the matter, all the same s/he must align his/her position with the popular will. Under cohabitation, the nature of the relationship between the two poles of the executive changes and there is a more equal sharing of powers, resulting in a transfer of power from the President to the Prime Minister. In other words, the power of the President is reduced to the letter of the Constitution, that is, to mainly that of an arbitrator between powers (article 5 of the Constitution). The Prime Minister determines and leads in the implementation of the nation's policy, a policy from which the President is excluded. This is translated in all institutional mechanisms such as, for example, within the Council of Ministers, where

45 Jacques Chirac Speech, 14 July 1997, TV Interview addressing the Jospin Government's plans, the need to reduce the budget deficit, the President of the Republic's powers, and cohabitation.

the work programme is essentially set by the government. Consequently, the Prime Minister's political accountability vis-à-vis the Head of State no longer holds, which makes the Prime Minister "unremovable" (i.e., s/he cannot be dismissed).[46]

Exercise of presidential powers in times of crisis. In times of crisis, the Fifth Republic regime endows the President of the Republic with another "*pouvoir propre*," that of the exceptional powers regime, which is activated at the President's discretion in exceptional circumstances (article 16 of the Constitution). These exceptional circumstances relate to situations where it is necessary to ensure the defence of the state and its democratic regime in cases of extreme danger such as war or internal subversion. The exceptional powers regime organises a kind of "republican dictatorship"[47] aimed at protecting the Republic while, at the same time, allowing infringement of all its core principles. De Gaulle's concern, when he devised article 16 of the Constitution, was to avoid the repetition of the events of June 1940 when the then President of the Third Republic, Lebrun, was left powerless by the German invasion, leading to the demise of the Republic and the establishment of the French State (*État Français*). Another concern was that such a regime would give the President maximum leeway in case s/he had to use his/her prerogative to activate the "nuclear fire" (i.e., nuclear weapons). The exceptional powers regime entails the absence of separation of powers, hence allowing the President to take any measure—legislative, executive, or judicial—that is required under the circumstances.[48] The decision to trigger the exceptional powers regime is entirely in the hands of the President and is not subject to appeal or judicial review. Article 16 of the Constitution has been regarded as a controversial provision ever since it was used by De Gaulle from 23 April until 29 September 1961 during the Algerian War for allegedly too long a period of time.[49] The 2008 constitutional amendment set new limitations on the use of exceptional powers. This was regarded as significant given the large power afforded to the President when assessing the substantive conditions necessary

46 Observers have been surprised at the generally amicable rapport shared between the President of the Republic and his/her Prime Minister during a period of cohabitation. This phenomenon can be partly attributed to the Prime Minister's potential aspiration to assume the role of Head of State, thereby deterring any inclination to undermine the authority of the presidency.

47 A "republican dictatorship" in the sense that it had under Roman Antiquity. Under Roman law, a dictatorship was legally installed for a short period of time (e.g., less than a fortnight under Cincinnatus) and with a specific goal (i.e., to safeguard the Republic). Once the normal functioning of the institutions and republican order were restored, the dictator was to transfer his authority back to the state and resume his normal role. There is also a Jacobian inspiration derived from the *Comité de Salut Public*. The Committee of Public Safety was a political organ that gained dictatorial control over France, under Robespierre's leadership, during the Terror period (September 1793–July 1794).

48 The President of the Republic has full legislative powers, thereby granting him/her the ability to establish special courts. This prerogative was exercised by De Gaulle, who swiftly established six distinct courts between the years 1961 and 1963 for the purpose of political repression. Subsequently, these military courts were substituted with the State Security Court or *Cour de sûreté de l'État* (1963–1981). See Victor Delaporte, "Aux origines de la Cour de sûreté de l'État : La conquête d'un pouvoir de punir par l'exécutif (1960–1963)" (2018) 140 (4) *Vingtième Siècle. Revue d'histoire* 137.

49 The authorities successfully suppressed the rebellion instigated by the coup staged by the generals in a span of fewer than three days. Therefore, the prolongation of the exceptional powers under article 16 of the Constitution for all these months can be deemed as a clear misuse of power and, for some, even constituted a genuine overthrow of the government. See Frédéric Rouvillois, "La V République, un coup d'état de tous les jours ?" in Christophe Boutin & Frédéric Rouvillois, *Le coup d'État : Recours à la force ou dernier mot du politique ?* (F-X de Guibert 2008) 204–205.

to trigger the crisis regime. These substantive conditions impose that the independence of the nation, the integrity of its territory, or the fulfilment of its international obligations is under grave and immediate threat, on the one hand, *and* that the proper functioning of the constitutional public authorities has been interrupted, on the other hand (article 16 paragraph one of the Constitution). The two branches of the conditions are cumulative. However, the phrasing of these substantive requirements is sufficiently imprecise as to leave some margin of appreciation to the President, which obviously represents a danger for fundamental freedoms and democracy in cases of abuse. Formal requirements include the obligation to consult the Prime Minister, the presidents of both Houses of Parliament, and the president of the Constitutional Council, whose reasoned opinion is published in the Official Journal (article 16 paragraph one of the Constitution). Once the conditions are fulfilled and consultations have been carried out, the President informs the nation of the implementation of exceptional powers (article 16 paragraph two of the Constitution). Other guarantees exist during implementation, which include the obligation to submit the measures taken by the President to the Constitutional Council for an opinion and the fact that these measures must all aim at re-establishing the normal functioning of constitutional order. Another guarantee, albeit limited, is the judicial review exercised by the supreme administrative judge of measures that fall within the regulatory domain, and of individual implementing measures.[50] Also, Parliament shall sit as of right (article 16 paragraph four of the Constitution), and the National Assembly cannot be dissolved during the use of the exceptional powers (article 16 paragraph five of the Constitution). Parliament can legislate and control the action of the government but without interfering with the measures taken by the President when implementing the exceptional powers. The Constitution cannot be amended (article 89 paragraph four of the Constitution). Lastly, the Constitutional Council decides whether the exceptional powers should continue to apply at the request of either president of the Houses of Parliament, or at the request of 60 deputies or 60 senators within 30 days of implementation. The Council gives its opinion on whether the exceptional powers continue to apply, as of right within 60 days of implementation, and at any time after 60 days of implementation (article 16 paragraph six of the Constitution). The opinion of the Constitutional Council is not legally binding, although it would be politically difficult for the President to overlook a negative opinion of the Council. Furthermore, in the event that the President misuses the exceptional powers bestowed upon him/her, there is a high probability of the situation escalating into a coup d'état, ultimately leading to the President's removal through impeachment by the Parliament.

The Constitution and the law provide other crisis frameworks, namely the state of siege and the state of emergency. Unlike the exceptional powers regime, these regimes do not grant the President of the Republic expanded powers (see Table 4.1 Crisis regimes under the Fifth Republic).

Firstly, the state of siege aims at situations of armed conflict and specifically applies "in the event of imminent danger resulting from a foreign war or an armed insurrection" (article 36 of the Constitution).[51] The President holds some authority in this matter because the state of siege is implemented through a decree deliberated in the Council of Ministers, which is presided over

50 CE, Ass., 2 March 1962, *Rubin de Servens*, Rec. Lebon 143 (regulatory measures); and CE, 23 October 1964, *d'Oriano*, Rec. Lebon 486 (individual implementing measures).

51 See also article L 2121-1 of the Code of Defence. Article 36 of the Constitution finds its origins in legislative provisions, namely the Law of 9 August 1849 on the state of siege, and the Law of 3 April 1878 on the state of siege.

TABLE 4.1 Crisis regimes under the Fifth Republic

	Crisis Regimes under the Fifth Republic			
	Exceptional Powers	*State of Siege*	*State of Emergency*	
			Security	*Health*
Legal source	*Article 16 of the Constitution*	*Article 36 of the Constitution*	*Act of 3 April 1955*	*Act of 23 March 2020*
Criteria	Two cumulative substantive conditions: 1 Alternative condition: Serious and immediate threat • to the institutions of the Republic, the independence of the nation, the integrity of its territory, • to the fulfilment of its international obligations. 2 The proper functioning of the constitutional public authorities is interrupted. Two cumulative formal conditions: 1 The President of the Republic must consult the Prime Minister, the presidents of both Houses of Parliament, and the Constitutional Council. 2 The President of the Republic shall address the nation and inform the nation about measures taken.	One formal condition: Decree adopted by the Council of Ministers	Two alternative substantive conditions: 1 imminent danger resulting from serious threats to public order, 2 events which, by their nature or seriousness, constitute a public disaster.	One substantive condition: A health disaster which, by its nature and seriousness, endangers the health of the population.
			One formal condition: Decree adopted by the Council of Ministers	
Executive power	The President of the Republic takes whatever measures are required by the circumstances without regard to the normal division of powers.	Police powers are exercised by military authorities with increased powers.	Strengthening the powers of the executive.	
Legislative power	• Parliament shall sit as of right. • The National Assembly shall not be dissolved during the exercise of such exceptional powers.		• A state of emergency may only be extended beyond 12 days by law. • The National Assembly shall be dissolved during the exercise of the state of emergency.	

Approval	• After 30 days, the presidents of both Houses of Parliament, 60 deputies, or 60 senators may refer the matter to the Constitutional Council to check that the conditions for application have still been met. • After 60 days, the Constitutional Council carries out this review as of right.	A state of siege may only be extended beyond 12 days by law.	• A state of emergency may only be extended beyond 12 days by law. • Proceedings before the administrative courts.	
Application	1961: attempted coup by the generals in Algiers	X	• 1955: French Algeria • 1958: coup in Algiers • 1961: attempted coup by the generals in Algiers • 1984: New Caledonia riots • 2005: riots in the suburbs • 2015: Paris terrorist attacks	Covid-19

by the President. This decree identifies the specific territory to which the state of siege applies and sets the duration of its implementation. If the state of siege is to continue beyond 12 days, it must be authorised by Parliament. Similar to martial law, the state of siege involves transferring the responsibilities of maintaining order and exercising police powers from civilian authorities to military authorities. It may also impose restrictions on civil liberties and fundamental freedoms. For instance, it may prohibit the publication of certain material or the holding of public gatherings that pose a risk to public order. Notwithstanding the state of siege, the rights guaranteed by the Constitution remain intact unless their exercise is temporarily suspended.[52]

Secondly, the declaration of a state of emergency encompasses "the whole metropolitan territory, or part of it, in overseas departments, in overseas territories governed by article 74 of the Constitution and in New Caledonia."[53] This declaration occurs either in the face of an imminent danger resulting from serious breaches of public order or in the presence of events that possess the nature and severity of a public calamity.[54] Under the state of emergency regime, the constitutional powers, including those vested in the President of the Republic, remain unchanged. However, there is an expansion of police powers exercised by civil authorities. Notably, this regime allows restrictions on fundamental rights and liberties of individuals suspected of posing a threat to public security. For instance, the state of emergency empowers the prefect and the minister for Home Affairs to impose limitations or prohibitions on road traffic and public gatherings, temporarily close certain public areas, authorise administrative searches, and implement house arrests. In response to the devastating Islamist attacks that took place in Paris and Saint-Denis on 13 November 2015, the state of emergency was declared during a Council of Ministers meeting on the same night.[55] This state of emergency was subsequently extended six times by Parliament until its conclusion on 1 November 2017. The end of the state of emergency coincided with the enactment of the Law of 30 October 2017, which aimed to strengthen domestic security and intensify the fight against terrorism.[56]

Government and Parliament

> « *Nul gouvernement ne peut être longtemps solide sans une redoutable opposition.* »[57]
>
> « *Le comptoir d'un café est le parlement du peuple.* »[58]

Under the Fifth Republic, the division of power within the executive branch follows a dualist approach. The executive branch is split between the President of the Republic, elected by direct

52 Articles L 2121-1 to L 2121-8 of the Code of Defence.

53 Article 1 of Law No 55-385 of 3 April 1955 relating to the state of emergency, as amended in July 2017.

54 Ibid.

55 Before November 2015, the state of emergency was declared five times: three times in relation to the Algerian troubles—in 1955 in the departments which formed French Algeria, and in 1958 and 1961 in the metropolitan territory; once in 1984 in relation to overseas troubles in New Caledonia; and once in 2005 to put an end to riots in a number of French suburbs which concerned 25 departments, including the entire Île-de-France (i.e., suburban areas outside Paris).

56 Law No 2017-1510 of 30 October 2017 strengthening domestic security and the fight against terrorism. Some of the laws, which prolonged the state of emergency from November 2015 till November 2017, also amended aspects of the regime.

57 Benjamin Disraeli (1804–1881), British Prime Minister (1868; 1874–1880) [No government can be long secure without a formidable opposition].

58 Honoré de Balzac (1799–1850), French novelist [The counter of a café is the parliament of the people].

universal suffrage, and the government, appointed by the President and held accountable to Parliament. While the President is endowed with significant powers and serves as a driving force for governmental actions, s/he does not possess the necessary legal and administrative means to independently make executive decisions or directly intervene in the legislative process. In fact, the President's ability to enact reforms relies heavily on his/her determination and persistence, as political decisions cannot be implemented without the support of the government and, in particular, the Prime Minister. It should be noted that the effectiveness of the executive duo greatly depends on the respective personalities of these individuals. Thus, the President must demonstrate strong resolve and perseverance in order to successfully advocate for reforms. This section aims to provide an overview of the government and parliamentary institutions, as well as their interrelationships.

The government

The provisions of the Constitution on the government (Title III) promptly ensue after the title on the President of the Republic (Title II). This sequential arrangement aligns with the fundamental logic of the Fifth Republic centred on a dualist executive where the President holds a position of paramount importance. This subsection outlines the structure and functions of the government.

Organisation of the government. The government is led by the Prime Minister, who serves as the Head of Government, and it functions as a collective and structured body. To comprehend the principles of collegial decision-making and hierarchical structure, it is necessary to understand the composition of the government.

The composition of the government is not laid down in the Constitution but is gathered from the decrees of appointment. The government is composed of the Prime Minister and of other members, primarily ministers. The appointment and the resignation of the Prime Minister are first examined. The Prime Minister is appointed by the President of the Republic, as one of his/her key prerogatives (article 8 of the Constitution). Two issues are generally associated with this appointment: a political issue and a legal issue. The political issue is about the choice of the individual to be appointed Prime Minister. Although the President has great freedom in his/her choice, s/he must choose someone who can effectively act as the head of the executive while also enjoying the support of the National Assembly. If the parliamentary majority is the same as the President's political orientation, the President enjoys a wide choice. S/he can appoint, as is generally the case, the leader of the majority party (i.e., the party who has the most seats in the National Assembly). However, the President is free to depart from this and can choose another key leader, as did Macron when he appointed Prime Minister Philippe in 2017. Philippe was then a member of the National Assembly (2012–2017). Unusually, he was a member of *Les Républicains* (right-wing), although he campaigned for Macron's party *La République en Marche !* (centre-left) during the 2017 legislative elections. In cases where the parliamentary majority is not the same as the President's political hue, the President's leeway is greatly reduced, and his/her choice is guided by the wishes of the parliamentary majority. The legal issue about the appointment of the Prime Minister relates to what s/he must do immediately after his/her appointment, whether s/he has the obligation, or not, to present the government programme to the National Assembly with a view of asking for a vote of confidence (see below).

In terms of resignation, the Prime Minister presents the resignation of his/her government to the President of the Republic, who then formally removes him/her from office (article 8 paragraph one of the Constitution). In other words, the resignation of the Prime Minister always entails the removal of the entire government. This occurs because of a vote of no confidence in the National Assembly on the government's programme or on one of its general policy declarations. The resignations that have occurred since 1958 have displayed interesting features that can be described as follows.[59] A first kind of resignation is the voluntary resignation resulting, for example, from a disagreement between the Prime Minister and the President (e.g., Chirac in 1976 or Valls in 2016). A second kind of resignation is the "courtesy resignation," which occurs after an unfavourable result in the presidential or legislative elections, even though the Prime Minister can possibly be reinstalled in his/her role in the newly constituted government. A third kind is the resignation that is imposed when the government fails to obtain the confidence of the National Assembly (e.g., Pompidou in 1962). Lastly, there is also the resignation that is imposed or provoked by the President who wants to replace the Prime Minister and constrains him/her to present his/her resignation. Most of the resignations under the Fifth Republic have fallen into that latter category. This is problematic since it amounts to an actual removal on the initiative of the President, which is not what was constitutionally intended and provided for. Such a practice, apart from the fact that it leads to the troublesome practice of Cabinet reshuffles, is a direct challenge to the principles of government accountability: a government can only be dismissed on the Prime Minister's initiative and following an unfavourable result from the elections. Again, the main consideration for this type of resignation to be acceptable is that the President and the Prime Minister are close, politically speaking.

Other government members are appointed by the President of the Republic on a proposal by the Prime Minister (article 8 paragraph two of the Constitution). The initiative of these eminently political appointments constitutionally belongs to the Prime Minister but is politically decided by the President. When the presidential majority is aligned with that in Parliament, the President enjoys significant leeway to impose his/her choice of who to appoint in government. However, the situation is different in a period of cohabitation where the Prime Minister has a real say in the choice of government members, who then must align with the majority in Parliament. In that situation, the President can only oppose the appointments that s/he is not comfortable with, notably those concerning ministerial portfolios key to his/her activity. The term of office of government members is terminated by a decision of the President on a proposal by the Prime Minister (article 8 paragraph two of the Constitution). Ministers and other members of the government can also resign on an individual basis. This is why a distinction is made between a collective resignation of the government when the Prime Minister initiates it, and an individual resignation when one minister decides to leave the government. The collective resignation of the government is either the result of the pressure exercised by the President on the Prime Minister forcing him/her and his/her government to resign or the result of an unfavourable vote of non-confidence (article 49 of the Constitution). The resignation of an individual member of government, on his/her own initiative or at the request of the Prime Minister, generally comes from a political disagreement with the President and/or the Prime Minister. Some resignations are very quick to happen after the appointment and generally originate in a disgraceful attitude of the concerned member. This was the case, for example, of the

59 Ferdinand Mélin-Soucramanien & Pierre Pactet, *Droit constitutionnel* (39th edn, Sirey 2021) 480.

resignation of Thévenoud, secretary of state for External Trade, which occurred in September 2014 only nine days after his appointment, due to his embroilment in an inglorious tax avoidance scandal. The changes in members of government provoked by these resignations are not unusual. Government reshuffles often allow the space to give a new impetus to the governmental team. The practice has even tended to be somehow normalised with the idea of the "permanent reshuffle," notably since Sarkozy's presidency when, for example, between 2012 and 2017, Fillon, Sarkozy's Prime Minister, resigned on four occasions: in 2007, after the legislative elections; in 2008, after the local elections; in 2009, after the European elections; and in 2010, in order to actively prepare for the 2012 presidential election. The possibility for members of government to be deputised while in governmental office has certainly contributed to easing these reshuffles because the sacked members of government are guaranteed to regain their seats in the National Assembly or in the Senate (article 25 paragraph two of the Constitution).[60]

The government is a collegial body that operates on the principle of collective political accountability. The accountability of the government to the National Assembly serves as the foundation for its legitimacy. The principle of collegiality implies that the government, represented by the Council of Ministers, is separate from its individual members. Ministers are individually responsible for their own actions, as well as collectively responsible for the policies implemented by the government. This idea is supported by the idea of political solidarity, which complements collegiality. As a result of this solidarity, a minister who disagrees with government actions must resign, as it would be untenable for them to support such actions in Parliament. This is why decisions within the Council of Ministers are made unanimously, as majority decisions would be illogical in a collective entity. However, the inclusion of ministers from different political perspectives, especially since Sarkozy's presidency ("*ministres d'ouverture*"), has made the practice of governmental solidarity more complicated. These ministers often express opinions that do not align with the mainstream views of the government.

The government is also a hierarchical body. The Prime Minister is the primus inter pares (i.e., first among equals) and has authority over the other members of government. S/he proposes their appointment to the President of the Republic, as well as their removal from office should they fail to respect governmental solidarity or act in a manner incompatible with governmental action. The Prime Minister is also entitled to settle any disagreement which may occur between ministers in, for example, the preparation of the budget between the minister for Finance and other ministers. Apart from the Prime Minister, and the minister for Justice (article 65 of the Constitution), the Constitution does not contain any provision about the structure of the government. Each government is free to determine the number of its members and the remit of their attributions. Generally, the government consists of several categories of members structured on a hierarchical basis. At the top of the hierarchy are the ministers of state (*ministres d'État*), who enjoy an honorary title, often because of their prominence in the political majority, and who head a ministerial department. A second category are the full ministers (*ministres de plein exercice*), who have oversight of a ministerial department and sit at the Council of Ministers meetings. A third category comprises the deputy ministers (*ministres délégués*), who report to the Prime Minister, or relevant minister in their area of competence, and act on delegation from them. Like ministers, deputy ministers head their ministerial department and take part in the Council of Ministers. A minister heads a particular

60 The possibility of deputisation is an innovation of the Constitution.

ministerial department and, as such, has responsibility for organising its services. Lastly, the secretaries of state (*secrétaires d'État*)[61] report to the Prime Minister, or relevant minister in their area of competence, and are often in charge of a specific role. They do not sit in the Council of Ministers meetings except when meetings concern matters in their remit. In recent years, successive governments have tended to diversify their different areas of competences by creating an increasing number of ministerial portfolios for reasons pertaining to increasing intervention of the state but also for reasons of pure political strategy. For example, the second Borne Government (2023–2024) is composed of 40 members, excluding the Prime Minister, divided into 16 ministers, 15 deputy ministers, and nine secretaries of state, plus a multitude of ministerial advisers.[62] This figure is relatively high compared to other governments of the Fifth Republic which have generally comprised about 30 members—only the Rocard Government (1988–1991), the Raffarin Government (2004–2005), and the Castex Government (2020–2022) comprised a record number of ministers with, respectively, 49 members, 44 members, and 43 members.

The government sits in different formations. The main formation is the Council of Ministers (*Conseil des Ministres*), where all important decisions are made. Such decisions include proposing government bills, endorsing ordinances, and engaging the government's responsibility. The Cabinet Council (*Conseil de Cabinet*) convenes the ministers under the chairmanship of the Prime Minister. Although not constitutionally mandated, the Cabinet Council is seldom observed in practice, except during a cohabitation when the Prime Minister regains leadership. The inter-ministerial committees (*comités inter-ministériels*) bring together ministers responsible for a specific matter to facilitate coordination and decision-making under the Prime Minister's supervision as regards the actions of their respective ministries. The select ministerial councils (*conseils restreints*) are overseen by the President of the Republic and bring together numerous government members and senior officials concerned with a particular issue.

The government formally makes its decisions within the Council of Ministers while the preparatory work is done beforehand. The Council of Ministers is the equivalent of the Cabinet where the principle of ministerial solidarity applies. Each member of the Council of Ministers must support the decisions made, even if s/he personally disapproves of them, or, failing to support such decisions, s/he must resign. As Head of the Government, the Prime Minister directs the action of the government and, in this respect, sets out its essential political orientations which, apart from periods of cohabitation, are those defined by the President of the Republic. The Prime Minister must also ensure the coordination of government action and avoid, through arbitration, different ministers taking initiatives in opposite directions. In other words, the Prime Minister makes sure that the principle of ministerial solidarity is respected among government members. The Prime Minister is assisted in his/her role by the Cabinet and the General Secretariat of the government, the latter in charge of preparing the agenda for the Council of Ministers in cooperation with the General Secretariat of the presidency. Other

61 This is not to be confused with the Secretary of State in the USA. In the American system, the Secretary of State is attached to the executive branch and holds no political accountability, except before the US President. The US Secretary of State is the equivalent of the minister for Foreign Affairs and holds the highest position among the Cabinet secretaries.

62 At the start of his first mandate, Macron limited the number of advisers in ministerial cabinets. See Decree No 2017-1063 of 18 May 2017 relating to ministerial cabinets. Macron had also campaigned for a "small-sized government limited to fifteen members maximum" during the 2017 presidential campaign…

consultative bodies, such as the Council of State in its consultative role, and the Economic, Social and Environmental Council, assist the Prime Minister in the decision-making process via their consultative or mandatory opinions.

Members of government are subject to several obligations and incompatibilities. Moreover, they are held accountable under a specific regime of criminal liability. In terms of obligations, and as part of promoting greater transparency in public affairs, government members are required to fulfil obligations of a financial nature. Within the first two months of their appointment, as well as within two months after leaving office, government members are required to disclose their assets and interests in a declaration to the High Authority for Transparency in Public Life (*Haute Autorité pour la Transparence de la Vie Publique*).[63] These declarations are made available to the public. In addition, upon appointment, government members undergo a tax audit and during their tenure, they delegate the management of their financial interests to a third party.

In terms of incompatibilities, a ministerial office is incompatible with a number of other functions and activities such as a parliamentary mandate, a professional representative function at national level, and any public office or professional activity in the private sector (article 23 paragraph one of the Constitution). Firstly, a ministerial office is incompatible with that of a parliamentary mandate, whether in the national Parliament or European Parliament. The incompatibility with a mandate in Parliament represents a departure from the traditional parliamentary regime whereby ministers are generally picked within members of Parliament and do not lose their parliamentary seat. Government members are free to exercise other types of political functions though, such as, for instance, leader of a political party or a local mandate, although the latter is also controversial. Incompatibility does not mean ineligibility though, and a minister can stand for parliamentary elections. Once elected, the minister has one month to opt for his/her seat in Parliament or to hold onto his/her ministerial position. In the latter case, s/he will be replaced, while in office, by his/her substitute in the National Assembly or in the Senate. The minister will regain his/her seat in Parliament when s/he leaves the government (article 25 paragraph two of the Constitution).[64] The issue of compatibility with a local mandate is a sensitive question. The proponents of compatibility between the position of minister and that of a local elected official justify the holding of multiple offices by the necessity for the minister to maintain grassroots activity with his/her constituency. On the contrary, the opponents, who militate for the prohibition of multiple mandates, invoke the necessity for the minister to fully commit to his/her office and not be distracted by, or overloaded with, another workload.[65] The prohibition of holding several mandates at a time would also arguably allow the opportunity for other aspiring politicians to stand for parliamentary elections in a renewed political landscape. While there is yet to be any legislation in the area, the practice of recent

63 The declaration of assets is neither an income tax return nor a wealth tax return. The declaration covers all the government member's own property, as well as property held in common for married persons under the community regime, and undivided property. The spouse's, or partner's, own property need not be declared.

64 Organic Law No 2009-38 of 13 January 2009 implementing article 25 of the Constitution.

65 Two proposals were put forward containing such a prohibition: one in March 2013, under Hollande's presidency, aiming at inscribing in the Constitution the incompatibility of a ministerial position with the exercise of any executive function in local government and in certain types of public authorities; this was reprised in a government bill tabled under Macron's first presidency, in May 2018, in relation to a constitutional reform aimed at ensuring "a more representative, accountable and efficient democracy." None of these proposals were adopted.

governments in relation to multiple mandates has been quite uneven. Secondly, in order to ensure their independence and full commitment to their function, ministers cannot exercise any other activity of a public or private nature.

Members of the government are criminally liable for offences committed while in office (articles 68-1 and 68-2 of the Constitution).[66] However, ordinary jurisdictions are not competent to deal with cases of ministerial responsibility. Instead, a special court, namely the Court of Justice of the Republic (*Cour de Justice de la République*), decides on these cases. The Court of Justice of the Republic is made up of 15 judges, namely 12 members of Parliament (i.e., six deputies and six senators) and three sitting judges from the Court of Cassation, one of whom presides over the Court. Proceedings before the Court of Justice of the Republic are brought by any individual who claims that his/her rights have been infringed by a government member. An investigative committee consisting of professional judges decides on whether to dismiss or to refer the case to the Court of Cassation, which then decides to formally refer the case to the Court of Justice of the Republic. For example, in September 2021, in the context of the Covid-19 pandemic, a former minister for Health was charged by the Court of Justice of the Republic's investigating committee for endangering the life of others due to her overall management of the health crisis. After referral by the investigating committee, the case was dropped and did not reach the Court of Justice of the Republic because the Court of Cassation decided in January 2023 that the offence of life endangerment was not characterised; none of the texts to which the investigating committee referred to indict the former minister provided for any particular obligation of prudence or security which is necessary in such a case. As it stands, the minister remains involved in the proceedings as a special witness but is no longer directly accused of an offence, thus making it impossible to refer her to the Court of Justice of the Republic for trial.[67] The possibility for the victim of governmental criminal action to bring judicial proceedings certainly represents an improvement in the rule of law. However, the procedure has also been criticised in several respects. For instance, the aggrieved individual parties cannot take part in the proceedings; moreover, the separation of those proceedings from the proceedings concerning top administrators which are brought before ordinary administrative courts makes it difficult to bring ministers to testify. The suppression of the Court of Justice of the Republic has been on the cards for some time (see below).

Role of the government. The government determines and conducts the policy of the nation (article 20 paragraph one of the Constitution). The Prime Minister is responsible for guiding the government's actions (article 21 of the Constitution). The Prime Minister has some leeway in directing the action of government members and, generally, when steering and coordinating the implementation of national policies. The Prime Minister is assisted by administrative services, including the General Secretariat of the government, which was established back in 1935. Acting as an equivalent to a general staff for civil matters, the General Secretariat operates with a streamlined organisational structure and employs highly skilled personnel. Their role in facilitating coordination between the government and Parliament in legislative

66 Government members also bear responsibility for managing finances, as they are responsible for authorising both expenses and income related to their respective ministerial departmental budget.

67 C. cass, Ass. Plén., 20 January 2023, No 22-82.535.

matters is crucial. When it comes to matters of national defence, the General Secretariat of national defence operates directly under the Prime Minister's supervision.

The role of the government is quite varied. First of all, the government assists the Prime Minister in the implementation of the policy determined by the President of the Republic (when the President is supported by his/her majority in Parliament) or determined by the Prime Minister (during cohabitation). Members of government, except secretaries of state, contribute to the decisions taken within the Council of Ministers. Another significant role of the government is to oversee the administration (article 20 paragraph two of the Constitution).[68] The *appareil administratif* is a powerful tool consisting of a considerable mass of the active population.[69] The state administration is governed by the principle of hierarchical authority and by the principle of territorial delocalisation. According to the principle of hierarchical authority, the top of the hierarchy is occupied by the Prime Minister. Since the administration is at his/her disposal, all state public agents must follow his/her orders and instructions under penalty of disciplinary sanctions. According to the principle of territorial delocalisation, state powers are delegated by the central administration to local state agents (in principle, the prefects) which allows state decisions to be taken and applied closer to the citizens (*les administrés*).[70] Given that the administration aims at implementing governmental policy, its action should guarantee the prevalence of the general interest over the multiple private interests of natural or legal persons. Administrative law thus endows the administration with powers, or prerogatives, derogating from ordinary law. These prerogatives outside the scope of ordinary law (*prérogatives exorbitantes du droit commun*) favour the administration and allow public authorities to unilaterally impose their decisions via different regimes such as the public service decision-making regime and enforceability of decisions regime.

The other powerhouse of the government is the financial tool since everything that the government accomplishes is conditioned by a budget. In deciding on the public budget, the state determines public expenditures before it determines its revenues. The process of adjustment between expenditures and revenues is called the budget. This budget is legally translated into a finance law (*loi de finances*) that is voted annually. In principle, the social welfare budget is dealt with by the employers and employees trade unions. However, the ever-increasing deficit of the social welfare regime has forced the state to take care of its budget. This is why the government votes annually a Social Security financing law (*loi de financement de la Sécurité Sociale*), which aims at balancing the accounts in that area. The economy and finances of the state are placed under the leadership of the eponymous ministry under the authority of the Prime Minister. The minister for the Economy and Finance oversees the preparation and implementation of finance laws for the financial year (i.e., state budget) and also of the supplementary finance laws (*lois de finances rectificatives*) and settlement finance laws (*lois de*

68 In addition to the administration, the government is also responsible for the armed forces (see below).

69 The French public service is made up of three parts, namely the state public service, the local (or territorial) public service, and the health public service attached to public hospitals. At the end of 2019, these services employ together 5.61 million agents (excluding subsidised contracts), that is, one in five employees in France. The state civil service has 2.49 million agents (44%), the territorial civil service 1.94 million (34%), and the hospital civil service 1.18 million (21%). See *Rapport annuel sur l'état de la fonction publique*, 2021, accessible at <https://www.fonction-publique.gouv.fr/rapport-annuel-sur-letat-de-la-fonction-publique-edition-2021>.

70 In addition, the government exercises administrative oversight (*tutelle*) over decentralised authorities and territories.

règlement).[71] The minister has a say in all financial matters of the state. Firstly, laws that have financial implications—and most of the laws have—must be signed by the minister who can impose his/her view on such texts as overseen by the Prime Minister. Secondly, during the preparation of the state budget, the minister decides on appropriations between the different ministries. This represents an important power in his/her hands since the amount of the approved lines of credits determines what the different ministries (other than the ministry for the Economy and Finance) can concretely do. Thirdly, as regards the implementation of the budget, the minister oversees, with the assistance of financial controllers and accountants, the accuracy and fairness of public accounts.

The government possesses various purely governmental powers such as the power to decide to resort to the referendum (article 11 of the Constitution) and declare the state of siege (article 36 of the Constitution). Furthermore, the government wields legislative and financial powers in relation to the elaboration laws and the elaboration and implementation of finance laws and Social Security financing laws, specifically outlined below.

The government has regulatory powers as well as powers in national defence and foreign affairs. Concerning regulatory powers, a distinction is made under the Constitution between the autonomous regulatory power, which belongs to the Prime Minister, and the regulatory power relating to the implementation of laws, which belongs to the government. Additionally, there is a residual regulatory power that applies to ministers under specific circumstances.

The a*utonomous regulatory power* of the Prime Minister relates to the adoption of acts via his/her regulatory power (article 37 of the Constitution). Such regulatory acts must be countersigned by the relevant minister(s) in charge. For those acts (i.e., decrees) deliberated in the Council of Ministers, the signature of the President of the Republic is also required. A decree deliberated in the Council of Ministers can only be amended via the same procedure. The requirement of the President's signature has de facto diminished the regulatory power of the Prime Minister. As for the r*egulatory powers necessary for the implementation of laws*, the government exercises it via ordinances (article 38 of the Constitution). Ordinances allow the government to take, within a limited time frame, measures of legislative nature in order to implement its programme.[72] Ordinances are characterised by a specific legal regime. Parliament must vote an enabling law, at the request of the government, in order to trigger the power to make ordinances since the initiative of issuing ordinances cannot come from Parliament.[73] The enabling law must fulfil the following substantive requirements: ordinances should only aim at the implementation of the government's programme; the power to issue ordinances is limited in time since, according to the enabling law, the government is expressly required to act during a certain period before being bound to table a ratification bill before Parliament; ordinance may only concern a number of areas of legislative nature but not all of them as this would be regarded as unconstitutional. Once the enabling law is enacted, ordinances are formally adopted in the Council of Ministers after consultation of the Council of State. Ordinances are signed by the President of the Republic, albeit the President is not legally bound to do so. After the expiry of the enabling period, the government cannot have recourse to new ordinances on the basis of the enabling law. Existing ordinances are deemed null and void should the

71 Organic Law No 2001-692 of 1 August 2001 relating to finance laws.

72 Ordinances were formerly known under the previous Republics as "decrees-laws" (*décrets-lois*).

73 Decision No 2004-509 DC of 13 January 2005 *Loi de programmation pour la cohésion sociale.*

government fail to table them for ratification before Parliament within the ratification period. Conversely, ordinances are deemed valid should they be expressly ratified by Parliament within such a period. The legal status of ordinances therefore evolves over time depending on which course of action is taken. Ordinances are regarded as regulatory acts and, accordingly, their legality may be reviewed by the Council of State. Once ratified by Parliament, they acquire a legislative nature once ratified by Parliament. Individual ministers are not entitled to exercise any regulatory power unless this power is expressly delegated to them by the Prime Minister or unless such power results from the express provisions contained in an enabling legislative or regulatory act. Ministers countersign the decrees taken by the Prime Minister in their area of competence, as well as the decrees enacted in the Council of Ministers and signed by the President of the Republic.

Concerning powers in national defence and foreign affairs, the government shares these powers with the President of the Republic with a degree of overlap between the two institutions. In practice, these areas have traditionally been the exclusive preserve (*domaine réservé*) of the Head of State. Again, the situation is different in cases of cohabitation where power-sharing as defined under constitutional provisions applies. Nonetheless, while the idea of an exclusive preserve was prevalent during the De Gaulle presidency (1959–1969), it has progressively lost its relevance in more recent presidencies. This was confirmed by President Chirac in his speech of 14 July 1997, who contended, at the time, that there was no presidential preserve but emphasised the particular role of the Head of State in preserving the role of France in the world, as well as maintaining the European and social *acquis*.[74] Overall, powers in the area of diplomacy and defence depend on the functioning of the regime (i.e., cohabitation or not). It also depends on the personality of the President, whether s/he is willing to give leeway to the government in those sensitive areas in order to avoid exposure or, on the contrary, to intervene as actively as s/he chooses fit. In relation to national defence, as seen above, while the government has power over the armed forces (article 20 paragraph two of the Constitution) and the Prime Minister is responsible for national defence (article 21 paragraph one of the Constitution), the President of the Republic is the Commander in Chief of the armed forces and presides over the higher councils and committees for national defence (article 15 of the Constitution). The 2008 constitutional amendment introduced a degree of parliamentary control over the decision to send military troops abroad. The President must inform Parliament within three days of sending the troops. Parliament may debate, but not vote, on such a decision. The extension of the military intervention is subject to parliamentary approval, with the final word to the National Assembly, after four months (article 35 paragraphs two and three of the Constitution).[75] The only exception, even in cases of cohabitation, is the power to resort to nuclear weapons, which belongs exclusively to the President.[76] Concerning powers in foreign affairs and diplomacy, while

74 Jacques Chirac Speech, 14 July 1997, TV Interview addressing the Jospin Government's plans, the need to reduce the budget deficit, the President of the Republic's powers, and cohabitation.

75 The article 35 procedure was used to approve the following military deployments or external operations (*opérations extérieures* or *OPEX*): Afghanistan (September 2008); Chad, Central African Republic, Côte d'Ivoire, Lebanon, and Kosovo (January 2009); Libya (July 2011); and Mali (April 2013).

76 Decree No 64-46 of 14 January 1964 relating to strategic air forces. The strategic air forces are in fact the nuclear strike force. If the President of the Republic has direct command over them, the mission, the organisation, and the conditions of engagement of strategic air forces are decided by the Defence Council. For more details, see Marie-Luce Paris, "The President as Commander in Chief in a Comparative Constitutional Perspective under French and US Law" (2021) 59 (2) *The Military Law and Law of the War Review* 196.

the President is responsible for negotiating and ratifying international agreements (article 52 paragraph one of the Constitution), there is a degree of overlap since the government, in charge of national policy, is also necessarily involved in international relations.

The government plays a crucial role in its interaction with Parliament. In that regard, it is worth noting the primary role of the Prime Minister in facilitating this relationship. The Prime Minister holds a central position in the legislative process, as s/he is responsible for proposing government bills, determining which amendments should be presented to Parliament on behalf of the government (article 44 of the Constitution), and convening a joint parliamentary committee to resolve disagreements between the two Houses of Parliament (article 45 of the Constitution). Additionally, the Prime Minister, after consulting with the Council of Ministers, has the authority to request a vote of confidence from the National Assembly, in order to assess support for their government (article 49 of the Constitution). Furthermore, the Prime Minister has the power to refer a law to the Constitutional Council for a judicial review (article 61 of the Constitution).

The government has powers in relation to referendums. While the legislative referendum (article 11 of the Constitution) can be categorised as a non-shared power, other types of referendums are shared between the two branches of the executive. Firstly, the ratification of a treaty concerning the accession of a new member state to the EU must receive the approval of the French citizens through a referendum. If the government issues the bill granting such a ratification, it is then put to a referendum by the President of the Republic (article 88-5 paragraph one of the Constitution).[77] The other type of referendum concerns the President's power to consult the people of an overseas territory on matters relating to its organisation, competencies, or governance. This can be initiated through a proposal from the government or a joint proposal from both Houses of Parliament (article 72-4 paragraph two of the Constitution).[78]

Other powers of the government comprise appointment powers and powers in times of crisis. Barring those powers assigned to the President of the Republic according to the Constitution under the Constitution, the Prime Minister has a role in the appointment to top civil and military positions (article 21 paragraph one of the Constitution). While the President holds exceptional powers to handle crises (article 16 of the Constitution), the government may also employ extraordinary measures to address them. The state of siege (article 36 of the Constitution) and the state of emergency (1955 Law) are two examples of such measures.

Parliament

The French Parliament has its origins deeply rooted in history, going back to the fourteenth century. Starting from 1302, a consultative gathering was regularly organised at the behest of the King of France, bringing together representatives from various sectors of society—the clergy, the nobility, and the so-called "*tiers état*" or Third Estate, which consisted of individuals not

77 While the referendum route was the only route when the constitutional provision was inserted, the 2008 constitutional amendment opened the parliamentary route. By voting on a motion adopted in identical terms by each House by a three-fifths majority, Parliament may authorise the adoption of the ratification bill under the procedure provided for in article 89 paragraph three of the Constitution, which is when Parliament is convened as Congress (article 88-5 paragraph two of the Constitution).

78 For more details on referendums, see Chapter 5 on political parties, elections, and referendums.

belonging to the clergy or nobility.[79] This consultative assembly, known as *Les États Généraux*, was a sort of representative non-democratic (yet) national forum. The *États Généraux* convened in Versailles in 1789, when the three orders were merged on the occasion of the abolition of feudal privileges on 4 August 1789. This pivotal moment ultimately gave rise to the birth of France's first constituent assembly.

The title of the Constitution on Parliament (Title IV) comes last in the titles on the main institutions of the Fifth Republic. From a comparative perspective, such a relegation of Parliament contrasts with the layout in other constitutions where the institution of Parliament is at the forefront. For example, the 1787 US Constitution's first article is dedicated to Congress. In Germany, the provisions on basic rights (articles 1–19) and on the Federation (articles 20–37) in the 1949 Basic Law are immediately followed by the constitutional provisions on the Bundestag (articles 38–49), representing the citizens, and Bundesrat (articles 50–53), representing the Länder. The 1937 Constitution of the Republic of Ireland is specific in this regard. Although the provisions on the President of the Republic of Ireland (articles 12–14) precede the provisions on the *Oireachtas* (articles 15–27), it must be borne in mind that the institution of the President is relatively powerless in the Irish political and constitutional system. The provisions dedicated to the *Oireachtas* form an ensemble together with the liminary provisions on the nation (articles 1–3) and the state (articles 4–11) to describe the nature of the state and its regime.

The Fifth Republic deliberately relegates Parliament behind the executive branch of power. Such a relegation marks a departure from the previous regimes which were characterised by governmental instability and too powerful a legislature. The so-called "rationalisation" of the parliamentary system has resulted in a shift in the centre of gravity of the decision-making power from the legislature to the executive—this is so despite the parliamentary-rooted basis of the regime. Parliament now appears like a "rubber-stamping House" of the action of the government as indeed only a minority of laws are generally initiated by members of Parliament. Most of the French legislation originates in government bills. Also, the formation of political majorities within the National Assembly that support the government has meant that the power of deputies to control the action of the executive has lost most of its relevance. Besides, Parliament is not in full control of important national choices since these are often influenced by European norms and policies. The 2008 constitutional amendment attempted a shift in the other direction to reinforce the role of Parliament in the legislative decision-making process. However, in a parliamentary system based on a strong political majority, stemming from directly elected deputies as well as a directly elected Head of State, there is no reason to put so much constraint on Parliament; successive political majorities benefit from the alignment of legitimacies (i.e., that of the President of the Republic and that of the National Assembly) to be able to govern to the fullest. The only caveat is that the Prime Minister, whose position was more prominent before 2008, now finds himself/herself more compelled to cooperate with his/her majority in Parliament. In a nutshell, the steady decline of the influence of the French

79 Originally, the *États Généraux* were summoned to address a disagreement between King Philip IV and Pope Boniface VIII. This disagreement arose in the latter part of the thirteenth century when Boniface decreed that all secular leaders must seek his approval before imposing taxes on the clergy within their territories. Understandably, the King of France was dissatisfied with this move and wanted to retain control over his realm, which housed many secular rulers. The King refused to let the Church dictate who had the power to levy taxes within his territory, thus leading to the ensuing dispute.

Parliament over national policy has resulted in a redefinition of its role. The organisation and role of Parliament are presented in turn.

Organisation of Parliament. The organisation of Parliament, within the framework of the French political system, refers to rules governing the selection and legal positions of its members. This encompasses considerations surrounding their immunities and incompatibilities. In addition, the topic covers the workings of Parliament, which include matters such as its agenda, sessions, and voting procedures. Prior to delving into these aspects, some observations about bicameralism and the Senate are provided.

A two-house Parliament and the issue with the Senate. The French Parliament is a bicameral Parliament comprising two houses, namely the National Assembly and the Senate. Members of the National Assembly and of the Senate are elected according to different rules, determined by law, but having the same legal status. Calls to constitutionalise the rules governing parliamentary elections have been made to prevent them from being influenced by the majority in power. However, this idea has not been implemented yet. The electoral system for the Parliament has remained largely unchanged since the establishment of the Fifth Republic, with only a few modifications for the National Assembly during Mitterrand's first term (1981–1988). To be eligible to stand for election in Parliament, a citizen must be at least 18 years old for the National Assembly and at least 24 years old for the Senate. In addition, the candidate must possess all their civil and political rights and should not have been deprived of these rights or deemed legally incapable or ineligible. While deputies (members of the National Assembly) are elected through direct universal suffrage as representatives of the French people, senators (members of the Senate) are elected through indirect universal suffrage and represent the local authorities of the Republic.

French bicameralism is unequal in the sense that the National Assembly has more power than the Senate. This is due to the more democratic mode of election of deputies, who are direct representatives of the people. The pre-eminence of the Lower House of Parliament concerns the accountability of the government that can be challenged by the National Assembly only. Also, while a bill must be passed in identical terms before becoming a law, the government has the possibility of authorising the National Assembly to have the final say on the text. By reason of its indirect mode of election—unchanged since the Third Republic—and its limited powers, the Senate has been the object of recurrent criticisms, even challenging its raison d'être. The indirect mode of election of senators favours an overrepresentation of small local constituencies which are traditionally more conservative. This has been exemplified by the almost non-interrupted domination of a right-wing majority, bar the 2011–2014 period which saw a brief left-wing majority. In fact, the combination of an overrepresentation of rural municipalities, with a lengthy mandate of six years, has arguably shaped the Senate into a conservative assembly seemingly out of touch with people's concerns. The following quotes reveal how problematic the image carried over by the Senate has been perceived over the years: "A senator is a deputy who persists" (Robert de Jouvenel, journalist, 1882–1924); "The Senate is an assembly of men with fixed ideas fortunately corrected by a high mortality rate" (Edgar Faure, politician, 1908–1988); "A House [of Parliament] such as the Senate … is an anomaly in contemporary democracies" (Lionel Jospin, former Prime Minister from 1997 to 2002). However, and after being reformed on several occasions,[80] the Senate has survived until now. The institution has proved to be, including recently, a useful political counterweight to the National Assembly as, for instance, illustrated by the active scrutiny exercised by the senators during the Covid-19 pandemic (March 2020–July 2022).[81] Its defenders emphasise that such a "high council of the *communes* of France" has always ensured the guarantee of the republican institutions. Besides, its mode of election can conversely be seen in a positive way. Because of its indirect mode of election, the Senate is not dependent on the vagaries of political elections associated with a shorter mandate based on direct elections.

The National Assembly. The 577 deputies of the National Assembly are elected through department constituencies for a period of five years.[82] The boundaries of electoral constituencies are reviewed at regular intervals in order to account for demographic changes. Under the 2008 constitutional amendment, an independent commission seeks public opinion on any alterations to constituency boundaries and the subsequent distribution of seats in the National Assembly.[83] Deputies are elected through direct universal suffrage using a two-round single-majority voting system. In the first round, a candidate must secure an absolute majority of the votes and represent at least 25% (i.e., one-fourth) of the registered voters in order to be elected outright. In the second round, candidates are required to have attained a minimum of 12.5% of the votes cast from registered voters in the initial round to be eligible for candidacy. The candidate who ultimately receives majority support from the votes cast emerges as the elected representative.

The financing of legislative electoral campaigns is strictly regulated.[84] The regulatory framework concerns management and fundraising rules as well as rules on expenses and reimbursement. The year before the election and in anticipation of any fundraising, the candidate must appoint a designated financial agent (i.e., natural person or association).[85] The financial agent is tasked with lodging all the funds raised during the campaign in a dedicated bank account. S/he is also in charge of recording the candidate's income, including dona-

80 In 1969, an initial attempt at reform was made by De Gaulle, who presented a proposal to merge the Senate with the Economic and Social Council, transforming it into a consultative entity without any veto power. Interestingly, the Socialist Party's programme for the 2007 presidential election incorporated a similar idea, suggesting the amalgamation of the Senate and the Economic and Social Council.

81 Catherine Deroche, Bernard Jomier & Sylvie Vermeillet, *Rapport fait au nom de la Commission d'enquête « Evaluation des politiques publiques face aux pandémies »*, Report No 199 (2020–2021), Senate, 8 December 2020.

82 The number of deputies is fixed in the Constitution since the 2008 constitutional amendment (article 24 paragraph three of the Constitution). The Philippe Government (2017–2020) proposed to reduce the overall number of members of Parliament by 30%, or about one-third, as part of a larger constitutional and institutional reform.

83 The independent commission comprises one member appointed by the President of the Republic, one member appointed by the president of the National Assembly, one member appointed by the president of the Senate, a judge from the Council of State elected by his/her peers, a judge from the Court of Cassation elected by his/her peers, and one member from the national Court of Auditors elected by his/her peers. The commission is chaired by a president appointed by the President of the Republic pursuant to the procedure under article 13 of the Constitution.

84 Organic Law No 2011-410 of 14 April 2011 on the election of deputies and senators. See also Chapter 5 on political parties, elections, and referendums.

85 The candidate themselves cannot serve as their own proxy, and if they use an election financing association, they are prohibited from being a member of that association as well. In addition, a candidate is limited to having only one proxy at any given time, and that proxy is authorised to act on behalf of a single candidate exclusively.

tions and funds received from political parties, and expenditures. The financial agent generally manages all expenses. This campaign account cannot be in deficit and is forwarded two months after the election to the National Commission of Campaign Accounts and Political Financing (*Commission Nationale des Comptes de Campagne et des Financements Politiques* or *CNCCFP*). The *CNCCFP* is an independent administrative authority whose main role is to control campaign accounts in all—not just legislative—elections and, more broadly, to ensure that political parties and candidates respect their accounting and financial obligations. Rules concerning fundraising allow a candidate to raise funds from political parties. However, in order to increase transparency and avoid external pressure, fundraising rules explicitly prohibit donations from any other legal persons such as private companies, trade unions, associations, charities, and foreign states. Natural persons may contribute to campaign fundraising by making donations, albeit capped at 4,600 euros for the entire campaign. Campaign expenditures are limited according to the number of inhabitants, which is, for the legislative elections, capped at 38,000 euros (plus 0.15 euros per inhabitant of the constituency). This limit is updated each year according to the cost-of-living index.[86] If this limit is exceeded, the campaign accounts may be subject to rejection by the *CNCCFP*, which leads to the non-reimbursement of electoral expenses as well as, as appropriate, to the ineligibility of the candidate for the next three years. Under certain conditions, the state will reimburse the electoral expenses of the candidate should s/he obtain at least 5% of the votes cast. Besides, to benefit from the reimbursement, these expenses must be electoral expenses (i.e., official leaflets, posters on electoral boards, and bulletins), and the candidate's campaign account must have been approved by the *CNCCFP*. The reimbursed amount is decided by the *CNCCFP* within the limit of 47.5% of the limit set for each constituency.

The electoral system implemented by the National Assembly has been successful in establishing strong majorities. This has, in turn, contributed to the bipolarisation of political life. However, smaller political formations have consistently called for some level of proportional voting in legislative elections to ensure a more diverse representation of various political affiliations and thus better represent the citizens. This becomes particularly significant when considering the 12.5% rule, which effectively eliminates smaller political parties before they can progress to the second round. Over the years, several attempts have been made to propose a system that combines majority voting with proportional representation. One such proposal was made in 2012 by the Commission on the Renewal and Ethics in Public Life (also known as the *Jospin Commission*). Their proposal involved electing a small percentage (i.e., 58 out of 577) of deputies through a party-list voting system with proportional representation.[87]

86 The finance law for 2012 has frozen this limit until the balance of public finances is restored. See Law No 2011-1977 of 28 December 2011 on finances for 2012 and Organic Law No 2012-272 of 28 February 2012 relating to the reimbursement of campaign expenditures for the presidential election.

87 Commission de rénovation et de déontologie de la vie publique, *Pour un renouveau démocratique*, November 2012, accessible at <http://www.ladocumentationfrancaise.fr/var/storage/rapports-publics/124000596.pdf>. More recently, the Philippe Government (2017–2020) put forward a more ambitious proposal recommending that 15% of deputies be elected by proportional voting.

The Senate. The 348 senators of the French Senate are elected for six years, with a partial renewal occurring every three years.[88] The election process is carried out through indirect universal suffrage, wherein an electoral college comprised of elected representatives, such as senators, deputies, regional councillors, departmental councillors, and local councillors, participates. The voting system employed varies depending on the number of senators to be elected in a particular constituency. Generally, a majority two-round system is used, except in departments where the requirement is to elect at least four senators. In such cases, a proportional voting system is adopted, wherein the highest average of votes cast prevails. Senatorial elections are subject to similar regulations as legislative elections concerning the financing of the election campaigns. These regulations encompass the appointment of a financial agent, the establishment of a campaign account, the scrutiny of accounts by the *CNCCFP*, and the imposition of expenditure limits. Nonetheless, certain adjustments may be made to accommodate specific circumstances.

The legal status of members of Parliament. The current legal status of members of Parliament is the result of a long evolution. According to the tenet of national sovereignty, the parliamentary mandate cannot be imperative; the mandate is representative and collective. Members of Parliament do not represent the electorate as such; rather, they represent the entire nation and speak on its behalf and in its interest. Deputies and senators must provide a statement listing their assets to the High Authority for Transparency in Public Life (*Haute Autorité Pour la Transparence de la Vie Publique* or *HATVP*), the national "anti-corruption body."[89] This statement must be handed in at the start, and again at the end, of the parliamentary mandate, as well as during the mandate in the event of changes in the patrimonial situation of any deputy or senator. The regime of these statements is almost similar to those made by ministers except that members of Parliament's statements are not published but only made available for consultation in the prefectures. Several rules have been put in place over the years to protect the independence of members of Parliament against the executive power. The most significant of these rules is the regime of incompatibilities attached to the parliamentary mandate as enshrined in the Constitution (article 23 of the Constitution) and as regulated by organic law (article 25 of the Constitution).

The general principle relating to parliamentary incompatibilities dictates that it does not hinder a member of parliament, be it a deputy or a senator, from seeking election for a different position than their current one. However, it does compel them to make a decision on which

88 The number of senators is fixed in the Constitution since the 2008 constitutional amendment (article 24 paragraph four of the Constitution).

89 The High Authority for Transparency in Public Life was established in 2013 as an independent administrative authority. It has a three-fold role: firstly, to review the statements of assets of the highest-ranking elected and appointed public officials (since 2013, the High Authority has reviewed the statements of some 15,000 public officials); secondly, to seek to prevent conflicts of interest between public officials and private interlocutors; thirdly, to counsel and train public officials on ethical principles. The High Authority may impose criminal sanctions and refer serious cases of maladministration (e.g., corruption, bribery, jobbery and influence peddling, electoral and tax frauds) to the relevant administrative or judicial authorities.

mandate they wish to pursue and consequently abandon the other.[90] These incompatibilities are applicable to both public offices and roles undertaken in the private sector.

Concerning public offices, a distinction is made between elective public offices and other public functions. Concerning elective public offices, there is a general prohibition of the accumulation of a parliamentary mandate with another elective public office mandate or any other elective public function.[91] That means that a deputy cannot be, at the same time, a senator, or a minister, or a member of the Constitutional Council, or a member of the Economic, Social and Environmental Council.[92] A deputy, or a senator, cannot be either an EP member. A deputy cannot hold more than one local public mandate (i.e., be elected as regional councillor, departmental councillor, or local councillor of a municipality of at least 3,500 inhabitants). In addition, according to rules limiting the accumulation of local elective mandates, no elected individual can hold more than two local mandates (i.e., mandates of regional councillor, departmental councillor, or local councillor).[93]

Despite these prohibitions and limitations, the accumulation of mandates (i.e., the possibility for members of Parliament to hold more than one electoral mandate concurrently) has been a recurrent and singular feature under the Fifth Republic. In 2012, 476 out of 577 deputies (82%) and 267 out of 348 senators (77%) held at least one other elective mandate, mainly at local level as a mayor, president of a Departmental Council, or president of a Regional Council. The proportion of members of Parliament holding multiple mandates is much lower on average in the rest of Europe (20%).[94] A further set of laws tightened the framework of parliamentary incompatibilities as regards local executive mandates in particular.[95] This was part of an ongoing effort, which started under the Sarkozy presidency and was pursued under the Hollande presidency, to improve the working and transparency of political institutions.[96] Also, since the parliamentary mandate has effectively become a full-time activity, it has been considered that such incompatibilities would contribute to raising the profile of the work of Parliament. The general incompatibility between a parliamentary elective mandate and an executive local mandate came into force in 2017 as regards deputies and senators, and in 2019 as regards members

90 If there is a European or local mandate, it is mandatory for members of Parliament to relinquish their oldest mandate. This refers to the mandate that they have held for the longest duration.

91 These prohibitions and limitations are laid down in a series of measures: Organic Law No 2000-294 of 5 April 2000 on incompatibilities between electoral mandates; and Law No 2000-295 of 5 April 2000 on the limitation of multiple electoral mandates and functions and their conditions of exercise.

92 The last three prohibitions in the enumeration are also valid for a senator.

93 Article L 46.1 of the Electoral Code. There is also an incompatibility concerning the accumulation of more than one *executive* function for holders of elective local mandates (i.e., president of the Regional Council, president of the Departmental Council, or mayor of a municipality), and concerning *executive* functions for holders of elective local mandates with holding a parliamentary mandate in the European Parliament. In other words, if an individual is elected deputy (or senator) or elected to an executive function at local level, s/he must end their EP mandate. S/he can cumulate his/her EP seat with a local mandate but with no executive function.

94 See François-Noël Buffet & Georges Labazée, *Rapport d'information fait au nom de la délégation aux collectivités territoriales et à la décentralisation sur le cumul des mandats*, Report No 365, Senate, 14 February 2012, accessible at <https://www.senat.fr/rap/r11-365/r11-365_mono.html>.

95 Organic Law No 2014-125 of 14 February 2014 prohibiting the cumulation of local executive functions with the mandate of deputy or senator, and Law No 2014-126 of 14 February 2014 prohibiting the cumulation of local executive functions with the mandate of representative in the European Parliament.

96 Comité de réflexion et de proposition sur la modernisation et le rééquilibrage des institutions de la Ve République, *Une Ve République plus démocratique*, JORF No 252 of 30 October 2007, accessible at <https://www.legifrance.gouv.fr/jorf/id/JORFTEXT000000467267>.

of the European Parliament.[97] The possibility for a member of Parliament to choose the mandate s/he wishes to keep is discontinued; the new rule is that the s/he retains the most recent mandate and renounces de facto the older mandate. These measures have been criticised under diverse claims. The first claim has denounced the perverse effect of such incompatibilities because one of their effects seemingly cuts off members of Parliament from their grassroots, thereby making it more difficult for them to fully appreciate their fellow citizens' concerns. According to other claims, these incompatibilities, on the contrary, do not go far enough in prohibiting multiple mandates. One suggestion has been made to limit the number of mandates per individual member of Parliament to three consecutive elective mandates. This would arguably also encourage access of a new generation of politicians to elective functions at national level.[98]

As regards other public functions, the incompatibility is total: the parliamentary mandate is incompatible with any other public function, whether national or international, whether civilian or military. This incompatibility with the exercise of all public functions also applies to the managing positions held in state-owned or nationalised companies. The logic behind such incompatibility lies in the requirement of independence attached to the parliamentary mandate. Such a requirement of independence, from the government in particular, would not be fulfilled if, for instance, a member of Parliament was required to abide, as a civil servant, by his/her superiors in a state-owned or nationalised company.[99] There are exceptions to such incompatibility concerning deputies in the National Assembly: deputies can cumulate their elective mandate with a professorial activity at university, or with the function of religious minister in the territory of Alsace-Moselle. Besides, it is also possible for members of Parliament to be tasked by the government with a clearly defined temporary six-month mission without it affecting their mandate.

Concerning positions in the private sector, the opposite rule applies: it is possible to hold a parliamentary mandate alongside a private office, with some exceptions. However, in an attempt to prevent collusions between business and politics, an increasing number of exceptions have been introduced without, however, yielding entirely satisfactory outcomes. As a result, there are certain private professional activities that are incompatible with a parliamentary mandate due to potential conflicts of interest. For example, individuals cannot serve as chairpersons or members of the Board of Directors for private companies that receive public aid, or for companies exclusively engaged in financial activities or involved in public offerings.[100]

Any of the incompatibilities examined above may arise when a member of Parliament is elected or while they are carrying out their responsibilities. In such cases, the member of Parliament must inform the bureau of their respective House about the specific activity they intend to continue and must cease any incompatible activity within 30 days of being elected.

97 The incompatibility is also between a parliamentary elective mandate and more than one of the following mandates: regional councillor, departmental councillor, member of the Assembly of Corsica, member of the Assembly of the capital city of Paris, local councillor of municipalities of more than 3,500 inhabitants.

98 The reform was about prohibiting three "consecutive, identical and full termed" mandates, except for mayors of small municipalities (i.e., fewer than 9,000 inhabitants). It was part of the package of institutional and constitutional reforms proposed by the Philippe Government (2017–2020) in 2018.

99 An exception is made for professors in higher education since they have statutory rights guaranteeing their independence, including academic freedom.

100 Those activities are enumerated under article LO 146 of the Electoral Code. Lawyers who serve as members of Parliament are restricted from practising their profession in specific situations where there is a potential conflict of interest.

If there is any uncertainty regarding an incompatibility (or if there is disagreement between the bureau of Parliament and the member of Parliament), the president of the relevant House of Parliament, the minister for Justice, or the member of Parliament themselves may refer the matter to the Constitutional Council. The Council will exercise its discretion to determine whether an incompatibility exists. If the concerned member fails to rectify their activities within 30 days of the Council's decision, the Council will declare that they have automatically resigned from office.

Immunities aim at guaranteeing the independence of members of Parliament. They establish a derogatory regime protecting them in the exercise of their functions in case they have caused civil or criminal damage. Two categories of immunities are to be distinguished, namely unaccountability and inviolability. Firstly, members of Parliament are not subject to "any prosecution, investigation, arrest, detention or trial for the opinions or votes expressed by them while in office" (article 26 of the Constitution). This unaccountability, which is absolute and permanent, exempts members of Parliament from all judicial civil and criminal proceedings by reason of all acts they accomplish during their mandate (e.g., interventions, votes). For example, a deputy or senator cannot be prosecuted for defamation, although s/he must still abide by the rules of his/her House. Secondly, inviolability extends to acts committed outside of the parliamentary function but concerns only acts of a criminal nature and is limited to the duration of the mandate. The aim is to avoid a member of Parliament being the object of pressure or other kind of influence undermining his/her actions as national representative. Deputies or senators can be charged by a judicial authority but cannot be remanded in custody or be the object of any measure involving deprivation of liberty without the authorisation of the bureau of their respective House, except when caught red-handed or on the basis of a previous conviction by a final judgment.[101]

To ensure that members of Parliament can work independently and without financial pressure of any kind, a generous parliamentary allowance is provided. This is also an essential factor in the democratisation of the political system, which allows every citizen to enter Parliament without relying on personal wealth or other (dubious) financial arrangements. Moreover, the necessary financial autonomy of members of Parliament, long symbolised by the payment of a parliamentary indemnity, has been reinforced alongside the reinforcement of the executive power, by various facilities and endowments in individual or collective material means. This trend reflects a growing professionalisation of the parliamentary mandate. The parliamentary allowance is aligned with the average "off-scale" remuneration of top civil servants, and is complemented by a duty allowance which is one-fourth of the remuneration thereof.[102] Deputies also receive a monthly fixed allowance for secretarial expenses and are allowed a credit for the remuneration of their staff.[103] In cases where this credit is not spent entirely, the available share

101 The House of Parliament has, however, the possibility of suspending the criminal measures during the parliamentary session.

102 Ordinance No 58-1210 of 13 December 1958 on the Organic Law on the allowance of members of Parliament. The parliamentary allowance has three components, namely a basic parliamentary allowance, a residence allowance, and a duty allowance. Since January 2019, the monthly gross allowance of deputies is 7,239.91 euros (net allowance 5,679.71 euros). The parliamentary allowance is taxable. The allowance can be cumulated with another allowance attached to a local elective mandate within the limits of a certain amount (at 2,811.62 euros per month per deputy in 2023).

103 As of January 2018, the monthly amount of the allowance for secretarial expenses has been 5,373 euros gross. The credit for staff remuneration is calculated in principle for three employees but may, at the discretion of the

shall be forfeited to the budget of the National Assembly or may be transferred by the deputy to his/her political group for the staff remuneration of that group.

The workings of Parliament. The rules governing the functioning of Parliament are provided for in the rules of procedure adopted by each House. Together with the relevant provisions of the Constitution[104] and several organic laws,[105] these rules of procedure constitute the specific branch of parliamentary law (*droit parlementaire*). The independent enactment of rules of procedure marks the autonomy of Parliament from the government. Each House of Parliament can amend its own rules of procedure at the majority of votes cast.[106] These rules of procedure must be referred, upon adoption, to the Constitutional Council for review of their conformity with the Constitution (article 61 paragraph one of the Constitution). The Council follows an extensive interpretation of the constitutional norms of reference when it comes to exercising such a review. These norms encompass not only the Constitution and relevant organic laws but also include a set of legislative measures relating to the institutions. The review exercised by the Council is strict.[107] Rules of procedure cannot be interpreted as going further than, or deviating from, what is provided for under the Constitution, whether it is to counter an extensive interpretation of their prerogatives by the Houses of Parliament or to protect the Houses of Parliament from waiving part of their prerogatives to their detriment. For example, the Constitutional Council held that the Houses of Parliament were not allowed to extend their prerogatives concerning the oral questions to the government or agenda setting, or, conversely, that they could hold non-public (secret) meetings.[108] Developments below concern the structures and working bodies of Parliament as well as parliamentary sessions, the determination of the parliamentary agenda, and parliamentary voting procedures. The focal point of the work of Parliament essentially revolves around the work of the National Assembly given its pre-eminence.

Both Houses of Parliament are organised around a number of internal bodies, namely the president of the House, the bureau of the House, and the conference of the presidents. The president of the National Assembly is elected for the duration of the parliamentary term (i.e., five years) unless anticipated elections are held after dissolution of the House, for example. The

member of Parliament, be paid out to a number of staff ranging from one to five. The member of Parliament has the status of employer and recruits and dismisses her/his staff as well as fixes their working conditions and salaries. The monthly amount of the credit is 10,581 euros.

104 The constitutional provisions that directly concern the working of Parliament are articles 27, 28, 29, 30, 31, 32, 33, 39, 43, 44, and 48 of the Constitution. In 1958, the main objective was to avoid a return to a *régime d'assemblée* by implementing several restrictions on the functioning of the Parliament through carefully crafted and well-defined rules.

105 Mainly Organic Law No 58-1100 of 17 November 1958 on the functioning of parliamentary assemblies, as amended; also, Organic Law No 2009-403 of 15 April 2009 relating to the application of articles 34-1, 39 and 44 of the Constitution.

106 Both the National Assembly and the Senate have overhauled their rules of procedure after the 2008 constitutional amendment. See rules of procedure of the National Assembly, 27 May 2009, and rules of procedure of the Senate, 2 June 2009. More recent modifications were made at the start of parliamentary term, in 2014 and in 2019. Each set of rules of procedure is completed by general instructions, equivalent of the Salient Rules of the Chair in the Oireachtas, issued by the bureau of each House which deals with the everyday functioning of Parliament.

107 See Chapter 6 on constitutional justice and rights protection.

108 Decision No 59-2 DC of 24 June 1959 *Règlement de l'Assemblée nationale.*

president of the Senate is elected every three years when one-third of the House's membership is renewed.[109] The presidents of both Houses of Parliament belong to the political majority of their respective House and are often leading political figures. They enjoy powers of two types, constitutional and parliamentary. Concerning their constitutional powers, the presidents of both Houses of Parliament are consulted upon dissolution of the National Assembly, or in the case of the application of the exceptional powers. They appoint three members of the Constitutional Council and may refer a law to the Council before its entry into force. Besides, the president of the Senate will also act as the acting President of the Republic in cases of vacancy of the presidency (see above). Concerning parliamentary powers, both presidents play a key role in the law-making process. Such a role includes organising parliamentary debates, acting as the equivalent of whips—albeit as regards all members of Parliament and not just as regards those in the majority—by giving the floor to members of Parliament and reminding them of the discipline of the House. They also ensure the security and safety of the House. In this role, presidents of the Houses of Parliament must show strict impartiality vis-à-vis all members, which is generally well observed. Each House of Parliament is administered by a bureau (or office) which is headed by the president of the respective House. Each bureau consists of elected deputies or senators, according to the representativity of their political group in the House, and civil servants.[110] Acting as the collegial management body of the legislature, the bureau directs parliamentary work and can, for example, decide upon the admissibility of a private member's bill or an amendment to a private member's bill, or decide upon the arrest of a member of Parliament. The conference of the presidents in each House of Parliament consists of the president of the relevant House, its vice-presidents, the presidents of the standing committees, and the presidents of the parliamentary groups.[111] The conference of the presidents plays a significant role in many aspects of the law-making process which include the determination of the calendar of parliamentary work and the agenda of parliamentary sessions. The conference of the presidents also ensures, for example, that the procedure for tabling a government bill before Parliament has been lawfully respected.

The plenary assembly, also known as the *assemblée plénière*, holds supreme authority within each House of Parliament in France. It possesses the exclusive power to enact legislation and oversee government activities. However, most parliamentary work takes place within parliamentary committees and political groups.[112] Both Houses of Parliament accommodate

109 The selection of the president occurs via a secret ballot among the members who are physically present in both Houses of Parliament. In the initial two rounds, an absolute majority is required, while a simple majority suffices in the third round, if needed.

110 The bureau consists of vice-presidents and an ensemble of administrative staff such as quaestors in charge of the internal administration of the House, and secretaries in charge of controlling the voting procedure and the drafting of minutes.

111 The conference in the National Assembly also includes the general rapporteur of the standing committee on Finance, the president of the parliamentary delegation for the EU. In the National Assembly and the Senate, it also includes, as appropriate, the presidents of the ad hoc committees.

112 There are also parliamentary offices and delegations, for example, for the EU (established in 1979), for the evaluation of scientific and technical choices (established in 1983), for gender equality and equality of opportunity between men and women (established in 1999), and for intelligence services (established in 2007). The offices for the evaluation of legislation and of public policies (established in 1996) were merged and eventually replaced by a stand-alone body for the evaluation and control of public policies as consecrated by the National Assembly's rules of procedure.

two distinct types of committees, namely standing committees and committees of inquiry, while additionally allowing for the establishment of ad hoc committees.

The number of standing committees in each House of Parliament cannot exceed eight. Each individual member of Parliament can be a member of only one standing committee. The appointment of members of Parliament in these committees is proportional to the representativity of political groups.[113] The National Assembly has eight standing committees, namely on Cultural Affairs and Education; on the Economy; on Foreign Affairs; on Social Affairs; on National Defence and the Armed Forces; on Sustainable Development and Urban Planning; on Finance, the Economy, and Budgetary Control; and on Constitutional Laws, Legislation, and General Administration of the Republic. The Senate has six standing committees, namely on Foreign Affairs, National Defence and the Armed Forces; on Social Affairs; on Cultural Affairs, Education, and Communication; on the Economy, Sustainable Development, and Urban Planning; on Finance; on Constitutional Laws, Legislation, Universal Suffrage, and General Administration. The role of standing committees, as small-sized parliamentary units, working behind closed doors, is to prepare the work of the main House by examining bills before these are debated and voted on at the plenary session. Therefore, such committees play a key role in the law-making process by assisting in the elaboration of the law without, however, being able to interfere in ministerial activity or to control the action of the government.[114] The role of these committees was reinforced by the 2008 constitutional amendment: their respective House can discuss and vote on government bills as amended by these committees, and not as first tabled by the government. Another aspect of the role of standing committees is the organisation of expert hearings on different topics on the model of the US Congress committees.

The existence of committees of inquiry was constitutionally recognised by the 2008 constitutional amendment. Committees of inquiry are temporary, set up to last up to six months. They consist of a maximum of 30 deputies in the National Assembly and 21 senators in the Senate. They are established according to the rules of procedure of each House of Parliament whereas rules governing their organisation and operation are defined by law. The key principle is that these committees cannot run in parallel with judicial proceedings on the same matter. Committees of inquiry allow deputies and senators to collect information and investigate on a particular issue, such as the management of a public service, or of a public company, or an overall societal issue. These committees have specific investigative powers and may summon ministers, but not the President of the Republic,[115] in order to question them. To ensure transparency, hearings before such committees and their reports are made public unless decided otherwise. The recommendations contained in their reports may be translated into legislation. At the time of writing, 86 committees of inquiry have been set up by the French Parliament since 1958. The first committee of inquiry established by the National Assembly was on the energy situation after the energy crisis in 1974, and the most recent one was on the dysfunctions and shortcomings of prison policy in France in 2021. The first committee of inquiry established by the Senate was on the French Radio and Television Broadcast Service in 1967, and the most recent one was on the violent incidents during the 2021–2022 Champions League

113 The majority decides on who chairs each standing committee. However, since 2007, the chairperson of the important standing committee on Finance in the National Assembly is allocated to a member of the opposition.

114 Ministers may attend meetings of the standing committees. They can also be heard at their request.

115 For example, Sarkozy was not heard by the committee of inquiry about his role concerning the liberation of the Bulgarian nurses detained in Libya in 2007.

final at the Stade de France in 2022. The most infamous committee of inquiry was the one on the *Outreau* scandal in 2005–2006. Labelled by President Chirac as "an unprecedented judicial disaster," the case was about alleged sexual abuse of children in northern France which produced 17 indictments, four convictions, and 12 acquittals. The case was built around the testimony of one of the co-defendants who lied about the involvement of the others. The committee of inquiry was established to examine between January and April 2006, through the testimonials of the acquitted individuals, the dysfunctional judicial system leading to the wrongful convictions, especially the judicial decisions taken by Judge Burgaud, who was the investigative judge on the case at the time.[116]

Ad hoc committees may be established, at the request of the government or at the request of the House of Parliament concerned, with a view to examining a specific government bill or a private member's bill. In practice, such committees are rarely used.

Political groups consist of the grouping of members of Parliament according to their political affinity. As such, they represent national political parties within Parliament except for those independent members who do not belong to any group, the so-called non-registered deputies or senators.[117] The formation of a political group does not require any formality other than lodging a political declaration with the president of the relevant House of Parliament and gathering a minimum of 15 members per group. The political declaration contains the objectives that the group wishes to attain and the means to reach these objectives. This is a pure formality as the House does not assess the content of such a declaration.[118] Political groups play a key role in the activity of Parliament. They are involved in the appointment of members of the bureau, in the work of the committees as well as in, among other things, the determination of the agenda and allocation of speaking time. Political groups determine the official political stance on important votes and expect their members to follow the party line. In other words, political groups represent an essential cog in the functioning of the democratic regime.[119]

The determination of the parliamentary calendar is key for the working of Parliament. Legislative elections mark the start of a new parliamentary term or legislature (*législature*).[120] Different provisions of the Constitution govern the regime of parliamentary sessions (*sessions parlementaires*), on the one hand (articles 28 and 29 of the Constitution), and the regime of parliamentary sittings (*séances parlementaires*), on the other hand (article 33 of the Constitution). Both Houses of Parliament sit simultaneously. Parliament does not sit permanently, and its sessions are limited. This is useful to provide a safe period during which

116 See André Vallini & Philippe Houillon, *Rapport fait au nom de la Commission d'enquête chargée de rechercher les causes des dysfonctionnements de la justice dans l'affaire dite d'Outreau et de formuler des propositions pour éviter leur renouvellement*, Report No 3125, National Assembly, 6 June 2006, accessible at <https://www.assemblee-nationale.fr/12/rap-enq/r3125.asp>.

117 Non-registered deputies and senators may nevertheless choose to be associated or affiliated (*apparentés*) with a political party. This means that these members of Parliament keep their independence while enjoying the benefits of being part of a group, such as the ability to join a parliamentary commission. Additionally, this affiliation benefits the party by expanding its membership.

118 Decision No 71-42 DC of 18 May 1971 *Résolution tendant à modifier les articles 2, 3, 5, 6, 7, 8, 11, 13, 14, 17, 21, 22, 29, 32, 36, 42, 45, 59, 72 et 108 du règlement du Sénat, à le compléter par un article 29 bis et un article 109 et à abroger l'article 84 dudit règlement.*

119 See also Chapter 5 on political parties, elections, and referendums.

120 At the time of writing, we are under the XVIth Legislature since 22 June 2022. The duration of a legislature is not provided for under the Constitution; however, it typically spans a period of five years.

the government cannot be held accountable. Parliament shall sit as of right during ordinary sessions (article 28 paragraph one of the Constitution). The number of sitting days of each House does not exceed 100 per ordinary session. However, the schedule of the weeks of parliamentary sessions shall be decided by each House (article 28 paragraph two of the Constitution). The rules of procedure of each House of Parliament determine the frequency and length of parliamentary sessions. Two weeks are monthly assigned to the examination of bills and items on the governmental agenda; one week is monthly assigned to the control of governmental action and to the evaluation of public policies; one sitting day is assigned to the agenda determined by opposition groups and minority groups; and a minimum of one session per week is assigned to questions to the government. *Ordinary sessions* take place during the working civil year, complemented, if need be, by extraordinary sessions over the summer. Ordinary sessions commence on the first working day of October and end on the last working day of June with a cap of 121 sitting days. Additional sessions may be decided at a majority of members of Parliament in either House of Parliament, or at the request of the Prime Minister after consultation of the House concerned. The President of the Republic, at the request of the Prime Minister or at the request of the majority of deputies in the National Assembly, may convene Parliament in *extraordinary sessions* (article 29 of the Constitution).[121] Parliament is automatically convened in *sessions as of right* under certain circumstances as provided for in the Constitution, such as after dissolution of the National Assembly (article 12 paragraph three of the Constitution), during the application of the exceptional powers (article 16 paragraph four of the Constitution), or to listen to the message delivered by the President (article 18 paragraph three of the Constitution). The 2008 constitutional amendment has given back to Parliament a certain control over its own agenda with an equal allocation of two weeks per month between the government and the Houses of Parliament.[122] Two weeks per month are allocated in priority to government bills and other texts that the government wishes to be tabled. For the other two weeks of the month, Parliament is free to set up its own agenda within the double constraint that, on the one hand, one week per month is allocated to the control of governmental action and to the evaluation of public policies, and, on the other hand, one session per month is used by minority groups and opposition groups (article 48 of the Constitution). Also, one session per week at least is reserved as priority to questions to the government. *Oral questions* are asked in writing by members of Parliament to members of the government who reply orally. Oral questions generally concern current affairs, and their broadcast provides a useful source of information

121 Most extraordinary sessions are convened at the request of the Prime Minister. When an extraordinary session is convened at the request of the majority of deputies, the session must not be prolonged further than what is necessary to deal with the set agenda, and must end, in any case, after 12 days (article 29 paragraph two of the Constitution). Besides, no new extraordinary session can be requested within the same month but at the request of the Prime Minister (article 29 paragraph three of the Constitution).

122 The agenda is split into two sections: a priority section and a complementary section. In the priority section, the government has the freedom to present its own bills, as well as any private members' bills that are approved by the government. This is an essential prerogative for the government to prioritise its own texts, as well as those of its political allies, while impeding the progress of texts it opposes, particularly those proposed by the opposition. The complementary section of the agenda is determined by the proposals put forth by the conference of the presidents.

for the House and the public.[123] *Written questions* are by far the most frequent.[124] The reply by the government must be published in the Official Journal within one month of the publication of the question.

As a corollary to the prohibition of the imperative mandate, the vote of deputies and senators is personal (article 27 paragraphs one and two of the Constitution). The possibilities of delegation or proxy voting are limited, and no member of Parliament shall be given more than one proxy vote (article 27 paragraph three of the Constitution). However, busy members of Parliament most often circumvent their obligation to vote in person. This is compounded by a very liberal interpretation of proxy voting possibilities (i.e., when a member of Parliament is ill, when s/he is in charge of a temporary mission at the request of the government, when s/he takes part in an international assembly, or when s/he is abroad at the time of an extraordinary session, and generally all *force majeure* situations). Except in the case of votes on personal appointments (e.g., election of the president of the National Assembly at the beginning of the parliamentary term), all votes are public. As a rule, the vote is by a show of hands, unless an uncertainty in the count requires a vote by distinguishing between members standing as opposed to those members who remain seated. Public voting is by ordinary ballot (via an electronic vote), or by ballot in the gallery, or in the adjoining rooms of the House. Members of Parliament have the choice between three voting options, namely "for," "against," or "abstention."

Role of Parliament. The role of Parliament is multi-faceted. Throughout history, it has primarily served four purposes: representing the citizens, enacting laws, approving tax levies, and overseeing the government.[125] In the case of the French Parliament, its authority is confined to the powers granted to it by the Constitution. These powers can be classified in three categories, namely the power to elaborate and pass laws, the power to control the government, and the responsibility of evaluating public policies (article 24 paragraph one of the Constitution). Since these powers involve interactions with the government, they will be examined in the next section on the relationships between the government and Parliament.

Relationships between the government and Parliament

Under the Fifth Republic, Parliament and the government are closely interrelated, in terms of both their organic makeup and their functioning. Prior to 1958, the relationship between the two institutions was mainly organic, ministers being most of the time also deputies or senators, and vice versa. Additionally, all members of Parliament potentially had the opportunity to become part of the government. However, this arrangement led to well-known perverse effects, such as a blurring of roles and interests, excessive partisanship, and governmental instability. Seeking

123 Oral questions are generally not followed by a debate. Oral questions with debate have become obsolete and do not appear in the rules of procedure anymore.

124 During the 2021–2022 session of the XVth legislature (2017–2022), a total of 45,764 questions were asked with 34,331 replies by the government. See <https://www2.assemblee-nationale.fr/15/statistiques-de-l-activite-parlementaire-sous-la-xve-legislature>.

125 The appointment of government is another role afforded to Parliament according to Bagehot.

to break away from this situation, the drafters of the Constitution sought to maintain a purely functional relationship, although this has not been completely successful.

Title V of the Constitution (articles 34 to 51-2) stands as the lengthiest title within the Constitution. It primarily deals with the intricate relationships between Parliament and the government. Under the Fifth Republic, both institutions maintain a close collaboration in two respects: a collaboration that concerns the law-making process, and a collaboration that concerns Parliament's oversight of the government's actions, namely in its evaluation of public polices and by holding the government accountable. The subsequent developments follow the tripartite division as laid down under the Constitution on the role of Parliament (article 24 of the Constitution): elaboration of, and voting on, laws; monitoring of the government's actions; and evaluation of public policies.

Collaboration in the elaboration of the law. In principle, the law is the work of Parliament. Parliament votes the law, thus underpinning the principle of the sovereignty of the law and the institution attached to it. However, this assertion must be qualified. The law has lost its sovereignty in two respects. Firstly, unlike under the previous Republics, the area of the law is limited under the Fifth Republic. Parliament may legislate only within the confines of its area of competence (article 34 of the Constitution), whereas the government has the competence to make decisions on "all areas that do not fall under the area of the law" (article 37 paragraph one of the Constitution). Parliament has therefore a residual legislative competence (*compétence d'attribution*), whereas the government has, under its autonomous regulatory power, the general normative competence (*compétence de droit commun*). Secondly, even within its area of competence, the action of Parliament is limited by two series of factors. Not only is the French legislature bound by EU norms under the principles of supremacy and direct effect, but the government also enjoys several prerogatives in the law-making process that make it the real "master of the legislative game." The principle of legislative collaboration thus gives pre-eminence to the government over Parliament. The 2008 constitutional amendment sought somehow to rebalance this collaboration to the benefit of Parliament. It did so by, firstly, giving a more modern and complete definition of the role of Parliament (amended article 24 of the Constitution), and secondly, enhancing the role of Parliament in the determination of the parliamentary agenda, the examination of texts, and the organisation of debates, among others. However, the law-making process largely remains in the hands of the government.

The general characteristics of legislative collaboration. As under the previous Republics, law-making requires constant collaboration between the legislative bodies (i.e., the National Assembly and the Senate) and the executive bodies (i.e., the government and the President of the Republic, who intervenes at the end of the process by promulgating the law). However, this collaboration is unequal to the benefit of the government. This was so wished by the 1958 constituents in order to rationalise the parliamentary system, including the legislative procedure. This rationalisation manifests itself in both political and institutional terms. Politically speaking, the parliamentary majority supports, in principle, the government's programme and votes on government bills. Institutionally speaking, the Constitution provides the government with a set of prerogatives that facilitate the government in tabling bills and progressing them without too much turbulence until the final vote. These constitutional prerogatives are of two types: those prerogatives that allow the government to oppose unfavourable private members' bills, on the one hand; those prerogatives that allow the government to have its own bills adopted and any other private member's bill that the government favours, on the other hand. Besides, part of the parliamentary agenda (i.e., two week-long sessions out of four sessions) is reserved as a matter of priority, and in the order determined by the government, to the examination of drafts and to the discussions that the government so requests to be placed on the agenda (article 48 of the Constitution). Also, the specific "49.3" procedure allows the government to force the adoption of the text of a bill unless it is dismissed by a vote of no confidence before the National Assembly (article 49 paragraph three of the Constitution). In the context of parliamentary rationalisation, it should be emphasised that the Constitution has limited the legislative field by determining what the matters are that fall within the scope of the law (article 34 of the Constitution) by, concomitantly, recognising an autonomous power of the government to enact regulations (article 37 of the Constitution). The demarcation of the legislative field represents a break from the French tradition that previously granted an unlimited field to legislate for Parliament.

Definition of the law. Under the current Constitution, the law is defined under a formal requirement as well as under a substantive requirement: the law is an Act adopted by Parliament (formal requirement) that falls under one of the areas specifically laid down under article 34 of the Constitution (substantive requirement). The substantive definition of the law consists of an enumeration of areas that fall under the competence of the legislature. The sphere of competence of Parliament (article 34 of the Constitution) is therefore clearly distinct from the sphere of competence assigned to the government in its power to adopt regulations (article 37 of the Constitution). While the former is the exception, the latter stands as the rule. The law determines the rules relating to areas such as civil rights and fundamental freedoms; freedom, pluralism, and the independence of the media; limitations to citizens' rights and property by reason of national defence; nationality, status, and capacity of legal persons, matrimonial regimes; the definition of criminal offences and the penalties applicable to them, criminal procedure, the establishment of new orders in the court system, and the status of judges; and tax and currency regimes. The law also determines the fundamental principles as regards matters such as the general organisation of national defence; the free administration of local authorities, powers, and resources; education; the protection of the environment; property rights; employment law, trade union law, and the social security regime. New areas may be added to this list by an organic law.[126]

The Constitution provides for mechanisms aimed at ensuring that the proposed law falls within the legislative area as defined under article 34 of the Constitution. There are two facets to the issue. Firstly, the Constitutional Council reviews the respect by Parliament of the regulatory area, in other words that it does not act ultra vires in areas which are not of its competence. The government and, since the 2008 constitutional amendment, the president of either House of Parliament, have the possibility to declare that a private member's bill, or an

126 The Constitution seems to distinguish between areas for which the law determines the *rules* and those areas for which it determines the *fundamental principles*. The Constitutional Council has not been overly strict about such a distinction. See, for example, Decision No 59-1 FNR of 27 November 1959 *Proposition de loi déposée par MM. Bajeux et Boulanger, sénateurs, tendant à la stabilisation des fermages (et à abroger le décret n° 59-175 du 7 janvier 1959 relatif au prix des baux à ferme).*

amendment to it, is inadmissible if its provisions are outside the confines of article 34 (article 41 of the Constitution). In the event of a disagreement between the government and the president of the House concerned, the bill in question is referred to the Constitutional Council for the purpose of determining its legislative or regulatory character. Overall, the approach of the Constitutional Council has been in favour of the government and the Council has ruled, in several cases, in favour of the regulatory character of the bill under discussion.[127] Besides, the Constitutional Council may decide to "de-legalise" (i.e., deprive them of their legislative character) provisions of a law adopted which fell within the regulatory area (article 37 paragraph two of the Constitution). Such a decision aims at allowing the government to amend the text in question by decree, therefore discarding its legislative nature.[128] Secondly, the Council of State, under administrative law, may annul a regulatory act which pertains to the legislative area.

The law-making process. The law-making process consists of three stages: namely, the tabling of bills through legislative initiative; the voting on the law following parliamentary debates; and finally, the promulgation of the law.[129]

Legislative initiative and tabling of bills. The right of legislative initiative belongs concurrently to the Prime Minister and to members of Parliament (article 39 paragraph one of the Constitution). The Prime Minister tables government bills (*projets de lois*), and members of Parliament table private members' bills (*propositions de lois*). Before being tabled in one or the other of the two Houses, government bills[130] must first be discussed in the Council of Ministers and submitted to the Council of State for their mandatory opinion.[131] The government may also request an opinion from the Economic, Social and Environmental Council concerning both government bills and private members' bills, and such an opinion is a mandatory requirement concerning bills bearing economic, social, or environmental implications. Deputies or senators may table private members' bills, and amendments thereof, either individually or, as is often the case, collectively on behalf of the members of a parliamentary group. The government is constitutionally obligated to conduct an impact study before tabling bills before Parliament (article 39 paragraph three of the Constitution).[132] This is in order to rationalise parliamentary

127 Before 2008, article 41 of the Constitution was rarely invoked by the government. This was not regarded as a particularly strategic move since it deprived the government of an area of action and added to the areas of Parliament's activity.

128 Similarly to article 41 of the Constitution, this has been seldom used.

129 The ordinary legislative procedure must be distinguished from the extraordinary legislative procedure. The ordinary procedure is characterised by a number of prerogatives in the hands of the government in order to facilitate the deliberation and voting on the bills put forward by the government.

130 Finance bills and Social Security financing bills must be tabled before the National Assembly in the first place (article 39 paragraph two of the Constitution). Without prejudice to article 44 paragraph one of the Constitution, government bills whose main object relates to the organisation of local authorities should be first tabled before the Senate.

131 Decision No 2003-468 DC of 3 April 2003 *Loi relative à l'élection des conseillers régionaux et des représentants au Parlement européen ainsi qu'à l'aide publique aux partis politiques*, pt 7. The request for an opinion of the Council of State is facultative as regards private members' bills at the initiative of the president of either House of Parliament, except when the instigator of the bill is against such a request.

132 As supplemented by Organic Law No 2009-403 of 15 April 2009 relating to the application of articles 34-1, 39 and 44 of the Constitution. Government bills introduced in the National Assembly or in the Senate must meet a

work by sparing Parliament discussion about irrelevant, costly, or frivolous legislative proposals. Impact studies were originally required as regards government bills in the area of the environment. This requirement has been extended to all government bills—bar finance bills, Social Security bills, programming bills, and bills relating to constitutional amendments. It also applies to a bill relating to the extension of emergency measures, and to a bill authorising the ratification of an international agreement. Failure to conduct such an impact study, or failure to conduct it properly, may result in the bill not being put on the parliamentary agenda.

The right of legislative initiative is limited by a number of factors. Firstly, most domestic laws have "an EU origin" given that the scope of EU action, binding in domestic law, largely covers the legislative field. This has the effect of limiting the legislative initiative of both the government and Parliament. Secondly, and similarly to most parliamentary regimes, domestic legislation has mainly a governmental origin. This is understandable in a system where the government benefits from a majority in Parliament as well as from the support of the administration which assists in carrying out government action—private members' bills are de facto limited since their chance of being adopted is less than that of government bills.[133] That being said, the right of amendment certainly represents the most effective tool of legislative action for Parliament in that it allows deputies and senators to put pressure on the government during the legislative process. Thirdly and more technically, private members' bills must deal with matters within the confines of the law as defined under the Constitution and must not encroach on the regulatory field of the government. Besides, any proposed text may, under certain conditions, be declared inadmissible. The first type of legislative inadmissibility is provided for under article 40 of the Constitution. If a private member's bill, or amendments thereof, does have implications in terms of public spending, this is regarded as a ground for inadmissibility. Such a bill will be outrightly rejected and declared inadmissible if it leads to an increase in public spending or a decrease in public income. Article 40 represents the most serious obstacle to parliamentary initiative because all legislation is deemed to have a financial effect, direct or indirect. In reality, parliamentary practice has been quite flexible on that matter. The second type of legislative inadmissibility is provided for under article 41 of the Constitution. Any private member's bill, or amendments thereof, that would not be within the domain of the law as determined under article 34, or that would be contrary to a delegation granted under article 38 relating to ordinances, is declared inadmissible.

Legislative procedure. The legislative procedure commences with the tabling of the proposed legislation (i.e., government bill or private member's bill) and concludes with the vote of the bill into law. A bill is firstly examined within a standing (or specific) parliamentary committee. Such examination aims at preparing the bill for further scrutiny by the entire house during the plenary session. The bill undergoes public scrutiny, firstly as a whole, and then each individual

number of requirements. These requirements encompass the provision of a statement of reasons for proposing the bill, an evaluation of its financial, environmental, economic, and social impact, as well as analysis of its conformity with European law and the intended methodology for the implementation of the future law. Only after complying with these requirements can the conference of presidents of the relevant House declare the bill admissible.

133 Less than 10% of laws voted in France originate in Parliament.

article of the bill is scrutinised.[134] Throughout the debating stage, the bill can be subject to multiple amendments (see below). To avoid hasty decisions, a "cooling-off" period of six weeks is mandated between the tabling of the bill and its discussion in the plenary session.[135]

The right of amendment. The debate in Parliament is based on the bill adopted in committee (without distinction between government bills and private members' bills) or, failing that, on the text introduced in each House (article 42 paragraph one of the Constitution). This means that amendments can be introduced at committee stage, except in the case of finance bills, Social Security bills, and bills relating to constitutional amendments. This is a significant change which has contributed to an increase in parliamentary committee work, allowing in-depth debate of the proposed legislation while avoiding the time constraints of plenary sittings. As a general principle, the right of amendment belongs to members of Parliament and the government (article 44 paragraph one of the Constitution). It means that members of Parliament and the government may suggest changes (i.e., additions or deletions) to the text of the bill under discussion. Amendments cannot however change the nature of (i.e., "denature") the bill. A recurring problem has been the tabling of massive amendments by members of Parliament considered as a practice of parliamentary filibustering. Nonetheless, the right of amendment is strictly circumscribed under the Constitution and parliamentary law. Firstly, express constitutional provisions on inadmissibility act as powerful restrictions in this regard (articles 40 and 41 of the Constitution). Secondly, further restrictions are put on the right of amendment pursuant to the conditions laid down by the Rules of Procedure of the Houses of Parliament, within the framework determined by an organic law (article 44 paragraph one of the Constitution).[136] Thirdly, any amendment proposed must have a link, whether direct or indirect, with the bill under discussion (article 45 paragraph one of the Constitution).

Parliamentary debates. The debating phase represents a key moment in the law-making process. The government may intervene by using different procedures provided for in the Constitution, notably to put an end to the debate which has become stalled. Before the bill is voted in its entirety, each provision is discussed and voted on. At that stage, the government may request what is called the so-called *vote bloqué* (article 44 paragraph three of the Constitution). The "blocked vote procedure" allows the House in which the bill is being debated to decide, by a single vote, to retain only the amendments proposed or accepted by the government on all or part of the text under discussion. This procedure is clearly extremely favourable to the government. The "blocked vote procedure" has been described by a former president of the National Assembly as a process whereby the government is able at any time, and generally

134 At this stage, members of Parliament may trigger various procedures in order to interrupt the debating process. Firstly, they may directly vote on a bill without engaging in prior discussions, if necessary. Also, a bill may be declared inadmissible on the grounds of unconstitutionality. Additionally, members of Parliament may request that a bill be referred to the committee stage.

135 A four-week period is allowed between the submission of the bill from one House of Parliament to the other House and its examination thereof. These periods of reflection do not apply to finance laws, Social Security financing laws, or government bills relating to crisis measures.

136 Organic Law No 2009-403 of 15 April 2009 concerning the application of articles 34-1, 39 and 44 of the Constitution.

at a difficult time, to move on from the technical level, about which a thousand reservations and many criticisms can be made, to the higher political level. By imposing such a vote, the government de facto "blocks" any further debate. Aimed at rallying the majority around the government, the "blocked vote procedure" clearly restrains the freedom of action of members of Parliament, who must accept the bill as it stands, or not accept it at all, and also prevents them from denaturing the bill too much through unrequested amendments. The "blocked vote procedure" is akin to a motion of confidence, albeit one which does not entail holding the government accountable.[137] Another procedure is the so-called "49.3 procedure." Even more radical than the "blocked vote procedure," the "49.3 procedure" allows the government to constrain members of Parliament into adopting a law without any discussion and without any vote (article 49 paragraph three of the Constitution). It is part of the mechanisms whereby the government may be held accountable before the National Assembly (see below). The procedure aims at tackling filibustering attempts by the opposition. It can also be used to discipline the parliamentary majority when this majority has taken to dismantling the bill proposed by the government. In that context, the deputies face the tough alternative of either approving the text as it is or, by rejecting it, dismissing the government and provoking the dissolution of the National Assembly. Another occurrence during parliamentary debate is the request by the government (or any member of Parliament) for a second deliberation of the proposed text.

The vote on the bill. The voting phase consists of the approval of the bill that is voted on as a whole by members of Parliament after listening to representatives from various political parties. The vote is conducted based on a majority of the votes cast unless the Constitution mandates a qualified majority. The voting is carried out in two stages, starting with the deputies and followed by the senators, or vice versa depending on the initial examination of the bill in either House. At this stage, the Prime Minister may engage the government's responsibility before the National Assembly (see below).

Parliamentary shuttle. Since a bill must be voted on identical terms by both Houses of Parliament, constitutional mechanisms are put in place in the eventuality of a disagreement between the two Houses. In the first place, the bill may "come and go" between the two Houses until agreement is reached on a common text, hence the so-called mechanism of the "parliamentary shuttle" (*navette parlementaire*). In the second place, and in the event of a disagreement between the two Houses of Parliament on a government bill, and after two readings by each of the Houses,[138] the Prime Minister may convene a "joint parliamentary committee" (*commission mixte paritaire*) (article 45 of the Constitution).[139] The joint parliamentary committee, which consists of an equal number of deputies and senators, is tasked with accommodating the disagreement and with coming up with a common text. In

137 Decision No 59-5 DC of 15 January 1960 *Résolution modifiant les articles 95 et 96 du règlement de l'Assemblée nationale*.

138 The procedure applies except in cases of accelerated procedure. Since the 2008 constitutional amendment, the conference of the presidents of the Houses of Parliament may oppose the implementation of the accelerated procedure.

139 The right to convene a joint parliamentary committee can also be decided jointly by the presidents of both Houses of Parliament as regards a private member's bill.

cases where the committee succeeds in doing so, the government submits the agreed text to both Houses for voting. However, if the text is not approved, the government gives the last word to the National Assembly, which then votes on the last version of the bill as voted by the deputies, and possibly amended by the senators. In cases where the government does not so proceed, the "shuttle" procedure resumes. If the joint parliamentary committee fails to come to an agreement, the government may, after a final reading by the National Assembly and the Senate, request the National Assembly to finally approve the text.[140] This part well illustrates two features of the legislative process, namely the unequal bicameralism which gives the last word to the directly elected House of Parliament, and the stronghold of the government on the legislative process. This last point is crucial since the government can also use the blocked vote procedure and/or the "49.3 procedure" (see below).

Exceptional legislative procedures. Certain laws require specific law-making procedures for their enactment. These include organic laws, finance laws, Social Security financing laws, and programming laws as well as treaties and international agreements (see Table 4.2 Types of laws).

Organic laws pertain to the organisation and the functioning of public powers and are provided for by the Constitution. In principle, the procedure for adopting organic laws is similar to that of ordinary laws, albeit with a few exceptions and peculiarities. Organic laws may be examined and voted on only a fortnight after they have been tabled before Parliament. When the National Assembly has the last word on the vote, organic laws must be approved by a majority vote. When it comes to organic laws concerning the Senate, they must be adopted in the exact same terms by both Houses of Parliament. This effectively provides the Senate with a veto power over the adoption of organic laws, hence preserving a form of equal bicameralism. Lastly, organic laws are mandatorily subject to review by the Constitutional Council to ensure their conformity with the Constitution.

Finance laws are adopted under the conditions prescribed by an organic law. Discussion and approval of the overall public budget take place within a 70-day period, with 40 days being reserved for debate before the National Assembly, 20 days before the Senate, and ten days for inter-house coordination, or "parliamentary shuttle." Following the expiry of the 70-day time frame, the public budget is enforced by way of ordinance. Such a short period of time has arguably the advantage of guaranteeing that the state budget is up and running at the beginning of each financial year, in contrast to the previous situation where, without capping the delay, the adoption of the budget could be delayed by several months.

Social Security financing laws aim at governing the conditions for maintaining a balanced budget within the Social Security system. These laws determine the expenditure objectives based on projected income, as specified by the organic law. The procedure for the enactment of these laws is quite similar to the procedure outlined earlier for finance laws. Social Security financing laws are also tabled before the National Assembly in the first place. Due to the significant impact on public finances of these laws (i.e., finance laws and Social Security financing laws), the government possesses several privileges when it comes to their adoption. These laws are tabled by priority; additionally, the standard periods of reflection that apply to ordinary

140 This can only apply as regards ordinary and organic laws because constitutional laws must be passed by both Houses of Parliament in identical terms.

TABLE 4.2 Types of laws

	Constitutional law	*Referendum law*	*Organic law*	*Ordinary law*	*Finance law*	*Social Security Financing law*	*Programming law*	*Enabling law*	*Ratification law*		*Law of the land (loi du pays)*
Legal source	Article 89	Article 11	Article 46	Article 34	Article 34 §5	Article 34 §6	Articles 34 & 70	Article 38	Article 53 §1 *(international commitments)*	Article 38 *(legislate by decree)*	Organic Law No 99-209 of 19 March 1999 & Organic Law No 2004-192 of 27 February 2004
What is it?	Law establishing a new Constitution or amending the current Constitution.	Law adopted by referendum.	Act supplementing and clarifying the Constitution at the express request of the constituent.	Act adopted by Parliament (or, more exceptionally, by the electorate in an article 11 referendum or, even more exceptionally, by the President of the Republic under article 16).	Determines the nature, amount, and allocation of the state's resources and expenditure, as well as the budgetary and financial balance.	Determines the general conditions for the financial equilibrium of the Social Security system and sets spending targets.	Determines the objectives of the state's action and defines multi-year public finance projects.	Act of Parliament authorising the Government to take measures that fall within the scope of the law by means of decrees.	Incorporates the stipulations of a treaty into the legal system.	Gives legislative force to a decree.	Only for New Caledonia and French Polynesia. Laws of the land are quasi-legislative acts that remain administrative by nature.

laws do not apply in this case; furthermore, the "49.3 procedure" (see below) may be applicable without any limitation.

Programming laws aim at providing the government's framework for medium- and long-term specific actions in the economic and social areas, as well as offering multiannual guidelines on public finances. These laws, although lacking normative force, follow a procedure similar to ordinary laws. However, they possess a distinct feature, requiring the submission of their bills to the Economic, Social and Environmental Council for evaluation and opinion (article 70 of the Constitution).

Treaties and international agreements are ratified or approved by Parliament before they can be ratified by the President of the Republic. The Constitution contains specific provisions that are applicable to various types of treaties and agreements, such as peace treaties, trade agreements, agreements with international organisations, agreements related to state finances, agreements related to personal status, as well as those that amend legislative provisions or involve the transfer, exchange, or acquisition of territory (article 53 of the Constitution). Once a treaty is signed, it cannot be amended. Therefore, the role of Parliament is limited to either approving or rejecting the treaty. However, in cases where a treaty, though not contradicting the Constitution, could impact the functioning of the institutions, Parliament may seek the authorisation (article 11 paragraph one of the Constitution).

Promulgation and publication of the law. The law-making process ends with the promulgation and publication of the law. The responsibility of the *promulgation* lies with the President of the Republic, who must so proceed within 15 days of the law being forwarded to the government (article 10 paragraph one of the Constitution).[141] Promulgation is defined as "the act by which the Head of State certifies the existence of the law and requests all public authorities to observe and enforce it therewith."[142] A number of contingencies may occur within the 15-day period, between the vote of the law and its promulgation. Firstly, the President may request the law to be reconsidered by Parliament (article 10 paragraph two of the Constitution). Such a possibility has been rarely exercised since 1958, having been used only three times.[143] This intervention of the President represents an interesting option in that it allows the Head of State, despite not being directly involved in the legislative process, to influence Parliament's position. The President is unable to make changes to the law personally, except in cases where Article 16 of the Constitution applies. However, the Prime Minister's countersignature is required for the promulgation to be valid.

Secondly, there is the possibility of a law being referred to the Constitutional Council for judicial review (article 61 paragraph two of the Constitution). The ex-ante constitutional review (or a priori control of the constitutionality of the law) is much more frequent in practice than the request for a second deliberation by Parliament. It has sometimes been claimed that the Council, by exercising its review, participates in the elaboration of the law.

141 The 15-day period applies to all types of laws (i.e., ordinary laws, constitutional laws, referendum laws, and organic laws).

142 CE, Ass., 8 February 1974, *Commune de Montory*, Rec. Lebon 93.

143 Article 10 paragraph two of the Constitution was used in 1983 (about the Universal Exhibition of 1989), in 1985 (about a law relating to the evolution of New Caledonia), and in 2003 (about a law on the election of regional councillors and EP members).

This is a fallacy since the review, while certainly preventive, is of a judicial, and not legislative, nature. Besides, such a review is exercised on an already voted law. Nonetheless, the intervention of the Constitutional Council arguably exercises a salutary influence on public authorities. Public authorities have indeed an interest in complying pre-emptively with constitutional requirements to avoid a ruling of unconstitutionality, some commentators considering this as the "deterring effect" of constitutional review.[144] Subject to these two possibilities (i.e., second parliamentary deliberation and judicial review), the President of the Republic *must* promulgate the law as it is a mandatory competence (*compétence liée*). This is a shared power of the President because the decree of promulgation is countersigned by the Prime Minister and the ministers who are the main promoters of the text. The *publication* of a law is carried out by inserting the decree of promulgation in the Official Journal. The date of a French law is the date of the signature of the decree of promulgation which includes the mandatory final provision: "This law shall be executed as law of the state." Publication in the Official Journal signals when the law starts to have a legally binding effect on citizens.[145]

Parliamentary scrutiny of government action. The primary purpose of parliamentary scrutiny is to oversee and evaluate government action. This entails ensuring that the government is held accountable for its decisions and policies, as well as requesting pertinent information from the government. Apart from these methods, other forms of scrutiny exist.

Principles of political accountability. The principles of political accountability of the government before Parliament are detailed below. In 1958, the constituents wanted to establish a true parliamentary regime. However, the constituents also wanted to take necessary precautions to prevent a return to governmental instability that plagued the previous Republics. Hence, they innovated by rationalising procedures of governmental accountability. The first principle of governmental accountability is that the government is responsible before the National Assembly only, and unaccountable before the Senate. The rationale for this exclusive power of the National Assembly is twofold. Firstly, only the National Assembly is directly elected by the citizens, thereby making it the only legitimate political institution entrusted with the power to overthrow the government. Secondly, because the Senate cannot be the object of dissolution, senators cannot be entrusted with the power of holding the government accountable since it would create an undesirable discrepancy in the mutual means of pressure between the Senate and the government. While the government may request the approval of the Senate on a declaration of general policy, an unfavourable vote would not entail any legal obligation for the government to resign (article 49 paragraph four of the Constitution). When the government is held accountable under the conditions provided for in the Constitution (except under article 49 paragraph four, which concerns the Senate), the Prime Minister is under the obligation to submit the resignation of the government to the President of the Republic, who is, in principle, bound to accept it (article

144 Louis Favoreu, "L'effet dissuasif du recours préventif en inconstitutionnalité" in *Mélanges Dmitri-Georges Lavroff, La Constitution et les valeurs* (Dalloz 2005) 151–160.

145 The law is published in the Laws and Decrees edition of the Official Journal.

50 of the Constitution). The National Assembly may hold the government accountable in three distinct ways.

Firstly, the government may be held accountable on its programme or on a general policy declaration after a *vote of confidence* before the National Assembly (article 49 paragraph one of the Constitution). A negative vote of the majority of the votes cast results in the resignation of the government. Regarding the procedure, two main elements should be noted. Firstly, the decision belongs to the Prime Minister, who may consult the President of the Republic, but the agreement of the latter is in no way required. However, since the Prime Minister's decision commits the entire government as a collegial body, it is logical that there is a deliberation in the Council of Ministers about the decision to engage the government's accountability. Secondly, the calculation of the majority votes is based on the votes in favour of the vote of confidence, leaving aside the votes against *and the abstentions*; if the government does not obtain a majority of the votes cast, it must resign. It has been argued that a distinction should be made between accountability regarding *a programme* and accountability regarding *a declaration of general policy*; while the former compels the government to ask for a vote of confidence, the latter leaves some discretion to the government as to whether to request such a vote. There is, however, a difficulty in identifying what exactly constitutes a programme and what constitutes a declaration of general policy. This has somewhat rendered the whole distinction moot.

As for the scope of this first way to hold the government accountable, it depends on the two modes of operation of the Fifth Republic, namely whether it is the normal operation of the regime or under a cohabitation. Under the former mode, since the Prime Minister draws his/her legitimacy from the President of the Republic, who appoints him/her, it is desirable that the Prime Minister requests a vote of confidence before the National Assembly with a view to establishing a relation of trust from the start as a sort of courtesy towards the elected representatives of the people. Under the latter mode (i.e., cohabitation), with the Prime Minister deriving his/her legitimacy only from the existence of a majority in the National Assembly, which is opposed to that of the President, it is normal that s/he requests a vote of confidence to solidify political support. In short, the vote of confidence appears to be a weapon intended to test the solidity of the relations between the Prime Minister and his/her majority. Instances of votes of confidence have been quite uneven in practice. In general, governments have never overused the vote of confidence since most of them were assured of the solidity of their parliamentary majority. Several governments asked for a vote of confidence as soon as they were formed while others waited several months after their formation; almost always, votes took place on a declaration of general policy. However, it seems that, since 1993, the practice has been for all governments to seek the confidence of the National Assembly within a few days of their appointment. All in all, since 1958, there have been 39 uses of the vote of confidence without one having had a negative outcome so far.

Secondly, the government may be held accountable when the National Assembly votes on *a motion of no confidence* or *motion of censure* (article 49 paragraph two of the Constitution).[146]

146 The procedure, as amended by the 2008 constitutional amendment, provides that: "The Prime Minister may, after deliberation of the Council of Ministers, request a vote of confidence before the National Assembly on a finance bill or a Social Security financing bill. In such a case, the bill shall be deemed adopted unless a vote of no confidence, tabled in the following twenty-four hours, is passed pursuant to the conditions provided for in the

The motion of censure represents the classic weapon of Parliament against the government in parliamentary regimes which the Fifth Republic, as a mixed regime, arguably is not. Such a tool is a survival of the previous regimes but with more restraint in order to avoid overthrowing the government too easily. The motion of confidence procedure is therefore subject to strict parliamentary rules. A motion must be set down for debate by at least one-tenth of the deputies calculated on the number of seats filled.[147] From the moment a motion is tabled, no more signatures are accepted, and existing signatures cannot be withdrawn. A deputy cannot table more than three motions per ordinary parliamentary session unless the government takes the initiative to engage its responsibility under the "49.3 procedure" (see below). A motion of censure can only be tabled during parliamentary sessions and cannot be tabled during times of crisis, such as during the interim presidency and during the application of the exceptional powers. Deputies vote on the motion after a period of reflection of 48 hours from the moment the motion has been tabled. No withdrawal of the motion is possible after it has been debated. In addition, for the calculation of the votes, only the votes cast in favour of the motion are counted towards the final ballot, which must be at the absolute majority of the deputies voting in the National Assembly—in other words, abstentions will count against the motion, and in favour of the government. The final ballot therefore gives a clear indication of whether the government faces an overly hostile majority or, on the contrary, benefits from a strong and constructive majority. If the motion is adopted, the Prime Minister and his/her government must resign. If the motion is not adopted, the government stays in place. Motions of censure have primarily been used by the deputies in the opposition to criticise the majority in government and stimulate debates on general policy issues rather than as a way to overthrow the government. Since 1958, there have only been a very limited number of motions of censure and only one motion has been passed so far, the one that resulted in the demise of the Pompidou Government in 1962.

Thirdly, the National Assembly may pass on a motion of no confidence which has been triggered by the government's decision to resort to the "*49.3 procédure*" (article 49 paragraph three of the Constitution). The "49.3 procedure" is a key mechanism to ensure the stability of the regime. However, each time it has been used, the "49.3 procedure" has been criticised by the opposition and sometimes the wayward faction of the majority because of the radical way it seeks to put pressure upon Parliament. This is why its operation is strictly regulated. Whereas, since 1958, the "49.3 procedure" could be applied without limit to any bill, the 2008 constitutional amendment has limited its use to the most important types of bills, namely finance bills, Social Security financing bills, plus one bill (whether government bill or private member's bill) per parliamentary session. The general idea of the procedure is that, because the bill in question is considered so important by the government to implement its policy, the Prime Minister cannot envisage the bill not being adopted. Therefore, the Prime Minister and his/her government are ready to be held accountable. Once the "49.3 procedure" is put in motion, the bill will be deemed adopted by the National Assembly with a very limited possibility of reversing such a

above paragraph. The Prime Minister may, in addition, resort to the procedure thereof in relation to one government bill or one private member's bill per session."

147 Motions of censure typically contain the underlying rationale and justification behind their proposal.

presumption of adoption. While the conditions to vote on the motion of confidence are similar to those explained above,[148] there are three possible outcomes to the "49.3 procedure."[149]

A first possible outcome is when no motion is tabled in the 24 hours following the decision of the Prime Minister to engage the accountability of his/her government before the National Assembly. In that case, the proposed bill is deemed adopted, without the deputies even having to vote on it. Such outcome makes sense since it means that less than one-tenth of the deputies object to the bill in question and that the bill is overwhelmingly supported, or that the opposition knows that a vote would be futile in that situation. A second possible outcome is when a motion is tabled but does not receive an absolute majority of the votes cast. In that case, the proposed bill is still deemed adopted. In short, those who have not expressly spoken out against the government are deemed to have tacitly expressed their support. Again, such an outcome makes sense. Considering the bill as sufficiently important to engage its accountability before the National Assembly, the Prime Minister is legitimate to think that not only would the majority not want to oust the government by voting against the bill, but also that the deputies in the majority would take a clear stance by voting in favour of the bill. The last possible outcome is when a motion of censure is regularly tabled and adopted (i.e., the motion collects the votes cast of the absolute majority of deputies composing the National Assembly). In that case, and in that case only, the bill is rejected, and the government overthrown.

The novelty of the "49.3 procedure" is that the law is deemed voted and approved if no motion of no confidence is tabled in the National Assembly, or if, in cases where such a motion is tabled, it is not approved.[150] In short, the existence of the government and the fate of the bill under discussion are inextricably linked—if the bill is not adopted, the government goes. The "49.3 procedure" represents a very effective political weapon—the supreme weapon of rationalised parliamentarianism—against the National Assembly. Among the means of pressure at the disposal of the government, the "49.3 procedure" ranks just below the "blocked vote." However, because it prevents deputies from expressing their vote except in the most extreme way, the "49.3 procedure" has been regarded as going against the principle of representative democracy. Besides, by the way in which the government has arrogated to itself the legislative role for the sake of "governmental efficiency,"[151] the "49.3 procedure" has been criticised for circumventing the separation of powers principle. A more frequent use from the 1980s to discipline the parliamentary majority or to stop obstruction from the opposition has compounded such criticism of the "49.3 procedure," with the latest episode occurring when the Borne Government passed its controversial reform on the pension system in March 2023 after two motions of censure filed by opposition groups. Still, no government has ever resigned on

148 It is possible for a deputy to cast his/her vote in favour of a motion of no confidence more than three times per session in the context of the "49.3 procedure." In other words, the limitation that restricts the number of times a deputy can vote on motions of no confidence under the ordinary procedure does not apply in the context of this procedure.

149 For a good illustration of the use of the "49.3 procedure," see the saga around the 2023 Pension Reform Law and decision No 2023-857 DC of 14 December 2023 *Loi de programmation des finances publiques pour les années 2023 à 2027.*

150 The "49.3 procedure" also offers the benefit of preserving the government's initial text while avoiding any debate on amendments.

151 Raymond Barre, former Prime Minister (1976–1981), cited in Frédéric Rouvillois, *Droit constitutionnel : La Vème République* (4th edn, Flammarion 2014) 289.

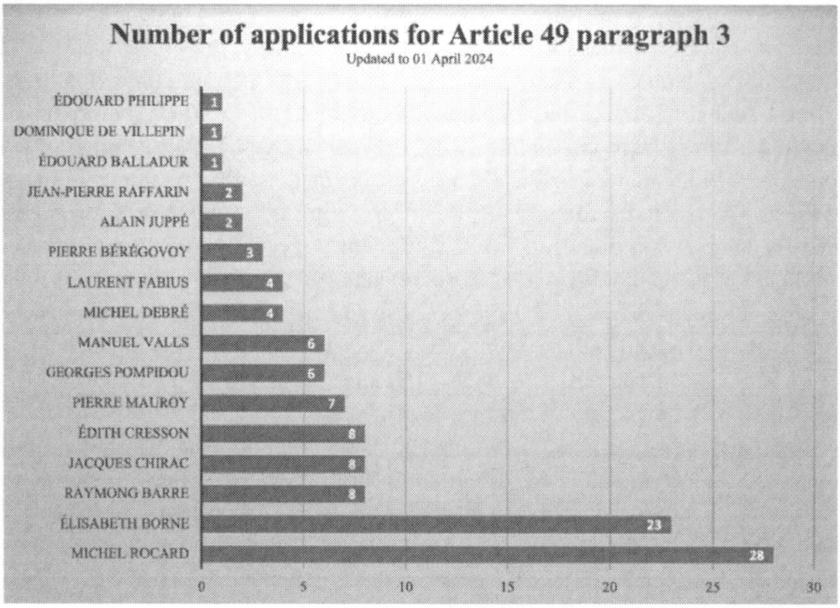

FIGURE 4.2 Article 49.3 applications

the basis of a successful vote of no confidence under the "49.3 procedure" so far.[152] (See Figure 4.2 Article 49.3 applications).

In the eventuality of a vote of no confidence, or a negative vote on the government's programme or on a declaration of general policy, the government must resign (article 50 of the Constitution). Should that happen, the outgoing government deals with current business until the installation of the new government. In any case, a ministerial crisis may prompt the President of the Republic to anticipate a possible resignation of the government by triggering the dissolution of the National Assembly. In other words, before the threat of a government's departure materialises, it often appears preferable to call on the electorate to end the rift between the government and the National Assembly by voting for a renewed majority. The dissolution then appears as a means to mitigate the drastic consequences of a government's resignation. However, the current state of affairs seems to defy such logic as there seems to be no intention from Macron to dissolve the National Assembly even though the majority is in shambles and the Borne Government (2022–2024) has encountered many difficulties.

The right to request information from the government. The right to request information from the government represents another form of parliamentary scrutiny. The effectiveness of

152 The "49.3 procedure" has been used in over 85 instances in connection with more than 50 bills. The Rocard Government (1988–1991) currently holds the highest record for using the "49.3 procedure," a total of 28 times. The Borne Government (2022–2024) has come close to this record by using the procedure 23 times within a span of 18 months.

this scrutiny greatly depends on the quality of the information that is presented to Parliament. Members of Parliament may gather information on governmental actions via several channels.

Firstly, with respect to the exercise of the monitoring and evaluation mission of Parliament, committees of inquiry can be set up within each House of Parliament (article 51-2 of the Constitution). As seen above, these committees will, under the conditions provided for by law, collect information on matters such as the administration of a public service (e.g., the state of prisons, the dysfunction of the justice system, the functioning of the intelligence services in the monitoring and surveillance of armed radical movements), the management of a national company, or the handling of a particular social issue (e.g., immigration, working hours, AIDS, energy). Each House can establish a committee of inquiry by adopting the proposal of one of its members (i.e., parliamentary resolution), thus making it possible to have such a committee in each House on the same matter. Under the separation of powers principle, no parliamentary investigation can be conducted into facts that are already the subject of ongoing legal proceedings. A committee of inquiry includes members of Parliament from all political groups, up to 30 deputies and up to 21 senators, and lasts up to six months maximum. A period of one year must separate the establishment of two commissions investigating identical facts within the same House. Committees of inquiry enjoy specific powers such as the power to summon, to organise hearings under oath, and to collect evidence, on location by the rapporteur if need be. The hearings of the committee can be made public via television broadcast. Failure to respect the investigative powers of the committee may result in criminal prosecution. Reports of the committees of inquiry are published, unless the House of Parliament concerned objects. These reports may be subject to a debate in the House without a vote. These reports often lead to recommendations and, sometimes, to the tabling of a bill thereof. The follow-up to be given to the work of these committees of inquiry is however subject to the agreement of the government.

Secondly, members of Parliament may ask questions to the government. While the practice of written questions has been widely used, that of oral questions has been less successful. *Written* questions may be addressed to any minister, including the Prime Minister, who is then requested to answer within a month. The practice of written questions is used as a means to obtain useful and diverse information from the government, on legal issues in particular. As for *oral* questions, the government addresses them on a weekly basis. These can be followed by a debate, although oral questions with a debate are seemingly waning. Questions to the government allow members of Parliament to prepare their questions in advance, albeit at short notice (i.e., two hours at the latest before the parliamentary session). The time allocated to the various members of Parliament is proportional to the political representation of the group to which they belong.[153]

Thirdly, members of the government may make *formal declarations* before the National Assembly. While these declarations may be followed by a debate, and possibly by a vote if the government so requests, the government cannot, in principle, be held accountable in that context because that would amount to making it an issue of confidence (article 50-1 of the Constitution). It cannot be excluded, however, that the government threatens to resign in the event of an unfavourable vote on a declaration. Generally speaking, members of government may access Parliament where they can be heard upon request (article 31 paragraph one of the Constitution).

153 The questions by deputies of the National Assembly are broadcast.

Parliamentary scrutiny takes on various forms, one of which involves the implementation of *parliamentary resolutions*. The 2008 constitutional amendment reinstated the practice of resolutions whereby the Houses of Parliament may give an opinion on a topical issue. However, the adoption of these resolutions is carefully regulated by law to prevent any abuses observed under the previous Republics.[154] As a result, parliamentary resolutions have no legally binding effect, and any resolutions that could potentially challenge government actions are deemed inadmissible (article 34-1 paragraph two of the Constitution). For instance, the socialist group of the National Assembly adopted a resolution on 2 December 2014, urging the French Government to officially recognise the Palestinian State.

In addition, the monitoring of EU law, including the respect of the principle of subsidiarity, refers to another type of control of governmental action (articles 88-1 to Article 88-7 of the Constitution). Informing Parliament is necessary in this context because laws enacted by the EU institutions are directly applicable into domestic law, as is the case for EU regulations for example, without having transited via or having been examined by Parliament. Only the government is in a position to provide EU-law related information to Parliament since the government is the direct interlocutor of EU institutions. Successive EU Treaties have strengthened the role of national parliaments in this context, notably the Protocol on The Role of National Parliaments in the European Union attached to the 1999 Treaty of Amsterdam. The duty to inform Parliament on EU law is now enshrined in the Constitution whereby the government forwards to the National Assembly and to the Senate, as soon as they are forwarded to the Council of the EU, any draft of EU legislative acts and other drafts of EU acts (article 88-4 paragraph one of the Constitution).[155] Although initially weak, the means of action of Parliament have been reinforced with the possibility of voting resolutions on EU legislative proposals, either within parliamentary delegations, or within the parliamentary standing committees, or even in the plenary House (article 88-4 paragraph two of the Constitution). Also, the National Assembly or the Senate have the possibility to issue an opinion regarding compliance by the EU institutions with the principle of subsidiarity when they forward a draft European legislative act to the French government (article 88-6 of the Constitution). In general terms, the principle of subsidiarity aims to favour the lower level of decision-making power as long as the higher level is not able to act more effectively. As a legal guiding principle of EU action, the principle of subsidiarity ensures that EU decisions are taken at the most relevant level and as close as possible to the citizens, as explained in the Treaty on European Union (article 5 paragraph three), which states:

> Under the principle of subsidiarity, in areas which do not fall within its exclusive competence, the [European] Union shall act only if and in so far as the objectives of the proposed action cannot be sufficiently achieved by the member states, either at central level or at

154 The inclusion of parliamentary resolutions was not initially specified in the Constitution. This omission was intended to prevent the act of questioning the government's decisions regarding a bill that would have been disapproved by Parliament and that could make the government accountable should it wish to obtain a favourable vote on the bill in question.

155 France first established a parliamentary delegation dedicated to the EU in both Houses of its Parliament in 1976. These delegations were subsequently amended in 1990. There is now a Committee on European Affairs in each House of Parliament.

regional and local level, but can rather, by reason of the scale or effects of the proposed action, be better achieved at Union level.

Evaluation of public policies. The collaboration in the evaluation of public policies is another aspect of the relationship between the government and Parliament. Evaluation of public policies is an essential tool of governance in modern democracies and is particularly developed in the UK, Ireland, and Scandinavian countries, for example.[156] The principle of evaluating public policies is not new under French constitutional law since it was already provided for under a number of parliamentary rules of procedure. The 2008 constitutional amendment enshrined such a role in the Constitution as the third element of the three-fold role of Parliament (i.e., voting the law, scrutinising government action, and evaluating public policies). The evaluation of public polices "aims to assess the effectiveness of such policies by comparing their results with their intended objectives and the implemented means."[157] The effectiveness of such a role lies in the mechanisms put in place in that regard to assist Parliament. These mechanisms are constitutional and parliamentary. Constitutional mechanisms comprise the assistance of the Court of Auditors (article 47-2 of the Constitution), and the possibility of committees of inquiry (article 51-2 of the Constitution). The *Court of Auditors* assists Parliament in its task of scrutinising government action. The Court also assists Parliament and the government in scrutinising the execution of finance laws and the implementation of Social Security financing laws. In addition, the Court of Auditors provides assistance in assessing public policies, and its public reports contribute to informing citizens on these matters. *Committees of inquiry* can be set up to gather information, as appropriate, and under the conditions provided for by law, by each House of Parliament. The composition of such committees aims to reflect political pluralism since their members are appointed according to the political representation of parliamentary political groups, with the chair or rapporteur automatically being attributed to a member of the opposition or of a minority group (see above).

The Rules of Procedure for the Houses of Parliament establish a parliamentary mechanism known as the Committee on Evaluation and Control of Public Policies of the National Assembly (*Comité d'Évaluation et de Contrôle des Politiques Publiques de l'Assemblée Nationale*).[158] This Committee serves as a dedicated monitoring body. It consists of 17 members representing the various governing formations of the National Assembly,[159] along with 15 ordinary deputies (five from the majority and ten from the opposition). The Committee primarily assesses, on its own motion as need be, public policies that span multiple areas. Additionally, the Committee is informed about any expert fact-finding missions carried out by Parliament and is invited to provide its input on the impact studies accompanying a proposed legislation. The Committee exercises its role within the limits of what is constitutionally acceptable, that is, without

156 See, for Ireland, the work of the Irish Government Economic and Evaluation Service (IGEES) in OECD, *The Irish Government Economic and Evaluation Service: Using Evidence-Informed Policy Making to Improve Performance*, OECD Public Governance Reviews (OECD Publishing 2020).

157 Decree No 98-1048 of 18 November 1998 relating to the evaluation of public policies.

158 Articles 98-1 and 146-2 to 146-7 of the Rules of Procedure of the National Assembly.

159 These representatives are the president of the National Assembly, as chair, the presidents of the parliamentary standing committees, the president of the standing committee on European affairs, the general rapporteur of the finance committee, the presidents of the political groups, and the presidents of various particular parliamentary committees.

infringing the separation of powers principle and without the power to issue injunctions to the government.[160]

Other Institutions

« *Quel mal a éprouvé la France à stabiliser ses institutions !* »[161]

The institutional framework of the Fifth Republic is comprised of various entities that complement the existing main institutions, namely the President of the Republic, the government, and Parliament. These institutions operate checks and balances on the state apparatus, commonly known "*appareil d'État.*" While some of these institutions are endowed with competence to act judicially, all of them, including several independent administrative authorities, are characterised by their independence from the main powers. This section presents the Economic, Social and Environmental Council in the first place followed by the examination of several "courts," namely the High Court and the Court of Justice of the Republic as the political courts, and the Court of Auditors. The Council of State is also presented in its advisory role. The last developments deal with the independent administrative authorities, including the Defender of Rights.

The Economic, Social and Environmental Council

The Economic, Social and Environmental Council (*Conseil économique, social et environnemental* or *CESE*) is enshrined in the Constitution under Title XI (articles 69 to 71 of the Constitution).[162] As an advisory body to the public authorities, the *CESE* represent key economic, social, and environmental sectors. Its primary aim is to foster cooperation between different socio-professional interest groups and ensure that these take part in the elaboration and evaluation of public policies. In 2021, the *CESE* underwent a substantial reform, granting it the authority to conduct public consultations, resulting in its designation as the "House of Public Consultations."[163] The CESE has indeed a very specific status in French constitutional law. As apart from Parliament but whose existence is recognised under the Constitution, the *CESE* could arguably be regarded as an atypical third House of Parliament. It is not the case, however, as *CESE*'s members are appointed and not elected, therefore not representing the entire nation. The composition, organisation, and role of the *CESE* are further elaborated below.

160 Decision No 2009-581 DC of 25 June 2009 *Résolution tendant à modifier le règlement de l'Assemblée nationale*, pt 61.

161 Édouard Balladur, Prime Minister (1993–1995) [How difficult it was for France to stabilise its institutions!].

162 The *CESE* traces its origins back to bodies that were established during the Third and Fourth Republics, namely the National Economic Council, which spanned from 1925 to 1940, and the Economic Council from 1946 to 1959. During the Fourth Republic, the *CESE* was granted a formal status as an advisory body at the disposal of both the National Assembly and the Council of Ministers for guidance and support.

163 Organic Law No 2021-27 of 15 January 2021 relating to the Economic, Social and Environmental Council. The *CESE* has undergone several reforms over the years, with the most recent being in 2008, 2010, and 2021. The 2008 constitutional amendment sought to improve the *CESE*'s representativity and accessibility.

Composition and organisation. The *CESE* consists of 175 members (233 members pre-2021 reform) appointed for a five-year term. Members cannot serve more than two consecutive terms. Membership is divided up into four categories.[164] The first category groups 52 members representing the employees appointed by trade unions. Each of the two main trade unions, namely the French Democratic Confederation of Labour (*Confédération française démocratique du travail* or *CFDT*) and General Confederation of Labour (*Confédération générale du travail* or *CGT*), appoints 14 employees. The second category consists of 52 members coming from companies, farming and agricultural activities, the craft industry, private insurance companies, unions and cooperatives, consular chambers, and other professions in the private sector. The third category represents 45 members for social and territorial cohesion and community life (with representatives of family associations, and representatives of other associations, charities, and organisations including those operating in overseas territories). The last category relates to the environment and nature conservation grouping representatives of environmental organisations (e.g., National Federation of Hunters, French League for the Protection of Birds etc.). Membership of the *CESE* requires being at least 18 years old, to have been carrying out an activity for at least two years within the relevant sector of appointment, and meeting the requirements to be an elector. In terms of organisation, the *CESE*'s working methods are close to those of Parliament. The *CESE* sits permanently with plenary sessions twice a month. Its working groups, which include sections, delegations, and temporary commissions (e.g., commission on the state of France), are tasked with preparing studies and draft opinions within their respective field. The plenary assembly of the *CESE* votes on the opinions prepared by the sections. Members of the government may attend plenary sessions of the *CESE* and take part in the debate on an opinion falling into their area.

Role. As a purely advisory body, the *CESE* delivers opinions (about 25 to 30 a year) but does not issue any legally binding act. Although not legally binding on the government, opinions issued by the *CESE* enjoy significant authority. The opinion of the *CESE* may be sought in various settings. Firstly, the government *must* consult the *CESE* for its opinion (*compétence liée*) on plans or programming bills of an economic, social, and environmental nature. The government *may* ask the *CESE*'s opinion on any government bills, drafts of ordinances, or decrees as well as on private members' bills falling within its area of competence. The government may consult the *CESE* for any programming bill laying down the multi-annual guidelines for public finances. In more general terms, the *CESE* may be consulted for its opinion by the government (or by Parliament) on any economic, social, or environmental matter. However, this last possibility is likely to be a moot point since the Council of State is the real advisor of the government including as regards economic, social, or environmental matters. Secondly, and since the 2008 constitutional amendment, citizens may also address the *CESE* by way of petition. Such petitions dealing with any question of an economic, social, or environmental nature must collect at least 150,000 signatures (500,000 signatures pre-2021 reform).[165] The *CESE* delivers its opinion within one year of receiving a valid petition. The

164 The 2021 reform got rid of the so-called qualified individuals appointed by the government.

165 Other conditions exist regarding citizens' petitions in order to screen them effectively. Petitions are limited to issues of general interest falling within the remit of the *CESE*'s areas of competence. Formally, the petition must be written in French and can be submitted either by mail or digitally. The petition must be presented in the same

Prime Minister, the president of the National Assembly, and the president of the Senate, as well as the representative of the citizens, are notified of the opinion on a petition. The opinion is also published in the Official Journal. Thirdly, the *CESE* may self-refer any matter concerning economic, social, or environmental objectives which it deems in need of reform. Fourthly, in order to widen citizens' participation in public life and in line with its role of advising public authorities, the *CESE* may, on its own initiative, or at the request of the Prime Minister, the president of the National Assembly, or the president of the Senate, have recourse to public consultation in matters falling within its competence. The *CESE* is entitled to organise such a public consultation, including the procedure of drawing lots to determine the participants of the consultation. Such a procedure must present guarantees of sincerity, equality, transparency, and impartiality. As the advisor to the government and to Parliament, the *CESE* fulfils other corollary functions, namely allowing the participation of representatives of the various professional categories in the economic, social, and environmental policy of the nation, promoting collaboration between these different professional categories and thus facilitating the reconciliation of their positions, and promoting constructive dialogue and cooperation with advisory bodies created within local governments, with its counterparts in the EU and other countries. The *CESE* also assists in informing citizens through the publication of its opinions and reports in the Official Journal.

The political courts

The High Court (*Haute Cour*) and the Court of Justice of the Republic (*Cour de Justice de la République*) constitute the so-called political courts as they are competent to judge political authorities, the President of the Republic for the former, and members of the government for the latter. The High Court and the Court of Justice of the Republic are examined in turn in this subsection.

The High Court. The High Court is enshrined in the Constitution under Title IX (articles 67 and 68 of the Constitution).[166] The role of the High Court is to pronounce the removal of the President of the Republic from office in the event of a breach of his/her duties manifestly incompatible with the exercise of his/her mandate. This is the only court that can deal with cases concerning the President during the exercise of his/her mandate, hence it is more a political body than a criminal court. The removal procedure arguably compensates the extended protection enjoyed by the President. The Court is composed of members of the National Assembly and members of the Senate and is chaired by the president of the National Assembly. The procedure for removal is as follows. A two-thirds majority of each House of Parliament is required to

---

terms by all signatories aged 16 or above (compared with 18 pre-2021 reform). Additionally, signatories must either be French citizens or hold regular residence in France. The collection of petitions must be overseen by a representative who acts as the intermediary connecting the citizens with the *CESE*.

166 See also Organic Law No 2014-1392 of 24 November 2014 implementing article 68 of the Constitution. The High Court was put in place by Constitutional Law No 2007-238 of 23 February 2007 amending Title IX of the Constitution, to replace the High Court of Justice (*Haute Cour de Justice de la République*). The former Court comprised members of Parliament and was entrusted to judge the President of the Republic for the crime of "high treason." The Senate was competent to judge the President under the Third Republic, and the National Assembly under the Fourth Republic.

convene the formation of Parliament as the High Court. The Court has then one month to rule, by a two-thirds majority of its members, on the removal of the President from office. The vote is personal and secret. Proxy voting is not permitted in that situation. The decision of the Court is of immediate effect. The procedure is similar to that of the impeachment procedure of the President of the USA in the American system. The procedure has never been used so far in France.[167]

The Court of Justice of the Republic.[168] The Court of Justice of the Republic is enshrined in the Constitution under Title X (articles 68-1 to 68-3 of the Constitution). The Court decides on the criminal liability of members of the government for offences committed while in office. Offences committed by government members that are unrelated to the conduct of the nation's policy fall within the jurisdiction of ordinary criminal courts. The Court of Justice of the Republic is made up of 15 judges, namely 12 members of Parliament (i.e., six deputies elected by the National Assembly, and six senators elected by the Senate), and three sitting judges from the Court of Cassation with one of them presiding over the Court. Proceedings before the Court are brought by any individual, whether French or foreign, who claims that his/her rights have been infringed by a government official in the performance of his/her duties. A complaints commission, consisting of professional judges from the Court of Cassation, the Council of State, and the Court of Auditors, decides on whether to refer the case to the Court of Cassation for formal referral to the Court of Justice of the Republic or to dismiss the case. The complaints commission acts as a filter mechanism to prevent the procedure from being used as a political weapon against governmental action. Should the complaint be declared admissible, an inquiry committee composed of three Court of Cassation judges hears the officials charged and those who declare themselves victims. The inquiry committee then decides whether to refer the case to the Court of Justice of the Republic. The Court rules by an absolute majority and by secret ballot on the guilt of the accused as well as, should the guilt be recognised, on the application of the sentence. Judgments of the Court may be appealed to the Court of Cassation. The Court of Justice of the Republic has dealt with several cases such as, for example, the tragic contaminated blood case, which started in the mid-1980s. The case ended up with the conviction of one government official, Edmond Hervé, former secretary of state for Health. Two other higher ranked members were acquitted, namely Georgina Dufoix, former minister for Social Affairs, and Laurent Fabius, former Prime Minister (1984–1986) and current president of the Constitutional Council. The famous quote by Dufoix (i.e., "I certainly feel responsible; however, this does not mean that I feel guilty," translated into the saying "*responsable mais pas coupable*") is symptomatic of the kind of disconnect that exists between the actions of government members and their effective accountability. While the possibility of initiating judicial proceedings has been regarded as an improvement for the victims of governmental criminal acts, the procedure has indeed been criticised in several respects. One criticism has been about the impossibility for individual parties to take part in the proceedings. Another

167 The accountability of the President of the Republic is dealt with above.
168 The Court of Justice of the Republic was established in 1993 in line with the recommendations of the Vedel Committee, established by President Mitterrand in 1992 as a response to the devastating contaminated blood scandal that occurred during the mid-1980s. See Constitutional Law No 93-952 of 27 July 1993 revising the Constitution of 4 October 1958 and amending its Titles VIII, IX, X and XVIII.

criticism has been in respect of cases concerning top administrators. These cases are dealt with before ordinary administrative courts, and it has proved difficult to bring these administrators to testify. The suppression of the Court of Justice of the Republic has been on the cards for some time as the Court represents a privilege for ministers which no longer has any raison d'être.[169] Members of the government should be tried by the ordinary criminal courts, including for acts performed in the exercise of their functions.

The Council of State

The Council of State is the highest administrative court in France, competent for settling disputes between the administration and the citizens. In addition to its judicial role,[170] the Council of State also serves as an advisory body, which was historically its primary mission. Formally installed in 1799, the Council of State reprised the responsibilities previously held by the Council of the King. This earlier Council, composed of close advisers to the monarch, was responsible for managing the administration of the Kingdom. Following the 1789 Revolution, the Council of State was tasked with upholding the principle of the separation of powers by acting as a special judicial order to judge the administration. This historical background explains the manner in which members of the Council of State are appointed and why the Council is considered as the first public body of the state. In this subsection, the composition and organisation of the Council of State are explained as well as its advisory role.

Composition and organisation. The Council of State consists of ordinary members and extraordinary members. *Ordinary* members are the auditors (*auditeurs au Conseil d'État*), senior auditors (literally, masters of requests or *maîtres des requêtes*), and councillors of state proper (*conseillers d'État*). Auditors are recruited by competitive examination, that of the National School of Administration (*École Nationale d'Administration* or *ÉNA*) with, each year, a certain number of auditors' positions (between four and six) being offered to students leaving the *ENA*. Around three-quarters of the senior auditors are recruited from among the auditors who have some seniority (i.e., between three and four years of seniority). Two-thirds of the councillors of state are recruited from among the senior auditors. For the remaining senior auditors and councillors of state, an external pathway recruitment (*tour extérieur*) is open to external candidates who have a certain seniority (i.e., the last quarter of the remaining senior auditor jobs are filled by external candidates aged 30 and above, with at least ten years of public service; and the remaining third of the councillors of state are appointed among external candidates aged 45 and above. With the exception of certain senior positions reserved solely to councillors of state (i.e., vice-president of the Council of State, presidents of sections, and presidents of sub-sections within the litigation section), auditors and senior auditors perform work that is similar to that of councillors of state. *Extraordinary* members of the Council of State include, among others, 12 councillors of state appointed by the government by decree in

169 One of the last attempts at removing the Court of Justice of the Republic was in April 2018, under the Philippe Government (2017–2020), as part of major constitutional and institutional reform wished by Macron.

170 The judicial role of the Council of State is examined under Chapter 6 on constitutional justice and rights protection.

the Council of Ministers for a four-year mandate. These extraordinary members can only take part in the advisory activities of the Council of State.

The internal organisation of the Council of State reflects the duality of its role: the Council of State sits in two formations: a judicial section (*section du contentieux*) when sitting in a judicial capacity, on the one hand,[171] and a number of administrative sections (*sections administratives*) when sitting in an advisory capacity. There are five specialised administrative sections, namely the section on the Administration, the section on Internal Affairs, the section on Public Works, the section on Finance, and the section on Social Matters. A further section on Reports and Studies is in charge of preparing the annual report, coordinating research projects, keeping up to date with developments in EU law, and monitoring issues related to the enforcement of the Council's decisions. Attached to this section is the international relations delegation, which coordinates the cooperative efforts of the Council of State, both bilateral and multilateral, with foreign jurisdictions and international associations, such as the International Association of Supreme Administrative Courts and the Association of the Councils of State and Supreme Administrative Courts of the EU. Members of the Council of State, whether sitting as administrative judges or in the administrative sections, belong statutorily to high public service but enjoy guarantees of independence.[172]

Advisory role. The Council of State is the adviser to the government responsible for giving its opinion on the legality and appropriateness of bills and certain draft decrees. The Council of State is consulted in a number of situations, either as a mandatory requirement or as a non-mandatory requirement. The Council of State *must* be consulted before the enactment of ordinances (article 38 paragraph two of the Constitution) and before the deliberation of government bills within the Council of Ministers (article 39 paragraph two of the Constitution). While not legally binding, the Council of State's opinions are generally followed by the government. The Council of State *may* also be consulted, at the request of the president of the National Assembly or the president of the Senate, on any private member's bill (article 39 paragraph five of the Constitution). The government may also request an opinion from the Council of State on any proposal and on any legal issue of interest or on any administrative matter. The procedure for forming an opinion is as follows. A rapporteur is assigned to gather the relevant legal documentation and to study the relevant issue. The officials and top civil servants from the ministerial departments concerned, also known as Government Commissioners, provide the Council of State with the necessary clarifications concerning the general scope of the text, the conditions of its elaboration, and the reasons for the choices made by the ministerial departments. The rapporteur then submits

171 The judicial section is composed of ten chambers—formerly known as subsections (*sous-sections*)—which are themselves specialised in different areas of public law. The plenary chamber of the judicial section (*Assemblée du Contentieux*) rules on difficult legal issues of principle.

172 This independence results from a few texts (i.e., articles 13, 37, and 39 of the Constitution) as well as practice.

the case to the relevant department for discussion, and the ministerial department votes on any potential amendments.

The Court of Auditors

The Court of Auditors is the supreme financial jurisdiction in charge of monitoring the appropriate use and efficient control of public funds in France. Its existence is enshrined in the Constitution (article 47-2 of the Constitution).[173] The Court's composition, features, and role are examined in turn.

Composition. The Court of Auditors is composed of members, appointed by decree of the President of the Republic. The Court also comprises auditing staff, including private sector experts, as well as civil servants who are specifically assigned to assist with the auditing and administrative management tasks. The hierarchical composition of the Court's members is as follows: the leading judge, known as the first president, who presides over the whole Court; the chief auditors (*conseillers-maîtres*); the senior auditors (*conseillers référendaires*); and the junior auditors (*auditeurs*). To ensure smooth functioning, the Court is divided into seven chambers and is equipped with a General Prosecutor's Office.[174]

Features. Competent for monitoring the state and Social Security accounts, evaluating the regularity of public policies, and informing Parliament, the government, and all citizens, a number of principles apply to the Court of Auditors, primarily the principle of independence from both the government and Parliament. This independence is based on its status as a Court, which it holds since it was founded in 1807.[175] The independence of the Court of Auditors was reinforced when the Court became self-governing and took charge of certifying the state's accounts, thus making it inappropriate for it to continue to be managed by the Department of Finance, which produces these accounts. Such independence also stems from the independence of its members who are permanent judges.[176] Independence is also a state of mind which is now firmly established within the institution owing to its long-standing practice and acquired prestige in the conduct of the audits. Respect of the principle of collegiality and of a number of procedural principles (such as the adversarial principle) are other principles that the Court abides

173 Also, article 15 of the 1789 Declaration: "Society has the right to call any public official to account for their administration."

174 In 2023, the average workforce in the Court of Auditors was 798 staff. One thousand and twelve staff is the average workforce employed by the Regional and Territorial Chambers of Accounts, of which 13 are located in metropolitan France and ten overseas.

175 Decision No 2001-448 DC of 25 July 2001 *Loi organique relative aux lois de finances*, pt 106: "Considering that under the Code of Financial Jurisdictions, the Court of Auditors is an administrative court; that, as stated above, the Constitution guarantees its independence from the legislative and executive powers; whereas, although some of its tasks, notably auditing and management, are not of a judicial nature, they may reveal irregularities calling for the implementation of court proceedings."

176 In 2006, significant enhancements were made to the statutory guarantees of members of the Court of Auditors with regards to recruitment, appointment procedures, promotions, and remuneration. These guarantees ensure a strong foundation for the functioning of the Court. Additionally, a code of practice has been established to provide further guidance and regulations for non-judicial inspection personnel, including rapporteurs, experts, and assistants.

by, all of which guarantee the quality and impartiality of the Court's role. In its proceedings, the Court of Auditors respects the principle of a fair hearing (i.e., audi alteram partem principle). Members of the Court carry out their audit based on documents and on-site investigations. The audited party has the right to give their point of view on the provisional document supplied to them by the Court. Methods for applying the fair hearing principle to the Court's proceedings have changed over the years. Successive reforms have sought to strike a balance between the obligation to hear the point of view of the individual being investigated, and the need to conduct an audit within a reasonable time frame in the interest of efficiency. Auditing is an individually focused process though, and the financial judge investigates "for the prosecution and for the defence" by simply suggesting what outcome ought to be followed and whether there may be legal consequences. However, and in order to eliminate personal preferences, ruling on auditing matters is a collegial decision. Moreover, each person's position is covered by the principle of confidentiality of judicial proceedings. Even though it is not regarded as a general procedural principle in French law, the principle of collective responsibility is therefore another important principle as regards the Court's legitimacy and credibility.

Role. The role of the Court of Auditors is multifaceted. Firstly, the Court judges the regularity of the accounts drawn up by state accountants (i.e., state civil servants or public officers accredited to manage public funds).[177] This is a very technical control essentially consisting of overseeing the regularity of income and expenditure and verifying that the specific rules imposed on public accountants are respected. The Court then releases the accountant from liability in cases where the accounts are correct or, on the contrary, declares them in default in cases where income has been lost or improper expenditure has been made. Although its activity as a court is the Court's longest-standing mission, it no longer represents a major part of its activity.[178] Secondly, in its auditing role, the Court of Auditors monitors the proper use and proper management of public funds, including as regards bodies that do not have public accountants. The Court of Auditors also assesses de facto accountants (i.e., persons who improperly handle public funds). All in all, the Court has jurisdiction over some one thousand accounts. Technically, it means that the Court reviews the conformity of public funds management with legislation and regulations, including EU legislation and regulations. The Court also checks that the relationship between public activities and the related resources used or mobilised is as good as possible, and that the use of public funds complies with the stated objectives. Each year, the Court carries out desk-based or on-site investigations. At the end of these investigations, the Court draws up a report intended to the minister concerned, which points out the failures or mismanagement observed in the administration concerned.[179] Thirdly, the Court of Auditors certifies the regularity, sincerity, and accuracy of state accounts. Far from being a solely technical matter, certification represents a vast field of competence for the Court, whose objective is to provide a more reliable, transparent, and comprehensive account of the

177 The financial records maintained by the accountants responsible for overseeing the finances of local authorities and their public establishments are overseen and audited by the Regional and Territorial Chambers of Accounts (*Chambres Régionales et Territoriales des Comptes*). The Court of Auditors is, in this case, judge of appeal.

178 The Court's procedures were thoroughly modernised in 2005, 2006, and 2008. However, the Court still does not have authority to assess the authorising officer, that is, the person who gives the instruction to pay or receive payment from the accountant.

179 This activity is also reflected in the publication of the annual report of the Court of Auditors.

financial reality of the state, as well as of the Social Security general regime.[180] Fourthly, the Court of Auditors assists the government and Parliament in the evaluation of public policies, either by praising the positive aspects of a particular policy or by drawing attention to its negative impact. When these policies are conducted nationally and locally, the Court conducts joint enquiries with the Regional and Territorial Chambers of Accounts (*Chambres Régionales et Territoriales des Comptes*). Since 2011, and in order to strengthen the means of Parliament in terms of monitoring government action and evaluating public policies, the president of the National Assembly and the president of the Senate may request the Court of Auditors to provide for evaluation reports that must be handed in within one year of their request.[181]

Independent Administrative Authorities and the Defender of Rights

Several independent administrative authorities assist the state across various sectors and scopes of operation, including the relatively recently established Defender of Rights.

Independent Administrative Authorities. Independent *administrative* authorities (*Autorités Administratives Indépendantes* or *AAI*) are institutions of the state responsible for ensuring the regulation of sectors that are considered essential and in which the state wishes to avoid intervening too directly. There are also independent *public* authorities (*Autorités Publiques Indépendantes* or *API*) which have legal personality. The list of independent administrative authorities and independent public authorities is determined by law.[182] The 17 independent administrative authorities cover a wide range of sectors such as competition (i.e., Competition Authority, *Autorité de la concurrence*), data protection (i.e., National Data Protection Commission, *Commission nationale de l'informatique et des libertés*, also known as *CNIL*), defence and security (i.e., National Defence Secret Commission, *Commission du secret de la défense nationale*, and National Commission for the Control of Intelligence Techniques, *Commission nationale de contrôle des techniques de renseignement*), energy (i.e., Energy Regulation Commission, *Commission de régulation de l'énergie*), nuclear energy (i.e., Nuclear Safety Authority, *Autorité de sûreté nucléaire*), education (i.e., High Council for the Evaluation of Research and Higher Education, *Haut Conseil de l'évaluation de la recherche et de l'enseignement supérieur*), and gaming (i.e., National Gaming Authority, *Autorité nationale des jeux*). Other independent administrative authorities are mentioned in this book such as the National Commission of Campaign Accounts and Political Financing (*Commission nationale des comptes de campagne et des financements politiques*), the National Commission for Public

180 Organic Law No 2001-692 of 1 August 2001 relating to finance laws. Since 2013, the Court of Auditors certifies the accounts of both Houses of Parliament by transmitting to their respective president an annual report on the regularity of the accounts thereof.

181 Law No 2011-140 of 3 February 2011 to strengthen the means of Parliament in terms of monitoring government action and evaluating public policies.

182 Law No 2017-55 of 20 January 2017 on the general status of Independent Administrative Authorities and Independent Public Authorities.

Debate (*Commission nationale du débat public*), and the High Authority for Transparency in Public Life (*Haute Autorité pour la transparence de la vie publique*).[183]

Independent administrative and public authorities are collegial bodies, with a few exceptions such as the Defender of Rights (see below). The members of these bodies are typically experienced civil servants who have a thorough understanding of the administration they are responsible for regulating. This expertise is crucial for ensuring the efficiency of their regulatory tasks. The appointment of members is for a specific term, typically ranging from three to six years, and can be renewed once, while also being irrevocable (except in the event of a serious breach of their legal obligations or permanent incapacity).[184] The chairperson of each authority oversees its services, sets the agenda for meetings, and may be entrusted with specific powers.

Independent administrative and public authorities are placed outside the traditional administrative structures and are not bound by hierarchical authority. Public authorities cannot address them orders, instructions, or even simple advice. Their members are not revocable. Independent administrative authorities have three features. Firstly, as *authorities*, they have a number of powers including the power to issue recommendations, make decisions, enact regulations, and impose sanctions. Secondly, due to their *administrative* nature, they act on behalf of the state, thereby assuming certain responsibilities delegated to them by the administration (e.g., regulatory power). Thirdly, they are *independent* not only from the sectors they oversee but also from public authorities, albeit with a certain reliance on their allocated budget, which is linked to the overall budget of the relevant ministry.[185]

The rationale behind the installation of independent authorities is to reconcile two imperatives: to ensure the regulation, that is to say the harmonious functioning, of a specific sector while, at the same time, providing a way for the government not to intervene too directly because of the sensitivity of the sector in question. An area is regarded as sensitive because of potential political implications (e.g., audio-visual and freedom of the press) or economic impact (e.g., telecommunications and competition between operators). A too direct intervention of the government in such areas would constitute a potential threat to civil and economic liberties. Hence the installation of intermediary institutions to help overcome this apparent contradiction. Independent administrative and public authorities thus meet three needs. Firstly, they ensure rapid state intervention, often adapting to changing needs and markets. Secondly, they offer a greater guarantee of the impartiality of state intervention. Thirdly, they allow for greater

183 The seven independent public authorities are the French Anti-Doping Agency (*Agence française de lutte contre le dopage*), the Financial Markets Authority (*Autorité des Marchés Financiers* or *AMF*), the Transport Regulatory Authority (*Autorité de régulation des transports*), the High Authority of Health (*Haute Autorité de santé*), the High Council of the Statutory Auditors (*Haut Conseil du commissariat aux comptes*), and the National Energy Ombudsman (*Médiateur national de l'énergie*). In the communication sector, the former Audio-visual Superior Council (*Conseil supérieur de l'audiovisuel*, also known as *CSA*) merged with the High Authority for the Dissemination of Works and the Protection of Rights on the Internet (*Haute Autorité pour la diffusion des œuvres et la protection des droits sur internet*, also known as *HADOPI*) to become the Audio-visual and Digital Communication Regulatory Authority (*Autorité de régulation de la communication audiovisuelle et numérique*, also known as *Arcom*).

184 Membership of independent administrative and public authorities is not compatible with holding certain other positions and offices, as determined by law. Besides, the accumulation of mandates within different several independent authorities is strictly prohibited, unless explicitly permitted by the law.

185 The situation is different for those independent public authorities which, such as the Financial Markets Authority, have been recognised as a legal entity and therefore enjoy financial autonomy.

participation of individuals of diverse origins and skills, in particular professionals from the regulated sectors concerned. Concretely, the regulatory role of the independent authorities involves actions to organise the sector in question by subjecting the various companies and other stakeholders to rules and obligations, but also considering their demands and needs as appropriate. This is one of the particularities of these authorities which, more than the ordinary administration, establish relationships of trust with the stakeholders in the sectors that they are responsible for regulating.

The Defender of Rights. The institution of the Defender of Rights is enshrined in the Constitution under Title XI bis (article 71-1 of the Constitution).[186] The Defender of Rights is an independent administrative single authority. Referring both to the institution and to the person who directs it, the Defender of Rights aims at providing a non-judicial remedy to citizens for the protection of their rights and freedoms against the action of the state, of local authorities, and of any public body or other body entrusted with a public service mission. The institution was modelled on equivalent authorities in other European jurisdictions such as the Ombudsman in Sweden and Finland, the *Defensor del Pueblo* in Spain, or the *Provedor de Justiça* in Portugal. The areas of competence of the French Mediator (*Médiateur de la République*), the Children's Ombudsman (*Défenseur des Enfants*), the Equality and Anti-Discrimination Authority (*Haute Autorité de Lutte contre les Discriminations et Pour l'Égalité*), and the National Commission on Security Ethics (*Commission Nationale de Déontologie de la Sécurité*) were merged within the area of competence of the Defender of Rights in order to facilitate and simplify access to these areas by citizens.[187] The Defender of Rights is assisted by Deputy Defenders of Rights, who are responsible, under the supervision of the main Defender of Rights, for their respective areas of competence, namely children's rights, anti-discrimination and equality, and security ethics. The Defender of Rights' team is made up of civil servants who have a good knowledge of the public authorities that the citizens are in conflict with, thus contributing to facilitating the resolution of issues. The Defender of Rights is appointed by the President of the Republic for a non-renewable and irrevocable six-year term.[188] S/he shall report to the President and Parliament.

The role of the Defender of Rights is to oversee the protection of citizens' rights and freedoms, to promote equality, and to ensure that rights are accessible to all. Anyone, whether a natural person or a legal entity, has the right to bring a case to the attention of the Defender of Rights free of charge. The Defender of Rights can also initiate a case on their own initiative. In carrying out their responsibilities, the Defender of Rights possesses investigative powers

186 The Defender of Rights was established by the 2008 constitutional amendment, as completed by Organic Law No 2011-333 of 29 March 2011 and Law No 2011-334 of 29 March 2011 relating to the Defender of Rights. In the developments below, the different paragraphs of article 71-1 of the Constitution are not expressly pinpointed.

187 Other authorities, such as the Office of the Controller-General for Places of Deprivation of Liberty (*Contrôleur Général des Lieux de Privation de Liberté*), the Commission on Access to Administrative Documents (*Commission d'Accès aux Documents Administratifs* or *CADA*), and the National Agency for Information Technology and Civil Liberties regulating data protection (*Commission Nationale de l'Informatique et des Libertés* or *CNIL)*, were not merged within the competence of the Defender of Rights because of their particularity. Such an overall concentration of authorities would have been regarded as an arguably harmful rationalisation in terms of rights protection.

188 Claire Hédon (2020–2026) is the current Defender of Rights, preceded by Jacques Toubon (2014–2020) and Dominique Baudis (2011–his death in 2014).

and the ability to intervene in settling disputes. Firstly, as part of their investigative power, they have the right to request any information deemed useful to investigate the case, provided no criminal prosecution is underway for the same matter. They also have the authority to conduct interviews, on-site verifications, and examinations as necessary. For matters concerning administrative law, the Defender of Rights is allowed to seek interpretation guidance from the Council of State. Secondly, in resolving disputes, the Defender of Rights can make recommendations that might include potential legislative or regulatory changes, or they can facilitate mediation. The Defender of Rights can also impose a binding solution in cases of misconduct or of proven wrongdoing. This can involve supporting a civil or criminal transaction, requesting disciplinary action against a public official, providing observations in court on behalf of a claimant, or recommending administrative sanctions against individuals or entities responsible for discrimination. Importantly, the Defender of Rights operates independently from the government and the administration. Their autonomy and independence, which are guaranteed by law, ensure that they do not take instructions from any authority, party to a case, or other individuals or pressure groups. Their duties cannot be prematurely terminated, except in the event of an unexpected obstacle ascertained by the highest courts. Additionally, the Defender of Rights cannot be subject to legal proceedings, arrested, or brought before a court based on their opinions or actions while fulfilling their duties.[189] Lastly, to further uphold their independence, the Defender of Rights cannot hold any electoral mandate, occupy any other public office, or engage in any other professional activity while in office.

SELECTED FURTHER READINGS

Jean-Luc **Albert** & Thierry Lambert, *La Cour des comptes : Un pouvoir rédempteur ?* (LGDJ 2017)
Michel **Ameller**, *L'Assemblée nationale* (2nd edn, PUF 2000)
Philippe **Ardant**, *Le Premier ministre en France* (Montchrestien 1997)
Pierre **Avril**, Jean Gicquel & Jean-Éric Gicquel, *Droit parlementaire* (6th edn, Montchrestien 2021)
__________, *Un Président pour quoi faire ?* (Seuil 1965)
Philippe **Blachèr**, *Le Parlement en France* (LGDJ 2012)
Bernard **Branchet**, *La fonction présidentielle sous la Vème République* (Dalloz 2008)
Sophie **de Cacqueray**, Sophie Hutier & Sophie Lamouroux, *Le Parlement depuis 2008 : Renforcement, statu quo ou retour aux fondements de la Vème République* (LGDJ 2020)
Jean-Pierre **Camby** & Pierre Servent, *Le travail parlementaire sous la Ve République* (6th edn, Montchrestien 2021)
________________, *La Loi* (LGDJ 2015)
Matthieu **Caron**, *Droit gouvernemental* (LGDJ 2020)
Florence **Chaltiel Terral**, *Le Conseil d'État, acteur et censeur de l'action publique* (LGDJ 2017)
Marie-Anne **Cohendet**, *Le président de la République* (2nd edn, Dalloz 2012)
Damien **Connil**, *Les groupes parlementaires en France* (LGDJ 2016)
Delphine **Dulong**, *Premier ministre* (CNRS Éditions 2021)
Marc **Frangi**, *Le président de la République : Arbitrer, diriger, négocier* (L'Harmattan 2018)
Michel **Gentot**, *Les autorités administratives indépendantes* (2nd edn, LGDJ 1994)
Richard **Ghevontian**, Xavier Magnon & Marthe Stéfanini (eds), *Pouvoir exécutif et Parlement : De nouveaux équilibres ?* (PUAM 2012)
Aline **Gonzales** & Dominique Grandguillot, *L'essentiel des institutions politiques et administratives en France* (18th edn, Gualino 2023)
Dominique **Grandguillot**, *Le Défenseur des droits* (Gualino 2011)
Jean **Guarrigues** et al. (eds), *Histoire du Parlement de 1789 à nos jours* (Armand Colin 2007)

189 The legal immunity of the Defender of Rights is similar to that enjoyed by members of Parliament.

Pascal **Jan**, *Institutions administratives* (6th edn, LexisNexis 2021)
________, *Le gouvernement* (3rd edn, La Documentation française 2015)
________, *Le président de la République au centre du pouvoir* (La Documentation française 2011)
Jean-François **Kerléo** (ed.), *Le règlement de l'Assemblée nationale commenté* (LGDJ 2022)
Bruno **Latour**, *La fabrique du droit : Une ethnographie du Conseil d'État* (La Découverte 2004)
Jean **Massot**, *Chef de l'État et chef de gouvernement. Dyarchie et hiérarchie* (La Documentation française 1993)
Bertrand **Mathieu**, *La Loi* (Dalloz 2010)
Jean-Luc **Mathieu**, *L'institution du Défenseur des droits* (L'Harmattan 2020)
Marcel **Morabito**, *Le chef de l'État en France* (2nd edn, LGDJ 1996)
Benjamin **Morel**, *Le Sénat et sa légitimité* (Dalloz 2018)
Julien **Mouchette**, *La magistrature d'influence des autorités administratives indépendantes* (LGDJ 2019)
François **Pillet**, *Le Sénat, gardien des libertés* (Mare & Martin 2017)
Pouvoirs, *Le régime semi-présidentiel : Enjeux et controverses*, No 184 (Seuil 2023)
_______, *L'Élysée*, No 180 (Seuil 2022)
_______, *De Gaulle*, No 174 (Seuil 2020)
_______, *Le Sénat, Pour quoi faire ?* No 159 (Seuil 2016)
_______, *Le renouveau du Parlement*, No 146 (Seuil 2013)
_______, *La candidature à la présidentielle*, No 138 (Seuil 2011)
_______, *Le contrôle parlementaire*, No 134 (Seuil 2010)
_______, *Le Conseil d'État*, No 123 (Seuil 2007)
_______, *La Loi*, No 114 (Seuil 2005)
_______, *L'Opposition*, No 108 (Seuil 2004)
_______, *La responsabilité des gouvernants*, No 92 (Seuil 2000)
_______, *La cohabitation*, No 91 (Seuil 1999)
_______, *Le Premier ministre*, No 83 (Seuil 1997)
_______, *Qui gouverne la France ?* No 68 (Seuil 1994)
_______, *Le Président*, No 41 (PUF 1987)
_______, *Le Ministre*, No 36 (PUF 1986)
_______, *Les pouvoirs de crise*, No 10 (PUF 1979)
Nicolas **Roussellier**, *La force de gouverner : Le pouvoir exécutif en France, XIXe XXIe siècles* (Gallimard 2015)
Olivier **Rozenberg** & Éric Thiers (eds), *Traité d'études parlementaires* (Bruylant 2018)
Jean **de Saint Sernin**, *Système majoritaire et bicamérisme sous la Vème République* (Dalloz 2019)
Pierre **Servent**, *Les présidents et la guerre 1958–2017* (Perrin 2017)
Maxime **Tandonnet**, *Histoire des Présidents de la République* (Perrin 2013)
Pauline **Türk**, *Les institutions de la Ve République* (16th edn, Gualino 202__________,
Le cumul et la durée des mandats: Débats, réformes et pratiques (Mare & Marin 2020)
__________, *Le contrôle parlementaire en France* (LGDJ 2011)
Jean-Claude **Zarka**, *Le Président de la Ve République* (2nd edn, Ellipses 2007)

5

POLITICAL PARTIES, ELECTIONS, AND REFERENDUMS

Classic constitutional law is concerned with elected representatives, comprising members of Parliament and local representatives. Their status and election process are governed by various principles. A subset of this area, known as political law, or law of politics (*droit politique*),[1] has emerged from a growing acknowledgment of political parties and the regulation of their funding, as well as from the increasing regulation of electoral campaigns. This chapter will introduce readers to key principles about political parties, elections, and referendums within the framework of French constitutional law.

Political Parties

> « *Pour ma part, je dirais simplement : oui aux partis politiques, mais non à l'esprit de parti.* »[2]

The raison d'être of political parties is to *acquire* and wield political power through electoral tactics, in contrast to interest groups and lobbyists whose main goal is to *sway* public power and promote specific policies using various direct and indirect means.[3] While it is difficult to pinpoint a legal definition of what a political party is, this section delves into the concept in

1 Some authors deal with *droit politique* separately, such as Portelli and Ehrhard. See Hugues Portelli & Thomas Ehrhard, *Droit constitutionnel* (14th edn, Dalloz 2021) 415–458 (Chapter 16 "Le droit de la vie politique").

2 Raymond Barre (1924–2007), French Prime Minister (1976–1981) [For my part, I would simply say that I fully support political parties, but I strongly oppose partisanship].

3 On political parties, lobbies, and interest groups, see Marie-Luce Paris, *Constitutional Law in France*, International Encyclopaedia of Laws (Wolters Kluwer 2024) 85–93 (paras 131–140). The developments below partly draw from this book.

DOI: 10.4324/9781003268871-7

relation to its evolution over time. The other parts of this section outline the rules and principles concerning the status and funding of political parties.

Definition and historical development

This subsection addresses the definition of political parties, tracing their evolution through history and offering insights into the present-day political landscape of France.

Definition of political parties. Political parties may be described as organised groups of citizens which rally around a common ideology, defend the interests of these citizens as well as provide the necessary financial and logistical means to the candidates representing these groups at the various elections. Political parties are different from parliamentary groups and other political factions. A parliamentary group is a group of political parties, and a political faction is a subgroup within a political party. Political parties have two main functions: the first function is to serve as a go-between the people and state power; the second function is to direct the policy of the nation by implementing their political project once they are in power. As a member of a political party, or of a parliamentary group, the individual politician supports the general interest of the electorate and must refrain from favouring partisan politics and electoral strategies at the risk of encouraging a so-called "partisan regime" (*régime des partis*) with the appropriation of political power by the party system. A majority party is a political party that has sufficient electoral strength to be able to regularly win control of a government and, when defeated, to constitute the main opposition to the party in power. A minority party is a political party whose electoral strength is so small as to prevent its gaining control of a government except in rare and exceptional circumstances and, as such, plays a smaller role in a country's politics and elections. The ruling party, or governing party, in a democratic parliamentary or presidential system is the political party or coalition of political parties or groups holding a majority of elected positions in Parliament in the case of parliamentary systems, or holding the executive branch in presidential systems. A political party that opposes, primarily for ideological reasons, the proposals of a government in place is called an opposition party.

There is no definition of political parties under French law, whether under constitutional or legislative provisions. However, the National Commission for Campaign Accounts and Political Financing (see below), supported by the Constitutional Council and the Council of State that have identified "through their concordant case law" several criteria in this regard, has considered that a political party is "a legal person under private law which has assigned as its mission a political goal."[4]

Historical development of political parties. In their modern form, political parties originated in Europe and in the USA in the nineteenth century along with development of the electoral

4 Commission Nationale des Comptes de Campagne et des Financements Politiques, Opinion relating to the general publication of the accounts of political parties and groups for the 2011 financial year [*Avis relatif à la publication générale des comptes des partis et groupements politiques au titre de l'exercice 2011*], 29 November 2012, accessible at <https://www.legifrance.gouv.fr/jorf/id/JORFTEXT000026836142>.

and parliamentary systems.[5] The development of political parties is largely the corollary of the democratisation of the right of suffrage. Political parties are of different types, and scholars have proposed typologies. Duverger, for example, proposed the distinction between "cadre political parties" (*partis de cadre*) and "mass political parties" (*partis de masse*).[6] The first type of political parties refers to elite-based parties which emerged thanks to the influence of their representatives at local or national level. *Partis de cadre* were regarded as the direct successors of nineteenth-century parties composed of bourgeois or *notables*. These parties were traditionally not very structured nor centralised since they were of a relatively modest size, depending on a leader in Parliament and on generous funding from their sponsors to pursue concrete political actions. Political parties of the second type refer to mass-based parties which emerged at the start of the twentieth century with the socialist and Marxist ideologies such as the Radical Socialist Party, the *SFIO* (*Section Française de l'Internationale Ouvrière*) Party, and the Communist Party established in 1901, 1905, and 1920, respectively.[7] Their development was very much linked to the development of universal suffrage when popular masses could exercise their right to vote. However, since these voters could not provide as much funding as the well-established benefactors of elite-based parties, the objective was to gain as many adherents as possible. Mass political parties favoured dissemination of people's ideas and values. As the end objective was to transform society towards more equality for the popular masses, these parties required a rigorously structured and hierarchical organisation in order to channel ideas and win elections, often implying that voters should be instructed on how to vote. The classical Duverger distinction gradually lost its relevance. After the Second World War, the French political landscape witnessed the gradual emergence of a new generation of political parties whose main aim was to bring together adherents around common shared values rather than strict ideological party lines. The Union for the New Republic (*Union pour la Nouvelle République* or *UNR*), established in 1958 and aimed at supporting De Gaulle, is one example of this new generation of parties.

Current political parties in France. Generally speaking, political parties are more or less numerous, whether reflecting a multiparty system, a two-party system, or even a two-and-a-half party system. These types of political systems present the advantage of protecting political and individual freedoms by guaranteeing the freedom to choose among different political ideologies, although sometimes the alliances formed between parties in power may not align with the wishes of the electorate. The constitution guarantees the role of political parties in certain jurisdictions, ensuring their importance in the political landscape.[8] An instance of the multi-party system can be found in the current French political landscape, which shows, in addition to the majority party of the President of the Republic, a diverse range of other political parties at the centre as well as at the extremes of the political spectrum. The US system epitomises the two-party system where the Democrats and the Republicans dominate

5 Political parties initially originated from the 1789 Revolution via the clubs (e.g., *club des Jacobins* 1789, *club des Cordeliers* 1790, *club des Girondins* 1791) with already the first signs of the right–left divide. This was continued with the practice of private club meetings organised by members of Parliament under the *Restauration* (1814–1830).

6 Maurice Duverger, *Les partis politiques* (Collection Points 1981, Armand Colin 1951). See also Jean Charlot, *Les Partis politiques* (Armand Colin 1971).

7 The *SFIO* Party changed its name to the Socialist Party in 1969.

8 See, for example, article 4 of the French Constitution and article 49 of the 1947 Italian Constitution.

political life, making it difficult for other formations to stand, let alone win a national election. The political system in Ireland presents the interesting example of a system which has been historically characterised as a two-and-a-half party system. This means that two major catch-all parties, *Fine Gael* on the centre-right and *Fianna Fáil* in the centre, have long dominated the political scene. The Labour Party stands as the "half-party," playing a smaller role in comparison with, however, *Sinn Féin* claiming a place of choice in recent times when it became the largest party in the *Dáil* after the 2020 general election.

Unlike the multi-party and two-party systems found in liberal democracies, the one-party system is predominantly seen in authoritarian states. This setup grants full power to a single political party, while simultaneously outlawing any potential competition from other parties, whether through legal means or in practice. The single-party system represents a rejection of democracy (e.g., Italian fascism or Nazi regime), and in the context of developing countries, it can also be regarded as a hindrance to development. In such a system, the single party generally embodies the state as well as the social organisation. It is characterised by a strict hierarchical organisation with the clear goal of directing the lives of the people and limiting political and individual freedoms. For example, the Communist Party of China, as the founding party of the People's Republic of China, is the sole party legally allowed to exist and to rule in the PRC, as is the Communist Party of Cuba for Cuba. In the Democratic People's Republic of Korea (North Korea), a ban on competing political parties ensures that the Workers' Party of Korea is the sole ruling party in this jurisdiction.

Political parties exhibit varying degrees of organisation, often structured through committees, sections, or other entities, which are influenced by the prevailing socio-economic conditions and the electoral system in place. The ideological or political objectives they adhere to also play a significant role in shaping their structure. Additionally, political parties serve as reflections of social, ethnic, or religious sensitivities. For example, the Trotskyist-Socialist party of People Before Profit in Ireland, the Christian democratic parties found in Belgium, Germany, Italy, and other European countries, or, in a different vein, the Turkish secular party (Republican People's Party) alongside various Islamic-conservative factions, including Erdoğan's Justice and Development Party, illustrate the diverse nature of political parties across the globe.

French political parties have traditionally been organised around a right–left divide. The same political majority (of the right) was in power for a long period of time—23 years without interruption between 1958 and 1981—under the presidencies of De Gaulle, Pompidou, and Giscard d'Estaing. This changed with the election of Mitterrand of the Socialist Party in 1981, which opened the way to a political *alternance*. The last four decades have been marked by the multiplication of political formations and parties, not all in power or represented in Parliament but voicing various specific and, often local, concerns of the French people. At the time of writing, the French political landscape is made up of many (i.e., more than 500) political parties, some with high visibility, others almost unknown. Not long ago, the political landscape was divided between two main political parties, namely The Republicans (*Les Républicains* or *LR*) and the Socialist Party (*Parti Socialiste*). This quasi-two-party system was itself relatively recent under the Fifth Republic since other political formations used to gravitate around the two main political forces: *LR*, successors of the Gaullists, were also associated with the centre-right party of the Union for the French Democracy (*Union pour la Démocratie Française* or *UDF*), absorbed by *LR*; the Communists (*Parti Communiste Français* or *PCF*) were associated, at some stage, in government with the Socialist Party before being progressively weakened in the early 1980s. The election of Macron in 2017,[9] with the support of his movement *En Marche !*, transformed this landscape with the result of placing the majority party, currently *Renaissance*, further at the centre of the political spectrum in a purportedly cross-party position.[10] The Republicans endured severe setbacks after the 2017 and 2022 presidential elections, as did the Socialist Party.[11]

Today, the most well-known political parties are those whose candidates are elected in almost all types of elections. Political parties are generally categorised according to the ideology that they purport to adhere to. At the far-left end of the political spectrum are *La France Insoumise* (*LFI*) and the Communist Party (*Parti Communiste* or *PC*). The left-wing parties are the Socialist Party (*Parti Socialiste*), *Europe Écologie Les Verts* (*EELV*), as well as the *Parti Radical de Gauche* (*PRG*) and *Divers Gauche* (*DVG*). At the time of writing, the party of the presidential majority, *Renaissance*, with 71 deputies out of 577 in the National Assembly,[12] is arguably considered centre left, as is the Democratic Party (*Mouvement Démocrate* or *MoDem*). On the centre-right of the political spectrum, the best-known parties are The Republicans, the Union of Democrats and Independents (*Union des Démocrates et Indépendants* or *UDI*), and *Divers Droite* (*DVD*). Finally, the far-right parties are the National Rally (*Rassemblement National* or *RN*, former National Front), *Debout La France* (*DLF*), and the nationalist party *Reconquête*. The *Rassemblement National* currently stands as the first opposition party in France with 88 seats in the National Assembly.[13] The New People's Ecological and Social Union (*Nouvelle Union Populaire Écologique et Sociale* or *NUPES*) has more seats in the National Assembly with 150 deputies in total but is a *coalition* of political parties, as opposed to a party proper, grouping *La France Insoumise* (75 deputies), the Ecologist Pole including *Europe Écologie Les Verts* (23 deputies), the Communist Party (31 deputies), and the Socialist Party (31 deputies).[14] The *NUPES* came into being because of the absence of a left-wing candidate in the second round of the last two presidential elections in 2017 and 2022, which opposed Macron and Le Pen on both occasions. The objective of the left-wing coalition was to present joint candidacies for the 2022 legislative elections, which followed the re-election of Macron to a second presidential term.[15] *Reconquête* is a newcomer party which caused a surprise in the first round of the 2022 presidential elections, scoring more than the votes of The Republicans and the Socialist Party combined, at 7% (see Figure 5.1 Composition of the 2022 National Assembly).

9 Macron was the minister for the Economy, Industry and Digital Affairs (2014–2016) under the socialist Hollande (2012–2017).

10 The movement formalised into a real political party under the name of *La République En Marche !* (*LREM*) in the 2017 legislative elections and changed to *Renaissance* in 2022 for the legislative elections that year.

11 The Republican candidate obtained less than 5% of the votes (i.e., 4.78%) in the first round of the 2022 presidential election, and the Socialist Party candidate less than 2% (i.e., 1.75%).

12 For numbers of deputies per political group during the XVIth legislature, see the National Assembly website accessible at <https://www2.assemblee-nationale.fr/instances/liste/groupes_politiques/effectif>.

13 The *Rassemblement National* obtained 23.15% of the votes in the first round of the 2022 presidential election, and 41.45% of the votes in the second round.

14 The rest of the deputies in the political groups of the National Assembly are as follows: 51 deputies for the Democrats (*MoDem* and Independents), 29 deputies for *Horizons* and affiliated members, and 21 deputies for *Libertés, Indépendants, Outre-mer et Territoires* (*LIOT*), and four non-affiliated independent deputies.

15 The same happened concerning the presidential party, *LREM*, then renamed *Renaissance*. Predicting bad results in the 2022 legislative elections, they decided to form a coalition with *MoDem* and *Horizons* under the name *Ensemble !*.

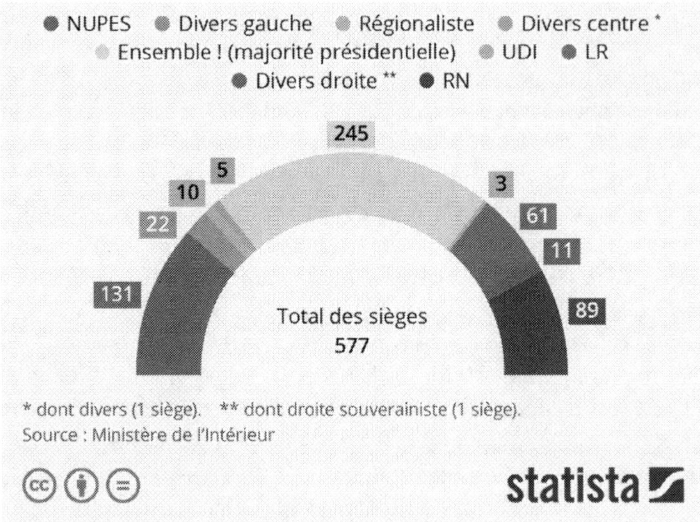

FIGURE 5.1 Composition of the 2022 National Assembly

Source: https://fr.statista.com/infographie/21758/repartition-des-deputes-sieges-par-groupe-politique-assemblee-nationale/. Licence Creative Commons CC BY-ND 3.0

TABLE 5.1 Outcome of the 2022 legislative elections

Ensemble! (centre-left electoral alliance, including the President's party)	*245*
NUPES (*Nouvelle Union populaire écologique et sociale*, left-wing electoral alliance)	131
RN (*Rassemblement National*, nationalist, right-wing populist party)	89
LR (*Les Républicains*, right-wing moderate party)	61
Divers Gauche (left-wing candidates)	22
Divers Droite (right-wing candidates)	11
Régionaliste (regionalist parties)	10
Divers Centre (centrist candidates)	5
UDI (*Union des Démocrates et Indépendants*, centre to centre-right political party)	3

Smaller political parties, though they may be minor in size, play a significant role in the political landscape. They are valuable as they often align with larger parties and help fund certain candidates' campaigns. This support is made possible through member donations and contributions to their preferred candidate. In some instances, their main goal is solely to aid in financing French politics, which validates their existence.

There are a total of 577 seats in the National Assembly. The outcome of the 2022 legislative elections is as follows:

Status of political parties

As an essential instrument of political participation allowing the expression of the will of the people, the legal status of political parties is obviously significant. However, it was not until after the Second World War that European constitutions started to acknowledge them in various provisions. For instance, the 1949 German Basic Law, the 1947 Italian Constitution, the 1976 Portuguese Constitution, and the 1978 Spanish Constitution all included provisions related to political parties. In France, the 1901 Law on Associations marked a significant step by allowing political parties to be established freely. This was followed by the recognition of parliamentary groups in the 1946 Constitution. It was only with the current Constitution that the existence and role of political parties were explicitly acknowledged for the first time. Over time, the constitutional and legislative status of political parties has been strengthened, highlighting their importance in the political landscape.

Constitutional status. The Constitution determines the role and obligations of political parties. Its article 4 states that "political parties and political groups contribute to the expression of suffrage." Political parties can be established and exercise their activity freely provided they respect the principles of national sovereignty and democracy. In its original drafting, article 4 of the Constitution emphasised as much the freedom of establishment of political parties derived from the freedom of association recognised under French law as the limitations to such freedom should one party infringe basic constitutional principles. No political party has ever been prohibited on this ground under the Fifth Republic, though. Subsequent constitutional amendments furthered the role of political parties in the political life of the nation with respect to the principle of gender equality between men and women and the principle of pluralism.

Concerning the principle of gender equality, political parties should seek to contribute to promote the principle in public life within the conditions determined by law. As for the principle of pluralism, it receives its expression through the equitable participation of political parties in the democratic life of the nation.[16] Also, the 2008 constitutional amendment recognised the existence of political parliamentary *groups*. Political groups are regarded as expressing the different political ideas of parties and formations within the National Assembly and allow the deputies to form groups according to their affinities. Rules relating to the establishment and organisation of these parliamentary groups are different from those applicable to political parties. To form a parliamentary group, the opposition only needs to make a formal declaration. This declaration is to be handed, by its president, to the president of the National Assembly. By contrast, a minority parliamentary group is simply declared into existence by a group that has not made such a declaration. Such an enhancement of the role of political parties, and political groups, has implied a number of changes in the electoral system and parliamentary law, such as the specific protection of the rights of the opposition and of minority political groups by the rules of the Houses of Parliament (article 51-1 of the Constitution). The case law of the Constitutional Council has been instrumental in interpretating article 4 of the Constitution. For example, in its 1990 decision on the law limiting electoral expenses, the Council noted that, while the state may grant financial aid to political parties or groups which contribute to the expression of the vote, the said aid "must, in order to comply with the principles of equality and freedom, comply with objective criteria; (…) moreover, the aid mechanism adopted must not result either in establishing a link of dependence of a political party vis-à-vis the state, or in compromising the democratic expression of the various currents of ideas and opinions."

16 See, respectively, Constitutional Law No 99-569 of 8 July 1999 on equality between women and men, and Constitutional Law No 2008-724 of 23 July 2008 on the modernisation of the institutions of the Fifth Republic.

Indeed, according to the Council, "the requirement of pluralism of ideas and opinions (…) constitutes the foundation of democracy."[17]

Legislative status. The Law of 1988 relating to financial transparency in political life (together with further pieces of legislation on their finances referred to below) frames the operational regime of political parties by recognising their legal personality and the different rights attached to it. Such rights comprise the right to institute proceedings before a court of law, the right to acquire property, and any act that comes within their political role (e.g., to publish a newspaper).[18] For a long time, political parties in France have enjoyed wide freedom as regards their creation. They could be created de jure under the general provisions of the 1901 Law on Associations or be regarded as de facto associations, which was traditionally the way leftist political parties established themselves. However, because political parties are endowed with legal personality and are in receipt of public funding, it was considered necessary to specify their obligations, hereby contributing to refining the legal framework in the area especially as regards financial obligations.

Financing of political parties

As part of the enhancement of their status, the legislative framework as regards the requirements for more transparency in political parties' financial activities and sources of funding has been tightened up. This was prompted by a series of scandals involving illegal and covert funding incriminating a number of political formations in the 1980s. A first set of laws was adopted at the end of the 1980s and start of the 1990s to govern the public funding of political parties.[19] These laws were further refined in 1995 with a law that prohibited the financing of political parties by legal persons.[20] Subsequently, in 2000, additional legislation was introduced to promote gender equality by reducing funding to political parties that did not adhere to the principle of gender parity when selecting candidates for elections.[21] Following more scandals in the 2000s, a new set of laws was enacted in 2013, leading to the establishment of the High Authority for Transparency in Public Life (*Haute Autorité pour la Transparence de la Vie Publique* or *HATVP*).[22] In 2016, the "moralisation of public life" legislation was introduced, introducing more stringent regulations on the financing of political parties and election campaigns.[23] Furthermore, in 2017, legislation was passed to instil confidence in political life,

17 Decision No 89-271 DC of 11 January 1990 *Loi relative à la limitation des dépenses électorales et à la clarification du financement des activités politiques*, pt 12.

18 Organic Law No 88-226 of 11 March 1988 relating to financial transparency in political life, as complemented by Law No 88-227 of 11 March 1988 relating to financial transparency in political life, as amended.

19 Law No 88-227 of 11 March 1988 relating to financial transparency in political life, as amended by Law No 90-55 of 15 January 1990 on the limitation of election expenses and the clarification of the financing of political activities.

20 Law No 95-65 of 19 January 1995 relating to the financing of political life.

21 Law No 2000-493 of 6 June 2000 aimed at promoting equal access of women and men to electoral mandates and elective functions.

22 Organic Law No 2013-906 of 11 October 2013, as complemented by Law No 2013-907 of 11 October 2013, relating to transparency in public life.

23 See, among others, Law No 2016-1691 of 9 December 2016 relating to transparency, the fight against corruption, and the modernisation of economic life; Organic Law No 2016-506 of 25 April 2016 on the modernisation of

which included guidelines on loans to political parties and the creation of a mediator to allocate funds to both parties and candidates during elections.[24] However, the compliance of political parties with financial oversight is necessarily limited by the need to uphold their "constitutionally guaranteed freedom."[25]

Political parties may receive public as well as private funds and bear significant obligations as regards the transparency of their financial activities.

Public funding. Public funding comes directly from the state and is divided up into two fractions. The first fraction is awarded to all political parties and political groups under certain conditions (i.e., parties must present candidates at elections in at least 75 constituencies) and is proportional to the number of votes obtained in the legislative elections. The second fraction is limited to the political parties represented in the National Assembly and is proportional to the number of elected representatives. These conditions aim at preventing moot political parties and groups looking to benefit from public funding, but which do not exercise any political activity. As such, the amount of public funding allocated to political parties and groups was set for the year 2022 at 66,155,387.84 euros, divided into 32,081,868.13 euros for the first fraction, and 34,073,519.71 euros for the second fraction.[26]

Private funding. Private funding[27] is sourced from private donors and is closely monitored to ensure transparency. Donations from foreign states are prohibited. The 1995 Law prohibits private donations from legal persons such as companies, limiting funding to individual donors. These donations are typically solicited during election periods, and not in the normal course of party operations, and are limited to 7,500 euros per person per year.

Principles and rules of financial transparency. The financial accounts of political parties are approved and certified yearly by auditors. They are transmitted to the National Commission for Campaign Accounts and Political Financing (*Commission Nationale des Comptes de Campagne et des Financements Politiques* or *CNCCFP*) in the first semester of the year following the financial year, and the accounts are published by the Commission. The Commission is an independent administrative authority whose main role is to control campaign accounts in all elections and, more broadly, to ensure that political parties and candidates respect their accounting and financial obligations. Rules regarding fundraising allow a candidate to raise funds from political parties but, in order to improve transparency and avoid external pressure,

---

the rules applicable to the presidential election; and Law No 2016-508 of 25 April 2016 on the modernisation of various provisions applicable to the elections. The other measures concern the exemplary character and probity of elected officials, the prevention of conflicts of interest, and, generally, transparency in political life. Another relevant piece of legislation is Law No 2019-828 of 6 August 2019 on the transformation of the public service.

24 Law No 2017-286 of 6 March 2017 aimed at reinforcing the accounting obligations of the political parties and the candidates; and Law No 2017-1339 of 15 September 2017 relating to confidence in political life. For example, the September 2017 Law prohibits loans from states or banks located outside the EEA.

25 CE, Sect, 9 June 2010, *Association CAP SUR L'AVENIR 13*, No 327423.

26 Decree No 2022-94 of 31 January 2022 on issued for the application of (…) Law No 88-227 of 11 March 1988 as amended relating to financial transparency in political life.

27 This is outside of the traditional subscriptions from members and elected representatives of political parties and groups. These subscriptions are generally of a low amount, not sufficient to meet operating expenses.

explicitly prohibit donations from any other legal persons such as private companies, foreign states, trade unions, or associations and charities. Should the Commission identify any irregularity in the accounts, the political party concerned loses the right to public funding. Overall, the legal framework in their financial activities is quite constraining for political parties but represents the flip side of their access to public funding and is also explained, to a large extent, by the numerous abuses committed by a number of political parties and political leaders over the years. The financial transparency of political parties has been complemented by rules concerning the financial transparency of the state at the start of the 2000s. The former "special funding" part of annual finance laws was replaced by a more streamlined system. Such a rationalised system allocates funding to security operations only under the formal control of a special committee composed of two deputies, two senators, and two members of the Court of Auditors. In the same vein, the remuneration of ministers has been set up in line with the salaries of top civil servants and is subject to taxation; also, the remuneration of the President's and ministers' cabinet personnel is no longer unofficial but takes the form of a special allowance.[28]

Elections and Referendums

> « *C'est une bonne idée d'avoir choisi le référendum, à condition que la réponse soit oui.* »[29]

In the first paragraph of article 3 of the Constitution, it is affirmed that "[n]ational sovereignty belongs to the people who shall exercise it through their representatives or by way of referendum." The sovereign people of France are thus entrusted to vote at regular intervals in the different elections. By their vote, voters, or electors, choose which political party or coalition they support. This section examines the right to vote and its progressive democratisation. It also explores the different elections that take place within the country, such as the presidential election, as well as the issue of referendums.

The right to vote

In a democratic society, the right to vote, or right of suffrage, is necessarily universal, meaning that it is available to all citizens without any form of discrimination. However, individuals looking to exercise their right to vote must meet specific criteria such as age, nationality, and mental capacity. This subsection discusses the importance of universal suffrage and the qualifications necessary to become an eligible voter or candidate in various electoral processes. Additionally, principles such as gender equality, financial transparency, and fairness in political communication are also examined, as they play a pivotal role in ensuring fair and transparent elections.

The principle of universal suffrage. In France, the right to vote has been gradually democratised, starting with the introduction of universal suffrage for all men in March 1848.

28 Law No 2001-1275 of 28 December 2001 on finances for 2002.

29 Valéry Giscard d'Estaing (1926–2020), President of the Republic (1974–1981), on the occasion of the vote on the Treaty establishing a Constitution for Europe in 2005 [It is a good idea to have chosen the referendum, provided the answer is yes].

The first vote by universal suffrage resulted in the election of the first President of the French Republic, Louis Napoléon Bonaparte, under the Second Republic.[30] This was followed by a decree in April 1848 abolishing slavery in the French colonies and thus opening up the right to vote to the "new citizens" or "new freemen" (i.e., emancipated slaves).[31] The right to vote was first granted to French women in 1944 (see Box 5.1 De Gaulle on women's right to vote).[32] This is quite late compared with other democratic states which granted equal voting rights to women much earlier in Europe (i.e., in 1922 in Ireland under the Irish Free State, and in 1928 in the UK) and elsewhere in the world (i.e., in 1893 in New Zealand, and in 1920 in the USA). The lowering of the electoral majority to 18 years old in 1974 is another step in the movement of democratisation of suffrage.[33] Lastly, EU citizens who reside in France have been entitled to vote in local and European elections since 1998, thus opening the right to vote to another fraction, although not national, of the population.[34]

Universal suffrage implies the respect of the principles of pluralism, equality, and freedom. It is important that political regimes ensure that these material conditions of the right to vote are fulfilled, as does the Constitution in its article 3 paragraphs three and four: "The right of suffrage shall be direct or indirect under the conditions laid down in the present Constitution. This right is always universal, equal, and secret. All French nationals over eighteen years of age of both genders and enjoying their civil and political rights are entitled to vote, under the conditions determined by the law."

Political pluralism is a principle upheld in French law dating back to the 1789 Declaration, even though its implementation has often been challenged. The Constitutional Council further solidified this principle in the realm of audio-visual communication by expressly referring to article 11 of the 1789 Declaration in its landmark 1989 decision.[35]

The principle of equality means that electoral law must not discriminate between citizens, and between different categories of citizens. As regards the prohibition of discrimination between citizens, the equal right to vote is encapsulated in the expression "one elector, one vote." An unequal voting system allows for a plural vote, meaning that an elector can vote for several candidates, or in several constituencies, depending on the wealth and educational or family status of such an elector. This is not allowed under French law. As regards

30 Decree of 5 March 1848 convening electoral assemblies and fixing the number of deputies to be elected. The concept of universal suffrage for men was initially proclaimed in 1792 during the establishment of the First Republic. It was also included in the 1793 Constitution. However, due to the tumultuous events of the Terror period and the failure to implement the 1793 Constitution, the idea of universal suffrage for men was not fully integrated into the electoral system.

31 Decree of 27 April 1848 relating to the abolition of slavery in the French colonies and possessions. The 1848 Decree was promoted by Victor Schœlcher, deputy at the National Assembly. Slavery was illegal in metropolitan France at the time under the old Middle Age principle of "*privilège de la terre de France*" (i.e., no one is a slave in France), although this was very unevenly respected and applied. The 1848 Decree generalised this principle to all colonies and possessions of the Republic.

32 Ordinance of 21 April 1944 on the organisation of public authorities in France after the liberation.

33 Law No 74-631 of 5 July 1974 setting the age of legal majority at eighteen.

34 Organic Law No 98-404 of 25 May 1998 determining the conditions for the application of article 88-3 of the Constitution relating to the exercise by citizens of the European Union residing in France, other than French nationals, of the right to vote and stand as a candidate in municipal elections, and transposing Directive 94/80/EC of 19 December 1994.

35 Decision No 88-248 DC of 17 January 1989 on *Loi modifiant la loi n° 86-1067 du 30 septembre 1986 relative à la liberté de communication*, pt 5.

the prohibition of discrimination between different categories of citizens, progressive changes came about in domestic law with the extension of the right to vote to women in 1944, as seen above, to military personnel in 1945,[36] to descendants of former reigning families in 1950,[37] and to all inhabitants of the overseas territories in 1956.[38] Also, the principle of equal vote may be undermined by the uneven division of constituencies. In theory, constituencies must include an approximately equal number of inhabitants (voters). In practice, however, this equality is rarely achieved. The electoral division can become a means of undermining the equality of citizens' right to vote, the best example being the practice of *gerrymandering*.[39] Originating in the USA, such a practice consists in severing an electoral bastion from a constituency and attaching it to a neighbouring constituency favourable to the majority in power. This is obviously prohibited under French law. On the basis of the principle of equality, the Constitutional Council decided that the delimitation of electoral boundaries should respect the principle of equal representation of the people and be done according to the demographic weight of each constituency based on the number of inhabitants (nationals and non-nationals), and not on the number of electors.[40]

Freedom of suffrage means that the vote is personal, not mandatory, sincere, and secret. The personal character of the right to vote means that electors vote, in principle, in person and, by exception, by proxy. Proxy voting is open, under conditions, to voters who cannot attend the electoral day(s) and cannot vote in person in their usual electoral constituency because they are away on annual leave or because of other conflicting commitments.[41] Some adaptations to the electoral rules were made during the Covid-19 pandemic allowing, for example, the possibility of two votes by proxy in France instead of one normally allowed, for the local elections of June 2020 and June 2021. Postal votes and online votes are not allowed under French law, except as regards French nationals residing abroad in certain elections and under certain conditions.[42] Voter registration is automatic as soon as any French national reaches 18 years of age.

36 Ordinance No 45-1839 of 17 August 1945 relating to the electorate and the eligibility of the military, amending article 33 and repealing article 31 last paragraph of the Law of 5 April 1884 relating to municipal organisation. It provides that: "The soldiers of the three armies are electors under the same conditions as other citizens." This breaks with the practice in force since 1872 which barred military personnel from voting and being elected.

37 Law No 50-728 of 24 June 1950 repealing the Law of 22 June 1886 relating to members of families who reigned in France, as amended by Law No 2011-525 of 17 May 2011 on the simplification and improvement of the quality of law. This breaks with the "law of exile" in force since the Third Republic, which barred the heads of the families having reigned in France, as well as their direct heirs in the order of primogeniture, from residing and voting in France.

38 Law No 56-619 of 23 June 1956 on measures to ensure the development of territories under the Ministry for Overseas France. Although inhabitants of the overseas territories were declared French citizens in 1946, and the status of the indigenous abolished, the right to vote was not yet recognised to all. See Law No 46-940 of 7 May 1946 proclaiming all nationals of overseas territories citizens.

39 The amusing etymology behind the term "gerrymander" comes from the combination of the name "Elbridge Gerry," the governor of Massachusetts, with the word "salamander." This last expression was due to the peculiar shape of the constituency in question (Essex County, Massachusetts) which Governor Gerry was attempting to manipulate in order to benefit his political party, resulting in a resemblance to the amphibious creature.

40 Decision No 86-208 DC of 2 July 1986 *Loi relative à l'élection des députés et autorisant le Gouvernement à délimiter par ordonnance les circonscriptions électorales* (*Découpage électoral*), pt 21. See also Decision No 2008-573 DC of 8 January 2009 *Loi relative à la commission prévue à l'article 25 de la Constitution et à l'élection des députés*, and Decision No 2010-618 DC of 9 December 2010 *Loi de réforme des collectivités territoriales*.

41 Articles L 71 to L 78 Electoral Code.

42 Law No 75-1329 of 31 December 1975 amending certain provisions of the Electoral Code. See also Law No 2013-659 of 22 July 2013 relating to the representation of French people living outside France.

However, the newly registered elector must still have his/her status (i.e., nationality, identity, and place of residence) checked at the city hall of his/her residence. Contrary to other countries where the vote is mandatory (e.g., Australia, Belgium, Brazil, Egypt, Gabon, Greece, Lebanon, Luxembourg), voting is optional in France, except for the senatorial elections under penalty of a fine of 100 euros. The elector is free to abstain from voting. Abstention has been an interesting variable in the French electoral landscape depending on the significance of the election. It is generally very low in the presidential election (between 15 and 20%) but much higher in the elections to the EP (around 50%), in some local elections, and in referendums. This is typically the case in referendums where there is not much at stake for the majority of the population such as, for example, the 1988 referendum on New Caledonia (63.1% abstention) or the 2000 referendum on the five-year presidential term (nearly 70% abstention). To this worrying abstentionism trend must be added the growing issue of blank and invalid votes, which are conflated under French law. A blank vote is a ballot paper which does not contain any choice of a candidate or list or answer. An invalid vote is a ballot paper which does not meet the requirements of a regular ballot paper because it contains, for example, irregular annotations or signs, or because the ballot envelope is empty. The secrecy of the vote is regarded as a constitutional principle. As noted by the Constitutional Council, the ignorance of such a fundamental principle may lead to the cancellation of all the votes cast in the polling station in question—in that case, a polling station which did not provide any voting booths.[43]

The elector. To be able to vote, that is, to have electoral capacity, the elector must fulfil four distinct requirements, namely to be a French national, to be over 18 years of age, to not be deprived of his/her voting rights, and to be registered to vote. The first three requirements pertain to the entitlement to vote (*jouissance du droit de vote*) while the fourth requirement concerns the exercise of the right to vote (*exercice du droit de vote*). Only nationals, by birth or naturalised, are entitled to vote in French elections. Foreigners are not entitled to vote except EU citizens domiciled in France as seen above. Electoral majority is at 18 years of age since 1974 as seen above. Certain citizens can be deprived of their right to vote due to their criminal conviction or due to their status as mentally ill persons.[44] In application of the principle of the individual nature of penalties, this deprivation of the right to vote cannot be automatic.[45] In addition to these substantial requirements, there is the formal requirement that the elector must be registered to vote on the electoral lists of the locality where s/he is domiciled. The elector can also expressly request to be registered in the locality in which s/he has been resident for at least the last six months, or where s/he has been paying local taxes for the last five years.[46] Voter registration is automatic since 1997,[47] but the elector is still required to bring proof of his/her nationality, identity, and residence to the local authorities, which a large number of (young) electors fail to do, thus increasing the non-registered proportion of the electorate. For

43 Decision No 88-14 REF of 9 November 1988 *Proclamation des résultats du référendum du 6 novembre 1988*, pt 2.

44 Article L 5 Electoral Code. This category refers to adults who have been legally placed under guardianship (known as *majeurs en tutelle*), typically representing individuals with severe mental illness.

45 Decision No 2010-6/7 QPC of 11 June 2010 *M. Stéphane A. et autres [Article L 7 du code électoral].*

46 Articles L 9 to L 15-1 Electoral Code. For French electors residing abroad, the rules vary depending on the election.

47 Law No 97-1027 of 10 November 1997 relating to the automatic registration of persons aged eighteen on the electoral lists.

not-yet registered citizens aged 18 or more, registration is still optional and on the initiative of the potential elector. An electoral administrative commission oversees voters' registration and reviews the list of voters every September to December each year. Litigation concerning the regularity of voter registration pertains to the ordinary judicial courts, whereas litigation concerning the regularity of the process followed by the electoral administrative commission pertains to the administrative courts.

The candidate. To be able to stand for elections, the candidate must fulfil the same requirements as the elector as well as being eligible to run for election.[48] Ineligibility rules may be permanent or temporary. The first type of ineligibility—permanent ineligibility—concerns the nationality of the candidate, his/her age (24 years of age to run for the senatorial elections, and 18 years of age for all other elections, including the presidential election and the elections to the EP), his/her legal capacity, and certain criminal convictions (i.e., crimes and offences of a sexual, financial, or economic nature) that make the candidate ineligible. The second type of ineligibility—temporary ineligibility—is linked to the professional occupation of the individual concerned; for example, military personnel can run for local elections under certain conditions,[49] and prefects, judges, police commissioners, and other civil servants cannot be elected in a constituency where they have been in post in the years preceding the election concerned. A temporary ineligibility is also the result of the penalties that have been inflicted on the candidate by the electoral judge, and this includes the penalty of ineligibility inflicted by their state of origin on EU nationals running for elections in France under the conditions of French law.[50]

Principle of gender equality. Under the constitutional principle of equal access to elective mandates, the 1999 constitutional amendment introduced the principle of gender equality.[51] Such a principle, also called the principle of "parity" (*parité hommes/femmes*), revised article 4 of the Constitution to state that: "[Political parties] shall contribute to the implementation of the principle laid down under the second paragraph of the First Article 3 [The law shall promote equal access by women and men to electoral mandates and elective functions…] within the conditions determined by law." Changes were also made to electoral laws, particularly regarding the party-list proportional representation system. These changes were necessary to address the objections raised by the Constitutional Council, which initially viewed positive discrimination towards women as a contentious issue (the so-called "women quotas case law").[52] This was complemented by a 2000 legislation that requires party-lists to balance the numbers of male and

48 EU citizens living in France can participate in local elections and serve as local council members; however, they are not eligible to hold positions as mayors or deputy mayors.

49 Article L 4121-3 Code of Defence.

50 Article LO 230-2 Electoral Code. Besides, EU citizens residing in France who are municipal councillors (or members of the Council of Paris) may neither be members in any capacity whatsoever of the senatorial electoral college nor participate in the election to this college of delegates, additional delegates, and substitutes (see article LO 286-1 Electoral Code).

51 Constitutional Law No 99-569 of 8 July 1999 on equality between women and men.

52 Decision No 82-146 DC of 18 November 1982 *Loi modifiant le code électoral et le code des communes et relative à l'élection des conseillers municipaux et aux conditions d'inscription des Français établis hors de France sur les listes électorales* (*quotas de femmes*), and Decision No 98-407 DC of 14 January 1999 *Loi relative au mode*

female candidates based on the type of election.[53] Furthermore, since 2013, gender equality has become a compulsory criterion in the election of departmental councillors. Each departmental constituency (*canton*) must present a pair of candidates, one male and one female, who will run together as a team.[54] Overall, these legal and legislative amendments are designed to further strengthen gender equality by ensuring that both men and women have fair opportunities to engage in political life and seek elective roles without experiencing any form of discrimination on the basis of gender.

Principle of financial transparency. In parallel with the introduction of the regulation on the financing of political parties (see above), the regulation of electoral campaigns emerged in the mid-1980s. The core principle in this area is that such regulation aims exclusively at the candidate (and the elected official) and not the political parties involved, at least not directly. Such regulation covers all elections at national level, including senatorial elections since 2014. Under the financial and legal mechanisms put in place, the candidate for an election has the obligation to appoint a designated financial agent (i.e., natural person or association) responsible for managing the funds raised during the electoral campaign and, generally, for monitoring all campaign expenses. The candidate, through his/her financial agent, opens a bank account dedicated to the electoral campaign, which must be certified by a chartered accountant responsible for tracing the origins of all funds received and all expenditures incurred. The National Commission for Campaign Accounts and Political Financing monitors the campaign accounts with a right of appeal to the electoral judge, with the exception of the presidential election, which falls exclusively to the Constitutional Council. The Commission rules on a candidate's campaign account within six months of receiving it. Adversarial proceedings before the Commission may result in the approval, rejection, or rectification of the account concerned. Referral to the electoral judge is only made should the Commission reject the account, although its observations as an administrative authority are not binding. Non-respect of the rules on financial transparency may result in three kinds of sanctions, namely pecuniary, criminal, and electoral: the pecuniary sanction results in the non-reimbursement by the state of the refundable part of the public funding and payment of any excess to the tax office; the criminal sanction results in a fine and a jail sentence of one year maximum; and the electoral sanction takes the form of ineligibility lasting one year, except for the presidential candidate and except in cases where the judge accepts that the candidate acted in good faith.

Principle of fairness in political communication. The legislator has successively regulated print media, audio-visual media, and opinion polls. Print media is now closely supervised by the National Commission, ensuring that propaganda materials such as flyers and bills are handled appropriately. Commercial advertising is strictly prohibited in the three months leading up to an election, to maintain a level playing field. Audio-visual communication is monitored by the

d'élection des conseillers régionaux et des conseillers à l'Assemblée de Corse et au fonctionnement des Conseils régionaux.

53 Law No 2000-493 of 6 June 2000 aimed at promoting equal access of women and men to electoral mandates and elective functions.

54 Law No 2013-403 of 17 May 2013 relating to the election of departmental councillors, municipal councillors and community councillors, and modifying the electoral calendar.

Audio-visual and Digital Communications Regulatory Authority (*Autorité de Régulation de la Communication audiovisuelle et numérique* or *Arcom*), which guarantees equal speaking time for candidates on public channels during presidential and legislative elections. *Arcom* also ensures that there is a balance of viewpoints on private channels. In addition, opinion polls have been regulated since 1977 in elections and referendums.[55] A special commission oversees their accuracy and transparency. Certain technical details must be included in the polls to verify their reliability. Since 2002, opinion polls cannot be issued the day before the ballot and on the actual day of the ballot, although results estimates are authorised after the closing of the last polling station in mainland France. Overall, these regulations aim to uphold the principles of fairness, equality, and transparency in political communication.

BOX 5.1 DE GAULLE ON WOMEN'S RIGHT TO VOTE

☛ "Just as we claim to make France the one and only master at home, so we will ensure that the French people are the one and only master at home. At the same time that the French will be freed from external enemy oppression, all their individual freedoms must be restored to them at home. Once the enemy has been driven out of the territory, all the men and *all the women* of our country will elect the National Assembly which will decide sovereignly on the destinies of the country (emphasis added)."

Statement by General De Gaulle, 23 June 1942, published in clandestine newspapers.

The different elections

French political life under the Fifth Republic has been characterised by a growing frequency of voting events, except for referendum votes which have been infrequent. The introduction of the election of the President of the Republic by direct universal suffrage in 1962 and the creation of new elections, notably at European and local levels, have contributed to this trend. This subsection explores the various electoral cycles and voting systems used in different elections, with a particular focus on the significance of political parties and the influence of the media in shaping election outcomes. The different types of elections[56] are then examined, before concluding with developments in the status of elected officials.

Electoral cycles. Before 1962, the electoral cycles were organised around the legislative elections. This changed after the 1962 reform which introduced the election of the President of the Republic by direct universal suffrage and made the presidential election the most

55 Law No 77-808 of 19 July 1977 relating to the publication and dissemination of certain opinion polls, as amended by Law No 2002-214 of 19 February 2002 amending Law No 77-808 of 19 July 1977 relating to the publication and dissemination of certain opinion polls, and Law No 2016-508 of 25 April 2016 on the modernisation of various provisions applicable to elections.

56 Except for the local elections, namely regional, departmental, and municipal elections, which are not described here.

significant moment in French political life.[57] Should the President not obtain a majority in the National Assembly after the legislative elections, where participation and results depend on the presidential election, the dissolution of the Assembly is pronounced. This happened twice under Mitterrand's presidency, in 1981 and in 1988. However, the various situations of cohabitation (in 1986–1988, 1993–1995, and 1997–2002) somewhat modified the rules for forming governmental majorities in the aftermath of the legislation/presidential electoral cycle. This was rectified when the electoral calendar was changed to put the presidential election in the first place (election taking place generally in April for the first round, and May for the second round) and the legislative election in the second place (election taking place generally in June).[58] The victory of the right on two occasions in 2002 and 2007, as well as the victory of the left in 2012, and of the centre-left in 2017, were arguably facilitated by such a streamlined system. In addition to the significant change introduced by the election of the President of the Republic by direct universal suffrage, the introduction of the election of members of the EP and of regional councillors by direct universal suffrage created a set of new elections. The first European elections took place in 1979 and the first regional election in 1986. However, and contrary to the stakes implied by the presidential election, the electorate often manifests relative indifference towards European and regional elections, which explains the large and endemic abstention rate at such elections although the trend is clearly reversing concerning European elections (see below). Nevertheless, European and regional elections often represent the possibility for new political forces to rise and the opportunity for the elector to sanction either the governmental majority or the opposition s/he is not satisfied with at national level.[59] For example, the European elections of 1984 and 1989 saw the emergence of, respectively, the National Front and the Green Party. Other examples include the appearance of a new variety of anti-system political parties at regional level since 1992, as well as the win in the 2015 regional election of the National Front, which obtained the lead in the first round in six regions and 46 departments. Generally, electoral behaviours tend to follow different trajectories depending on the type of election, the voting system in place, as well as what is at stake for the electorate in a particular election. Overall, the picture that has emerged in the last few years is one where periods without electoral consultations are seemingly the exception in France.[60]

The voting system. Democratic regimes rely on different voting systems, each with their unique methods of calculating votes. The primary voting systems include the first-past-the-post system and the proportional representation system. In the first-past-the-post system, each election aims to fill one seat per electoral constituency, whereas the proportional representation system looks to fill multiple seats, allowing voters to select from a list of candidates and indicate their preferences. Under the proportional representation system, different techniques exist: either the list of candidates is pre-determined and the voter cannot change the order, or the voter can re-order candidates on the list according to their preference (i.e., preferential voting or single transferable vote). This last form of voting system is used, for example, in

57 Constitutional Law No 62-1292 of 6 November 1962 relating to the election of the President of the Republic by universal suffrage.

58 Organic Law No 2001-419 of 15 May 2001 modifying the end of the mandate and powers of the National Assembly.

59 Hugues Portelli & Thomas Ehrhard, *Droit constitutionnel* (14th edn, Dalloz 2021) 221.

60 Ibid 222.

Ireland across all elections (i.e., general, local, presidential, and European elections). In this system, candidates are listed alphabetically on the ballot paper, enabling voters to rank them based on their preferences (i.e., first choice, second choice, and so on). If a preferred candidate is eliminated, or elected with a surplus of votes, the voter is instructed that their vote is to be transferred to the second-choice candidate. Additionally, a less common technique known as "*panachage*" (or mixing) technique allows voters to select candidates from different lists, which is used, for instance, in local elections in small French towns with populations under 3,500.

Voting systems provide for one or two rounds. The one-round system is commonly found in Anglo-Saxon systems such as in the UK or the USA. This system favours the list or candidate that receives the most votes in the initial round. As such, this type of system is often seen as an "efficient" voting system which structures political life into two rival formations, preventing a third-party trend to emerge. On the other hand, the two-round system allows for some staggering of the winning strategy. In this system, candidates seek, in the first place, to win enough votes to be allowed to compete in the second round. Once in the second round, and after partisan negotiations, candidates strategise to secure the necessary number of votes to finally win the election. The two-round system is largely practised in, for instance, France for all types of elections, including presidential, general, and local, as is examined below. This system offers a more complex and dynamic approach to electoral politics, allowing for more strategic manoeuvring and negotiation among candidates.

As for the calculation of the number of votes, this is done according to majority voting or proportional voting. The majority voting system is evidently used in the first-past-the-post system where the seat(s) is(are) filled by the candidate, or the list, which obtains the highest number (i.e., majority)[61] of votes while the other candidates do not obtain any seats. The advantage of this system is that it procures efficiency, stability, and coherence by avoiding the dispersion of political forces and favours the emergence of strong majorities. Its drawback is that it favours representatives of the big parties to the detriment of more modest political forces, thus possibly neglecting an important part of the electorate. The proportional voting system is used when several seats are to be filled, in a one-round vote. The seats are filled by those lists or those candidates that obtain the most votes among themselves. The advantage of this system is the degree of representation it offers to smaller political forces, hence reflecting a fairer image of public opinion. The drawback is the risk of governing with fragile coalitions formed between different political forces and possibly resulting in political instability. Whatever the voting system, a number of factors are taken into account to make the final calculation of votes. These factors include the number of registered voters, the number of voters who attend the polling station,[62] and the number of voters who actually express their vote since blank and invalid votes do not, generally, count.

Overall, the choice of voting system, whether it be the first-past-the-post system or the proportional representation system, has significant implications because of its direct or indirect impact on citizen representation, the number of parties able to wield power, and the stability of political majorities and ease of governance. These systems can also be combined into

61 The voting system may require a simple (or relative) majority, meaning that the number of votes is higher than the one obtained by the opposing candidate or list, or an absolute majority, which is 50% of the votes plus one vote.

62 Those voters who do not attend the polling station form the abstention votes.

a so-called "mix voting system" to make use of the efficiency of first-past-the-post and the fairness of proportional representation. It is the case, for example, in elections to the German *Bundestag*, as well as in French regional and local elections for towns with over 3,500 residents.

Under the Fifth Republic, the main voting system is the two-round majority voting system with adaptations as regards certain elections based on the proportional representation voting system or on a mixed voting system. The two-round majority voting system is used for the two major domestic elections, namely the presidential election and the election of deputies. In the presidential election, the rule is that, should a candidate fail to obtain an absolute majority of the votes cast in the first round, the first two candidates who have obtained the majority of the votes cast run in the second round. This has resulted in the formation of coalitions around the two competing candidates who have generally represented, except for the 1969 and 2002 presidential elections,[63] the right and left wings. The ensuing bipolarisation of political life has been reinforced by the legislative elections which follow the same two-round majority voting system, except in the 1986 election, which applied proportional representation. Such bipolarisation has also somewhat simplified the political party system, facilitating the support for successive governments by strong majorities. The two-round majority voting system is also applied as regards the cantonal election which designates the departmental councillors. Again, the two-round majority voting system has resulted in stable majorities and probably explains why departments have retained a strong influence at local level despite the creation of the regions in 1982.[64]

The introduction of proportional representation in the French electoral system is linked to the introduction of the election of members of the EP by direct universal suffrage in 1976 with the first election in 1979. The Gaullist party at the time (*Rassemblement pour la République* or *RPR*) sought to diminish the political influence of EP members and so resorted to introducing a dose of proportional representation clearly aimed at limiting opposing political forces. The voting system was based on the highest average of votes within a single constituency, that of the national territory, thereby barring the party-lists that did not obtain at least 5% of the votes cast from being represented.[65] Mitterrand (1981–1993) was the first proponent of introducing proportional representation at national level. This has been done quite sporadically since 1981: it was applied in a mix form in the 1983 municipal election, and plainly in the 1986 legislative elections and regional elections. In recent times, in particular under the presidencies of Hollande (2012–2017) and Macron (since 2017), the introduction of "a dose of proportional representation" in the voting system has been discussed but to no avail so far.[66]

63 In the 1969 election, the candidates were Georges Pompidou (conservative right) and Alain Poher (centrist); in the 2002 election, the candidates were Jacques Chirac (moderate right) and Jean-Marie Le Pen (far right).

64 Law No 82-213 of 2 March 1982 relating to the rights and freedoms of municipalities, departments, and regions. The 1982 Law was followed by several other laws which completed the decentralisation process.

65 Law No 77-729 of 7 July 1977 relating to the election of representatives to the European Parliament, as lastly amended by Law No 2018-509 of 25 June 2018 relating to the election of representatives to the European Parliament.

66 See, for example, Claude Bartolone and Michel Winock, *Refaire la démocratie*, Report No 3100, National Assembly; and (aborted) Government Bill of 23 May 2018 for a more representative, accountable, and effective democracy.

The importance of political parties in elections. Although political parties represent only one means of contributing towards the suffrage, they have progressively acquired a central role in the most important domestic elections. As regards the presidential election for example, the legislation on endorsements (see below), which requires a candidate to obtain a certain number of supporters, makes it difficult, almost impossible, for any given candidate to stand for election as an independent candidate without the support—ideological, financial, and logistical—of a political formation. In the words of Duverger: "The choice of candidates to stand for the presidential election is as important as the choice between these candidates. This is the reason why no presidential election has ever been won in a developed nation by a candidate running as an independent."[67] The same is true for referendums. Despite being aimed at bypassing partisan lines in giving the vote directly to the people, referendums are based on a popular expression which is very much shaped by political parties since French law grants them the right to take part in the official referendum campaign in proportion to their representativity on the national scene (see below).

The role of the media in elections. The primary role which is played today by the radio, television, and the Internet has given rise to issues surrounding the status and control of the media, including social media.[68] In a pluralist regime, the principle dictates that the media should impart information without any political bias, as well as give equal and fair access to the media to all candidates. As for the broadcasting regime in particular, such a regime can either be based on the principle of freedom or be based on a public monopoly. The first model is used in the USA, for example, whereby any private actor may broadcast provided they have obtained a licence to do so from a special commission which reviews essentially technical requirements. The second model is the one practised in several countries in Western Europe, including France. Since the end of the 1980s, the trend has been towards a privatisation of part of the broadcasting network with, for example, one or two television channels remaining under state control while others enjoy different levels of licensing from the public authorities, rendering this system of "controlled liberalism"[69] rather complex. The overall principle remains that pluralism of opinions shall be guaranteed together with equal and fair access of political parties and candidates to broadcast. In France, the principles of freedom and pluralism in audio-visual communication were recognised by law in 1986.[70] *Arcom* is the regulatory body entrusted, by law, to enforce the principle of pluralism in audio-visual and digital media.[71] The principle of pluralism revolves around the notion of candidates' "speaking time" during electoral periods as well as in a non-electoral context. Such pluralism has been defined as

67 Maurice Duverger, *La monarchie républicaine, ou comment les démocraties se donnent des rois* (Robert Laffont 1974) 54–55.

68 Social media refers to online platforms and software that enable individuals to connect and exchange information on the Web through either a computer or a mobile device. Some popular social media platforms include Metaverse (formerly known as Facebook), Twitter, Instagram, LinkedIn, and YouTube.

69 Ferdinand Mélin-Soucramanien & Pierre Pactet, *Droit constitutionnel* (39th edn, Sirey 2021) 134.

70 Law No 86-1067 of 30 September 1986 on freedom of communication, as amended by Law No 2000-719 of 1 August 2000. See also Decision No 86-217 DC of 18 September 1986 *Loi relative à la liberté de communication.*

71 Instituted in January 2022, *Arcom* was born from the merger of the Higher Audio-visual Council (*Conseil Supérieur de l'Audiovisuel* or *CSA*) and the High Authority for the Dissemination of Works and the Protection of Rights on the Internet (*Haute Autorité pour la Diffusion des Œuvres et la Protection des Droits sur Internet* or *Hadopi*).

"internal," meaning that the balance between views and opinions must be respected by each television channel or radio station.

In electoral periods, *Arcom* sets the rules concerning the conditions of production, programming, and broadcasting of programmes relating to the election campaign that public radio and television stations are required to produce and broadcast. *Arcom* even intervenes before the opening of the official campaign by recalling the requirements of pluralism, requirements that may vary depending on the type of election. *Arcom* addresses, for the duration of the electoral campaign, recommendations to radios and television channels, as well as to local cable services, in order to fix the rules concerning the access of candidates to audio-visual and digital media. For each election, *Arcom* applies its 2011 general recommendation on the principle of political pluralism in radio and television services during an election period,[72] as well as a particular recommendation setting the list of the audio-visual services to be controlled. The guiding principles are those of, firstly, *quantitative* control of airtime and speaking time of the candidate and his/her supporters, and, secondly, *qualitative* control as regards the respect of ethical principles and the obligation for the broadcasters to act with moderation and honesty. Also, the respect of equity between candidates is part and parcel of pluralism.[73] Should *Arcom* find an obvious imbalance, it can ask the channel, including by written notification, to restore the balance between candidates, lists, or political parties. In the context of the fight against the dissemination of fake news, especially during electoral campaigns, the French Parliament adopted legislation in 2018.[74] These "anti-fake news" laws authorise a candidate or a political party to bring interlocutory proceedings to stop the dissemination of false information during the three months preceding a national election. Also, the main digital platforms have an obligation to report any sponsored political content by publishing the name of the author and the amount paid.

Outside of electoral periods, a specific system is established to monitor and track the speaking and broadcasting times of politicians, hereby consecrating a quantitative approach to ensuring political pluralism. According to the law, the speaking time of politicians on television and radio programmes that is recorded by *Arcom* is shared monthly with the presidents of both Houses of Parliament and with the leaders of the political parties represented in Parliament. Additionally, this information is made available to the public on *Arcom*'s website. In that framework, *Arcom* checks the respect of the so-called "principle of reference." This principle is based on the ternary rule that requires a fair distribution of speaking time among political party representatives in government, those in the majority, and those in the opposition. Since a 2000 reform, members of political parties not represented in Parliament also benefit from an equitable time in audio-visual programming and broadcasting. The speaking time of the President of the Republic is typically not counted towards the total time of their political party. However, this must be nuanced. Since 2009, although the President's constitutional role dictates that their words should not be attributed to a specific party, they can still

72 See *CSA* Recommendation No 2011-1 of 4 January 2011 on the principle of political pluralism in radio and television services during an election period, as amended, and *CSA* Deliberation No 2017-62 of 22 November 2017 on the principle of political pluralism in the radio and television media services.

73 The rules regarding the presidential election are a little different (see below).

74 Organic Law No 2018-1201 of 22 December 2018 and Law No 2018-1202 of 22 December 2018 relating to the fight against the manipulation of information.

be considered when evaluating political diversity in a non-electoral context. The exception is when the President is acting strictly in their capacity as Head of State.

The print media also exerts a considerable influence on public opinion which can only be meaningful within the context of a pluralist regime. Under a pluralist regime, healthy and unbiased competition between the different political parties must be guaranteed. There is always the danger though that this freedom is reduced by the dependence of print media on private benefactors or publicity providers, due to the cost. Also, this kind of press, except for larger groups which operate their own correspondents' network, is heavily dependent on news agencies, which are themselves controlled either by private actors or by the government. Such danger is exacerbated by the general decline of the political press to the advantage of news media, including social media. In several countries, including France, the former holds a relatively strong presence despite decreasing influence on public opinion. There is also a trend towards a concentration of media outlets with a decrease in the number of major daily newspapers, thus reinforcing the influence of large companies over the formation of public opinion. In French law, freedom of the press is protected by the seminal Law of 29 July 1881 (the 1881 Law). The 1881 Law defines the freedoms and responsibilities of the press and imposes a legal framework on publications as well as on the public display, peddling, and sale on the public highway. The 1881 Law has been amended several times to regulate this freedom beyond the rules relating to respect for the person, the protection of minors, the repression of insult, defamation, or invasion of privacy.[75] Recently, a private member's bill was tabled in the Senate in November 2022 proposing to enhance the freedom of the press by including the legal principle of adversarial proceedings in the 1881 Law and inserting the proposed provision: "a *publication can only be prohibited in application of a judicial decision rendered contradictorily*."

The presidential election. Before 1958, the President of the Republic was elected by Parliament and not by the people,[76] Parliament being the most pre-eminent institution under the previous regimes. With a President of the Council of Ministers at the centre of the decision-making process, the office of the President of the Republic was not of prime importance. The person holding such an office therefore reflected this, arguably explaining why, under the Third and Fourth Republics, the President was generally someone who lacked personality. The Fifth Republic changed this state of affairs. Between 1958 and 1962, the President was elected via *indirect* universal suffrage by an electoral college of around 80,000 representatives of the same type as the electoral college electing the senators. The electoral college was mainly made up of deputies and senators, general councillors, and representatives of local councils. Members of Parliament represented only a fraction of the electoral college. Besides, rural communities were overrepresented (i.e., 39,000 electors for 16 million inhabitants living in rural areas) in comparison to urban communities (i.e., 33,500 electors for 27 million inhabitants of urban areas). Based on the US model of the presidential Electoral College, this mode of election corresponded to De Gaulle's wish to see the presidential election escape the turmoil of political parties. De Gaulle's concern was to sever the connection with Parliament due to the

75 See also Law No 86-897 of 1 August 1986 on the reform of the legal regime of the press, and Law No 2010-1 of 4 January 2010 on the protection of journalists' sources.

76 Article 2 of Constitutional Law of 25 February 1875 under the Third Republic, and article 29 of the 1946 Constitution under the Fourth Republic.

deterioration of his relationships with a faction of its members. This was partly due to his appointment of Pompidou as Prime Minister in April 1962. The appointment of an outsider and virtual stranger, who was not a member of Parliament and had never been elected to a representative mandate, was regarded as an unfortunate choice by many at the time. Another reason was the hostile stance of De Gaulle towards the European integration project, which stirred up tensions in his relationships with loyal members of the majority party in government, the Popular Republic Movement (*Mouvement Républicain Populaire* or *MRP*), and forced some of its members to resign. Still, while departing from the system of the previous Republics, the election by an electoral college was not a direct election by the people. In fact, De Gaulle had been concerned about not hurting public opinion by too radical a move towards what could be perceived as reminiscent of the Bonapartist plebiscites. The indirect mode of election was used in the first presidential election of the Fifth Republic when De Gaulle was elected on 21 December 1958, with 78.5% of the votes cast by representatives of the electoral college.

This was drastically changed in 1962. The 1962 constitutional amendment, approved by referendum with a large majority of 62.25% of the votes cast, established the election of the President of the Republic by *direct* universal suffrage.[77] Although the aversion to the direct election of the Head of State stemmed far back in French constitutional history and was based on the fear of a personalisation of power, more immediate reasons could explain, at the time, the reluctance towards a direct election. Legally speaking, the President of the Republic was still the President of the so-called "Community" formed by the former French overseas colonies. Also politically, the Communist Party was still relatively strong. Both reasons represented unpalatable obstacles towards the direct election of the President of the Republic (i.e., votes by constituents in the colonies and by the communists!). Still, De Gaulle understood that, in a democracy, and outside of times of crisis, if the President of the Republic was to be a more pre-eminent institution than Parliament, s/he should have his/her own legitimacy. The way to gain such legitimacy was to be elected by the people and thus benefit from the "trust of the nation." The aim was clearly to make the President the central figure of the political system with a democratic legitimacy attached not only to the incumbent President but also to his/her successors.[78] The 1962 constitutional amendment had clear institutional and political implications. At the institutional level, the enhanced democratic legitimacy of the President changed the relationship with the Prime Minister; in fact, while the constitutional powers have remained unchanged, the President has been able to exercise them with more weight by imposing leadership in the areas of competence shared with the Prime Minister, such as in matters of defence policy. At the political level, the most obvious implication has been the polarisation of political life as mentioned above: the election of the President has become a key moment in this regard, pushing the different political parties to regroup, almost mechanically, into two camps to support the candidate who is the closest to their political ideas, hereby resulting in a right–left divide although the "trend towards the centre" of politics under Macron's last two mandates has somewhat unsettled the right–left paradigm. Besides, the phenomenon of bipolarisation has undoubtedly been a factor of regime stability compared to the multiparty

77 Constitutional Law No 62-1292 of 6 November 1962 relating to the election of the President of the Republic by universal suffrage. The 1962 Constitutional Law was adopted, exceptionally, by a referendum under article 11 of the Constitution.

78 De Gaulle's decision to push for the 1962 reform was also influenced by the unsuccessful assassination attempt known as *attentat du Petit Clamart* on 22 August 1962, from which he narrowly escaped.

system and the combinations it implied in previous regimes. In any case, the election by direct universal suffrage has had the effect of propelling the President of the Republic, endowed with strong powers, into the realm of day-to-day politics (see Table 5.2 The presidential election in France and in Ireland).[79]

Today, the President of the Fifth Republic is elected by direct universal suffrage, based on a single (i.e., voting for one candidate only) majority vote with two rounds, for a five-year term which can be renewed only once (articles 6 and 7 of the Constitution). A number of other points are traditionally associated with the study of the presidential election. These points concern the eligibility of the candidate, the support system around the candidate, and the rules governing the electoral campaign. These points also include the rules governing the voting system and how electoral disputes are dealt with. Generally, it is preferable that only candidates who have, if not necessarily chances of success, at least a national dimension representing strongly identified political ideas, run for the presidential election. Concerning eligibility requirements, the candidate must be a French national, be at least 18 years of age (23 years of age until 2011), without any prior conviction that would make him/her ineligible, and in compliance with his/her military, now civic,[80] obligations.[81] Given the solemnity of the office of the President, the other significant requirement is the obligation to obtain 500 endorsements (*parrainages*) from elected officials. Such an endorsement or sponsorship system aims at filtering candidacies so that only the most serious ones can enter the presidential race. The *parrainages* system has been criticised for various reasons (see Box 5.2 The system of *parrainages*). Among other reasons, such a system has tended to encourage some degree of manipulation when, for example, a candidate incites local representatives to endorse another candidate in order to weaken a third candidate, often a serious opponent. Another eligibility requirement is the obligation for the candidate to provide the Constitutional Council with a statement listing his/her assets. Only the statement of the successfully elected candidate is subsequently made public by publication on the website of the High Authority for Transparency in Public Life. The list of presidential candidates is issued by the Constitutional Council after verification of compliance with eligibility requirements. The list is then published in the Official Journal no later than on the sixteenth day preceding the first ballot.

The presidential electoral campaign starts on the day of the publication of the candidates' list and lasts a fortnight for each electoral round. Due to the nature of the presidential election—of national scope and very personalised—the electoral campaign is strictly regulated as regards electoral expenses and the presence of the candidates in the media. Expenses for

79 For these developments, see also Marie-Luce Paris, *Constitutional Law in France*, International Encyclopaedia of Laws (Wolters Kluwer 2024) 95 (para 145).

80 Compulsory military service, also known as conscription, was suspended in 1997 in France. The decision affected all French individuals born after 31 December 1978. The enactment of Law No 97-1019 of 28 October 1997 reforming the national service, is indeed a suspension only. The legislation clearly states that military service can be reinstated through a new law "at any time as soon as the conditions of the defence of the nation or the objectives assigned to the armies so require." In an attempt to revive some form of civic duty, the French government introduced the Universal National Service (*Service National Universel* or *SNU*) in 2018. This *SNU* is mandatory for all teenagers aged 15 to 17, with both a compulsory and an optional period. The "military obligations" now arguably concern only the mandatory part of the *SNU*. At the time of writing, a new reform of the *SNU* is still being discussed.

81 Articles L 1 to L 6, and articles L 9 to L 43 Electoral Code. There are no specific provisions on eligibility concerning the presidential election. General provisions of the Electoral Code apply.

TABLE 5.2 The presidential election in France and in Ireland

	France	*Ireland*
What is the presidential election about?	The election of the President of the French Republic (*Président de la République*) is by direct electoral suffrage for a term of five years. The President can run for another five-year term but may not serve more than two terms. (article 6 of the 1958 Constitution)	The election of the President of Ireland (*Uachtarán na hÉireann*) is by direct universal suffrage for a term of seven years. The President can run for another seven-year term but may not serve more than two terms. (articles 12. 2. 1° and 12. 3. 2° and 3° of the 1937 Constitution)
Who can vote in a presidential election?	To vote in a presidential election, the voter must be: • A French citizen • Aged 18 or over • Ordinarily resident in France (with special arrangements for French nationals residing abroad) • Not deprived of their voting rights • Registered to vote	To vote in a presidential election, the voter must be: • An Irish citizen • Aged 18 or over • Ordinarily resident in Ireland (with special arrangements for citizens on the Postal Voters List) • Registered to vote
Who can run for President?	To be eligible for election, the candidate must be: • A French citizen • Aged 18 years or over • Without any prior conviction that would make the candidate ineligible, and in compliance with military, now civic, obligations • Endorsed by at least 500 elected officials (*parrainages*) (Electoral Code) * The candidate must also declare their candidacy and provide an assets statement to the Constitutional Council.	To be eligible for election, the candidate must be: • An Irish citizen • Aged 35 years or over • Nominated either by at least 20 members of the Oireachtas and four local authorities (former or retiring Presidents can nominate themselves) (articles 12. 4. 1° and 2° of the 1937 Constitution)
How does the presidential election work?	Voting is by secret ballot and based on a single majority vote with two rounds. Voting is in person with possibility of proxy voting under strict conditions.	Voting is by secret ballot and based on proportional representation by the single transferable vote. Voting is in person with possibility of postal voting for certain individuals.
How much can a candidate spend?	The spending limit is 16.8 million euros per candidate in the first round, and 22.5 million euros in the second round, with reimbursement by the state of the public funding depending on the results obtained (i.e., more or less than 5% of the votes). Financial supervision is by the Constitutional Council.	The spending limit is 750,000 euros per candidate, with reimbursement of up to 200,000 euros by the state should the candidate be elected or obtain more than 25% of the quota in the election. Financial supervision is by the Standards in Public Office Commission (SIPO).
Who is the current President?	Emmanuel Macron (2017–2022; 2022–present) re-elected	Michael D. Higgins (2011–2018; 2018–present) re-elected

the presidential election campaign are capped.[82] Since 2009, electoral expenditures have been limited to 16,851,000 euros per candidate in the first round, and to 22,509,000 euros per candidate in the second round, with the possibility of updating these limits according to the cost-of-living index.[83] The presidential candidates may receive public funding and private funding. Concerning public funding, each candidate receives a flat-rate reimbursement depending on the results obtained (i.e., more or less than 5% of the votes). Concerning private funding, each candidate can collect such funding but donations and other benefits from legal persons, such as private companies and entities, are prohibited. Legal persons, except political parties or groups, are not allowed to fund a candidate's election campaign. Individual donations are limited to 4,600 euros per donor. Since 2017, only French nationals or (natural) persons residing in France can donate to a candidate. Each presidential candidate is responsible for appointing a special association or agent to manage campaign expenses as well as for providing a campaign account, which must extend to accounts held in the 12 months preceding the ballot. The Constitutional Council reviews the campaign accounts.

The principle governing media presence of the presidential candidates is that of *equality* of treatment from the public authorities. The principle applies to all candidates under the supervision of the National Commission in Charge of Controlling the Electoral Campaign relating to the Election of the President of the Republic (*Commission Nationale de Contrôle de la Campagne Électorale relative à l'Élection du Président de la République* or *CNCCEP*).[84] The Commission ensures the smooth running of the presidential campaign, in particular the preservation of the free expression of suffrage and fairness between the candidates standing for election. The same equality principle applies to the expression of candidates in the audio-visual media under the control of *Arcom*. While still based on the principle of political pluralism, the principle of *equity* has replaced the principle of equality in terms of airtime and speaking time in the period lasting from the publication of the candidates' list until the eve of the official 15-day presidential campaign.[85] Under the principle of equity, only the last two weeks before the election are subject to the rule of equal airtime and speaking time in radio and television media. This principle does not apply to social networks (e.g., Facebook/Metaverse, YouTube, LinkedIn, Twitter etc.) despite these being widely used by candidates (see Box 5.3 The presidential election campaign and social media).[86]

The presidential election takes place in two rounds. To be elected in the first round, a candidate must obtain an absolute majority of the votes cast (i.e., more than half of the votes). The

82 Constitutional Law No 62-1292 of 6 November 1962 on the election of the President of the Republic by universal suffrage, as amended by Organic Law No 2012-272 of 28 February 2012 relating to the reimbursement of campaign expenditures for the presidential election.

83 Decree No 2009-1730 of 30 December 2009 increasing the limit of election expenditures.

84 Article 13 of Decree No 2001-213 of 8 March 2001 implementing Law No 62-1292 of 6 November 1962 relating to the election of the President of the Republic by universal suffrage.

85 Organic Law No 2016-506 of 25 April 2016, as complemented by Law No 2016-508 of 25 April 2016, on the modernisation of various provisions applicable to the elections. See also the specific recommendations adopted by *Arcom* for the 2022 presidential election in its recommendation No 2021-03 of 6 October 2021 in relation to audio-visual communication services which supplements the general rules previously laid down.

86 See, for example, Fabienne Greffet, Stéphanie Wojcik & Gersende Blanchard, "S'engager dans la campagne présidentielle : Les formes multiples de la participation politique en ligne" (2014) 3 *Politiques de communication* 25; Fabienne Greffet & Stéphanie Wojcik, "Exploring Online Participation: The Case of the 2012 French Presidential Election Campaign" (2018) *Comunicazione Politica*.

second round is only between the two candidates who have obtained the highest number of votes in the first round (article 7 paragraph one of the Constitution). This is to ensure that the successful candidate obtains a consistent and solid majority in the final round. The results of the presidential election are proclaimed by the Constitutional Council (see Figure 5.2 Presidential election results in 2017 and 2022). The election can be disrupted by several occurrences such as the death of one of the candidates or other events preventing a candidate from participating in one of the election rounds. Constitutional provisions lay down the rules concerning such incidents, whether these occur before the declaration of candidacies, or in between this declaration and the first round, or in between the two rounds (article 7 paragraphs five, six, seven, and eight of the Constitution). The litigation of the presidential election is entrusted with the Constitutional Council (article 58 of the Constitution). The Council exercises its judicial review over the regularity of the presidential elections wherever appropriate, when a referral is made by the prefect regarding any alleged irregularity committed in the department or when a referral is made by any candidate regarding any alleged irregularity relating to electoral operations. The Council may also exercise its review on its own initiative, notably as a result of duly reported complaints by electors.

MACRON – LE PEN 2017	**66.10%** – 33.90% **20,743,128** – 10,638,475 votes cast	*registered voters 47,568,693 **25.44% abstention of registered voters
MACRON – LE PEN 2022	**58.55%** – 41.45% **18,768,639** – 13,288,686 votes cast	*registered voters 48,752,339 **28.01% abstention of registered voters

FIGURE 5.2 Presidential election results in 2017 and 2022

Source: Ministère de l'Intérieur et des Outre-mer, <https://www.archives-resultats-elections.interieur.gouv.fr/resultats/presidentielle-2022/FE.php> and <https://mobile.interieur.gouv.fr/Archives/Archives-elections/Election-presidentielle-2017/Resultats-globaux-du-second-tour-de-l-election-du-President-de-la-Republique-2017>

Parliamentary elections. The electoral regime of deputies and senators is determined by law. Article 34 of the Constitution prescribes that the law shall lay down the rules with respect to "the electoral regime of the Houses of Parliament, [of local assemblies and representative bodies of French nationals established outside France, as well as the terms and conditions for electoral mandates and elective offices held by members of deliberative assemblies in the local authorities]." Besides, an organic law was adopted in 2009 to implement article 25 of the Constitution, which covers the duration of parliamentary terms, the number of parliament members, their remuneration, eligibility criteria, and rules regarding ineligibility and conflicts of interest.[87] There have been calls, albeit to no avail so far, to constitutionalise the rules governing elections in Parliament so that these rules do not depend on the majority in power. The electoral framework for Parliament has remained relatively unchanged since the

87 Organic Law No 2009-38 of 13 January 2009 implementing article 25 of the Constitution. The provisions of the 2009 Organic Law are incorporated into various provisions of the Electoral Code.

establishment of the Fifth Republic, with only a few modifications made during the first term of President Mitterrand (1981–1988) concerning the National Assembly. Although having the same status, deputies and senators are elected according to different rules.

The legislative elections. The 577 deputies of the National Assembly are elected for five years by direct electoral suffrage.[88] To stand for election in the National Assembly, the candidate must fulfil the same requirements as the elector as well as being eligible to run for election. Notably, the candidate must be over 18 years of age and must enjoy all his/her civil and political rights, as well as not have been declared ineligible in law (see above). In practical terms, a candidate must declare that s/he is running for a seat in the National Assembly to the prefect of the department of his/her constituency. Besides, any candidate must stand for election together with his/her substitute member in case s/he is later called to exercise other functions incompatible with his/her parliamentary mandate. When presenting their candidate, political parties must ensure respect of the gender equality principle at risk of facing financial penalties. Candidates are elected from within a department constituency. In this regard, the determination of electoral boundaries is key. Such determination is guided by the principle of equality of suffrage, meaning that the National Assembly must be elected "on an essentially demographic basis."[89] As a consequence, the boundaries of electoral constituencies are reviewed at regular intervals in order to take into account demographic changes. Since the 2008 constitutional amendment, a public opinion is sought from an independent commission concerning any change in constituency boundaries and the correlative distribution of seats within the National Assembly.[90] The last division of electoral constituencies was made in 2010 with a few changes: out of the 577 seats in the National Assembly, 556 are allocated to the departments, ten to the overseas territories, and 11 to the constituencies concerning French nationals abroad. The 2010 division was used in the 2012, 2017, and 2022 legislative elections. As for the voting system, deputies are elected in a two-round single majority voting system.[91] To be elected in the first round, a candidate must obtain an absolute majority of the votes cast and represent at least 25% (i.e., one-fourth) of the registered voters. To stand for election in the second round, a candidate must have obtained at least 12.5% of the votes cast of the registered voters in the

88 The number of deputies is fixed in the Constitution since the 2008 constitutional amendment under article 24 paragraph three of the Constitution.

89 Decision No 86-218 DC of 18 November 1986 *Loi relative à la délimitation des circonscriptions pour l'élection des députés*, pt 7.

90 The independent commission on constituency boundaries comprises one member appointed by the President of the Republic, one member appointed by the president of the National Assembly, one member appointed by the president of the Senate, a judge from the Council of State elected by his/her peers, a judge from the Court of Cassation elected by his/her peers, and one member from the Court of Auditors elected by his/her peers. The commission is chaired by a president appointed by the President of the Republic pursuant to the procedure under article 13 of the Constitution. See Law No 2009-39 of 13 January 2009 relating to the commission provided for under article 25 of the Constitution and to the election of deputies.

91 In 1986, the traditional two-round majority voting system was briefly set aside by Mitterrand. Struggling to maintain political support, he opted to switch to a proportional representation voting system for the legislative elections that year. See Law No 85-890 of 10 July 1985 amending the electoral code and relating to the election of deputies (proportional representation change) and Law No 86-825 of 11 July 1986 relating to the election of deputies and authorising the government to delimit electoral constituencies by ordinance, followed by Law No 86-1197 of 24 November 1986 relating to the delimitation of constituencies for the election of deputies (change back to the majority voting system).

first round. The candidate who is eventually elected is the one who obtains the majority of the votes cast. As for the electoral campaign, the rules are very similar to those of the presidential election in terms of electoral expenses and use of media (see above). The funding of the legislative electoral campaign is strictly regulated.[92] The year before the election and before any fundraising, the candidate must appoint a designated financial agent (i.e., natural person or association). The financial agent is tasked with entering all the funds raised during the campaign into a dedicated bank account, with recording the candidate's income (including donations and funding by political parties) and expenditure, as well as with managing all expenses generally. The campaign account cannot be in deficit. The campaign account is forwarded, two months after the election, to the National Commission for Campaign Accounts and Political Financing. Natural persons may contribute to campaign fundraising by making donations, albeit capped at 4,600 euros for the entire campaign. Campaign expenses are capped according to the number of inhabitants and are, for legislative elections, capped at 38,000 euros per candidate (plus 0.15 euro per inhabitant of the constituency). This limit is updated each year according to the cost-of-living index. If this limit is exceeded, the campaign accounts may be subject to rejection by the Commission, which leads to the non-reimbursement of electoral expenses as well as, as appropriate, the ineligibility of the candidate for the next three years. Under certain conditions, the state will reimburse electoral expenses: the candidate must have obtained at least 5% of the votes cast;[93] these expenses must be electoral expenses (i.e., official leaflets, posters on electoral boards, and bulletins); and the candidate's campaign account must have been approved by the Commission. The reimbursement amount is a fixed reimbursement by the state equal to 47.5% of the capped expenses. The date of the legislative elections is determined by reference to the parliamentary term (article 25 of the Constitution). The parliamentary term is fixed as a five-year term, except in the event of a dissolution, in which case the legislative elections are held no sooner than 20 days and no later than 40 days after that dissolution (article 12 paragraph two of the Constitution).[94] The litigation concerning legislative elections is entrusted with the Constitutional Council. The Council intervenes once the election is over (i.e., after the two rounds of the election) and only if there is a dispute as regards an alleged electoral irregularity (e.g., doubt expressed about the eligibility of a candidate). Judicial review by the Council covers not only any irregularity about the vote itself but also any irregularity about the overall electoral operations.[95] All registered voters and all candidates may bring proceedings before the Council, and their appeal has no suspensory effect. The Council rules on the matter within ten days of the announcement of the election results by either dismissing the appeal or by annulling, or reforming, the election results.

The electoral system of the National Assembly has resulted in stable majorities which have contributed to the bipolarisation of political life as mentioned above. However, small political formations have regularly pushed for some degree of proportional voting in the legislative

92 Organic Law No 2011-410 of 14 April 2011 on the election of deputies and senators.

93 Presidential candidate Pécresse faced a significant defeat in the initial round of the 2022 presidential election, failing to secure even 5% of the votes. However, she sparked controversy by reaching out to her supporters and the general public, requesting assistance in recouping approximately five million euros that she had personally invested in her campaign.

94 Article LO 121 of Organic Law No 2001-419 of 15 May 2001 modifying the end of the mandate and powers of the National Assembly.

95 Decision No 81-1 ELEC of 11 June 1981 *Monsieur François DELMAS*.

elections to arguably ensure a better representation of the diversity of political affiliations and hence of the citizens. This is especially true as regards the 12.5% threshold rule, which has the effect of eliminating modest political parties before the second round. The proportional voting system was used on one occasion only, in the 1986 legislative elections. Mitterrand's decision to restore proportional representation for the first time in 30 years raised fears of a return to the parliamentary instability of the Fourth Republic. That was also a cause for political outrage since the opposition accused him of wanting to strengthen the National Front (*Front National*, ancestor of *Rassemblement National*) in order to weaken the Republican Right, which was faring favourably in the polls. Indeed, proportional representation was the only electoral system which was considered likely to allow the election of *FN* deputies. This is eventually what happened: the *FN* was able to form a parliamentary group for the first time with 35 elected members. This also marked the start of the first cohabitation under the Fifth Republic when the right-wing coalition eventually won the election. More recently, several attempts have been made to put forward a system combining majority voting with a dose of proportional voting. One such proposal was made in 2012 by the Commission on the Renewal and Ethics in Public Life (*Jospin Commission*), which proposed that a small portion (i.e., 58 out of 577, that is, around 10%) of deputies be elected by a list voting system with proportional representation.[96] The Philippe Government (2017–2020) made a more ambitious proposal by recommending that 15% of deputies be elected by proportional voting.

The senatorial elections. The 348 senators of the Senate are elected for six years, with partial renewal every three years.[97] The election is by indirect universal suffrage by an electoral college. The electoral college consists of elected representatives comprising deputies, regional councillors, departmental councillors, and delegates of local councils. In line with the role of the Senate, which is to represent "the local authorities of the Republic" (article 24 paragraph four of the Constitution), the composition of the electoral college ensures, in each department, the representation of the different categories of local authorities and the diversity of the municipalities, taking into account the population residing therein.[98] The eligibility requirements for senators are the same as for deputies except the minimum age, which is fixed at 24 years. The voting system varies according to the number of senators to be elected in any constituency, namely a majority two-round system for the constituencies presenting one or two candidates, and a proportional voting system at the highest average, without combined or preferential vote, for the constituencies presenting three or more candidates. Such a voting system reflects the intention of the constituent power to feature local representation in the Upper House of Parliament. The senatorial elections must comply with the same kind of rules as the legislative elections on electoral campaign funding, appointment of a financial agent, campaign accounts, and expenditure limits, albeit with a few adaptations. While litigation concerning the election of senators is entrusted with the Constitutional Council because it involves an election

96 Decree No 2012-875 of 16 July 2012 on the creation of a commission for the renovation and deontology of public life. See Commission de rénovation et de déontologie de la vie publique, *Pour un renouveau démocratique*, November 2012, accessible at <http://www.ladocumentationfrancaise.fr/var/storage/rapports-publics/124000596.pdf>.

97 The number of senators is fixed in the Constitution since the 2008 constitutional amendment under article 24 paragraph four of the Constitution.

98 Law No 2013-702 of 2 August 2013 relating to the election of senators.

of national dimension, litigation concerning the electoral college of senatorial delegates is entrusted with the administrative courts, with an appeal before the Constitutional Council.

Due to its indirect election process and limited powers, the Senate has faced ongoing criticism. The combination of a lengthy mandate and the overrepresentation of rural conservative municipalities have led to a predominantly right-wing majority, with only a brief left-wing majority from 2011 to 2014. This has led to the Senate being seen as a conservative institution, seemingly out of touch with people's concerns. The following quotes reveal how problematic the image carried over by the Senate in the history of the French Republic has been: "The Senate is an assembly of men with fixed ideas fortunately corrected by a high mortality rate";[99] "[a] House [of Parliament] such as the Senate (...) is an anomaly in contemporary democracies."[100] However, and after being reformed on a number of occasions,[101] the Senate continues to serve as a valuable political counterbalance to the National Assembly.

The elections to the European Parliament. The EP elections differ from national elections in that they do not aim to select representatives of sovereign nations. While no specific mention is made in the Constitution, European elections are governed by law.[102] However, in terms of politics, European elections share similarities with domestic elections, as they involve direct universal suffrage and the participation of similar political parties. The European elections involve a party-list proportional representation system, with no combination or preferential voting, in a single national constituency. French candidates' seats in the EP are allocated based on the percentage of votes each list receives, requiring a minimum of 5% to be eligible. The main feature of the European elections is the historically high rate of abstention. Despite a steady decline in voter turnout from 1979 to 2014, there has been a resurgence in participation in recent years with 42.6% turnout in 2014 and 50.6% in 2019. Projections suggest an even higher turnout of over 65% in the 2024 European elections.[103] Another notable feature of European elections at the national level is the rise of the far-right National Rally party, which emerged as the leading party in both the 2014 and 2019 elections.[104]

The status of elected officials. Elected officials (i.e., deputies, senators, mayors, various local councillors) enjoy a specific status. Such a status is not about regulating their political practice but about ensuring that elected officials enjoy certain rights. For a long time, the status of elected officials was not regulated under French law because of the different conceptions regarding the role of public representatives. Some believed that holding a public mandate did not necessitate particular attention let alone required any sort of remuneration, whereas others

99 Edgar Faure (1908–1988), Prime Minister (1952, and 1955–1956).

100 Lionel Jospin, Prime Minister (1997–2002).

101 The first of these reforms occurred in 1969 when De Gaulle put to referendum a proposal with a view to merge the Senate with the Economic and Social Council at the time into a purely consultative body with no veto power. The reform failed after a negative vote.

102 Law No 77-729 of 7 July 1977 relating to the election of representatives to the European Parliament, as amended by Law No 2018-509 of 25 June 2018 relating to the election of representatives to the European Parliament.

103 Eurobarometer, *EP Spring 2023 Survey: Democracy in Action: One Year Before the European Elections*, June 2023.

104 The National Rally obtained 23% of the votes cast and won 23 EP seats on a list led by the (young) successor of Marine Le Pen in 2019.

believed that regulating their mandate would make them "professional politicians" at odds with democratic principles. Nevertheless, while such a debate has largely abated since it started in the eighteenth century, affording a status to elected officials has emerged as a necessity for two main reasons. Firstly, because elected officials exercise elective public functions, they need to be competent and well trained to deal with public affairs, especially given the rise in legislative activity and the ever-increasing delegation of powers in the context of decentralisation. Secondly, the number of local elective mandates has increased considerably under the successive decentralisation reforms, approximating 520,000 local elected officials in 2022 (i.e., more than 1,900 regional councillors, just over 4,000 departmental councillors, and more than 500,000 local municipal councillors). A certain level of political distrust and the necessity to improve political accountability and transparency also explain the necessity to frame the legal mandate of the *élus*. A set of four laws, spanning the period 1990–2019, encapsulates the legal framework of the status of elected officials, all aimed at conciliating the obligations attached to their mandates with the enjoyment of a proper allowance and social protection, as well as the right to vocational training.[105] This legal framework has contributed to boosting local democracy by allowing citizens to run for, and be elected in, local elections without abandoning their profession. The discrepancies between local elected officials can indeed be significant. There is nothing in common, for example, between the mayor of Paris, or the president of a region, who benefit from a very generous allowance (i.e., gross monthly remuneration of 5,837.01 euros, as of July 2022), and the thousands of local officials who earn much less (e.g., 241.53 euros for local councillors of municipalities of fewer than 100,000 inhabitants, as of July 2022) who often have to cumulate their public role with a regular job.

BOX 5.2 THE SYSTEM OF *PARRAINAGES*

The endorsement system (or *parrainages* system) aims at limiting the number of candidacies by ruling out the most fanciful ones. During the first three presidential elections by direct universal suffrage, the endorsement of 100 elected officials was required. This rule effectively limited the number of candidates for the elections of 1965 (six candidates) and 1969 (seven candidates), but less so in 1974 (12 candidates). The endorsement legal regime has been reviewed several times, notably in 1976, which increased the number of signatures to *500*. The last two changes were made by two organic laws in 2016 and 2021.

The term "endorsement" (sometimes referred to as "sponsorship") may not be the most appropriate phrase to use, as it more accurately represents an individual "nomination" of the candidate by an elected official. Interestingly, the person being nominated does not necessarily have to have previously expressed their desire to run for President.

The elected officials authorised to endorse a candidate pertain to several representative institutions. These elected officials are deputies, senators, and EP members, as well as the different categories of local representatives such as mayors (including mayors of the Paris, Lyon, and Marseille *arrondissements*), departmental and regional councillors, and the councillors

105 Law No 92-108 of 3 February 1992 relating to the conditions for exercising local offices; Law No 2002-276 of 27 February 2002 relating to local democracy; Law No 2015-366 of 31 March 2015 aimed at facilitating the exercise, by local elected representatives, of their mandate; and Law No 2019-1461 of 27 December 2019 relating to the involvement in local life and the proximity of public action.

of Paris and the metropolis of Lyon. The list also includes a number of elected representatives of specific territorial entities such as the territorial councillors of Saint-Barthélemy, Saint-Martin, and Saint-Pierre-et-Miquelon; the elected members of the assemblies of Corsica, French Guyana, Martinique, French Polynesia, the provincial assemblies of New Caledonia, and the territorial assembly of Wallis-and-Futuna; and the president of the executive council of Corsica, the president of the executive council of Martinique, the president of French Polynesia, and the president of the government of New Caledonia. Lastly, the advisers to the Assembly of French nationals living abroad or the presidents of the consular councils can also endorse presidential candidates. This list amounted to some 47,000 elected officials in 2022.

In order to prevent candidates from only representing their local interests, the rule of 500 endorsements requires that endorsements come from a minimum of 30 diverse departments or overseas territories, with no more than one-tenth coming from the same department. The process of endorsing candidates is overseen by the Constitutional Council. The complete list of endorsements is released at least eight days prior to the initial ballot on the Council's website and in the Official Journal.

The endorsement system is the object of recurrent debate. Critics argue that despite the reforms implemented in 1976, the system has failed to curb the increasing number of candidates vying for an endorsement, with the number reaching 16 in 2002. Additionally, there are concerns that the system does not allow for the inclusion of popular candidates who may not be part of the established political network. There is also the issue of potential pressure on smaller municipality mayors from candidates seeking their endorsement, as well as the unsavoury possibility of elected officials haggling over their support. The Constitutional Council noted that the endorsement of a candidate is "a personal and voluntary act, which cannot give rise to bargaining or remuneration."

Several reforms have been proposed to improve the current system. Some of them are listed below:

- A radical approach: To establish a committee comprised of around 100,000 elected officials. These officials would then vote in secret to choose the candidates they want to see in the election.
- An improved approach: To increase the requirements for endorsements, such as raising the number of signatures needed to 1,000. Additionally, ensuring the secrecy of endorsements can help prevent any undue influence on certain local elected officials.
- A different approach: The introduction of a citizen endorsement system. In this system, candidates would need to gather a minimum of 150,000 endorsements from citizens in order to be eligible to compete.

BOX 5.3 THE PRESIDENTIAL ELECTION CAMPAIGN AND SOCIAL MEDIA

The principle is the complete ban on any paid advertising on social media platforms.

In other words, it is not permitted by law to pay for ads on social networks six months before a presidential election to target specific groups of people with sponsored messages. This prohibition is applicable to all candidates running for any election. In July 2023, the National Commission for Campaign Accounts and Political Financing, anticipating the European elections of June 2024, clarified that candidates cannot register, in the six months preceding the election, for Twitter Blue, for example, as the Commission considers that subscription to the social network, during the election period, "is a new form of paid advertising." Despite this restriction, candidates running for presidential elections have shown a strong inclination towards using social media to reach a wider audience with their campaign messages.

This issue came to light during the 2022 presidential election when President Macron, after announcing his candidacy in March 2022 through a letter addressed to the French people posted on his official social media accounts, transformed his social media presence from that of the "President of the French Republic" to that of "a presidential candidate seeking re-election."

The National Commission in Charge of Controlling the Electoral Campaign relating to the Election of the President of the Republic issued a statement on 28 February 2022 regarding the use of social media accounts by candidates in their campaign for the presidential election. The Commission recalled the general principles applicable to the electoral campaign, particularly the strict prohibition on using public resources during the campaign period. Furthermore, the Commission highlighted the importance of ensuring that candidates' social media accounts are not utilised in a manner that blurs the lines between their official duties and campaign activities. To address this concern, the Commission recommended that separate accounts dedicated solely to the electoral campaign should be created if the candidate or their supporters had been extensively using personal accounts to communicate messages related to their public role. Additionally, candidates were advised to ensure that no public resources are used for managing the personal social media accounts specifically created for the presidential campaign. This was to uphold the integrity of the electoral process and prevent any potential misuse of public funds in the pursuit of electoral objectives.

However, the matter was not settled. Macron's campaign team found a way to circumvent the Commission's recommendations. While Macron had created social networks accounts specifically for the electoral campaign (e.g., "Emmanuel Macron avec vous" @avecvous on Twitter), these were much less followed than those of Macron's official accounts as President of the Republic. Macron's team therefore opted to have their accounts on Twitter, Facebook/Metaverse, and Instagram entirely managed by the campaign team, with campaign resources, and posting mainly messages concerning the campaign. In the event of significant international news (i.e., the war in Ukraine from 24 February 2022), it had been agreed that "diplomatic messages" might be published but written by the community managers of the campaign team, and no longer by the *Élysée*. Political opponents were not satisfied and continued to allege that Macron's campaign team had been using accounts that had been funded by the *Élysée* services for the past five years, which ultimately benefited the presidential candidate. More information was subsequently requested from the Commission to provide further clarity on the matter.

In a press release on 11 March 2022, regarding guidelines for conducting election campaigns on social media, the Commission reiterated its stance from February 2022. In particular, the Commission noted that a tweet from the account @EmmanuelMacron, announcing his candidacy in the form of a "Letter to the French people," was considered part of the election campaign. Due to the account's history of primarily sharing messages related to the presidency, it was advised not to use it for campaign purposes. The Commission advised the candidate to delete the tweet and use a separate account specifically created for the presidential campaign instead.

Referendums

De Gaulle made extensive use of the referendum. He resorted to it on five occasions between 1958 and 1969 to hold three constitutional referendums, in 1958 (adoption of the 1958 Constitution), in 1962 (election of the President of the Republic by universal direct suffrage), and in 1969 (reform of the Senate and creation of the regions), and two legislative referendums on Algeria, in 1961 (self-determination) and in 1962 (independence). De Gaulle's successors have used it as much in total: Pompidou in 1972 (EEC enlargement), Mitterrand in 1988 (New Caledonia Agreements) and 1992 (Maastricht Treaty), and Chirac in 2000 (five-year presidential term reform) and 2005 (Treaty establishing a Constitution for Europe)—Giscard d'Estaing did not use it at all. No referendum has been held under the last three Presidents (Sarkozy, Hollande, and, so far, Macron). The decline in the use of the referendum in France can be explained by the change in its political significance especially marked by a Gaullist use in the early years of the Fifth Republic. De Gaulle had a strong stance as regards why and how he would use such an instrument of direct democracy and was ready to gamble away his mandate by asking the French people for their trust even if that meant facing the consequences of a negative result in the referendum vote. This is what happened when the French people voted "No" (at 52.4%) in the 1969 referendum on government decentralisation and reform of the Senate, leading to De Gaulle's resignation. However, linking the referendum vote and their political responsibility has not been the approach adopted by De Gaulle's successors, and no other President of the Republic has resigned as a result of a negative referendum. Besides, as a tool of direct democracy, the referendum is difficult to handle for the political power especially because of its limited scope under French constitutional law. De Gaulle widened the scope of the referendum by using, controversially, article 11 of the Constitution to conduct constitutional reforms. However, his successors were more hesitant to do so given the difficulty in finding an appropriate topic and suitable question to put to a referendum, as exemplified by Mitterrand's attempt in 1984 to use article 89 of the Constitution to revise article 11, or Chirac's intention in the early 2000s to hold a referendum on education but without being able to find the right question for it. It seems that both the wider scope of article 11, which now extends to environmental policy, and the introduction of a referendum of shared initiative, have not contributed to reviving referendum use. This subsection assesses the use of the article 11 referendum and of local referendums under various provisions of the Constitution. It does not deal with the article 89 referendum on the constitutional amendment procedure, which is examined in Chapter 3 (see Box 5.4 National referendums in France since the 1789 Revolution).

The referendum of article 11 of the 1958 Constitution.[106] The Constitution provides for a referendum under article 11, allowing the President of the Republic to submit government bills or private members' bills to a public vote. These bills can relate to "the organisation of public powers" or with "reforms relating to the economic, social or environmental policy of the Nation and the public services which contribute thereto," or "concerning the ratification of a treaty which, albeit not repugnant to the Constitution, would impact on the functioning of the institutions" (article 11 paragraph one of the Constitution). The bill in question can either originate from a government proposal during a parliamentary session or a joint proposal from both Houses of Parliament. In an effort to enhance semi-direct democracy, the 2008 constitutional amendment introduced the possibility of the "referendum of shared initiative" (*référendum d'initiative partagée*) between Parliament and the citizens (article 11 paragraph three of the Constitution). This initiative requires support from one-fifth of Parliament members and one-tenth of the registered electorate and cannot aim to repeal a law enacted less than a year ago.[107]

There are a few points of procedure about article 11. Firstly, there is an obligation to have a debate in Parliament should the proposal come from the government, which is generally the case, but also, logically, should the proposal emanate from both Houses of Parliament. The decision to follow through a governmental proposal or a parliamentary proposal for an article 11 referendum is a discretionary power of the President of the Republic. Such a decision does not require the approval of the Prime Minister or of the government. Thus, theoretically, if the initiative is *really* from the government or from Parliament, the President can refuse to put the proposal to a referendum, although this would put him/her in a difficult political position. If, on the contrary, it is the President who wishes to put a proposal to a referendum under article 11 but his/her government refuses (hypothesis of a cohabitation), the political hurdle may be insurmountable. The same would be true in the eventuality of opposition by the National Assembly. The situation is different concerning the referendum of shared initiative since the President seems to have the constitutional obligation to submit the proposal to a referendum (article 11 paragraph five of the Constitution). The voting procedure surrounding article 11 involves, in the first place, the preparation for the vote that is organised by the government that ensures, under the control of the Constitutional Council, the respect of the rules on referendum campaigns notably as regards the use of channels of communication. The voting procedure concerns, in the second place, the actual vote, the result of which is proclaimed by the Constitutional Council. Should the referendum result in the approval of the government bill (or private member's bill) by the French people, the bill will be enacted into law on its

106 These developments on article 11 of the Constitution draw from Marie-Luce Paris, *Constitutional Law in France*, International Encyclopaedia of Laws (Wolters Kluwer 2024) 59–60 (para 80).

107 The other paragraphs of article 11 of the Constitution detail the procedure of the referendum.

promulgation by the President of the Republic within 15 days of the proclamation of the result (article 11 paragraph seven of the Constitution).

Litigation surrounding the article 11 referendum can involve challenges through judicial review at various stages of the referendum process. These stages include decisions regarding the preparation for the referendum, the actual vote, and the implementation of the referendum law. Because of its discretionary nature, the decision of the President of the Republic to resort to the referendum is not subject to any appeal before any court. The Constitutional Council has also ruled itself incompetent to intervene in this matter.[108] Decisions regarding the preparation of the referendum fall under the government's jurisdiction, with oversight by the Constitutional Council according to its *Hauchemaille* case law.[109] The most common legal disputes concerning article 11 focus on the referendum vote itself, whose regularity can be reviewed by the Council (article 60 of the Constitution). Should the Council identify an irregularity pertaining to the referendum operations, it can make the necessary corrections or pronounce the annulation of the referendum result, in part or in whole. In principle, the enacted referendum law is typically immune from judicial review as affirmed by the Council. This law is considered different from ordinary legislation, and it would be problematic indeed to envisage the exercise of judicial review on a law which constitutes "the direct expression of national sovereignty."[110]

In terms of its use, article 11 was used by De Gaulle as a genuine means of communicating with the French people. He also combined this with a more political tactical motive of bypassing Parliament when an agreement with it would be dubious. In other words, article 11 was envisaged by De Gaulle as a way of triggering a vote of confidence in a difficult political situation. De Gaulle resorted to article 11 in relation to constitutional revisions for, paradoxically, two of the most significant constitutional amendments proposed under the Fifth Republic.[111] The first referendum under article 11 was to successfully introduce the election of the President of the Republic by direct universal suffrage in 1962, whereas the second referendum, which failed, was in relation to a bill relating to the regions and the modification of the Senate in 1969. In both instances, the hostility of Parliament towards the constitutional amendments proposed made the article 89 route risky. It appeared to De Gaulle that relying on article 11 was a better option, allowing him to bypass parliamentary opposition.[112] However, amending the Constitution on the basis of article 11 led to heavy criticism at the time. It was claimed that the use of this provision was inappropriate since the provision is primarily concerned with legislative bills. Constitutional amendments could only be carried out via the special procedure provided for under Title XVI of the Constitution on Revision.

108 Decision No 81-1 ELEC of 11 June 1981 *Monsieur François DELMAS*.

109 Decision No 2000-21 REF of 25 July 2000 *Monsieur Stéphane HAUCHEMAILLE*; Decision No 2000-23 REF of 23 August 2000 *Monsieur Pierre LARROUTUROU*; and Decision No 2005-31 REF of 24 March 2005 *Monsieur Stéphane HAUCHEMAILLE et Monsieur Alain MEYET*.

110 Decision No 62-20 DC of 6 November 1962 *Loi relative à l'élection du Président de la République au suffrage universel direct, adoptée par le référendum du 28 octobre 1962*, pt 2.

111 De Gaulle also used article 11 to hold a referendum on the self-determination of Algeria on 8 January 1961, and on the ratification of the Evian Agreements for independence on 8 April 1962. The outcome of both referendums saw a significant majority voting "Yes."

112 As with many other provisions, De Gaulle played a pivotal role in the introduction of article 11 in the Constitution. He believed in the necessity of having a mechanism in place for the President of the Republic to directly seek the opinion of the French people, bypassing the need to involve Parliament in certain circumstances.

On the contrary, proponents of the recourse to article 11 responded that, the French people being sovereign, the expression of their vote could not be subject to any specific procedure and that article 11 derived from article 3 of the Constitution on the sovereignty of the French people. Another argument invoked, albeit on more dubious grounds, was that the use of article 11 for the first time on the occasion of the 1962 referendum had somehow created a constitutional precedent which could be relied upon on the occasion of the 1969 referendum. After a long interruption, other article 11 referendums occurred with mixed results. The 1972 referendum on the accession of the UK, Ireland, and Denmark (and Norway) returned an average result, and the 1988 referendum on New Caledonia was marked by more than 65% abstention. The 1992 referendum on the Maastricht Treaty was a little more convincing with just 51% of "Yes" votes. The rejection of the Treaty establishing a Constitution for Europe in the 2005 referendum has arguably contributed to halting further resort to the referendum procedure. The record high participation rate at nearly 70% stood in contrast with the limited consequences that were faced by the President at the time, who just changed his Prime Minister but did not question the negative result further.

Local referendums. Article 53 of the Constitution provides for the possibility of a local consultation to obtain the consent of the people concerned by any transfer of, exchange of, or addition to, French territory. Progressively, the case law of the Constitutional Council had opened further possibilities of referendums for "the overseas people." Such possibilities were consolidated and given a legal basis by the 2003 constitutional amendment on the decentralised organisation of the Republic.[113] Generally, three types of local referendum regimes can be distinguished: a common type of regime applicable to all local authorities (articles 53 and 72-1 of the Constitution),[114] a regime applicable to overseas territories (articles 72-4 and 73 of the Constitution), and the special regime applicable to New Caledonia (articles 76 and 77 of the Constitution).

Concerning the common regime applicable to all local authorities, a few overseas territories have used the referendum provided for under article 53 of the Constitution. For example, Djibouti (referendums held on 19 March 1967 and 8 May 1977) and the Comoros (referendum held on 22 December 1974) used this method to assert their independence or, conversely, reaffirm their allegiance to the French Republic, as did the inhabitants of the island of Mayotte in the Comoros archipelago (referendum of 8 February 1976).[115] However, there is some uncertainty surrounding article 72-1 of the Constitution, as its implementation requires the passing

113 Constitutional Law No 2003-276 of 28 March 2003 relating to the decentralised organisation of the Republic.

114 This does not include the local consultations organised under article 72-1 paragraph three, which provides that, when it is envisaged to create a local authority with a special status or to modify its organisation, it may be decided by law to consult the voters registered within the local authority concerned. Voters may also be consulted on changes to the boundaries of local authorities under the conditions prescribed by law.

115 For an interpretation of article 53 of the Constitution, see Decision No 75-59 DC of 30 December 1975 *Loi relative aux conséquences de l'autodétermination des îles des Comores*, pts 2–4: "2. Considering that the provisions of [article 53] must be interpreted as being applicable, not only in the event that France cedes to a foreign state or acquires territory from it, but also in the event that a territory ceases to belong to the Republic to constitute an independent state or to be attached to it; 3. Considering that the island of Mayotte is a territory within the meaning of article 53, last paragraph, of the Constitution, this term not having in this article the same legal meaning as in the expression 'Overseas Territory' as used in the Constitution; 4. Considering, therefore, that this island [Mayotte] cannot leave the French Republic without the consent of its own population; …."

of an organic law. This provision, in its paragraph two, authorises a local authority to seek the opinions of voters on proposals or decisions that fall within its jurisdiction.

Concerning the regime applicable to overseas territories, the change of legal regime of such territories, or part of these territories, is made subject to the consultation of the voters concerned (article 72-4 paragraph one of the Constitution). The changes concerned are the ones that allow the passage from one regime to the other, as provided for in article 73 (regime of legislative identity) and article 74 of the Constitution (regime of legislative speciality). Under these provisions, French Guyana and Martinique voted, in a referendum on 24 January 2010, in favour of staying in the framework of article 73, which provides for the passage from an overseas department, or region, into a single overseas territory. This can go both ways, and the case of Mayotte illustrates the passage from a territory to a department when the Mahorais voted, in a referendum on 29 March 2009, in favour of a single-status local authority called the "department of Mayotte," the hundred and first department of France. Such constitutional provisions therefore allow multiple possibilities for differentiation and assimilation of the different territories of the Republic. The question of the accession to independence by these territories is arguably possible under these constitutional provisions although some uncertainties remain. Before the 2003 constitutional amendment on the decentralised organisation of the Republic, independence could be claimed under article 53 of the Constitution and also on the basis of the right of peoples to self-determination under the 1958 Preamble, as affirmed by the case law of the Constitutional Council.[116] Under the current organisation, and because of the express enumeration of overseas territories under article 72-3 of the Constitution, a claim to independence would certainly necessitate a constitutional amendment under article 89, hence a referendum at national level.

New Caledonia presents a unique situation that is covered by Title XIII of the Constitution on Transitional Provisions on New Caledonia (articles 76 and 77 of the Constitution). Currently, New Caledonia has a significant level of autonomy, but falls short of complete constitutional sovereignty. The 1998 Nouméa Agreement set a period of 15 to 20 years as a transition phase, during which the people of Caledonia would have the opportunity to vote on independence through a referendum. Between 2018 and 2021, three self-determination referendums were held. The first referendum took place in 2018, and the victory of the "No" meant that another referendum could be held as provided by the organic legislation envisaging up to three votes in the event of a negative result in the first referendum. The second referendum in 2020 also ended in a "No" outcome, though by a narrower margin.[117] In 2021, the third and final referendum saw a resounding victory for the "No" camp (96.50%), but with a lower turnout (43.87%) due to calls from separatists to boycott the vote. Despite three consecutive referendums rejecting full sovereignty, discussions on the future institutional framework of New Caledonia are ongoing.

116 Decision No 2000-428 DC of 4 May 2000 *Loi organisant une consultation de la population de Mayotte.*

117 In 2020, the votes cast were 53.26% of "No" votes and 46.74% of "Yes" votes, to be compared with 56.7% of "No" votes and 43.3% of "Yes" votes in 2018.

BOX 5.4 NATIONAL REFERENDUMS IN FRANCE SINCE THE 1789 REVOLUTION

August 1793 On the Constitution of Year I
September 1795 On the Constitution of Year III
September 1795 On the Decree concerning the method of re-election of two-thirds of the National Convention (the "Two-Thirds Decree")
January 1800 On the Constitution of Year VIII
June 1802 On the lifetime consulate of Napoléon Bonaparte
June 1804 On the Constitution of Year XII
May 1815 On the additional act to the constitutions of the Empire
20–21 December 1851 On the constitutional proposals of Louis-Napoléon Bonaparte
21–22 November 1852 On the Restoration of the Empire
8 May 1870 On the draft Constitution of 20 April 1870
21 October 1945 On the return to the Third Republic
21 October 1945 On the draft provisional constitutional law
5 May 1946 On the draft Constitution of 19 April 1946
13 October 1946 On the Constitution of the Fourth Republic
28 September 1958 On the Constitution of the Fifth Republic
8 January 1961 On self-determination in Algeria
8 April 1962 On the Evian Accords and the independence of Algeria
28 October 1962 On the election of the President of the Republic by direct universal suffrage
27 April 1969 On the organisation of the regions and the reform of the Senate
23 April 1972 On the enlargement of the European Communities
6 November 1988 On self-determination in New Caledonia
20 September 1992 On the ratification of the Maastricht Treaty
24 September 2000 On the five-year presidential term
29 May 2005 On the ratification of the treaty establishing a Constitution for Europe

SELECTED FURTHER READINGS

Éric **Agrikolliansky**, *Les partis politiques en France* (3rd edn, Armand Colin 2016)
Marion **Ballet** & Olivier Duhamel, *Les élections présidentielles* (Dalloz 2017)
Philippe **Blachèr** & Jean-Éric Gicquel, *Les grands textes de la déontologie de la vie publique* (LGDJ 2017)
Philippe **Blanchetier** & Jérôme Grand d'Esnon, *Le financement des campagnes électorales* (LGDJ 2019)
Christophe **Boutin** & Frédéric Rouvillois, *Le référendum* (La Nouvelle Librairie 2023)
________________________________, *Les parrainages* (La Nouvelle Librairie 2022)
Éric **Buge**, *Droit de la vie politique* (PUF 2018)
Yves-Marie **Doublet**, *Le financement de la vie politique* (2nd edn, PUF 1997)
Maurice **Duverger**, *Les partis politiques* (Collection Points 1981, Armand Colin 1951)
_______________, *La monarchie républicaine, ou comment les démocraties se donnent des rois* (Robert Laffont 1974)
Abel **François** & Éric Philippeau, *Le financement de la vie politique* (Armand Colin 2015)
Aline **Gonzalez**, *Les différentes élections en France* (Gualino 2020)

Jean-François **Kerléo**, Elina Lemaire & Romain Rambaud, *Transparence et déontologie parlementaire: Bilan et perspectives* (LGDJ 2019)
Jacques **Le Bohec** & Christophe Le Digol (eds), *Gauche/Droite: Genèse d'un clivage politique* (PUF 2012)
Michel **Offerlé**, *Les partis politiques* (PUF 2022)
Pouvoirs, *Les clivages politiques*, No 179 (Seuil 2021)
_______, *Les partis politiques*, No 163 (Seuil 2017)
Romain **Rambaud**, *Droit des élections et des référendums politiques* (LGDJ 2019)

6

CONSTITUTIONAL JUSTICE AND RIGHTS PROTECTION

The French judicial system plays a critical role in safeguarding individual freedoms and upholding the rule of law. This essential mission cannot be delegated or surrendered by the state. Serving as a public service on behalf of the French people, the justice system is primarily administered by public courts.[1] Rooted in the ideals of the 1789 Revolution, the French legal system is guided by domestic general principles and laws enacted by Parliament, as well as by European and international legal principles. Following an overview of the French court-system, this chapter will deal with key elements of constitutional justice. This will include a discussion on the role of the Constitutional Council and the process of constitutional review, as well as an examination of the fundamental principles of constitutional justice, as illustrated by pertinent case law.

In terms of principles governing French justice, certain principles of the organisation of the public service find application in the judicial field while other organisational principles are specific to judicial activity. Principles of the public service of justice include the principle of continuity and the principle of hierarchy: the former ensures the permanence of judicial services and severely limits the right to strike in the judiciary, while the latter concerns both the courts and the members of the judiciary as will be explained below. In addition, the public service of justice is structured, in its relations with its users, by a few operating principles such as the principle of equality which is directly linked to that of equality before the law; the principle of gratuity, which does not however exclude the existence of legal costs; and the principle of neutrality—a corollary of the requirement of impartiality and independence—which ensures that

1 As has been the case in many other jurisdictions, the development of processes of alternative dispute resolution (ADR), whereby private parties resolve their disputes without trial, has flourished in recent years, often encouraged by the French legislature. For more details, see Marie-Luce Paris, *Constitutional Law in France*, International Encyclopaedia of Laws (Wolters Kluwer 2024) 139–141 (paras 247–248).

DOI: 10.4324/9781003268871-8

the judge, in his/her application of the rule of law, is not influenced by external pressures or by his/her own opinions. As for the principles specific to judicial activity, these are the principle of collegiality and the principle of separation of functions: the former requires the intervention of several judges to deliberate on most decisions, and the latter is illustrated by the distinction between the two categories of professional judges in the French judicial system, namely the sitting judges and the prosecuting judges as explained below. Other rules specific to justice are the rule of publicity, which allows any citizen to attend most hearings, and the general rule of loyalty in judicial proceedings, which can be attached to the guarantee given to each party that their case will be heard fairly. The requirement of a fair trial is also linked to the principle of the presumption of innocence, the principle of a double level of courts and the possibility of appeal, the adversarial principle, and the principle of non-retroactivity of the law.

Constitutional justice has a specific role in the overall justice system. Constitutional justice aims at protecting freedoms against political power when such power abuses its prerogatives and is exercised in particular through the development of binding standards for citizens. Constitutional justice was at the heart of the reflections of the Enlightenment philosophers, such as Locke and Montesquieu, in the seventeenth and eighteenth centuries,[2] but also at the heart of the reflections of some twentieth-century academics, such as Charles Eisenmann.[3] The movement of constitutionalism addressed much of the questioning around the theoretical and legal bases of modern constitutional justice. In a liberal political system, that is to say, respectful of rights and freedoms, the rulers must be limited in their action by the constitution. As for the state, which produces law, it must also be subject to such limitations: this is called "the rule of law." For this framework to be effective, the public authorities in general, and the executive and legislative powers in particular, must respect the limits set by the constitution, which implies that the various standards are organised according to a hierarchical mode, called hierarchy of norms as explained below.

The French Court-System

> « *Le premier caractère de la puissance judiciaire, chez tous les peuples, est de servir d'arbitre. Pour qu'il y ait lieu à action de la part des tribunaux, il faut qu'il y ait contestation. Pour qu'il y ait juge, il faut qu'il y ait procès.* »[4]

The French court-system is comprised of a variety of courts endowed with various, often specialised, heads of jurisdiction. Its primary purpose is to uphold the law and protect the rights and freedoms of all individuals. The system is organised into three judicial orders: the ordinary judicial order, the administrative judicial order, and the constitutional judicial order. This section focuses on the ordinary and administrative judicial orders, beginning with a description

2 John Locke (1632–1704), English philosopher; Montesquieu (1689–1755), French judge and political philosopher.
3 Charles Eisenmann (1903–1980), French jurist.
4 Alexis De Tocqueville (1805–1859), French politician and political philosopher [The primary feature of judicial power, in all societies, is to act as a mediator. For there to be action by the courts, there must be a dispute. For there to be a judge, there must be a trial].

of the features of the court-system. The constitutional judicial order, responsible for delivering constitutional justice, will be examined in the subsequent sections.[5]

Features of the French court-system

Court-systems typically feature distinct types of courts that operate in a hierarchical order, starting from lower courts to appeal courts and ultimately to supreme courts. In addition to this hierarchical organisation, the French court-system is unique in that it operates on a dual organisation basis (see Figure 6.1 The French court-system). This sets it apart from other legal systems, such as the Irish court system, which follows a single-division structure with five different types of courts, starting with the district courts, the circuit courts, up to the High Court, the Court of Appeal, and the Supreme Court, all working together as a unified judicial body.

Dual judicial organisation. Since the 1789 Revolution, the French court-system has been divided into two orders. The distinction between the two orders is enshrined in the Law of 16–24 August 1790 on judicial organisation, which prohibits ordinary judges from hearing disputes relating to the administration or the work of civil servants.[6] Alongside ordinary courts (*ordre judiciaire*) competent to settle disputes between simple litigants, there are administrative

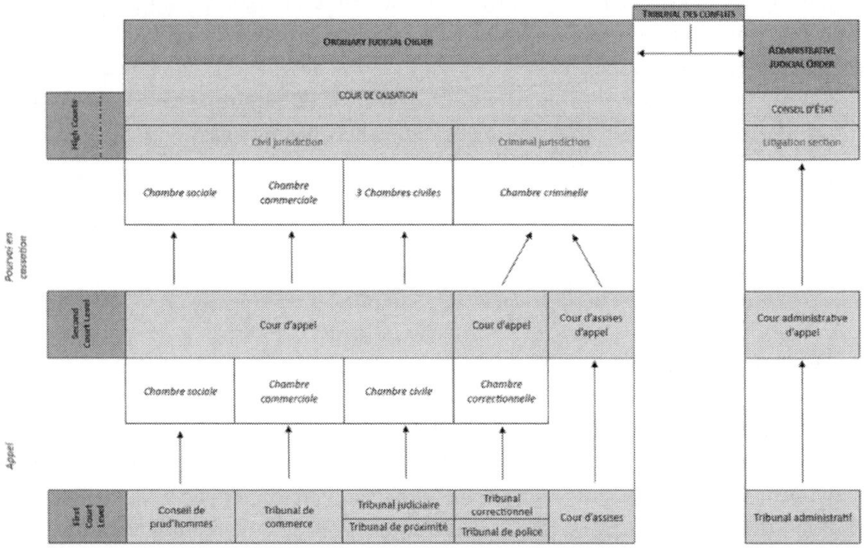

FIGURE 6.1 The French court-system

Source: Le Conseil départemental de l'accès au droit de la Côte d'Or, <https://cdad-cotedor.justice.fr/juridictions/organisation-de-la-justice/lorganisation-des-juridictions-francaises/>

5 Other types of courts exist. Because they are of a regulatory or political nature, they are examined in Chapter 4 on the institutions of the Fifth Republic. These are the Court of Auditors, which is a regulatory court, and the so-called political courts, namely the High Court, which judges the President of the Republic, and the Court of Justice of the Republic, which judges government members.

6 On the historical origins of the separation between the ordinary courts and administrative courts, see Marie-Luce Paris, *Constitutional Law in France*, International Encyclopaedia of Laws (Wolters Kluwer 2024) 141–142 (para 250).

courts (*ordre administratif*) competent to settle disputes between the administration and the citizens. Criminal justice is attached to the ordinary judicial order, albeit its object is to implement public power and enforce the law against particular litigants (i.e., those who have committed crimes). While this model of jurisdictional organisation has been replicated in some European countries, such as Greece or Luxembourg, it remains a peculiarity compared to most other western democracies. This dual organisation explains the existence of a Disputes Court (*Tribunal des Conflits*).[7] Established in 1872, the Disputes Court is a single court which does not belong to any judicial order. It consists of an equal number of members from the two supreme courts of each judicial order, namely the Court of Cassation for the ordinary judicial order and the Council of State for the administrative judicial order. The role of the Disputes Court is to rule on conflicts of jurisdictions between the two judicial orders. Different types of conflicts of jurisdictions may arise, whether it is to determine which court has jurisdiction in the first place or which decision is valid in cases of contrariety of final judgments. A positive conflict may occur when the administration, in the person of the state representative in the department, disputes the competence of an ordinary court to judge a case which has been put before it. On the contrary, a negative conflict is when the courts of each of the two judicial orders have irrevocably declared that they are incompetent to rule on a particular matter, without any of the court having referred the dispute to the Disputes Court. In that case, the interested parties may file a petition with a view to determining which court is competent to settle the dispute.[8] The Disputes Court is also competent in cases of conflicting decisions. Such a situation arises when the final judgments of, respectively, an administrative court and an ordinary court, in proceedings before the two orders of jurisdiction in disputes concerning the same subject matter, present a contrariety which leads to a denial of justice which is prohibited under article 4 of the Civil Code.[9] Also, the Disputes Court has a special competence in the event of excessive lengthy judicial proceedings. In that case, an action for damages may be brought before the Disputes Court if a claim relating to excessively long proceedings in the same litigation and between the same parties before the courts of both orders on account of the applicable rules of jurisdiction has been implicitly or explicitly rejected by the Ministry of Justice.

Hierarchical judicial organisation. Within each judicial order, the tribunals and courts operate in a hierarchy. At the basis are the trial courts or first-level courts (*tribunaux de*

7 The organisation and rules of procedure of the Disputes Court were amended by Law No 2015-177 of 16 February 2015 on the modernisation and simplification of law and procedures in the areas of justice and home affairs.

8 There is also the possibility that a court refers a matter to be decided by a court of the other judicial order after a final judgment has been made, called a "conflict on referral" (*conflit de renvoi*). More specifically, where a court of the ordinary or administrative judicial order has, by a decision which is no longer subject to appeal, declined the jurisdiction of the court to which it belongs on the grounds that the dispute does not fall within that judicial order, any court of the other order, to which the same dispute is referred, if it considers that the dispute arises out of the order of the court to which it was originally referred, must, by a reasoned decision, which is not subject to appeal even in cassation, refer the matter to the Disputes Court and stay proceedings until the jurisdictional matter is resolved by the said Court. The same is true when a court must decide on a case which involves the trial of either an action brought or an exception, a jurisdictional issue raising a serious difficulty involving the separation of the judicial orders. That court may, by a reasoned decision which is not subject to appeal, refer the matter to the Disputes Court for a decision on the question of jurisdiction.

9 Article 4 of the Civil Code: "The judge who refuses to rule, under the pretext of silence, obscurity or insufficiency of the law, may be prosecuted on the indictment of denial of justice."

première instance). The appellate courts or courts of appeal (*cours d'appel*) judge the appeals brought against the decisions taken by the first-level courts. There is no third level of appeal in France, contrary to appearances. At the top of each judicial order, a judge of cassation (*juge de cassation*), namely the Court of Cassation for the ordinary judicial order and the Council of State for the administrative judicial order, is responsible for controlling and harmonising the application of the law by the trial and appeal judges (*juges du fond*). When judicial proceedings reach the Court of Cassation, or the Council of State, via an appeal on points of law filed by the litigant (*pourvoi en cassation*), it is not a matter of judging the case a third time. Rather, the top judge will challenge the decision of the lower court judges on points of law only, that is, determine whether the decision violated the law or not. If the appellate or trial decision has violated the law, the supreme court judge will quash the lower court's decision in a *cassation* decision; if this is not the case, the supreme court judge will reject the cassation appeal in a *rejet du pourvoi en cassation* decision.

The ordinary judicial order

This subsection examines French ordinary courts and the court sitting at the top of the ordinary judicial order, namely the Court of Cassation, as well as the body which guarantees the independence of these courts, namely the Superior Council of the Judiciary.[10]

Ordinary courts. Ordinary courts of law are competent to try civil cases and criminal cases. In civil matters, judicial courts of law (*tribunaux judiciaires*) occupy a central place within the court-system.[11] Judicial courts of law have full competence in civil matters (*juridictions civiles de droit commun*) for all disputes that have not been entrusted to another court (i.e., commercial court, industrial tribunal, or joint tribunal for rural leases) regardless of the value of the dispute. Within this ensemble, certain disputes are entrusted to specialised judges (i.e., family court judge, protection litigation judge). A judicial court of law is seized by summons or by motion. The civil law judge may impose, as appropriate, a prior recourse to mediation. In criminal matters, courts are responsible for defending society by ensuring the repression of offences. Criminal justice is exercised at three levels depending on the category of offence committed. The term "offence" is a generic term that covers all breaches of criminal rules which are classified in increasing order of seriousness into contraventions (*contraventions*),[12] misdemeanours (*délits*),[13] and crimes (*crimes*).[14] Police courts (*tribunaux de police*) are

10 These developments partly draw from Marie-Luce Paris, *Constitutional Law in France*, International Encyclopaedia of Laws (Wolters Kluwer 2024) 142–148 (paras 251–261) and 157–158 (para 278).

11 Law No 2019-222 of 23 March 2019 on programming 2018–2022 and reform for justice. The major 2019 reform merged the former courts, namely the *Tribunaux de Grande Instance* (*TGI*) and the *Tribunaux d'Instance* (*TI*), into these new judicial courts of law. For practical reasons, former *Tribunaux d'Instance* that were not in the city of the headquarters of a *Tribunal de Grande Instance* were not abolished but became local chambers of the judicial court (*chambres de proximité*), except in Paris where there are no such local chambers as all courts are in the same city. There are currently 164 judicial courts of law and 125 local chambers.

12 Contraventions are punishable by a fine of 1,500 euros maximum, or 3,000 euros in the event of a repeat offence.

13 Misdemeanours are punishable by a prison sentence of less than, or equal to, ten years, or by a fine equal to, or of more than, 3,750 euros.

14 Crimes are the most serious offences and are punishable by a prison sentence ranging, depending on the seriousness of the crime, from 15 years to life.

competent in matters of contraventions, correctional courts (*tribunaux correctionnels*) in matters of misdemeanours, and the assize courts (*cours d'assises*) in matters of crimes. Police courts are attached to the civil judicial courts of law and are single-judge courts where a lawyer is not required. Correctional courts rule, in principle, in a public and collegial hearing, but an increasing number of cases are entrusted to a single judge. Representation by a lawyer is not compulsory for defendants and victims. Assize courts are not permanent courts and sit when in session. The opening date of the session is set whenever necessary on a proposal from the public prosecutor, and the list of cases to be heard in a session is decided by the first president of the court of appeal. Assize courts are attached to the department (*département*) and are composed of professional judges and popular jurors drawn by lot. Although their remit is for judging crimes, assize courts have full jurisdiction (*plénitude de jurisdiction*), meaning that they can hear any criminal case that is brought before them.[15] Verdicts of the assize courts can be appealed, and the law also authorises the prosecutor to appeal against judgments of acquittal before an assize court of appeal.

Should a litigant be unsatisfied with the first instance ruling handed down, they have the option to file an appeal. This process involves a second review of the case, known as the principle of double degree of jurisdiction (*double degré de juridiction*). The court of appeal (*cour d'appel*) serves as a higher court that hears appeals against decisions made by lower courts within its jurisdiction, such as judicial courts and a number of specialised courts such as commercial courts and industrial tribunals. The court of appeal assesses both the facts and the law involved in the case to ensure no legal errors have been made. The court may either confirm the original decision by the first judges, in an *arrêt confirmatif*, or overturn it partially or entirely, in an *arrêt infirmatif*. Appeals against the court of appeal's rulings can only be made through a cassation appeal or *pourvoi en cassation*. Courts of appeal, composed solely of professional judges, are divided into chambers and comprise judges called *conseillers*. Each court of appeal is led by a first president and a general prosecutor. The public prosecutor (*ministère public*) is represented in court by the general prosecutor (*procureur général*) or one of their deputies (*avocats généraux* or *substituts généraux*) during hearings before the court of appeal.[16]

The Court of Cassation. The *Cour de cassation* is the highest court of the French ordinary judicial order. The Court of Cassation sits in Paris, on the grounds of the Île de la Cité courthouse. The Court of Cassation is not a third level of jurisdiction. The Court's role is to ensure the correct application of the law by the trial and appeal judges, and to rule on matters of law only, not on the merits of the case.[17] As such, the Court of Cassation ensures the uniform interpretation and application of the law throughout the territory. In the event of *cassation*, that is, when the Court considers that the judge on the merits has not correctly interpreted and applied the law in an *arrêt de cassation*, the Court of Cassation must refer the case to another court of the same

15 To ease their caseload, the 2019 Law authorised, as an experiment for three years, assize courts without jurors. Composed of five professional magistrates, such courts are competent to try crimes punishable by 15- or 20-years' imprisonment, which represent 57% of criminal cases judged.

16 There are currently 36 courts of appeal whose jurisdiction, covering one or more departments, is specific and does not overlap with regional divisions.

17 Law No 2016-1547 of 18 November 2016 on the modernisation of justice in the twenty-first century. This allows the Court of Cassation to rule on the merits of a civil case when the interest of the proper administration of justice justifies it.

nature as the court which ruled on the quashed or "broken" ruling. If, on the contrary, the Court of Cassation dismisses the cassation appeal, it means that it upholds the impugned decision of the lower court in an *arrêt de rejet*. The Court of Cassation has other roles of a consultative and constitutional nature. Under its consultative role, lower ordinary courts may refer to the Court of Cassation for an opinion on a novel point of law which presents a serious difficulty, and which has arisen in numerous disputes.[18] The opinion of the Court of Cassation is not binding, not on the lower courts or on the Court of Cassation itself. However, by clarifying a particular point of law outside the context of a lawsuit, such an opinion may influence lower judges and hence contribute to further stabilising the case law. Under its constitutional role, the Court of Cassation may refer an issue of constitutionality to the Constitutional Council under the *QPC* (*question prioritaire de constitutionnalité*) procedure (see below). The Court of Cassation is organised into six specialised divisions or chambers, five handling civil law disputes and one handling criminal law disputes. There are three civil chambers proper, a commercial chamber and a financial chamber. The First Civil chamber deals with personal and family law, consumer protection, intellectual property, etc.; the Second Civil chamber with civil procedure, social security, elections etc.; the Third Civil chamber with real estate, leases, environment etc. The Commercial Chamber deals with bank, stock exchange, brands etc. The Social Chamber deals with labour law, training, staff representation etc. In the event of conflicts of interpretation between two or more chambers, the Court of Cassation may sit in a joint chamber formation which groups judges from two or more chambers known as *Chambres mixtes*, or it may sit as in a plenary hearing of 19 judges representing the different chambers and presided by the First President of the Court known as the *Assemblée plénière*. Each chamber is composed of a president and counsels, all belonging to the category of the sitting judges. The public prosecutor is represented by the General Prosecutor and substitutes of the General Prosecutor.

The Superior Council of the Judiciary. Originally established under the 1946 Constitution, the Superior Council of the Judiciary (*Conseil Supérieur de la Magistrature* or *CSM*) was re-established under the current Constitution. The *CSM* is the body responsible for assisting the President of the Republic in his/her function as guarantor of the independence of the judicial authority (article 64 paragraph two of the Constitution). As such, the *CSM* is primarily responsible for appointing and managing the careers of members of the judiciary, judges and prosecutors. However, the prominent role initially afforded to the President of the Republic vis-à-vis the *CSM* was greatly diminished by two constitutional amendments, in 1993 and in 2008 respectively: the President no longer chairs the *CSM* nor appoints all of its members; the minister for Justice no longer sits on the *CSM* either.[19] While these reforms have on the whole reinforced the autonomy of the *CSM* in accordance with the separation of powers, between the judicial and the executive powers, they have not dramatically increased the *CSM*'s powers vis-à-vis the executive power notably as regards public prosecutors. The *CSM* consists of two formations: one formation which is competent as regards sitting judges, on the one hand, and

18 Article L 441-1 of the Code of Judicial Organisation. The procedure applies to all ordinary courts, including criminal courts, except investigating courts and assizes courts.

19 Constitutional Law No 93-952 of 27 July 1993 revising the Constitution of 4 October 1958 and amending its Titles VIII, IX, X and XVIII, and Constitutional Law No 2008-724 of 23 July 2008 on the modernisation of the institutions of the Fifth Republic.

another formation which is competent as regards public prosecutors, on the other hand (article 65 of the Constitution). The First President of the Court of Cassation (equivalent to the Chief Justice) presides over the formation of the *CSM* which is competent as regards judges, while the General Prosecutor of the Court of Cassation presides over the formation of the *CSM*, which is competent as regards public prosecutors. Each formation consists of 15 members: the president (i.e., the First President of the Court of Cassation as regards judges, and the General Prosecutor of the Court of Cassation as regards prosecutors), six judges elected by their peers,[20] a member of the Council of State, a legal practitioner, as well as six external highly qualified persons appointed, respectively, by the President of the Republic, the president of the National Assembly, and the president of the Senate. Concerning the appointment of judges, the *CSM* makes proposals concerning high-ranked judges and gives its assent only concerning all other judges who are appointed by the executive power. As far as public prosecutors are concerned, the *CSM* gives its opinion on appointments concerning all public prosecutors, including the most important hierarchical positions, which was not the case before the 2008 constitutional amendment. The *CSM* also deals with disciplinary issues. In that role, the *CSM* sits in full capacity as the disciplinary body as far as judges are concerned.[21] The *CSM* delivers an opinion only on the penalty to be imposed by the minister for Justice as far as prosecutors are concerned. The *CSM* may sit in a plenary formation to consider requests for opinions formulated either by the President of the Republic, in his/her role as guarantor of the independence of the judicial authority, or by the minister for Justice in matters of ethics and good administration of justice.

The administrative judicial order

This subsection examines French administrative courts and the court sitting at the top of the unified administrative judicial system, namely the Council of State.[22]

Administrative courts. Administrative courts rule on disputes between the administration and citizens, as well as disputes between two public bodies. The administration encompasses all state and local authorities, public institutions, and private bodies carrying out public service functions. In every administrative court, a public rapporteur (*rapporteur public*, former *commissaire du gouvernement*) takes part in the proceedings and is responsible for giving, in total independence, his/her assessment on the facts of the case, on the applicable law, and on how the case ought to be decided. Administrative courts can be broadly categorised into those with general jurisdiction and those specialised in specific areas of law. Lower administrative courts (*tribunaux administratifs*) are the ordinary trial courts of first instance that handle disputes between individuals and the administration, as well as on labour disputes in the public sector.[23] Apart from their adjudicative role, administrative courts may offer advice when

20 The composition of the six judges varies based on the *CSM* formation. In the formation involving sitting judges, the *CSM* consists of five sitting judges and one public prosecutor. Conversely in the formation involving public prosecutors, there are five public prosecutors and one sitting judge.

21 One extra sitting judge sits in the disciplinary formation of the *CSM* in that case.

22 These developments partly draw from Marie-Luce Paris, *Constitutional Law in France*, International Encyclopaedia of Laws (Wolters Kluwer 2024) 148–151 (paras 262–267).

23 There are 42 administrative courts in France, at least one per region. The last administrative court established was that of Montreuil in Seine-Saint-Denis in 2009. Administrative courts were established in 1953 and succeeded,

requested by the prefects and other local administrative authorities within their jurisdiction. Typically, administrative courts consist of a panel of three judges, including an investigative judge responsible for examining the case. The proceedings involve two stages, namely an investigative phase and a judgment phase. In the past, the investigation phase was conducted solely in writing, but since January 2023, oral hearings during this phase are permissible.

Administrative courts of appeal (*cours administratives d'appel*) are competent to rule, at the request of a private party or at the request of the administration, on judgments rendered by the lower administrative courts, save a few exceptions in which appeals are directly referred to the Council of State.[24] Administrative courts of appeals are headed by a judge of the Council of State and are divided into chambers. The judgment formation is headed by the president of the chamber and four counsels, namely two chamber counsels, one counsel from another chamber, and a public rapporteur. A number of specific disputes fall under the jurisdiction of specialised administrative courts, at first instance and then on appeal. Their decisions may then be referred to the Council of State, which is the cassation court of the administrative judicial order. Some courts are specialised to rule on disciplinary matters of certain professions, such as the Superior Council of the Judiciary for judges of the ordinary judicial order, and disciplinary sections of professional bodies such as those concerning, for example, architects, auditors, veterinarians, doctors, dental surgeons, pharmacists, or midwives. Other courts are specialised in the litigation of foreign nationals with the task of granting, refusing, or withdrawing refugee status and subsidiary protection (i.e., the national Court of Asylum); others courts are competent in social matters (i.e., departmental committees and central welfare commissions as well as departmental and regional courts for military invalidity pensions), and in financial matters (i.e., regional courts of auditors and the national Court of Auditors, the enforcement committee of the Financial Markets Regulator).

The Council of State. The *Conseil d'État* is the highest court of the French administrative judicial order. The Council of State sits in Paris, in the Palais Royal since 1875, alongside the Constitutional Council.[25] The Council of State has had a pivotal role in maintaining the relationship between the citizens and public authorities and in developing administrative law as a judge-made law based on its seminal decisions.[26] The Council of State has competence to rule on cassation, on appeal, or "in first and last instances" (i.e., the only court hearing

with profound changes, the prefecture councils which had been created in each department by the Law of 28 Pluviôse Year VIII (17 February 1800) concerning the division of the French territory and the administration, which organised the prefectural system. See Law No 53-611 of 11 July 1953 relating to economic and financial recovery and Decree No 53-934 of 30 September 1953 on reforming administrative litigation. Administrative courts are organised and adjudicate in accordance with the provisions of the Code of Administrative Justice.

24 There are nine administrative courts of appeals in France. The ninth administrative court of appeal was established in Toulouse in 2022. Administrative courts of appeals were established in 1987 and are organised and rule in accordance with the provisions of the Code of Administrative Justice. See Law No 87-1127 of 31 December 1987 on reforming administrative litigation.

25 Formally installed in 1799, the Council of State assumed the responsibilities previously held by the King's Council, which, composed of trusted advisers to the monarch, was responsible for managing the affairs of the Kingdom. Post-Revolution, the Council was tasked with upholding the principle of the separation of powers by overviewing a special judicial order to adjudicate on administrative matters.

26 As well as on the decisions of the Disputes Court. See Guy Braibant, Pierre Devolvé, Bruno Genevois, Marceau Long & Prosper Weil (eds), *Les grands arrêts de la jurisprudence administrative* (23rd edn, Dalloz 2021).

the case).[27] The disputes before the Council of State range from disputes concerning public liberties, to disputes on the civil service, administrative police, taxes, public contracts, public health, competition rules, environmental law, and urban and regional development, to name just a few. Firstly, the Council of State is the judge of cassation of the judgments delivered by the administrative courts of appeals. The supreme administrative judge does not judge the dispute a third time but verifies compliance with the rules of procedure and the correct application of the law by the lower administrative courts and the administrative courts of appeals. In that role, and like the Court of Cassation for the ordinary judicial order, the Council of State contributes to the unity of the case law. Secondly, the Council of State is, exceptionally, an appellate judge notably in electoral matters at local level as regards municipal and cantonal elections.[28] Finally, the Council of State has a judicial review competence, in the first and last instances, as regards a number of administrative acts, including decrees and regulatory acts of ministers (e.g., circulars), as well as challenges against EU and regional elections results. Like the Court of Cassation, the Council of State has a constitutional law role and may refer an issue of constitutionality to the Constitutional Council under the *QPC* procedure (see below). The judicial section of the Council of State[29] is composed of ten chambers—called subsections (*sous-sections*)—which are themselves specialised in different areas of public law. Cases posing the least difficulty are delivered by one of the subsections or by two subsections, whereas more complex cases are decided by one of the solemn formations of the Council of State, namely the litigation section (*section du contentieux*) meeting in a court formation, or the litigation assembly (*assemblée du contentieux*) made up of the presidents of all sections including the vice-president of the Council of State.

The status of judges and the independence of the judiciary

The judiciary is known as the "guardian of individual freedom" according to article 66 of the Constitution. However, it is referred to as the judicial *authority* (*autorité judiciaire*) rather than the judicial *power*. The term "authority" has arguably a less commanding connotation than the term "power," highlighting the fact that in France, the judiciary is not on par with the executive and the legislative branches of power. This is due to deep-seated historical distrust from the other branches towards the judiciary.[30] The independence of the judiciary is guaranteed in the Constitution and is entrusted to the President of the Republic, the highest political figure in the state (article 64 of the Constitution). The President is supported in this role by the Superior Council of the Judiciary. However, given the prominent powers afforded to the President of the Republic, this has been problematic as regards the separation of powers principle. Reforms of the Superior Council of the Judiciary relegated the executive power's role, though, and the President of the Republic no longer chairs the Superior Council of the Judiciary. In this con-

27 The Council of State not only serves as a judicial authority but also has an advisory role as seen in Chapter 4 on the institutions of the Fifth Republic.

28 The Council of State was relieved of much of this appellate competence when the administrative courts of appeals were established in 1987.

29 The Council of State includes various administrative sections in its advisory role, as outlined in Chapter 4 on the institutions of the Fifth Republic.

30 For more details, see Marie-Luce Paris, *Constitutional Law in France*, International Encyclopaedia of Laws (Wolters Kluwer 2024) 141–142 (para 250).

text, the judiciary includes all civil, commercial, criminal, and social courts, which, under the supervision of the courts of appeal and the Court of Cassation, adjudicate on matters of private law. However, the status of French judges (*magistrats*) varies, with a distinction made between sitting judges (*magistrats du siège*) and prosecuting judges (*magistrats du parquet*) within the ordinary judicial system, as well as between ordinary and administrative judges.

In terms of comparison, there exist two primary models of judicial systems. In common law countries, where case law is an authoritative source of law, judges are selected from the most distinguished members of the bar. Becoming a professional judge is often seen as the pinnacle of a successful legal career and carries a high level of prestige. On the other hand, in continental law countries, notably France, there is a different approach known as the "career judiciary" (*magistrature de carrière*). Here, junior members are appointed after a rigorous competitive examination process. As a result, professional judges in these countries have a lower level of prestige compared to their counterparts in common law jurisdictions.

Judges of the *ordinary* judicial order are public officials remunerated by the state, but they have a separate status from that of other civil servants which allows the protection of the specific missions entrusted to them. Their status is set by a 1958 Ordinance relating to the status of the judiciary.[31] This status is based on constitutional principles and European law requirements aimed at guaranteeing the independence but also the competence, impartiality, and neutrality of members of the judiciary. Independence entails impartiality of the judges. As another fundamental feature of the judiciary, the importance of which is guaranteed under the ECHR, the principle of impartiality refers to the absence of prejudice which must characterise judges. This concerns the relations of judges with the other powers and constitutes a condition, necessary but not sufficient, of their impartiality in their relations with the litigants. Also, to guarantee the impartiality of judges, the law provides for a certain inability to judge in the case, for example, of a relationship between several judges of the same court, between a judge and a lawyer, or between a judge and a party. There is also a specific procedure which allows the parties to raise the issue of suspected bias of a judge. In general terms, the general independence of the judiciary results not only from constitutional provisions based on the separation of powers principle but also from statutory guarantees which protect judges from the pressures or threats that might weigh on their ability to judge. However, the independence enshrined in the Constitution concerns sitting judges only and does not extend to prosecuting judges. Due to their role as public prosecutors representing the interests of society, prosecuting judges, or prosecutors, have an organic link with the executive power. They may thus have to follow, in their written submissions, the instructions of their hierarchical authority, that is, the Ministry of Justice. The issue of the independence of public prosecutors has been recurrent in France.[32] Several lawyers and politicians have suggested aligning their status alongside that of ordinary

31 Ordinance No 58-1270 of 22 December 1958 on the Organic Law relating to the status of the judiciary. In 2019, France had approximately 8,600 ordinary judges, with women making up 66% of this total. When compared to other European countries, it is clear that the number of judges in France is insufficient and has been a point of criticism. France has half the number of judges and a quarter of the prosecutors per capita compared to the European average. However, there have been some efforts in recent years to increase the recruitment of judges in France.

32 On the general issue of the independence of the public prosecutors, see the case law of the ECtHR (ECtHR, *Moulin v France*, App No 37104/06, 23 February 2011), CJEU (*The Minister for Justice and Equality v OG and PI*, Case C-508/18, EU:C:2019:456, 27 May 2019), Court of Cassation (C. cass., Crim., 15 Dec. 2010, Bull. crim. I, 2010, No 207), and Constitutional Council (Decision No 2011-125 QPC of 6 May 2011 *Mr Abderrahmane L. [Transfer into the custody of the Public Prosecutor]*).

judges. By contrast, sitting judges do not bear the same obligation. Although they are public officials, sitting judges are not civil servants and are therefore not subject to the hierarchical authority of the minister. They are irremovable and, as such, cannot be transferred, even as a promotion, to another court without their consent. Their decisions can only be challenged in the context of the exercise of judicial remedies.

Administrative judges fall within the broader scope of the public service framework, with specific provisions ensuring their independence and security of tenure. Over time, members of administrative courts have been legally recognised as judges with the Constitutional Council granting them rights and guarantees similar to those of ordinary judges. As a matter of fact, lower administrative judges (i.e., those of the administrative courts and administrative courts of appeals) have an equivalent institution to the Superior Council of the Judiciary, known as the Superior Council of Administrative Courts and Administrative Courts of Appeal (*Conseil supérieur des tribunaux administratifs et cours administratives d'appel*). This Council, attached to the Ministry of Justice, deals with matters of career progression and disciplinary actions. As regards the Council of State, a few remarks must be added. First of all, the Council of State is constitutionally protected (e.g., articles 13, 37, and 39). Secondly, its members' status is governed both by law and by established practices. In terms of the law, the provisions of the Code of Administrative Justice[33] are very close to the legal framework of the public service where no irremovability is formally established with, however, several exceptions (e.g., no promotion scheme is established). The guarantees enjoyed by the members of the Council of State ultimately come from practice. Even if the law does not guarantee irremovability, in practice, this guarantee exists.[34] Also, if career progression is done, in theory, by choice, it obeys, in practice, seniority, which assures the members of the Council of State great independence, both regarding the political authorities and the authority of the Council of State itself. Generally speaking, the Constitutional Council has emphasised the importance of maintaining the independence of both ordinary and administrative courts, declaring that "the independence of the courts [both ordinary and administrative] is guaranteed as well as the specific nature of their functions which neither the legislature nor the government can encroach upon."[35] This separation of powers ensures that court rulings cannot be overridden or altered by the government or lawmakers.

The Constitutional Council

> « *Le Conseil [constitutionnel] n'est pas là pour rendre des services politiques, mais pour défendre le droit et protéger les libertés qui sont garanties par la Constitution.* »[36]

33 The Code of Administrative Justice results from Decree No 63-766 of 30 July 1963 on public administration regulation for the application of Ordinance No 45-1708 of 31 July 1945 and relating to the organisation and functioning of the Council of State.

34 Except in quite exceptional historical circumstances such as the period 1940–1944, under the Vichy regime.

35 Decision No 80-119 DC of 22 July 1980 *Loi portant validation d'actes administratifs*, pt 6.

36 Jean-Louis Debré, former president of the Constitutional Council (2007–2016) [The primary purpose of the [Constitutional] Council is not to cater to political interests, but to uphold the law and safeguard the freedoms enshrined in the Constitution].

The Constitutional Council is the court at the heart of constitutional justice in France. It is an innovative institution whose origins and evolution will be explained first before examining its organisation and role.[37]

Origins and evolution of the Constitutional Council

The concept of judicial review of legislation originated in the USA during the nineteenth century through landmark case law such as *Marbury v Madison* in 1803. In Europe, this practice began to take shape in the first half of the twentieth century through innovative constitutional provisions such as those found in the 1920 Austrian Constitution and 1937 Irish Constitution (see Table 6.1 Models of constitutional justice). While such judicial review expanded to other jurisdictions after the Second World War (e.g., Germany, Italy), it was not until the establishment of the Constitutional Council by the 1958 Constitution that constitutional review emerged in France, albeit in a limited form. The aim of this subsection is to explain the origins and the evolution of the Constitutional Council as an integral institution within the French legal system.

Origins of the Constitutional Council. The Constitutional Council traces its roots back to the establishment of the Fifth Republic in 1958, marking the first time in French history that there was a mechanism in place for the constitutional review of legislation. This development was a significant departure from the past due to several factors. This was owing, firstly, to a deep-seated distrust of judges whose influence was far too significant on the administration and the legislature in the *Ancien Régime*. Additionally, the sovereignty of the law and Parliament had been fiercely safeguarded during the Third and Fourth Republics, with the belief that the law was inherently infallible and that Parliament could do no wrong. In this context, the creation of the Constitutional Council in 1958 represented a real innovation. As part of an effort to "rationalise" the parliamentary regime, that is, to make it more efficient and less dysfunctional, the Constitutional Council was initially responsible for preventing any encroachment on the regulatory area by the legislature. Its role as a "weapon against the deviation of the parliamentary regime" was meant to ensure that the boundaries set forth in article 34 of the Constitution were respected. Although the Council's original purpose was to uphold these limits on legislative power, it has since evolved significantly over time.

Evolution of the Constitutional Council. The Constitutional Council has evolved significantly since its inception. Initially conceived as an auxiliary to the executive power, responsible for ensuring the protection of the regulatory domain against the encroachments of the legislative power, the Council has entirely redefined its role to become the guardian of fundamental

37 The developments below partly draw from Marie-Luce Paris, *Constitutional Law in France*, International Encyclopaedia of Laws (Wolters Kluwer 2024) 165 et seq. (paras 296 et seq.), Marie-Luce Paris, "The French Constitutional Council: Another 'Work-in-Progress'" in Emmanuel Guinchard & Marie-Pierre Granger (eds), *The New EU Judiciary: An Analysis of Current Judicial Reforms* (Kluwer Law International 2017) 47, and "The French System of Rights-Based Review: From Exceptionalism to Parochial Constitutionalism" in John Bell & Marie-Luce Paris (eds), *Rights-Based Constitutional Review: Constitutional Courts in a Changing Landscape* (Edward Elgar 2016) 302, 310 et seq.

TABLE 6.1 Models of constitutional justice

	American Model	*European Model (or Kelsenian)*
Which courts exercise the review?	Distributed or diffused review All courts have the power of constitutional review of laws.	Centralised review Only one court has the power of constitutional review of laws.
What is the nature of the review?	By way of exception The review is initiated in the course of ongoing proceedings, the main dispute of which is not about the constitutionality of the law.	By way of an action The review is initiated directly, and the main dispute is about the constitutionality of the law.
When is the review carried out?	Ex-post or a posteriori Review is exercised after the law comes into force.	Ex-ante or a priori Review is exercised before the law comes into force.
Are the facts taken into consideration?	Concrete review As the review is carried out in the context of a particular dispute, it takes into consideration the facts of the case.	Abstract review As the review is carried out in the context of a dispute whose only purpose is to review the constitutionality of the law, it does not take account of the facts, since there are none.
What authority does the judicial review decision have?	Relative res judicata *Inter partes effect* As the review is concrete, the authority of the decision is limited to the case at hand.	Absolute res judicata *Erga omnes effect* As the review is abstract, the authority of the decision is not limited to the case at hand.
What is the effect of the judicial review decision?	Non-application of the law While the law that is deemed unconstitutional stays in force in the legal system, it is not applied to the case in question.	Non-entry into force of the law The law that is deemed unconstitutional cannot be promulgated and hence cannot form part of the legal system.

freedoms. This transformation has elevated the Council to a level comparable to other constitutional courts in Europe. This is due to successive revisions which have widened both the Council's field of action and its mode of referral. Such a transformation is also owed to the Council itself, which, through dynamic case law, has acquired the means of action and a legitimacy that were unforeseen in 1958. The well-known 1971 decision on Freedom of Association (*Liberté d'association*) and the 1974 constitutional amendment have paved the way for the Council to assert its authority through a broader range of cases and an enhanced referral system.

In its groundbreaking 1971 Decision,[38] the Constitutional Council struck down, for the first time, a law for breach of fundamental rights. Instead of simply interpreting the basic Constitution, which did not explicitly address the right to freedom of association that was central to the case, the Council turned to the Preamble of the Constitution for guidance. By

38 Decision No 71-44 DC of 16 July 1971 *Loi complétant les dispositions des articles 5 et 7 de la loi du 1er juillet 1901 relative au contrat d'association* (*Liberté d'association*).

referencing the 1789 Declaration and the Preamble of the 1946 Constitution contained within the Preamble, the Council incorporated these principles into the constitutional framework. This decision gave birth to what scholars now refer to as the "block of constitutionality" (*bloc de constitutionnalité*).[39]

The 1974 constitutional amendment expanded the possibility to make a referral to the Council to 60 deputies or 60 senators, de facto to the opposition in Parliament.[40] The 1974 reform significantly increased the activity of the Council. As a result, the Council has come to test the constitutionality of many laws, touching upon some of the most significant political and societal issues of modern France such as, among others, bioethics, civil partnership, decentralisation, immigration, nationalisations and privatisations, the termination of pregnancy, the headscarf ban, and the participation of France in European integration. On these bases, the Council has stood on the one hand, as the protector of rights and freedoms earning the support of public opinion, and has become, on the other hand, the moderator in the relations between public powers, and between the majority and the opposition. Generally speaking, the Council has identified and guaranteed rights and freedoms according to a "deductive" method. It means that the Council has deduced from a general principle of constitutional value (e.g., the right to speak, to write, to print freely as declared in the 1789 Declaration) another more precise principle (e.g., the constitutional objective of pluralism in the media). Other examples include those relating to the principle of equality of citizens before the law which the Council has extrapolated to also guarantee the principle of equality before justice or equality before public charges or equality of suffrage; and those instances relating to the principle of freedom, which the Council has extrapolated to also guarantee the freedom of movement, freedom of enterprise etc.

The latest landmark in the evolution of the Council is the introduction of the priority preliminary ruling on an issue of constitutionality (known as *QPC*) procedure in 2008. This new procedure not only offers citizens another legal remedy for constitutional matters but also expands the role of the Constitutional Council by making its contentious procedure more robust and accessible to a wider range of participants, including citizens and their legal representatives, rather than just political figures. In essence, the transformation of its role has enabled the Constitutional Council to take a prominent place among French institutions.

Organisation of the Constitutional Council

This subsection examines the composition of the Constitutional Council, the status of its members as well as its structure and working methods.

Composition of the Constitutional Council. The Constitutional Council is composed of nine members appointed for a non-renewable term of nine years (article 56 of the Constitution). Members of the Council are appointed by political authorities: three are appointed by the President of the Republic, three by the president of the National Assembly, and three by the

39 The expression was coined by famous constitutionalist Professor Louis Favoreu.

40 Constitutional Law No 74-904 of 29 October 1974 amending article 61 of the Constitution; and Constitutional Law No 92-554 of 25 June 1992 adding to the Constitution a title: "European Communities and the European Union" concerning referral of international agreements.

president of the Senate. One-third of the Council is replaced every three years, meaning that the President of the Republic and the president of each of the Houses of Parliament each appoints one member to the Council every three years. In addition to these appointed members, the Council comprises the former Presidents of the Republic as ex officio members who serve de facto for life. The president of the Council is appointed by the President of the Republic, who may choose among appointed members or among ex officio members, although no president of the Council has ever been appointed in the latter category so far.[41] Since the 2008 constitutional amendment, the appointment procedure is subject to parliamentary scrutiny via the law standing committees (*commissions des lois*) of each House of Parliament (article 56 paragraph one of the Constitution). Each law standing committee is invited to give its public opinion on the nominee after a hearing. The law standing committees may oppose a veto (i.e., three-fifths of the votes in both committees) to the nominee of the President of the Republic, while it is not possible concerning the nominees of the presidents of either House of Parliament, who cannot be opposed. While some view the introduction of parliamentary scrutiny as a welcome change aimed at involving the democratic representation in the appointment process, others argue that it politicises it further by in effect requiring those who vote on the law to confirm those who will review it.

Membership of the Constitutional Council has long been criticised for various reasons. Firstly, one major issue is the automatic inclusion of former Presidents of the Republic as members, which is seen as unconventional.[42] While this arrangement was initially intended to ensure former Presidents a status worthy of their level of competence as well as being able to draw on their experience of the institutions, it no longer serves a valid purpose. Due to the transformation of the Council into a constitutional court subject to all the guarantees associated with a fully fledged court, including the guarantee of a fair trial under article 6 of the ECHR, there is no longer a need for ex officio membership for former Presidents. It is time to reconsider this outdated practice and allow the Council to operate without this unnecessary legacy.

Secondly, the appointment procedure of the other members has been criticised in two respects: the non-requirement of any qualification to be appointed, on the one hand, and the appointment by political authorities, on the other hand. The fact that the choice of the nominee is not subject to any qualification requirement, not even a legal qualification (i.e., it is not necessary to be a lawyer),[43] or age-related requirement, has been perceived as unusual when compared with other constitutional courts. It is true that most appointed members possess legal training and/or have substantial political experience with a good knowledge of the institutions, thus deflating, to some extent, criticism based on the absence of qualifications. Such criticism cannot be entirely dissipated, though. The political experience of appointed members generally means that they worked, before their appointment, in the highest spheres of political power.

41 The current president of the Constitutional Council is Laurent Fabius, former Prime Minister (1984–1986), who took office in 2016.

42 Former Presidents of the Republic Sarkozy (2007–2012) and Hollande (2012–2017) are, in principle, members ex officio on the Constitutional Council, albeit they have chosen not to sit on it. A few Presidents actually sat on the Council but later retired, such as Chirac, former President of the Republic (1995–2007), who sat on the Council from 2007 and later retired for health reasons in 2011.

43 Schnapper, for example, was a sociologist. She sat in the Constitutional Council from 2001 to 2010. She recounted her experience in Dominique Schnapper, *Une sociologue au Conseil Constitutionnel* (Gallimard 2010).

The composition of the current Constitutional Council is typical in that regard, being chaired by a former Prime Minister, Fabius, also former president of the National Assembly, deputy, and minister.[44] Besides, of the eight other members, there is another former Prime Minister, two former ministers, and two former parliamentarians. But the long political career of these members does not necessarily predispose them to controlling political activity and may even cast doubt on their impartiality because of a suspected enduring partisanship. This is linked to the second point about the political nature of the appointment. Overall, fears of a politicisation of the Council have arguably proven unfounded as the Council regularly reviews important texts regardless of the political hue of the government and of the political majority from which these texts originate. In a sense, one can be satisfied with the Council's independence because the Council decides constitutional cases, in principle, on considerations of law and not of politics, hereby acting as an efficient counter-power to the political power. However, one may disagree. On the contrary, in the name of the denunciation of "a government of judges," the Council has been arguably careful not to use the powers theoretically conferred upon it in its role. In other words, the Council has not acted as the efficient counter-power it should have been because of fears of "a government of judges," hereby losing sight of its raison d'être and role. The Covid-19 pandemic case law somewhat illustrates this: in its 2020 decision on the emergency regime to deal with the Covid-19 outbreak, the Council validated the vaccination and other measures despite the state of emergency regime clearly violating several fundamental freedoms recognised by the Constitution (e.g., freedom of movement, principle of equality) without however protecting public health. Besides, this was compounded by the wording of the decision, which reveals neither the violation of the Constitution, nor what is at stake in this violation, nor the result of the violation.[45]

Status of members of the Constitutional Council. The independence of members of the Constitutional Council is the primary concern as regards their status.[46] This has several implications. Members of the Council cannot be revoked[47] and their term in office cannot be renewed, hereby protecting them from all kinds of pressure. They benefit from a substantial salary in order to ensure their financial independence. Members of the Council must take an oath before the President of the Republic, swearing to uphold the Constitution impartially and to comply with a duty of discretion (*devoir de réserve*). This discretion prevents them from disclosing the contents of the Council's deliberations and from taking a stance in the public debate on an issue related to the case law of the Council. This was the case, for example, of Simone Veil, member of the Constitutional Council from 1998 to 2007, who, in 2005, withdrew from her duty when she took part in the referendum campaign concerning the Treaty establishing a Constitution for Europe. Also, any member must withdraw when s/he is involved

44 Fabius was involved in the contaminated blood criminal proceedings at the end of the 1990s. Tried together with two former members of his government before the Court of Justice of the Republic for crimes and misdemeanours committed in the exercise of their functions, he was acquitted.

45 Decision No 2020-799 DC of 26 March 2020 *Loi organique d'urgence pour faire face à l'épidémie de covid-19*. For a critical account, see Lauréline Fontaine, *La Constitution maltraitée* (Amsterdam 2023).

46 Ordinance No 58-1067 of 7 November 1958 on the Organic Law on the Constitutional Council.

47 Constitutional Council members have the option to step down either by submitting a voluntary resignation or being required to resign if they are no longer able to fulfil their duties due to physical incapacity or conflicts of interest.

in a case for which his/her neutrality would not be total, or s/he may be disqualified from sitting in the case. Besides, members of the Council are subject to a number of incompatibilities as a guarantee of their independence: they cannot exercise any electoral mandate and cannot be a member of the government or of the Economic, Social and Environmental Council; more generally, they are prevented from exercising any public function and any other professional or salaried activity, including being a member of the Bar, except those activities which do not call into question their independence (e.g., scientific, literary, or artistic activities).

Structure and working methods of the Constitutional Council. The Constitutional Council holds a unique level of autonomy in three key areas, namely administrative, regulatory, and financial.

Firstly, the Council is in charge of its administrative organisation under the leadership of its president. Another key figure of the Council is the Secretary-General. Often dubbed the "tenth member" of the Council, the Secretary-General is a lawyer of the highest standing, generally a member of the Council of State. S/he manages the different services of the Council, namely the Legal Service, including the Registry attached to it, the Research and Documentation Service, which runs legal research, the Administrative and Financial Service, responsible for the management of the institution, and the Press and External Relations Service, in charge of the Council's publications, of the relations with other courts, universities, and French institutions, and of international relations. Aside from these administrative functions, the Secretary-General directs the preparatory work of the Council and liaises with the different government ministries. The Council's size, which consists of a team of between 60 and 70 staff, is relatively modest compared to other equivalent courts. For example, members of the Council do not have personal advisers or collaborators apart from their secretariat. However, the Council has adjusted to expand at the margins, liaising with other institutions and for various purposes. For instance, the Council is assisted by delegates and rapporteurs during elections. Legal Service staff are generally hired from among members of the Council of State as well as a few coming from the Court of Cassation; it may also comprise clerks on secondment from Parliament and law academics; also, some *chargés de mission* (generally academics at non-professorial level) may be hired to deal with *QPC* cases, and some *stagiaires* may be hired among the best students in (mostly Parisian) law schools for specific research tasks.

Secondly, the regulatory autonomy of the Constitutional Council is provided for in a number of constitutional and organic laws, allowing the Council some discretion in its decisions.[48] Prior to the 2008 constitutional amendment, the regulatory framework was quite flexible, with only one court rule (adopted without a specific date) based on the 1958 Ordinance. It was only in 2010, with the introduction of the *QPC*, that the Council decided to adopt formal court rules.[49] Finally, in 2022, the Council ratified rules of procedure concerning ex-ante review decisions.[50]

48 All these laws, except the 1958 Ordinance, were referred to the Constitutional Council for review.

49 Decision No 2010-117 ORGA of 4 February 2010, *Décision portant règlement intérieur sur la procédure suivie devant le Conseil constitutionnel pour les questions prioritaires de constitutionnalité*, as amended.

50 Decision No 2022-152 ORGA of 11 March 2022 *Décision portant règlement intérieur sur la procédure suivie devant le Conseil constitutionnel pour les déclarations de conformité à la Constitution*.

Thirdly, in terms of financial autonomy, the Constitutional Council sets its own budget. While this budget may seem modest compared to other constitutional courts, it still represents a considerable amount of funding. There has been a notable increase in the budget since the last fiscal year (i.e., 15,9 million euros in 2022 compared to 11,7 million euros in 2018) partly due to the expanding workload concerning elections and the need to update the digital monitoring system for *QPC* cases.[51] The Council has some flexibility in managing its budget. Indeed, unlike other government entities, the Council's budget, which is included in the "Public Powers" mission of the Finance Bill, is approved by Parliament without any changes or discussions. Moreover, the Council is not required to provide a detailed account of its expenditures to the government or Parliament.

In terms of working methods, the judicial procedure before the Constitutional Council has been modelled on that of the Council of State. This procedure is not codified and has been, at least originally, mainly inquisitorial, that is, mostly written, secret, and collegiate, with a limited involvement of parties and limited publicity. Incremental changes, some at the initiative of the successive presidents of the Council and others made by law, such as the possibility for the rapporteur to hear representatives from the administration or members of Parliament who made the referral, have greatly increased the judicial nature of the Council's proceedings. The contentious nature of *QPC* proceedings has further boosted this progressive judicialisation with rules of procedure aimed at securing transparency, due process of law, and impartiality—all important conditions to satisfy the requirements of a fair trial under article 6 of the ECHR. Notably, parties and their counsels are now fully associated with *QPC* proceedings and are notified about all aspects of the case. Impartiality and transparency are further guaranteed by the oral and public nature of *QPC* hearings and by a system of abstention and recusation of members of the Council. The Council takes its decisions by a simple majority, in plenary sessions, with a quorum of seven members, which is essential to ensure the authority of the ruling. While the length of judicial proceedings is a negative trait of most supreme courts in Europe, including the ECtHR, the Council has been quite exemplary in rendering justice within prescribed timeframes, especially within the strict timeframe of one month in ex-ante review proceedings. The form of the Constitutional Council's decisions is modelled on that of the administrative jurisdictions and, despite their different types, follows the same format which is in line with the French concise style of drafting judgments (see below).

Role of the Constitutional Council

After some observations about the general competence of the Constitutional Council, this subsection examines the Council's advisory role and judicial role.

General principle of competence. The Constitutional Council enjoys a limited jurisdiction (*compétence d'attribution*) which is determined by the Constitution and various organic laws.

51 *Mission "Pouvoirs Publics", Projet de loi de finances pour 2022*, Commission des lois, Rapport du Sénat, 24 November 2021, 3. The increase is up by 32.81% compared to the last financial year. The provisional budget for 2022 is divided into five actions: constitutional review of norms (7.3 million euros), elections (2.5 million euros), external relations (1.6 million euros), maintenance and works (1.2 million euros), and general expenses (3.2 million euros).

The Council has emphasised that its jurisdiction is "strictly delimited by the Constitution; that it is likely to be clarified and supplemented by organic law only in compliance with the principles laid down by the constitutional text; that the Constitutional Council cannot be called upon to rule in cases other than those expressly provided for by these texts."[52] As the protector of the Constitution and of the area of the law (*domaine de la loi*), the Constitutional Council distinguishes between its roles as a constitutional authority and as a constitutional court. In the former capacity, the Council provides advice, while in the latter, it acts as an electoral court and a proper constitutional court.

Advisory role. In this role, the Constitutional Council delivers *opinions* and issues *declarations* as directed by the Constitution. As regards opinions, the Council issues them in electoral matters regarding, for example, the organisation of referendums. The Council may also issue opinions or observations on matters of its competence, opinions that it chooses to publish or not. For example, taking stock of the litigation related to the 2012 and 2017 legislative elections and the 2017 presidential election, the Council issued observations on the matter.[53] The Council is required to issue its opinion in the more extraordinary context of exceptional powers (article 16 of the Constitution) to verify that the conditions for their implementation are met. In that case, the opinion is mandatory, reasoned, and published but not legally binding, meaning that the President of the Republic is not required to follow the opinion of the Council. The Council's opinion is also required as regards each measure taken by the President of the Republic when implementing the exceptional powers; in that case, the opinion is also not legally binding (*avis simple*) but is not published.[54] In terms of declarations, the Council is responsible for declaring, or establishing, a factual situation resulting in legal effects such as, for example, when the Council, upon request by the government, ascertains the impediment of the President of the Republic to exercise his/her functions (article 7 paragraph four of the Constitution). In electoral matters, the Council has multiple occasions to intervene whether it concerns the President of the Republic or members of Parliament. Concerning the President of the Republic, the Council is in charge, for example, of announcing the results of the presidential election (article 58 of the Constitution) or of declaring the vacancy of the office of the President of the Republic or his/her permanent incapacity to continue in office (article 7 paragraph five of the Constitution). The role of the Council vis-à-vis members of Parliament is to declare their ineligibility or to acknowledge their resignation from office in the event of an incompatibility between mandates. Concerning other technical matters, the Council may, upon referral by the president of either

52 Decision No 2003-469 DC of 26 March 2003 *Révision constitutionnelle relative à l'organisation décentralisée de la République*, pt 1.

53 Decision No 2013-26 ELEC of 11 July 2013 *Observations du Conseil constitutionnel relatives aux élections législatives des 10 et 17 juin 2012*, and Decision No 2019-28 ELEC of 21 February 2019 *Observations du Conseil constitutionnel relatives aux élections législatives des 11 et 18 juin 2017* (for the legislative elections), and Decision No 2017-172 PDR of 20 July 2017 *Observations du Conseil constitutionnel sur l'élection présidentielle des 23 avril et 7 mai 2017* (for the presidential election).

54 Since the 2008 constitutional amendment, the Constitutional Council may be consulted after 30 days of implementation of the exceptional powers by the president of the National Assembly, the president of the Senate, 60 deputies or 60 senators, with a view to examining if the conditions for the implementation of article 16 are still met. The Council is required to reply promptly by delivering a public opinion. The Council proceeds to decide, as of right and under the same conditions as mentioned above, after 60 days of implementation of the exceptional powers, and at any time thereafter (article 16 paragraph six of the Constitution).

House of Parliament or the Prime Minister, decide, within the short period of eight days, on the conformity of government bills with the rules laid down under the 2009 Organic Law,[55] notably its part on impact study (article 39 paragraph four of the Constitution). For example, in a 2014 decision, the Constitutional Council validated, for the first time, an impact study that had been considered insufficient by the Senate. The Council considered that the government bill in question about various topics relating to regional and departmental elections, electoral constituencies in regions and departments, and the electoral calendar met the criteria provided for under the Constitution and the provisions of the 2009 Organic Law.[56] It also falls on the Council to declare the inadmissibility of a private member's bill where the enactment of such a bill may result in either a decrease in public revenue or the creation of or increase in public expenditure (article 40 of the Constitution).

Judicial role. The judicial role of the Constitutional Council entails jurisdictional powers, that is, the power to make legal decisions and judgments, which can be categorised into three main areas: overseeing electoral processes, ensuring that the separation of public powers is maintained, and conducting judicial reviews of norms.

Electoral court. In this role, the Constitutional Council acts as a regulator of elections at national level. In that regard, the Council is the guardian of democratic and constitutional principles, namely the principles of equality, fairness in voting, pluralism, and respect for opposition rights. In addition to its advisory and declaratory powers in electoral matters, the Council exercises powers of a contentious or judicial nature. This shift towards acting as a judicial body, known as jurisdictionalisation, allows the Council to play a more active role in ensuring the legality of presidential elections, parliamentary elections, and referendums. This development is seen as a significant advancement in the rule of law.

Concerning the presidential election, the Constitutional Council intervenes at two stages. Firstly, leading up to the elections, the Council oversees the regularity of the electoral process by examining the complaints, brought by voters, candidates, or prefects, relating to the list of candidates. The Council may also intervene by postponing or by annulling the election process at whatever stage in the event of any issue (i.e., death, impediment) that prevents a candidate from running in the election. Secondly, after the elections, the Council officially proclaims the results of the presidential election. Lastly, the Council also acts on appeal from the National Commission for Campaign Accounts and Political Financing (*Commission Nationale des Comptes de Campagne et des Financements Politiques* or *CNCCFP*), to check if the spending limit for electoral expenses has been respected by each candidate.[57]

55 Organic Law No 2009-403 of 15 April 2009 relating to the application of articles 34-1, 39 and 44 of the Constitution.

56 Decision No 2014-12 FNR of 1 July 2014 *Présentation du projet de loi relatif à la délimitation des régions, aux élections régionales et départementales et modifiant le calendrier électoral*, pt 6.

57 See, for example, Decision No 2013-156 PDR of 4 July 2013 *Décision du Conseil constitutionnel sur un recours de M. Nicolas Sarkozy dirigé contre la décision du 19 décembre 2012 de la Commission nationale des comptes de campagnes et des financements politiques*, on the invalidation of the campaign accounts of the candidate, later President of the Republic (2012–2017), Sarkozy.

Concerning the elections of deputies and senators, the Constitutional Council's review is two-fold. Firstly, the Council oversees the regularity of the electoral process by reviewing ineligibilities and incompatibilities of candidates and may declare the ineligibility of a member of Parliament or may formally acknowledge a member of Parliament's resignation should s/he fall under one of the incompatibilities determined by law. The Council may also annul parliamentary elections held in contravention with the Electoral Code or amend results of parliamentary elections. Secondly, and as for the presidential election, the Council is responsible for ruling over disputes about the financing of electoral expenses.

Concerning referendums, the Constitutional Council is responsible for ensuring the regularity of the referendum process whether the referendum is a legislative referendum (article 11 of the Constitution), an amendment to the Constitution referendum (article 89 of the Constitution), or an EU accession referendum (article 88-5 of the Constitution). Again, the Council intervenes at different stages of the referendum process. The Council is consulted by the government on the organisation of the referendum and may send delegates on the ground to check that the process is carried out according to the law.[58] The Council also deals with the complaints addressed by the prefects or the voters about the referendum process and may, as a result, decide to annul a referendum. However, the Council has always refused to review the conformity of the referendum law to the Constitution since such a law represents the "direct expression of national sovereignty."[59] At the end of the referendum process, the Council officially proclaims the results.[60]

Constitutional court. In that role, the Constitutional Council is tasked with a dual mission. Firstly, as the "guardian of [the area of] the law," the Council oversees the balance of powers between Parliament and the government, ensuring each stay within their designated roles. Secondly, as the "guardian of the Constitution," the Council reviews the conformity of certain norms (i.e., laws and treaties) to the Constitution.[61] The Constitutional Council's original role was to act as the "regulator of public powers," a role that the Council arrogated to itself thus marking its profound difference from other public powers.[62] As such a regulator, the Council ensures that Parliament does not encroach on the government's field of competence (article 37 of the Constitution) since the field of competence of Parliament is limited under the Fifth Republic (article 34 of the Constitution). The Council fulfils this role by using the mechanisms of the

58 Decision No 2000-24 REF of 23 August 2000 *sur une requête présentée par Monsieur Stéphane HAUCHEMAILLE*, pt 2.

59 Decision No 62-20 DC of 6 November 1962 *Loi relative à l'élection du Président de la République au suffrage universel direct*, pt 2, confirmed by Decision No 92-313 of 23 September 1992 *Loi autorisant la ratification du traité sur l'Union européenne* (*Maastricht III*), pt 2.

60 Since the 2008 constitutional amendment, the Council is also responsible for reviewing the conformity of a private member's bill, and the procedure carried out accordingly, to the Constitution in the context of the shared initiative referendum (article 11 paragraph four of the Constitution). See Organic Law No 2013-1114 of 6 December 2013 implementing article 11 of the Constitution.

61 The Constitutional Council may also examine the compliance of any government bill placed on the legislative agenda with article 39 of the Constitution.

62 Decision No 62-20 DC of 6 November 1962 *Loi relative à l'élection du Président de la République au suffrage universel direct, adoptée par le référendum du 28 octobre 1962* (*Loi référendaire*), pt 2.

so-called "delegalisation" (article 37 paragraph two of the Constitution)[63] and "inadmissibility" (article 41 of the Constitution)[64] which protect the regulatory area. These mechanisms also protect the area of the law by ensuring the intelligibility and quality of the legislation. As is well acknowledged, the Constitutional Council has developed a derivative role as the "guardian of the Constitution" by judicially reviewing norms, especially laws, for their conformity with the Constitution, also called control of the constitutionality of laws (*contrôle de constitutionnalité des lois*). This expanded role began with the groundbreaking 1971 decision on Freedom of Association concerning judicial review of non-promulgated laws (article 61 of the Constitution) and has since been enhanced by the 2008 constitutional amendment introducing judicial review of promulgated laws (article 61-1 of the Constitution).[65] This evolution of the Council's role will be explored further in the following section on constitutional review.

Constitutional Review

> « *À plusieurs reprises, la QPC a été l'occasion pour le Conseil [constitutionnel] de statuer sur des questions de société.* »[66]

The system of judicial review of legislation by the Constitutional Council has evolved over time, resulting in the relatively recent emergence of a fully fledged constitutional review system with its unique characteristics.[67]

Meaning of constitutional review

After briefly introducing the general meaning of constitutional review, this subsection delves into the specific model of constitutional review implemented in the French legal system.

General meaning. The term "judicial review" means "that a judge can examine a legal decision or a norm (…) and check its compatibility with a higher norm." In other words, judicial review is "a court's power to detect conflicts in law, and possibly to attach consequences to resolve such

63 The government can refer a promulgated law to the Constitutional Council with a view to "delegalising" it and declaring its regulatory character (i.e., declassifying the text from a law to a regulatory act amendable by decree). The Constitutional Council may also "declassify" a law adopted by the French Parliament in contravention to the provisions relating to the powers of the Polynesian authorities under Organic Law No 2004-192 of 27 February 2004 on the statute of autonomy of French Polynesia.

64 The government or the president of one of the Houses of Parliament may refer a private member's bill or an amendment to any such bill because it does not fall in the area of the law or is contrary to a delegation provided for under article 38 of the Constitution, and may request the Council to certify the inadmissibility, meaning that the bill cannot progress through the legislative process.

65 The same is true as regards international treaties (article 54 of the Constitution).

66 *Rapport d'activité 2022*, Conseil Constitutionnel, September 2022, 8 [On several occasions, the *QPC* was an opportunity for the [Constitutional] Council to rule on social issues].

67 The developments below partly draw from Marie-Luce Paris, *Constitutional Law in France*, International Encyclopaedia of Laws (Wolters Kluwer 2024) 162 et seq. (paras 289 et seq.), Marie-Luce Paris, "The French Constitutional Council: Another 'Work-in-Progress'" in Emmanuel Guinchard & Marie-Pierre Granger (eds), *The New EU Judiciary: An Analysis of Current Judicial Reforms* (Kluwer Law International 2017) 47, and "The French System of Rights-Based Review: From Exceptionalism to Parochial Constitutionalism" in John Bell & Marie-Luce Paris (eds), *Rights-Based Constitutional Review: Constitutional Courts in a Changing Landscape* (Edward Elgar 2016) 302.

conflicts."[68] Judicial review aims at reviewing executive and legislative acts, possibly leading to the invalidation of such acts, by the courts. In an administrative law context, judicial review is the process through which courts question the lawfulness of the action of public bodies. Put differently, judicial review serves to ensure that any delegated legislation is consistent with the scope of the power granted by Parliament to the government and the administration. In a constitutional law context, judicial review involves a superior court assessing the conformity of legislation enacted by Parliament to the Constitution. Constitutional review has now become "a dominant feature of modern constitutionalism" and "is now clearly a global phenomenon."[69]

The European model of constitutional review and the hierarchy of norms. In general terms, the constitution organises the relations between institutions and public authorities and sets out the rules for the exercise of political power. The constitution sits at the top of legal norms. Consequently, all other legal norms must conform to the constitution, hence the concept of the hierarchy of norms (*hiérarchie des normes*). The superior or supreme norm sits at the top of the (numerous) other lower norms at the bottom. For this reason, the image is also one of a pyramid of norms. The idea that each legal norm derives its legitimacy from a higher rule of law with which it must conform was inspired by Hans Kelsen (see Figure 6.2 The hierarchy of norms).[70] Kelsen based his theory on positivism, according to which the law is identified with

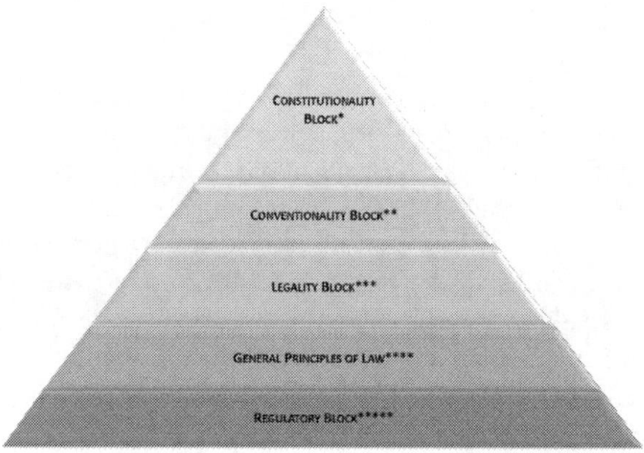

FIGURE 6.2 The hierarchy of norms

*Constitutionality Block: 1958 Constitution, 1789 Declaration, 1946 Preamble, 2004 Charter for the Environment, Fundamental Principles Recognised by the Laws of the Republic, Principles of Law Particularly Necessary to Our Time
**Conventionality Block: international agreements, EU law
***Legality Block: organic laws, ordinary laws, referendum laws, article 38 ordinances
****General Principles of Law: non-written general rules
*****Regulatory Block: regulatory acts and administrative acts (decrees, orders, circulars, and directives)

68 Aalt Willem Heringa, *Constitutions Compared: An Introduction to Comparative Constitutional Law* (4th edn, Intersentia 2016) 159.

69 Albert H Y Chen & Miguel Poiares Maduro, "The Judiciary and Constitutional Review" in Mark Tushnet, Thomas Fleiner and Cheryl Saunders (eds), *Routledge Handbook of Constitutional Law* (Routledge 2013) 97, 100.

70 Hans Kelsen, Austrian lawyer (1881–1973).

the sovereignty of the state and should not be limited by any superior rule. The requirement of conformity of any legal norm to the constitution is the raison d'être of judicial constitutional review. The French legal system adopts a European or *Kelsenian* model of constitutional review by entrusting to a constitutional court, the Constitutional Council, the task of ensuring the conformity of laws to the Constitution. Under French constitutional law, constitutional review concerns conformity to not only the text of the Constitution of the Fifth Republic but also to a range of norms and principles of constitutional value which, together with the Constitution, have formed what is called the "block of constitutionality" (see below).[71] However, the classical approach based on the hierarchy of norms has changed due to the emergence of a plurality of legal sources (i.e., hard law, soft law) and the pregnant influence of international and European law on domestic law. As a result, the approach, especially in the protection of fundamental rights, has shifted from being a hierarchical approach to one being pluralistic, articulating or combining legal norms which appear complementary or equivalent.

Types of constitutional review

Brief developments on French constitutional history shed light on the barriers that have prevented the implementation of judicial review of legislation in the French legal system. This subsection then presents the two main types of constitutional review which are currently in force, namely the longstanding ex-ante review established in 1958, and the newer ex-post review introduced in 2008.

French constitutional history. The history of judicial review of legislation in France has been full of paradoxes and failures.[72] A proper mechanism of constitutional review was not firmly established before the Fifth Republic in 1958, albeit limited initially to a mechanism of ex-ante review. This was further enhanced by the 2008 constitutional amendment and the introduction of ex-post constitutional review.[73] Historically, the reluctance to establish constitutional review in domestic law is explained by the so-called *légicentrisme* doctrine, which placed, at the time, the law at the centre of the hierarchy of norms. In strict legal terms, *légicentrisme* meant that the law was regarded as unlimited (i.e., no restriction on its scope), indivisible (i.e., no delegation of the power to make the law), and unquestionable (i.e., judicial immunity as judges were supposed to "serve" the law and not sanction it). This approach found its origins in the French conception of democratic sovereignty. According to article 6 of the 1789 Declaration, "[t]he Law is the expression of the general will." Combined with an historical hostility towards judges, *légicentrisme* made it difficult to envisage judicial review of legislation. However, from being an "inviolable" norm, the law has been progressively challenged with the advancement of constitutionalism. The realisation, especially after the Second World War and the abuses of

71 Administrative and ordinary judges have both ruled that the supremacy conferred by the Constitution to international agreements on the laws (as stated in article 55 of the Constitution) cannot, within the domestic legal order, apply "to provisions of a constitutional nature." See CE, Ass., 30 October 1998, *Sarran, Levacher et autres*, Rec. Lebon 368; C. cass., Ass. plén., 2 June 2000, *Fraisse*, Bull. Ass. plén. 2000, No 4.

72 Marie-Luce Paris, *Constitutional Law in France*, International Encyclopaedia of Laws (Wolters Kluwer 2024) 164 et seq. (paras 293 et seq.).

73 Ex-ante constitutional review is known as a priori constitutional review, while ex-post constitutional review is referred to as a posteriori constitutional review. The latter is commonly known in the French context as the *QPC* review.

totalitarian regimes during the twentieth century, that the law was unable to fulfil its role in securing individual and collective rights and freedoms and in providing for political stability, led to a shift in favour of the constitution. Envisaged as the supreme norm, the constitution was henceforth regarded as the norm capable of acting as a more solid bulwark for guarding against these risks. Therefore, the introduction of the constitutional paradigm, which considers the constitution as the expression of sovereignty, has been the result of an incremental evolution in the French legal order. The Fifth Republic resolutely broke from the previous tenet of the sovereignty of the law by curtailing the sovereignty of Parliament. The weakening of the law, and the ensuing recognition of the political and judicial authority of the constitution, are embodied in several provisions of the Constitution, namely article 34 on the delimitation of the scope of the law, article 55 on the supremacy of international law, and, prominently, article 61 on constitutional review of legislation.

The 1958 Constitution and the introduction of ex-ante judicial review. The establishment of the Constitutional Council in the early days of the Fifth Republic did not originally correspond to the introduction of a full mechanism of judicial review of legislation. The initial aim was to ensure that Parliament remained within the limits of its competence (article 34 of the Constitution) and did not infringe on the normative power granted to the government (article 37 of the Constitution). Nonetheless, and under its ex-ante review power, the Council gradually developed into an organ whose task was to ensure the supremacy of the Constitution over the law. The following quote from one of its decisions best embodies how the Council envisaged its role under domestic constitutional law: "[the law] is the expression of the general will albeit in the respect of the Constitution."[74] The endorsement of a full review of constitutionality by the Council, in contrast with its initial role as regards the division of normative competences, is the result of its 1971 decision on Freedom of Association.[75] The other turning point was, as seen above, the 1974 constitutional amendment which granted to 60 deputies or 60 senators the right to challenge the law before its promulgation, whereas this right was previously reserved to the President of the Republic, the Prime Minister, and the president of either House of Parliament.[76] By in fact opening the review to the members of the opposition, the 1974 reform notably increased the activity of the Council and raised its profile in the political landscape. Ex-ante referrals, although optional, have become quite systematic, testing the constitutionality of many laws touching upon some of the most significant political and societal issues of modern France. Ex-ante review is either mandatory or facultative, depending on the type of norms concerned. A finding of unconstitutionality leads to the censure of all, or part of, the law but not to its annulment since the law, not having been promulgated, is regarded as not yet in existence (see below).

The 2008 constitutional amendment and the introduction of ex-post judicial review. The introduction of a mechanism of exception of unconstitutionality was proposed several times

74 Decision No 85-197 DC of 23 August 1985 *Loi sur l'évolution de la Nouvelle-Calédonie*, pt 27.

75 Decision No 71-44 DC of 16 July 1971 *Loi complétant les dispositions des articles 5 et 7 de la loi du 1er juillet 1901 relative au contrat d'association* (*Liberté d'association*).

76 Constitutional Law No 74-904 of 29 October 1974 amending article 61 of the Constitution.

but was always opposed by the Senate.[77] The priority preliminary ruling on an issue of constitutionality (*question prioritaire de constitutionnalité* or *QPC*) procedure was eventually introduced as part of the 2008 constitutional amendment, hereby adding another constitutional remedy in the form of ex-post judicial review.[78] Under the added article 61-1 paragraph one of the Constitution, "if, during pending proceedings before a French court, it is argued that a legislative provision infringes the rights and freedoms guaranteed by the Constitution, the Constitutional Council may be seized of this issue by the Council of State or the Court of Cassation, which can decide on the matter within a specified period of time." So, the general mechanism of the ex-post judicial review is the following one: the issue of constitutionality is, firstly, raised before a first-instance court, an appeal court, or one of the supreme courts (i.e., Court of Cassation or Council of State); secondly, the issue is filtered by one of the supreme courts if coming from lower instances, and it is eventually decided upon by the Constitutional Council. A *QPC* is declared admissible, by a first-instance or an appeal judge, under four conditions: if, firstly, the allegedly unconstitutional provision is of a legislative nature; if, secondly, the application of such a provision is necessary for the outcome of the case; if, thirdly, such a provision has not been previously declared compatible with the Constitution by the Council (except for a change in circumstances of fact or law); and if, fourthly, the issue of constitutionality presents a "serious character." Should the *QPC* be declared admissible, the ordinary judge will then suspend the proceedings on the merits until a decision is reached by the Council on the constitutionality issue. In the eventuality that an issue of conventionality (i.e., an issue about the compatibility of the challenged law with the ECHR, or any other international convention) is raised during the same proceedings, the *QPC* should be dealt with as a priority. A provision that is declared unconstitutional on the basis of *QPC* proceedings is repealed from the moment of the publication of the decision of the Constitutional Council, or from a later date that is decided by the Council.

The introduction of the *QPC* procedure has been hailed as a success. Despite initial doubts and criticisms about its compatibility with European law and its precedence over conventional judicial review, the success of the *QPC* procedure has since been validated.[79] The 2022 report of the Constitutional Council points to the success of this "constitutional revolution," with the Council reaching its thousandth *QPC* ruling in 2022.[80] These rulings have addressed a wide array of topics including freedom of religion and secularism (*laïcité*), criminal procedure, tax litigation, environment and planning, health and bioethics, health and Covid-19, and local authorities. Notably, certain *QPC* rulings have even resulted in legislative reforms in key areas of French law such as, among others, the reform of the custody regime, pension system for veterans, involuntary confinement in mental hospitals, regulations for senior civil servants, and laws regarding sexual harassment. The *QPC* jurisprudence has, at times, sparked controversy but has ultimately demonstrated its significance in shaping French law.

77 For more details, see Marie-Luce Paris, "The French System of Rights-Based Review: From Exceptionalism to Parochial Constitutionalism" in John Bell & Marie-Luce Paris (eds), *Rights-Based Constitutional Review: Constitutional Courts in a Changing Landscape* (Edward Elgar 2016) 302, 316.

78 Law No 2008-724 of 23 July 2008 on the modernisation of the institutions of the Fifth Republic.

79 For more details, see Marie-Luce Paris, "The French System of Rights-Based Review: From Exceptionalism to Parochial Constitutionalism" in John Bell & Marie-Luce Paris (eds), *Rights-Based Constitutional Review: Constitutional Courts in a Changing Landscape* (Edward Elgar 2016) 302.

80 *Rapport d'activité 2022*, Conseil Constitutionnel, September 2022, 5 and 75.

Modalities of constitutional review

This subsection delves into how constitutional review is carried out within the framework of French law. It explores two main aspects: the norms that are the object of review, as well as the norms of reference used by the Constitutional Council when exercising its review, encompassed in the so-called "block of constitutionality." The features of constitutional review and constitutional review rulings are also covered.

The norms and object of review. The norms that are susceptible of constitutional review are described below. They are categorised according to whether they undergo ex-ante or ex-post review procedures.[81]

Under *the ex-ante constitutional review*, the review is mandatory as regards certain normative acts and is facultative as regards others. The normative acts for which review is *mandatory* are organic laws and the rules of procedure of the Houses of Parliament (article 61 paragraph one of the Constitution). Since organic laws complete and specify the provisions of the Constitution, they can never run the risk of being found unconstitutional, hence the mandatory referral to eliminate that risk. As for the rules of procedure of the Houses of Parliament, their mandatory review is also easily explained by the primary mission of the Constitutional Council, which is to regulate public powers. In line with the idea of parliamentary rationalisation, the Council ensures that Parliament does not encroach on the other branches of power. Also featured in this category are the legislative proposals to be submitted by way of a referendum of shared initiative. These proposals must be referred for constitutional review before they are submitted to the electors to gather their support (article 11 paragraph three of the Constitution).

The normative acts for which review is *facultative* are ordinary laws, international treaties, and laws of the land. Concerning ordinary laws (article 61 paragraph two of the Constitution), review by the Council consists in reviewing their procedural dimension (i.e., if the adoption of the law respected all procedural requirements) as well as their substantial dimension (i.e., if the legislature respected all the principles laid down in the Constitution). Even though facultative, the mere possibility of judicial review necessarily constrains the legislature to exercise a degree of self-restraint in order to anticipate and, primarily, to avoid censure by the constitutional court. Concerning international treaties (article 54 of the Constitution), the primacy of the Constitution in the domestic legal order means that treaties and international agreements can be judicially reviewed before their ratification, or their approval. In the event of incompatibility between the ratified or approved treaty and the Constitution, the latter will have to be amended. The 1992 Maastricht Treaty, the 1997 Amsterdam Treaty, the 1999 European Charter for Regional or Minority Languages, and the 2007 Lisbon Treaty were all referred to the Constitutional Council and necessitated an amendment to the Constitution. However, the 2012 Treaty on Stability, Coordination and Governance in the Economic and Monetary Union ("TSCG" or the so-called Fiscal Stability Treaty), aimed at controlling the public finances of

81 The process of ex-post review is essentially the same as the *QPC* procedure in French law. These terms will be used interchangeably throughout.

EU member states, did not require such a modification.[82] Concerning laws of the land, these are acts adopted in the legislative area by the deliberative assemblies of New Caledonia and of French Polynesia, both local authorities being endowed with a particular status. Since the end of the 1990s, laws of the land adopted by the New Caledonian Congress can be referred for review by the various local authorities and by the state representative in the territory.[83] The possibility of review is more limited concerning Polynesia. Constitutional review only consists in the possibility of "declassifying" a law adopted by the domestic legislature into a law pertaining to the local Polynesian legislature, should the domestic law in question encroach on the legislative area conferred upon the local legislature.[84]

Although most normative acts are subject to judicial review, there are certain exceptions. Firstly, regulatory acts and other normative acts that are not included in the above categories are generally not subject to review by the constitutional court as a matter of principle. However, these acts may still be subject to review by the administrative judge under the control of legality (*contrôle de légalité*). Secondly, constitutional laws and referendum laws are also excluded from judicial review. This exclusion is based on the fact that there is no legal basis for such reviews in these cases. Constitutional laws are seen as sovereign because the "constituent power is sovereign,"[85] while referendum laws are viewed as "the direct expression of sovereignty" as established by the case law of the Constitutional Council.[86]

The category of norms pertaining to EU law stands apart. In principle, the Constitutional Council has no competence to judicially review EU normative acts (i.e., regulations and directives) since this is the remit of the CJEU, although their implementation in domestic law is a constitutional requirement (article 88-1 of the Constitution). The case of domestic laws transposing EU law directives is specific. In principle, a domestic law transposing an EU directive should be immune from review, firstly, because the directive it is transposing is supposed, under the supervision of the CJEU, to respect rights and freedoms, and secondly, because it would represent an infringement of the implementation requirement set out under article 88-1 of the Constitution should the transposition law be censored by the Constitutional Council. However, the Constitutional Council enjoys some residual competence in the matter and can judicially review a transposition law in cases where such a law is outrightly incompatible with the EU directive such a law purports to transpose or if such a law does not constitute the exact transposition of the EU directive in domestic law. Besides, judicial review is open whenever the Constitutional Council considers that the transposition could affect constitutional provisions "inherent in the constitutional identity of France." Such provisions are the specific

82 Decision No 2012-653 DC of 9 August 2012 *Traité sur la stabilité, la coordination et la gouvernance au sein de l'Union économique et monétaire.*

83 Constitutional Law No 98-610 of 20 July 1998 relating to New Caledonia and Organic Law No 1999-209 of 19 March 1999 on New Caledonia.

84 Organic Law No 2004-192 of 27 February 2004 on the statute of autonomy of French Polynesia.

85 Decision No 92-312 DC of 2 September 1992 *Traité sur l'Union européenne* (*Maastricht II*), pts 19 and 34. The Constitutional Council has also clarified that it derives neither from article 61, nor from article 89, nor from any other provision of the Constitution, the authority to decide on the constitutionality amendment. See Decision No 2003-469 DC of 26 March 2003 *Révision constitutionnelle relative à l'organisation décentralisée de la République*, pt 2.

86 Decision No 62-20 of 6 November 1962 *Loi relative à l'élection du Président de la République au suffrage universel direct, adoptée par le référendum du 28 octobre 1962* (*Loi référendaire*), pt 2; and Decision No 92-312 DC of 2 September 1992 *Traité sur l'Union européenne* (*Maastricht II*), pt 2.

constitutional provisions that are unique to French law with no equivalent in other EU member states. For example, in a 2021 decision *Société Air France*, the Constitutional Council held that the prohibition "of delegation to private entities the general administrative police powers which are inherent in the use of 'public force' necessary for guaranteeing rights" constituted "an inherent principle of France's constitutional identity."[87]

Under the ex-post constitutional review, constitutional review is aimed at "a legislative provision [that] infringes the rights and freedoms guaranteed by the Constitution." Such legislative provision(s) may be contained in organic laws, ordinary laws, laws of the land, or ratified ordinances with legislative force. Administrative acts and non-ratified ordinances are excluded from the review. In the context of *QPC* proceedings, constitutional review covers not only the text of the provision but also its interpretation by the ordinary or administrative judge since both the text and its interpretation are regarded as inseverable. In other words, when the interpretation of a legislative provision, as upheld by the Court of Cassation or by the Council of State, arguably infringes the rights and freedoms guaranteed by the Constitution, a litigant is entitled to challenge such an interpretation by way of judicial review under the so-called "living law doctrine" (*doctrine du droit vivant*).[88] Rather than censuring the legislative provision in question, the Constitutional Council will rather issue a decision of compatibility "with a reserve of interpretation." The aim of such a "reserve of interpretation" is to direct the trial judge towards the correct interpretation of the law which is being judicially reviewed.[89] Concerning the laws transposing EU directives, the case law of the Constitutional Council stays in line with the principles set out for the ex-ante review as examined above.[90]

The norms of reference and the block of constitutionality. The Constitutional Council exercises its review against a number of norms of constitutional value. These norms comprise not only the Constitution but also several other texts and principles which, taken together, constitute the "block of constitutionality" (*bloc de constitutionnalité*). Contrary to other constitutions such as, the 1949 German Basic Law (*Grundgesetz*) in its articles 1 to 19, or the 1937 Irish Constitution (*Bunreacht na hÉireann*) in its articles 40 to 44, the French Constitution does not include a catalogue of fundamental rights although some provisions related to the protection of rights can be found in provisions such as article 1 about equality before the law or article 66 on individual freedom. The reason for the absence of such a catalogue in the current Constitution is that the 1789 Declaration and the Preamble to the 1946 Constitution already contain a list of fundamental rights to which the Preamble to the Constitution refers. The question is whether these two texts can be regarded as of constitutional significance too, on a par with the Constitution. As seen above, the Constitutional Council addressed this question in its seminal 1971 decision on Freedom of Association. In its ruling, the Council recognised the constitutional value of the 1789 Declaration and of the 1946 Preamble, thus consecrating the

87 Decision No 2021-940 QPC of 15 October 2021 *Société Air France [Obligation pour les transporteurs aériens de réacheminer les étrangers auxquels l'entrée en France est refusée]*, pt 15.

88 For example, Decision No 2010-52 QPC of 14 October 2010 *Compagnie agricole de la Crau [Imposition due par une société agricole]*, pt 4.

89 For example, Decision No 2013-340 QPC of 20 September 2013 *M. Alain G. [Assujettissement à l'impôt sur le revenu des indemnités de licenciement ou de mise à la retraite]*.

90 For example, Decision No 2010-79 QPC of 17 December 2010 *M. Kamel D. [Transposition d'une directive]*.

emergence of the block of constitutionality.[91] Besides, the Council ensures a balance between norms of constitutional value without, however, establishing a hierarchy between them. All constitutional principles have the same value, albeit some seemingly enjoy a higher level of protection (e.g., freedom of expression, right to asylum). What is included in the block of constitutionality and what is excluded from it is explained below (see Figure 6.3 The block of constitutionality).

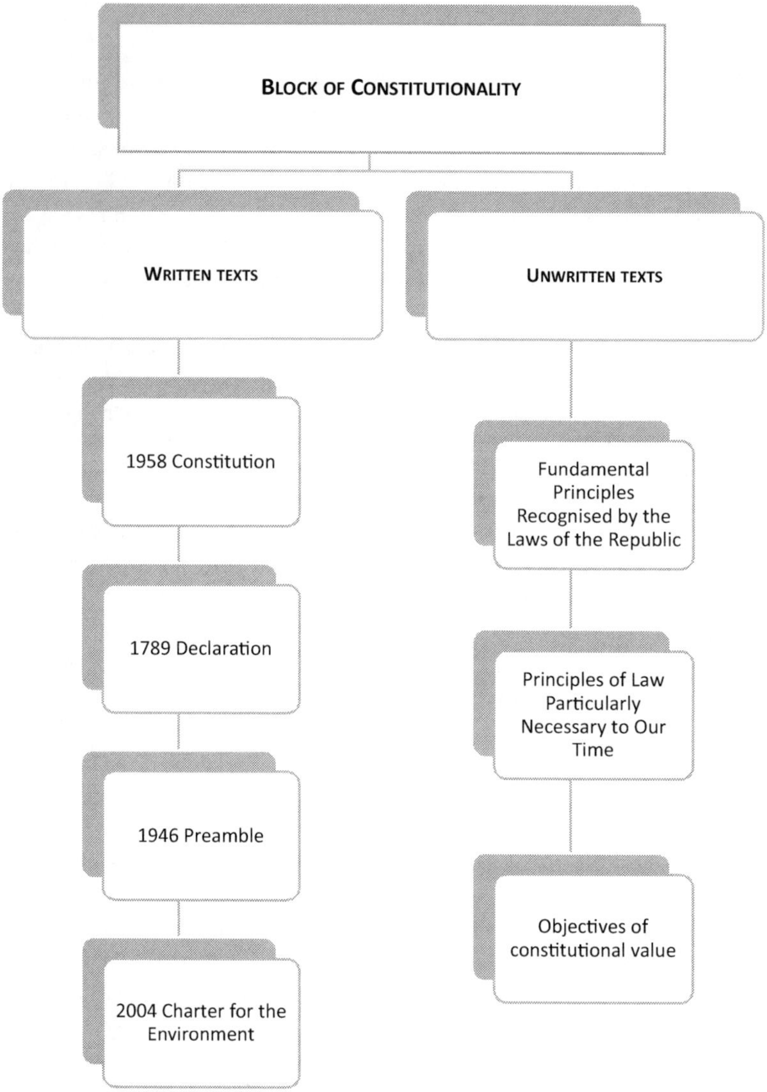

FIGURE 6.3 The block of constitutionality

91 Decision No 71-44 DC of 16 July 1971 *Loi complétant les dispositions des articles 5 et 7 de la loi du 1er juillet 1901 relative au contrat d'association* (*Liberté d'association*).

What is included in the block of constitutionality. The block of constitutionality includes all provisions of the Constitution, as well as the Preamble, which holds constitutional value. The Preamble to the Constitution states that "[t]he French people (...) solemnly proclaim their attachment to the human rights and the principles of national sovereignty as defined in the 1789 Declaration, as later confirmed and complemented by the Preamble to the 1946 Constitution, as well as to the rights and duties laid down in the 2004 Charter for the Environment." As a result, the 1789 Declaration, the 1946 Preamble as well as the 2004 Charter for the Environment are all part of the constitutional norms of reference considered by the Constitutional Council during judicial review of legislation.

Like the Preamble to the Constitution, the 1946 Preamble refers to other norms. These norms are deemed significant and are therefore included in the block of constitutionality due to their textual connection with the current Constitution. Firstly, the Preamble to the 1946 Constitution makes a reference to the 1789 Declaration. The 1789 Declaration guarantees civil and political rights such as, for example, the right to security and safety (article 7), freedom of opinion (article 10), freedom to communicate (article 11), and the right to property (article 17).[92] Such rights are regarded as "first generation rights."[93] Secondly, the Preamble to the 1946 Constitution enumerates a set of economic and social rights known as "second generation rights" and known as the "Principles of Law Particularly Necessary to Our Time" (*principes particulièrement nécessaires à notre temps*). These include social rights, notably the principle of equality between men and women (paragraph 3), the right to employment (paragraph 5), the right to strike (paragraph 7), the protection of the family (paragraph 10), as well as the protection of health, material security, rest, and leisure (paragraph 11). These principles also concern a number of political principles, such as the right to claim asylum (paragraph 4) and the respect for international law (paragraph 14). This comprehensive framework outlined in the Preamble reflects the values and principles that underpin the 1946 Constitution.

Furthermore, the 1946 Preamble mentions the "Fundamental Principles Recognised by the Laws of the Republic" (*principes fondamentaux reconnus par les lois de la République*). This category does not refer to any established list. It is therefore more controversially regarded since, by allowing the Constitutional Council a great discretion in their development, it carries the risk of judicial activism. Under the Fundamental Principles Recognised by the Laws of the Republic and drawing from key republican liberal laws of mainly the Third Republic, the Council has developed principles such as the right to education and freedom of thought,[94]

92 See, for example, Decision No 73-51 DC of 27 December 1973 *Loi de finances pour 1974* (*Taxation d'office*) pt 2, in which the Constitutional Council referred, for the first time, to a principle inscribed in the 1789 Declaration, that of equality before the law, to censure a legislation provision on tax. See also Decision No 81-132 DC of 16 January 1982 *Loi de nationalisation* (*Nationalisation*), pt 16, in which the Council declared that the principles enounced in the 1789 Declaration enjoy full constitutional value.

93 The categorisation of fundamental rights into, originally three, generations was introduced by Czech lawyer Karel Vašák in the late 1970s. See his seminal piece, Karel Vašák, "A Thirty-Year Struggle: The Sustained Efforts to Give Force of Law to the Universal Declaration of Human Rights" (1977) 30 (11) *The UNESCO Courier* 29–32.

94 Decision No 77-87 DC of 23 November 1977 *Loi complémentaire à la loi n° 59-1557 du 31 décembre 1959 modifiée par la loi n° 71-400 du 1er juin 1971 et relative à la liberté de l'enseignement.*

freedom of association,[95] the independence of administrative courts,[96] academic freedom,[97] the specificity of the criminal justice system for minors,[98] and the derogatory regime applicable in Alsace-Moselle.[99]

The Council has further refined the criteria used to identify the Fundamental Principles Recognised by the Laws of the Republic. Firstly, the principle must be embodied in a legislative text of general scope, bearing in mind that this text must have been adopted under the Republican regime to the exclusion of laws passed during either the monarchy or the First and Second Empires. In that context, the Council considers only laws that are anterior to the 1946 Constitution.[100] Secondly, constitutional value is not attributed to the laws as such. This only applies to a principle contained in the law. As indicated by the case law of the Council, such a principle must be linked to one of the three foundational principles of the Constitution, namely the guarantee of fundamental rights and freedoms, the principle of national sovereignty, or the organisation of public powers.[101] Thirdly, the principle must be fundamental. Even though the appreciation of this criterion involves a degree of judicial discretion, a principle can only be regarded as fundamental if it has been constantly applied over time. An exceptional period of nonapplication of the principle will prevent such a principle from being qualified as fundamental. Even though the Fundamental Principles Recognised by the Laws of the Republic have a textual link with the Constitution, this link can be tenuous due to the indeterminacy of the category. This may explain why the Council has abandoned the reference to this particular category of principles in its more recent case law. The difficulties associated with the weak link between the Fundamental Principles Recognised by the Laws of the Republic and the text of the Constitution are particularly emphasised when the Council has recourse to constitutional principles that are not grounded in a textual provision. In its case law, the Council has referred to different kinds of sources—namely constitutional principles, objectives of constitutional value, constitutional requirements, or legitimate objectives—without necessarily establishing their textual basis, in a very similar manner as the reasoning used by the Council of State as regards the development of general principles of law. For example, the Constitutional Council has developed in such a manner principles such as, for instance, the principle of continuity of the public service,[102] or the principle of the accessibility and intelligibility of the law.[103] However, the ex-nihilo creation of constitutional principles always carries the risk of exposing the Council to the criticism of judicial activism.

95 Decision No 71-44 DC of 16 July 1971 *Loi complétant les dispositions des articles 5 et 7 de la loi du 1er juillet 1901 relative au contrat d'association* (*Liberté d'association*).

96 Decision No 80-119 DC of 22 July 1980 *Loi portant validation d'actes administratifs.*

97 Decision No 83-165 DC of 20 January 1984 *Loi relative à l'enseignement supérieur* (*Libertés universitaires*); and Decision No 2010-20/21 QPC of 6 August 2010, *M. Jean et autres* (*Loi Université*).

98 Decision No 2002-461 DC of 29 August 2002 *Loi d'orientation et de programmation pour la justice.*

99 Decision No 2011-157 QPC of 5 August 2011 *Société SOMODIA [Interdiction du travail le dimanche en Alsace-Moselle].*

100 Decision No 88-244 DC of 20 July 1988 *Loi portant amnistie.*

101 Decision No 2013-669 DC of 17 May 2013 *Loi ouvrant le mariage aux couples de personnes de même sexe*, pt 21.

102 Decision No 79-105 DC of 25 July 1979 *Loi modifiant les dispositions de la loi n° 74-696 du 7 août 1974 relatives à la continuité du service public de la radio et de la télévision en cas de cessation concertée du travail.*

103 Decision No 99-421 DC of 16 December 1999 *Loi portant habilitation du Gouvernement à procéder par ordonnances, à l'adoption de la partie législative de certains codes, Rec.* 49.

Lastly, the 2004 Charter for the Environment, which was added to the Constitution through the 2005 amendment, constitutes another part in the block of constitutionality.[104] The 2004 Charter provides for the constitutional protection of "third generation rights," including the right to a healthy environment (article 1) and the right to access information and participate in environmental issues (article 7). Additionally, the 2004 Charter imposes obligations on the state and public authorities, such as following the precautionary principle, preventing environmental harm, and holding the state accountable for environmental issues.[105]

In addition, the Constitutional Council has established a number of principles of constitutional value (*principes à valeur constitutionnelle*) whenever no textual basis can be found in the texts mentioned above. The principle of the continuity of public services,[106] the principle of the protection of health and of safety of the public and of property,[107] and the guarantee of human dignity[108] are all principles of constitutional value developed by the Council. Some of them have been quite controversially, if not improperly, affirmed by the Council such as the principle of fraternity as regards the right to assist aliens, on humanitarian grounds, regardless of the legality of their stay on French territory.[109] Besides, the Council has used the notion of objectives of constitutional value (*objectifs de valeur constitutionnelle*) whether to enhance the protection of certain rights, to balance the protection of numerous and, often contradictory, rights, or, in some cases, to justify rights limitations. A good example is the conciliation that was operated by the Council during the Covid-19 pandemic between the health emergency regime and the respect of fundamental freedoms.[110] In a ruling dealing with the prorogation of the health emergency regime, the Council ruled that the Constitution did not exclude the

104 Constitutional Law No 2005-205 of 1 March 2005 on the Charter for the Environment.

105 For example, Decision No 2022-843 DC of 12 August 2022 *Loi portant mesures d'urgence pour la protection du pouvoir d'achat*, in which the Constitutional Council makes an interesting link between the emergency measures adopted for the protection of the purchasing power of French citizens and the constitutional requirement of prevention of environmental damage as regards the installation of a floating LNG platform and other installations for the production of electricity from fossil fuels in the context of the 2021–2023 energy crisis.

106 Decision No 79-105 DC of 25 July 1979 *Loi modifiant les dispositions de la loi n° 74-696 du 7 août 1974 relatives à la continuité du service public de la radio et de la télévision en cas de cessation concertée du travail.*

107 Decision No 80-127 DC of 20 January 1981 *Loi renforçant la sécurité et protégeant la liberté des personnes.*

108 Decision No 94-343/344 DC of 27 July 1994 *Loi relative au respect du corps humain et loi relative au don et à l'utilisation des éléments et produits du corps humain, à l'assistance médicale à la procréation et au diagnostic prénatal.*

109 Decision No 2018-717/718 QPC of 6 July 2018 *M. Cédric H. et autre [Délit d'aide à l'entrée, à la circulation ou au séjour irréguliers d'un étranger]* (*Délit de solidarité*), pt 8.

110 Decision No 2020-800 DC of 11 May 2020 *Loi prorogeant l'état d'urgence sanitaire et complétant ses dispositions.* Other examples include the preservation of pluralism in audio-visual communication (Decision No 82-141 DC of 27 July 1982 *Loi sur la communication audiovisuelle*), the right to avail oneself of decent housing (Decision No 94-359 DC of 19 January 1995 *Loi relative à la diversité de l'habitat*, as reaffirmed in Decision No 2015-470 QPC of 29 May 2015 *Société SAUR SAS [Interdiction d'interrompre la distribution d'eau dans les résidences principales]*), the preservation of public order (Decision No 93-325 of 13 August 1993 *Loi relative à la maîtrise de l'immigration et aux conditions d'entrée, d'accueil et de séjour des étrangers en France*, or *Maîtrise de l'immigration*), the principle of accessibility and intelligibility of the law (Decision No 99-421 DC of 16 December 1999 *Loi portant habilitation du Gouvernement à procéder, par ordonnances, à l'adoption de la partie législative de certains codes*), the protection of the environment (Decision No 2019-823 QPC of 31 January 2020 *Union des industries de la protection des plantes [Interdiction de la production, du stockage et de la circulation de certains produits phytopharmaceutiques]*), or the protection of intellectual property rights (Decision No 2020-841 QPC of 20 May 2020 *La Quadrature du Net et autres [Droit de communication à la Hadopi]*).

possibility for the legislature to establish such a regime. However, the Council added that the legislator had to ensure, within the framework of such a regime, the conciliation between the objective of constitutional value of health protection and the respect of the rights and freedoms recognised to all those who reside on French territory, in particular the right to freedom of movement, to respect for private life, to freedom of enterprise, as well as the right to collective expression of ideas and opinions.[111] While the Council validated several provisions of the health emergency regime, it also censured some and introduced some reserves of interpretation as regards certain provisions, notably as regards the processing of medical personal data collected for "tracing" purposes as well as the regime of quarantine and isolation measures.

Under the ex-post constitutional review, the norms of reference that are included in the block of constitutionality, whether they are textually based or case-law based, are the ones which aim at safeguarding rights and freedoms as guaranteed by the Constitution. This means that the Council can only consider constitutional provisions related to fundamental rights and freedoms during *QPC* proceedings, rather than provisions concerning the organisation of public powers or the functioning of institutions. For instance, articles such as the right to parliamentary amendment (article 44 of the Constitution), the recognition of regional languages (article 75-1), the requirement to transpose EU directives (article 88-1), the principle of no taxation without consent (article 14 of the 1789 Declaration), and the principle of sustainable development (article 6 of the 2004 Charter) are all examples of provisions that may be considered by the Constitutional Council during its review. These provisions must directly impact fundamental rights or freedoms in order to be included in the review process.

What is excluded from the block of constitutionality. The norms that are excluded from the block of constitutionality are those that do not display a textual link with the Constitution. Despite their significance, organic laws are not generally included in the block of constitutionality. In the specific situation when the Constitutional Council refers to organic laws, it does not refer to them as such because these organic laws are expressly referred to in the constitutional provisions examined by the Council.[112] In that case, an ordinary law, which is repugnant to an organic law, would be equally repugnant to the Constitution itself. For the same reason, the rules of procedures of the Houses of Parliament are not included in the block of constitutionality.[113] The issue of international law is more ambiguous. Based on the strict distinction between the review of constitutionality and that of conventionality, international norms are generally excluded from the block of constitutionality. However, this has been challenged by the development of EU law. Firstly, in its 1992 decision on the Maastricht Treaty, the Constitutional Council recognised the rule pacta sunt servanda on the basis of the fourteenth paragraph of the Preamble to the 1946 Constitution on the respect of international law.[114] More importantly, in the well-known litigation about the electoral status in France of EU citizens, the Council referred to both the TEU and the EU directive concerned in order

111 Decision No 2020-800 DC of 11 May 2020 *Loi prorogeant l'état d'urgence sanitaire et complétant ses dispositions*, pt 17.

112 Decision No 78-95 DC of 27 July 1978 *Loi complétant les dispositions de l'article 7 de la loi n° 60-791 du 2 août 1960 relative à l'enseignement et à la formation professionnelle agricole*.

113 Decision No 80-117 DC of 22 July 1980 *Loi sur la protection et le contrôle des matières nucléaires*.

114 Decision No 92-308 DC of 9 April 1992 *Traité sur l'Union européenne* (*Maastricht I*).

to review the conformity with the Constitution of the organic law in question.[115] However, this was done only on the basis of article 88-3 of the Constitution, which states that such an electoral status had to be granted in accordance with EU law. The Council thus took EU law into account because of its textual link with the Constitution. The affirmation that article 88-1 of the Constitution entails a constitutional requirement as to the implementation of EU directives generalises this state of affairs. The Council has ruled on the conformity of domestic laws with EU law provisions in an increasing number of cases.[116] However, this has not resulted in an incorporation of EU law as such into the block of constitutionality. EU law is merely taken into account in the constitutional review of legislation because of a constitutional referral and in order to enforce a constitutional provision. This explains why the Council has only censured manifest disregard of EU directives by implementing laws,[117] and that EU law has not been taken into account in the case of laws that do not aim at implementing EU directives.[118] In the same manner, the Council has excluded the constitutional requirement of implementation of EU directives from the rights and freedoms guaranteed under the Constitution, which is the basis of its review in the context of the review under *QPC* proceedings.[119]

Features of constitutional review. Constitutional review is a review of judicial nature (*contrôle juridictionnel*) that is entrusted to a constitutional court that decides, in principle, on considerations of law, and not of opportunity. Constitutional review under the ex-ante procedure (article 61 of the Constitution) is of an abstract nature and by way of action or main constitutional plea (*par voie d'action*) since the impugned law is reviewed, before its promulgation, independently of any judicial proceedings. The aim here is to prevent the entry into force of an allegedly unconstitutional text. The advantage of the ex-ante review is the legal certainty that it provides to the enacted law because, once such a law has been reviewed before its promulgation and "cleared" of its unconstitutional elements, it cannot be challenged again. Conversely, the major disadvantage of the ex-ante review is the non-systematic nature of the review and the risk that the law is promulgated while containing an "irreversible" unconstitutionality. However, and before the introduction of the *QPC* procedure, the Constitutional Council recognised the possibility of reviewing a promulgated law in specific circumstances following its "New Caledonia" case law. According to this case law, the Council considered that the constitutionality of a promulgated law can be usefully raised during the examination of any subsequent legislative provisions which modify it, supplement it, or affect its field, as opposed to when it comes to the simple application of the law in question.[120] On

115 Decision No 98-400 DC of 20 May 1998 *Loi organique déterminant les conditions d'application de l'article 88-3 de la Constitution relatif à l'exercice par les citoyens de l'Union européenne résidant en France, autres que les ressortissants français, du droit de vote et d'éligibilité aux élections municipales, et portant transposition de la directive 94/80/CE du 19 décembre 1994.*

116 Decision No 2006-543 DC of 30 November 2006 *Loi relative au secteur de l'énergie.*

117 Decision No 2006-540 DC of 27 July 2006 *Loi relative au droit d'auteur et aux droits voisins dans la société de l'information.*

118 Decision No 2006-535 DC of 30 March 2006 *Loi pour l'égalité des chances.*

119 Decision No 2010-605 DC of 12 May 2010 *Loi relative à la concurrence et à la régulation du secteur des jeux d'argent et de hasard en ligne.*

120 Decision No 85-187 DC of 25 January 1985 *Loi relative à l'état d'urgence en Nouvelle-Calédonie et dépendances*, pt 10; also, Decision No 2013-669 DC of 17 May 2013 *Loi ouvrant le mariage aux couples de personnes de même sexe*, pt 53.

the other hand, constitutional review under the ex-post or *QPC* procedure (article 61-1 of the Constitution) is of by way of exception (*par voie d'exception*) since the issue of constitutionality of the impugned law is raised during court proceedings the outcome of which depends on the determination of the constitutionality question.

Referral mechanism. The referral mechanism to the Constitutional Council presents two general features. Firstly, and as seen above, except for limited types of norms which *must* be referred to the Council (i.e., organic laws and rules of procedure of the Houses of Parliament), constitutional review of laws is never mandatory under domestic law. As a result, some laws are never reviewed by the Council. Secondly, access to the Council is never direct for the litigants whether it is under the ex-ante review or under the ex-post review procedure, although access has been enlarged as explained above. Under the ex-ante review procedure, access has been progressively enlarged from, originally, central political authorities only (i.e., the President of the Republic, the Prime Minister, the president of the National Assembly, and the president of the Senate) to a wider base of 60 deputies or 60 senators.[121] Referral by deputies or senators has arguably been regarded as the ultimate weapon in the hands of the opposition whereby they can challenge the law on the legal terrain, having failed to do so on political grounds. This was the wish of the instigator of the 1974 reform, former President of the Republic Giscard d'Estaing (1974–1981), who considered such a reform as a way to strengthen democracy. However, this was also denounced as an instrumentalisation of constitutional review being used for political purposes instead of being used to ensure the strict respect of the Constitution.[122] In practice, referrals of laws by the executive (i.e., President of the Republic and Prime Minister) are quite rare and mainly emanate from members of Parliament; this is reversed as regards referrals of international treaties. As explained above, the ex-post review procedure has further extended the possibility to refer a constitutional issue to the Council by providing an indirect access to litigants via the *QPC* procedure.[123]

Under the ex-ante review procedure, a referral is made after the vote on the impugned law but before its promulgation (or after the signature of the impugned treaty but before its ratification, in the case of constitutional review of international treaties). The Constitutional is required to make a decision within one month (or eight days in urgent cases) from the date of the referral. The referral process is suspensive, which means that the law in question cannot be promulgated until the Council has made its ruling. Applicants present their case to the Council through a written plea (*requête*) that outlines their legal arguments, often including implicit political arguments. The Council is not bound by the contents of the referral plea and can make a decision that goes beyond the specific arguments raised, by analysing other parts of the law that may be unconstitutional but were not mentioned in the applicant's plea. However, the Council cannot initiate a review of the constitutionality of a law or international treaty of its own accord.

Under the ex-post review procedure, a *QPC* referral to the Constitutional Council is made regarding a law that is already in effect. As explained above, the typical procedure of the *QPC* involves initially bringing up the issue of constitutionality in a lower court, an appellate

121 The 60 co-signatories of the referral must belong to the same House, either the National Assembly or the Senate.

122 Didier Maus et alii, *30 ans de saisine parlementaire du Conseil constitutionnel* (Economica 2006).

123 The only direct access to the Constitutional Council under the *QPC* procedure is for electoral matters.

court, or one of the supreme courts (Court of Cassation or Council of State). This issue is then reviewed by one of the supreme courts if it originated from a lower court or appellate court, and ultimately decided upon by the Constitutional Council. A filtering mechanism based on the utility, novelty, and seriousness of the issue of constitutionality is in place to avoid a flood of *QPC* cases. For a referral to be deemed admissible by a lower court or appellate judge, certain conditions must be met. Firstly, the provision being challenged must be of a legislative nature. Secondly, the application of the allegedly unconstitutional provision must be crucial to the outcome of the case. Thirdly, the provision must not have previously been deemed constitutional by the Council, unless there has been a significant change in circumstances of fact or law. Lastly, the issue of constitutionality must present a "serious character."

Ordinary and administrative judges are only responsible for filtering the issue of constitutionality and not for assessing it, even though filtering the seriousness of such an issue entails, to an extent, "pre-reviewing" the issue of constitutionality.[124] In addition, the court of trial may in practice determine the constitutionality of a law by not referring the issue of constitutionality to a higher court, meaning that the court acts as a "positive constitutional court" by determining what the law is. However, the court of trial cannot declare the unconstitutionality of a law, meaning that the court cannot act as a "negative constitutional court" by ascertaining what the law is not. At that stage, the Council may also receive external contributions from third parties, mainly lobbies and other interest groups. These contributions are the so-called *portes étroites*, drawn from the biblical metaphor and representing, in that case, the indirect and tight access of external parties to the Constitutional Council. Such "narrow doors" aim at bringing to the attention of the Council a number of observations that may influence its final decision. The Council decided to make these external contributions public by publishing them on its website, in 2017 as regards ex-ante proceedings and in 2019 as regards in *QPC* proceedings. Once the *QPC* referral from either the Court of Cassation or the Council of State reaches the Council, it must rule on the issue of constitutionality within three months.[125] Similarly to ex-ante proceedings, *QPC* proceedings have a suspensive effect, meaning that the case on the merit cannot be decided until the Council has ruled on the issue of constitutionality. The specific case of the so-called "moot referrals" (*saisines blanches*) illustrates an interesting, albeit worrying, development at the intersection of both types of constitutional reviews. Moot referrals are those that contain no specific grievance against the challenged law and that merely seek the approval of the Council, thereby neutralising any potential future *QPC* challenge once the law in question enters into force.[126] Moot referrals are now prohibited by the rules of procedure of the Council requiring the applicant to indicate in their referral the legislative provisions, or the clauses of the international treaty, on which the Council is invited to rule as well as the constitutional requirements that the law, or the treaty provisions, are likely to disregard.[127]

124 Organic Law No 2009-1523 of 10 December 2009 relating to the application of article 61-1 of the Constitution, and Decision No 2009-595 DC of 3 December 2009 *Loi organique relative à l'application de l'article 61-1 de la Constitution*.

125 The Constitutional Council typically delivers its *QPC* judgments within an average of 70 days, which is a little over two months.

126 Two examples are the referral made by Hollande about the Law No 2015-912 of 24 July 2015 relating to intelligence, and the referral made by Macron about Law No 2019-290 of 10 April 2019 aimed at strengthening and guaranteeing the maintenance of public order during demonstrations, one of the so-called "Anti-Thugs" laws.

127 Decision No 2022-152 ORGA of 11 March 2022 *Décision portant règlement intérieur sur la procédure suivie devant le Conseil constitutionnel pour les déclarations de conformité à la Constitution*, pt 2.

Constitutional review rulings. Decisions of the Constitutional Council, including constitutional review rulings, all bear the same structure which is in line with the French concise style of drafting judgments (see Box 6.1 Terminology on judicial decisions). At the top of the ruling, the *visa* contains the mention of the legal and regulatory texts which the Council refers to in the main part of the decision. This is followed by the *considérants* which embody the operative part of the ruling. These *considérants* are structured around several distinct paragraphs detailing the reasoning of the Council and justifying its decision, all starting with the phrase "considering that .... ." Finally, the ruling ends with the *dispositif* in the form of numbered articles in which the Council decides whether the provisions examined are constitutional or unconstitutional. The judicial style of the Council can be described as "hyperformalist," meaning that legal problems are to be solved exclusively through deduction of a particular conclusion in a given case from abstract and general premises, as opposed to the policy argument model of reasoning. Also, no dissenting opinions are issued; although they might be recorded, they are not publicly available. Disclosing such opinions would expose the divergences within the Council and affect the authority of its decisions. A Council's decision is a single collective decision, bearing only an indication of the members who sat in the judgment formation.[128]

Constitutional review rulings are either ex-ante review rulings or ex-post review rulings bearing, respectively, the abbreviation *DC* for decisions on constitutional conformity (*décisions de conformité*) and the abbreviation *QPC* for decisions on the issue of constitutionality (*question prioritaire de constitutionnalité*).[129] Constitutional review rulings must be motivated and are published in the Official Journal. They are binding on all public authorities which comprise, beyond the authorities involved in the particular case, political authorities, the administration, and courts at all levels (article 62 paragraph three of the Constitution). The legally binding force of the rulings does not only concern the operative part but also their ratio decidendi. The rulings have the authority of res judicata even though no actual enforcement procedure exists. Despite not considering themselves legally bound by the case law of the Council since the Council does not have normative powers, ordinary and administrative courts have generally conformed to constitutional review rulings and have adjusted

128 For more details, see Marie-Luce Paris, "The French Constitutional Council: Another 'Work-in-Progress'" in Emmanuel Guinchard & Marie-Pierre Granger (eds), *The New EU Judiciary: An Analysis of Current Judicial Reforms* (Kluwer Law International 2017) 47, 63.

129 The Constitutional Council renders decisions of other types, each bearing a distinctive abbreviation. In addition to the *DC* and *QPC* decisions, there are *LP* decisions for decisions on laws concerning New Caledonia (*Loi du pays de Nouvelle-Calédonie*), *LOM* decisions for decisions concerning the legislative competence of certain overseas territories, namely French Polynesia, Saint-Barthélemy, and Saint-Martin (*Loi Compétences Outre-Mer*), *PDR* decisions on the regularity of presidential elections (*Élection présidentielle*), *AN* and *SEN* decisions concerning respectively the regularity of the elections to the National Assembly and to the Senate, *L* decisions for decisions relating to declassification of laws (*Loi*), *D* decisions concerning the ineligibility of members of Parliament (*Déchéance*), *I* decisions concerning parliamentary incompatibilities (*Incompatibilité*), *OF* decisions concerning the non-respect by members of Parliament of their tax obligations (*Obligations Fiscales*), *ELEC* decisions concerning other electoral disputes (*Diverses Élections*), *FNR* decisions concerning various inadmissibilities under articles 39 and 41 of the Constitution (*Fins de Non-Recevoir*), *REF* decisions concerning referendums (*Référendum*), *RIP* decisions concerning the referendum of shared initiative, *ART16* decisions concerning the application of the emergency powers under article 16 of the Constitution, and *ORGA* decisions concerning the functioning of the Constitutional Council. A final category, *AUTR* decisions, relates to all other decisions of the Constitutional Council that cannot be categorised in the previous ones and include, for example, the Council's public opinions.

their own case law accordingly.[130] The legally binding force of constitutional review rulings also means that such rulings cannot be appealed or subject to any other judicial remedy, except a complaint before the ECtHR provided the rulings form part of the exhaustion of domestic remedies.

There exists a distinction between the impact of rulings on constitutional conformity and the impact of rulings on the issue of constitutionality, also known as *QPC* rulings. When it comes to constitutional conformity, the Constitutional Council has the authority to deem a voted-but-not-yet-promulgated law as unconstitutional, in whole or in part. In such cases, the law cannot be promulgated or enforced (i.e., it cannot come into existence in the legal order). The exception is where the unconstitutional provisions can be severed from the main text, which can then be promulgated as "amputated" of the unconstitutional provisions. Rulings on constitutional conformity are of general and absolute scope. On the other hand, when it comes to *QPC* rulings, the Constitutional Council may declare an applicable law unconstitutional, either in part or in its entirety. The law, or the unconstitutional parts of it, must be abrogated (i.e., it must cease to exist in the legal order) from the date of publication of the ruling, or at a later date as decided by the Council. However, when revoking the law, the Council must ensure the effectiveness or *effet utile* of the *QPC* ruling for the applicant. Indeed, should the Council decide to delay the effects of the ruling and apply the disputed law, the applicant may lose the benefits of the constitutional decision. Therefore, the Council must tailor the effects of its decisions based on the specific circumstances and legal context of each case. For instance, in a decision on the custody regime in 2010, the Council found certain provisions of the Code of Criminal Procedure related to police custody to be unconstitutional due to the absence of legal counsel for the suspect. Given the necessity to protect public order and to avoid creating a legal vacuum in the event of the abrogation of the regime altogether, the Council postponed the effects of its decision by a year, thus providing the legislature with the time to appropriately amend custody legislation. Eventually, this resulted in an overhaul of police custody law in 2011.[131]

BOX 6.1 TERMINOLOGY ON JUDICIAL DECISIONS

☛ In the French legal system, there are three distinct categories of court decisions that hold jurisdictional significance:

- The *jugement* is the decision rendered by lower courts (*tribunaux*) such as the ordinary and administrative courts.
- The *arrêt* is the decision issued by higher courts (*cours*) such as courts of appeal, assizes courts, administrative courts of appeal, the Court of Cassation, and the Council of State.
- The *décision* is the ruling handed down by the Constitutional Council.

These different types of court decisions serve as crucial components of the French legal system, each playing a unique role in shaping domestic case law.

130 Decision DC No 98-408 of 22 January 1999 *Traité portant statut de la Cour pénale internationale.*

131 Decision No 2010-14/22 QPC of 30 July 2010 *M. Daniel W. et autres [Garde à vue]*; and Law No 2011-392 of 14 April 2011 on police custody.

Principles of Constitutional Justice

« La Constitution est désormais l'affaire des citoyens. »[132]

Constitutional justice plays a crucial role in upholding democratic values, protecting human rights, and maintaining the rule of law.[133] The principles of constitutional justice are closely connected to the idea of a hierarchy of norms. Constitutional justice, understood as constitutional review including as regards human rights norms, presupposes the idea of a normative hierarchy because determining the normative hierarchy of a given legal system allows constitutional justice to be established within it. In a system that values constitutional justice, constitutional courts play a vital role in maintaining a balance of power that upholds the supremacy of the constitution. These courts ensure that authority is not concentrated solely in the hands of the executive branch but is shared among an independent judiciary and a representative Parliament. Through their interpretation of laws and boundaries of authority, constitutional courts hold state institutions accountable and contribute to the stability of the constitutional framework. Furthermore, constitutional courts also play a key role in fulfilling obligations under international law, including human rights standards. By ensuring compliance with international legal standards, these courts contribute to a global framework of justice and human rights protection.

In its role as a constitutional court, the French Constitutional Council fulfils these tasks. Perhaps more than other European constitutional courts due to its difficult beginnings, the Council has strived to eschew criticism and has affirmed its impartiality by, substantially, establishing a number of constitutional principles and by, procedurally, refining its judicial methods. Through these efforts, the Council has arguably managed to adapt its case law to the evolving legal, political, and social context of France. The following provides a summary of the important principles that have been developed thus far.

The principle of reconciling various fundamental freedoms

There is, in principle, no hierarchy between the different fundamental freedoms and rights protected under the Constitution. The legislature is responsible for finding a balance between fundamental freedoms and rights and for imposing, within the limits of the law, restrictions on those freedoms and rights. The legislature does so under the supervision of the Constitutional Council, which decides on the basis of constitutional principles. For example, in its 1982 decision on nationalisations, the Council upheld the constitutionality of the principle of nationalisation as stated in paragraph nine of the 1946 Preamble while, at the same time, reaffirming the importance of the right to property and freedom of enterprise contained in the 1789 Declaration. The Council thus considered that any component of the block of constitutionality has an equal status and refused to recognise the primacy of one over the other on the grounds

132 Jean-Louis Debré, former president of the Constitutional Council (2007–2016) [The Constitution is now the business of the citizens].

133 Article 1, *Revised Statute of the World Conference on Constitutional Justice* [CDL-WCCJ-GA (2017)010-e], as amended by the 2nd General Assembly, Vilnius, 12 September 2017, The European Commission for Democracy through Law (Venice Commission).

of chronological or hierarchical or other considerations.[134] The constitutional case law contains numerous other examples which reconcile, for instance, the exercise of freedom of communication with those objectives of constitutional value that are the safeguard of public order, the respect of freedom of others, and the principle of pluralism in sociocultural expression;[135] or, in the Covid-19 pandemic context, reconcile the constitutionally protected rights with the objective of constitutional value of health protection.[136] Overall, the Council has strived to balance the different constitutional principles in concreto by taking into consideration the particularities of each case.

The principle of a minimum level of rights protection

Due to the special attention given to certain fundamental freedoms by the Constitutional Council, they are afforded a higher level of protection. The legislature is prohibited from reducing this level of protection, as it could be subject to the Council's scrutiny, known as the "ratchet effect" (*effet-cliquet*).[137] For that reason, when enacting new laws under article 34 of the Constitution, the legislature must ensure legal safeguards are in place to uphold constitutional principles.[138] In that context, the Council has sanctioned the inaction of the legislature (*incompétence négative*), stating that failure to include adequate guarantees for rights protection would be considered a dereliction of duty, as it grants too much power to the regulatory power.[139]

The scope of constitutional review

The process of judicial review carried out by the Constitutional Council has become more rigorous and models the review conducted by the Council of State. There are three methods of judicial review that demonstrate this: firstly, the technique of the review of the manifest error of assessment (*erreur manifeste d'appréciation*) with an appreciation based on a manifestly disproportionate restriction to rights and freedoms;[140] secondly, a type of review that considers proportionality, allowing the Constitutional Council to clarify their decision and define the

134 Decision No 81-132 DC of 16 January 1982 *Loi de nationalisation (Nationalisation).*

135 Decision No 88-248 DC of 17 January 1989 *Loi modifiant la loi n° 86-1067 du 30 septembre 1986 relative à la liberté de communication.*

136 Decision No 2021-824 QPC of 5 August 2021 *Loi relative à la gestion de la crise sanitaire.*

137 Decision No 83-165 DC of 20 January 1984 *Loi relative à l'enseignement supérieur* (*Libertés universitaires*).

138 Decision No 2004-494 DC of 29 April 2004 *Loi relative à la formation professionnelle tout au long de la vie et au dialogue social.*

139 For example, Decision No 93-322 DC of 28 July 1993 *Loi relative aux établissements publics à caractère scientifique, culturel et professionnel* (*Statut des universités*), Decision No 2004-499 DC of 29 July 2004 *Loi relative à la protection des personnes physiques à l'égard des traitements de données à caractère personnel et modifiant la loi n° 78-17 du 6 janvier 1978 relative à l'informatique, aux fichiers et aux libertés* (*Protection des données personnelles*).

140 For a first mention of the manifest error of assessment, see Decision No 81-132 DC of 16 January 1982 *Loi de nationalisation* (*Nationalisation*), pt 20. See also, Decision No 2005-532 DC of 19 January 2006 *Loi relative à la lutte contre le terrorisme et portant dispositions diverses relatives à la sécurité et aux contrôles frontaliers*, pt 21: "Considering that, having regard to the purposes assigned by the legislator and to all the guarantees it has provided, the contested provisions [enhanced powers granted to police forces and customs to control individuals] are appropriate to ensure, between the respect for private life and the safeguarding of the public order, a reconciliation that is *not manifestly unbalanced* (emphasis added)."

boundaries set for the legislature;[141] thirdly, a more recent evaluation focusing on the necessity or suitability of the limitations imposed on rights and freedoms.[142]

The principle of conformity "subject to reservations"

Instead of censuring or annulling the impugned law, the Constitutional Council may opt for the technique of "reservations of interpretation." It means that, while upholding the constitutionality of the impugned law, the Council substantiates its ruling by adding directives on how to interpret the law in question. Such reservations of interpretation stand as a conditional constitutionality declaration, and it is up to the executive to correctly interpret the law when they apply it.[143] These reservations of interpretation have the same legally binding force as the decisions themselves. They are labelled differently in the literature depending on what they seek to achieve: neutralising reservations (*réserves neutralisantes*) aimed at suppressing the unconstitutional interpretation; constructive reservations (*réserves constructives*) aimed at filling a gap in the impugned law; directive reservations (*réserves directives*) prescribing a certain way on how to interpret the law; or interpretative reservations (*réserves interprétatives*) indicating the correct interpretation to be given to the impugned law. In some exceptional cases, rendered in the case of ex-ante or ex-post decisions, a reservation of interpretation may result in modifying the law, if not rewriting it. This was the case, for example, in a 2017 decision relating to the law enhancing end-of-life patients' rights in which the Council ruled that:

> With regard to a decision to stop or limit life-sustaining treatment leading to the death of a person unable to express his or her will, the right to an effective judicial remedy requires that this decision be notified to the persons from whom the doctor has inquired about the patient's wishes, under conditions allowing them to exercise an appeal in good time. This appeal must also be able to be examined as soon as possible by the competent court in order to obtain the possible suspension of the contested decision. *Subject to these reservations*, the complaint alleging breach of the right to an effective judicial remedy must be dismissed (emphasis added).[144]

141 For example, Decision No 2000-433 DC of 27 July 2000 *Loi modifiant la loi n° 86-1067 du 30 septembre 1986 relative à la liberté de communication*, pt 40: "… that, consequently, it is incumbent on the legislature, when laying down the rules tending to preserve the pluralist character of socio-cultural expression, to ensure that their application does not limit the freedom of enterprise in *excessive proportions* with regard to the constitutional objective of pluralism (emphasis added)."

142 See, for example, Decision No 2020-801 DC of 18 June 2020 *Loi visant à lutter contre les contenus haineux sur internet* (*Loi Avia on online hate speech*), pts 5 & 8: "… freedom of expression and communication is all the more precious since its exercise is a condition of democracy and one of the guarantees for the respect of the rights and freedoms of others. It follows that the interference with the exercise of this freedom must be *necessary, appropriate and proportionate* to the objective pursued (…) Therefore, the legislature has restricted freedom of expression and communication in a way that is not *appropriate, necessary and proportionate* to the aim pursued (emphases added)."

143 See, for example, Decision No 93-325 DC of 13 August 1993 *Loi relative à la maîtrise de l'immigration et aux conditions d'entrée, d'accueil et de séjour des étrangers en France* (*Maîtrise de l'immigration*), pt 28: "… that *subject to this interpretation*, the legislature has not, by disregarding the right to a normal family life of refugees, infringed the right to asylum (emphasis added)."

144 Decision No 2017-632 QPC of 2 June 2017 *Union nationale des associations de familles de traumatisés crâniens et de cérébro-lésés [Procédure collégiale préalable à la décision de limitation ou d'arrêt des traitements d'une personne hors d'état d'exprimer sa volonté]*, pt 17.

Avoiding the risk of political review

When it comes to making decisions on political or social issues such as bioethics or immigration, the Constitutional Council regularly makes it clear that its role is not to override the decisions made by the legislature or, according to the consecrated expression used in the case law, whether in ex-ante or in ex-post decisions: "Article 61 of the Constitution does not confer on the Constitutional Council a general power of assessment and decision identical to that of Parliament."[145] The Council's role is to rule on the conformity with the Constitution of the laws submitted to its examination, without getting involved in political considerations. This restraint is meant to prevent accusations of judicial activism, or "government of the judges" by a non-elected body in charge of limiting the power of the democratically elected legislature. Over time, the Council's role in upholding rights has only strengthened its position in the country's institutional framework.

SELECTED FURTHER READINGS

Pierre **Avril** & Jean Gicquel, *Le Conseil constitutionnel* (6th edn, Montchrestien 2011)

Jean-Jacques **Bienvenu** et alii (eds), *La Constitution administrative de la France* (Dalloz 2012)

Julien **Bonnet**, Pierre-Yves Gahdoun & Dominique Rousseau, *Droit du contentieux constitutionnel* (13rd edn, LGDJ 2023)

________________________________, *La question prioritaire de constitutionnalité* (PUF 2014)

Guy **Braibant**, Pierre Devolvé, Bruno Genevois, Marceau Long & Prosper Weil (eds), *Les grands arrêts de la jurisprudence administrative* (24th edn, Dalloz 2023)

Jean-Paul **Branlard**, *L'essentiel de l'organisation judiciaire en France* (5th edn, Gualino 2015)

Xavier **Braud**, *L'essentiel de l'organisation juridictionnelle* (4th edn, Gaulino 2023)

Jean-Pierre **Camby**, *Le Conseil constitutionnel, juge électoral* (8th edn, Dalloz 2022)

Thierry **Debard**, Serge Guinchard & André Varinard, *Institutions juridictionnelles* (16th edn, Dalloz 2021)

Laurent **Domingo** et alii [Louis Favoreu and Loïc Philip], *Les grandes décisions du Conseil constitutionnel* (20th edn, Dalloz 2022)

Guillaume **Drago**, *Contentieux constitutionnel français* (5th edn, PUF 2020)

Pierre **Espuglas**-Labatut, *Le Conseil constitutionnel* (9th ed., Dalloz 2020)

Louis **Favoreu**, *La politique saisie par le droit* (Economica 1988)

Karine **Foucher**, *L'apport de la QPC à la protection des droits et des libertés : Un bilan* (LGDJ 2020)

Hugues **Fulchiron** & Laurent Eck, *Introduction au droit français* (2nd edn, LexisNexis 2020)

Patrick **Gérard**, *La juridiction administrative* (2nd edn, La Documentation française 2022)

Léo **Hamon**, *Les juges de la loi : Naissance et rôle d'un contre-pouvoir* (Fayard 1987)

Fabrice **Hourquebie**, *Le pouvoir juridictionnel en France* (LGDJ 2010)

Xavier **Magnon** (ed.), *QPC : Principes généraux, pratique et droit du contentieux* (2nd edn, LexisNexis 2013)

Bertrand **Mathieu** et alii, *Les grandes délibérations du Conseil constitutionnel 1958–1986* (Dalloz 2014)

________________ & Dominique Rousseau, *Les grandes décisions de la question prioritaire de constitutionnalité* (LGDJ 2013)

Christine **Maugüe** & Jacques-Henri Stahl, *La question prioritaire de constitutionnalité* (4th edn, Dalloz 2023)

Marie-Luce **Paris**, "The French Constitutional Council: Another 'Work in Progress'" in Emmanuel Guinchard & Marie-Pierre Granger (eds), *The New EU Judiciary: An Analysis of Current Judicial Reforms* (Kluwer 2017) 47

145 Decision No 74-54 DC of 15 January 1975 *Loi relative à l'interruption volontaire de la grossesse* (*IVG*), pt 1.

_______________, "The French System of Rights-Based Review: From Exceptionalism to Parochial Constitutionalism" in John Bell & Marie-Luce Paris, *Rights-Based Constitutional Review: Constitutional Courts in a Changing Landscape* (Edward Elgar 2016) 302

Pouvoirs, *La question prioritaire de constitutionnalité*, No 137 (Seuil 2011)

________, *Le Conseil constitutionnel*, No 105 (Seuil 2003)

Thierry-Serge **Renoux**, *La justice en France* (La Documentation française 2013)

Jean-Éric **Schoettl**, *La démocratie au péril des prétoires : De l'État de droit au gouvernement des juges* (Gallimard 2022)

Didier **Truchet**, *Droit administratif* (10th edn, PUF 2023)

Michel **Verpeaux**, *Contentieux constitutionnel* (2nd edn, Dalloz 2020)

_______________ & Betrand Mathieu (eds), *L'autorité des décisions du Conseil constitutionnel* (Dalloz 2010)

Susan **Wright**, "The French *Conseil constitutionnel* under an Evolving Constitution" (2017) 23 (2) *European Public Law* 245

GENERAL BIBLIOGRAPHY

Listed below are references to French constitutional law and political institutions textbooks and other works that are not listed in the Selected Further Readings rubrics, as well as sections on relevant law periodicals and websites.

Publications in English

John **Bell** & François Lichère, *Contemporary French Administrative Law* (Cambridge University Press 2022)

________, *French Constitutional Law* (Oxford University Press 1995)

Sophie **Boyron**, *The Constitution of France: A Contextual Analysis* (Hart 2013)

Publications in French

Philippe **Ardant** & Bertrand Mathieu, *Droit constitutionnel et institutions politiques* (35th edn, LGDJ 2023)

Pierre **Avril** & Jean Gicquel, *Lexique de droit constitutionnel* (6th edn, PUF 2020)

Denis **Baranger**, *La Constitution* (Dalloz 2022)

Philippe **Blachèr**, *Droit constitutionnel* (10th edn, Hachette 2023)

Pierre **Brunet**, Francis Hamon & Michel Troper, *Droit constitutionnel* (44rd edn, LGDJ 2023)

Guy **Carcassonne** & Marc Guillaume, *La Constitution* (16th edn, Points 2022)

Carolina **Cerda-Guzman**, *Cours de droit constitutionnel et institutions de la Vème République* (7th edn, Gualino 2022)

Olivier **Duhamel** & Guillaume Tusseau, *Droit constitutionnel et institutions politiques* (5th edn, Seuil 2020)

Thomas **Ehrhard** & Hugues Portelli, *Droit constitutionnel* (15th edn, Dalloz 2023)

Louis **Favoreu** et al., *Droit constitutionnel* (26th ed., Dalloz 2024)

Jean **Gicquel** & Jean-Éric Gicquel, *Droit constitutionnel et institutions politiques* (36th edn, LGDJ 2023)

Olivier **Gohin**, *Droit constitutionnel* (5th edn, LexisNexis 2022)

Jean-Paul **Jacqué**, *Droit constitutionnel et institutions politiques* (14th edn, Dalloz 2022)

Anne-Marie **Le Pourhiet**, *Droit constitutionnel* (11th edn, Economica 2021)

Ferdinand **Mélin-Soucramanien**, *Constitution de la République française* (21st edn, Dalloz 2023)

__________________________ & Pierre Pactet, *Droit constitutionnel* (42nd edn, Dalloz 2023)

Stéphane **Rials**, *Textes constitutionnels français* (33rd edn, PUF 2022)
Frédéric **Rouvillois**, *Droit constitutionnel, 2. La Ve République* (7th edn, Flammarion 2023)
Jean-François **Sirinelli**, *La Ve République* (5th edn, PUF 2022)
Michel **Verpeaux**, *La Constitution* (3rd edn, Dalloz 2022)
Michel **de Villiers** & Armel Le Divellec, *Dictionnaire du droit constitutionnel* (13th edn, Sirey 2022)

Older Classics

Below is a selected list of landmark works by famous French constitutionalists.

Joseph **Barthélemy** & Paul Duez, *Traité de droit constitutionnel* (Dalloz 1933, rééd. Economica 1985)
Raymond **Carré de Malberg**, *Contribution à la théorie générale de l'État* (Sirey 1922, 2 volumes, rééd. Dalloz 2003)
Léon **Duguit**, *Traité de droit constitutionnel* (3rd ed., De Boccard 1927–1930, 3 volumes, rééd. 1972)
Maurice **Duverger**, *La Ve République* (PUF 1959)
Adhémar **Esmein**, *Éléments de droit constitutionnel français et comparé* (1896, 4th edn, Sirey 1906, rééd. LGDJ 2001)
Maurice **Hauriou**, *Précis de droit constitutionnel* (2nd edn, Sirey 1929)
Georges **Vedel**, *Cours de droit constitutionnel et d'institutions politiques* (Cours de droit 1958–1959, 1959–1960, 1960–1961)

Periodicals

Constitutions (est. 2010)
Droits (est. 1985)
Jus Publicum (online only, est. 2008)
Les nouveaux Cahiers du Conseil constitutionnel (est. 1997)
Pouvoirs (est. 1977)
Revue française de droit constitutionnel (est. 1990)
Revue du droit public et de la science politique en France et à l'étranger (est. 1894)

Websites

Constitutional Council [www.conseil-constitutionnel.fr]
DC decisions [www.conseil-constitutionnel.fr/les-decisions/type/DC]
QPC decisions [www.conseil-constitutionnel.fr/les-decisions/type/QPC]
Council of State [www.conseil-etat.fr]
Court of Cassation [www.courdecassation.fr]
Disputes Court [www.tribunal-conflits.fr]
Government [www.gouvernement.fr]
La Documentation française, la marque reconnue d'un éditeur public [www.ladocumentationfrancaise.fr] is a public publisher which specialises in publications in the area of law and public administration.
Légifrance, le service public de la diffusion du droit [www.legifrance.gouv.fr] offers comprehensive access to French legislation and case law.
National Assembly [www.assemblee-nationale.fr]
President of the Republic [www.elysee.fr]
Senate [www.senat.fr]
Service public, le site officiel d'information et de démarches administratives [www.service-public.fr].
Vie publique, au cœur du débat public [www.vie-publique.fr] gives access to many official publications and allows users to track legislation in progress.

INDEX

Note: For figure and box citations, page numbers appear in *italics*. For table citations, page numbers appear in **bold**.

FSC
www.fsc.org
MIX
Papier | Fördert
gute Waldnutzung
FSC® C083411

Kolibri 360 GmbH
Ferdinand-Jühlke-Straße 7
99095 Erfurt, Deutschland
produktsicherheit@kolibri360.de